Theory and Practice of Sociocriticism

10656781

DATE DUE FOR RETURN

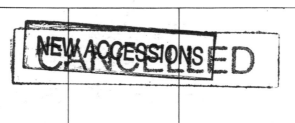

Theory and History of Literature
Edited by Wlad Godzich and Jochen Schulte-Sasse

Volume 53. Edmond Cros *Theory and Practice of Sociocriticism*
Volume 52. Philippe Lejeune *On Autobiography*
Volume 51. Thierry de Duve *The Readymade: Marcel Duchamp, Painting, and Modernity*
Volume 50. Luiz Costa Lima *The Control of the Imaginary*
Volume 49. Fredric Jameson *The Ideologies of Theory: Essays 1971–1986, Volume 2*
Volume 48. Fredric Jameson *The Ideologies of Theory: Essays 1971–1986, Volume 1*
Volume 47. Eugene Vance *From Topic to Tale: Logic and Narrativity in the Middle Ages*
Volume 46. Jean-François Lyotard *Le Différend*
Volume 45. Manfred Frank *What Is Neostructuralism?*
Volume 44. Daniel Cottom *Social Figures: George Eliot, Social History, and Literary Representation*
Volume 43. Michael Nerlich *The Ideology of Adventure, Volume 2*
Volume 42. Michael Nerlich *The Ideology of Adventure, Volume 1*
Volume 41. Denis Hollier *The College of Sociology*
Volume 40. Peter Sloterdijk *Critique of Cynical Reason*
Volume 39. Géza von Molnár, *Romantic Vision, Ethical Context*
Volume 38. Algirdas Julien Greimas *On Meaning: Selected Writings in Semiotic Theory*
Volume 37. Nicolas Abraham and Maria Torok *The Wolf Man's Magic Word: A Cryptonymy*
Volume 36. Alice Yaeger Kaplan *Reproductions of Banality: Fascism, Literature, and French Intellectual Life*
Volume 35. Denis Hollier *The Politics of Prose*
Volume 34. Geoffrey Hartman *The Unremarkable Wordsworth*
Volume 33. Paul de Man *The Resistance to Theory*
Volume 32. Djelal Kadir *Questing Fictions*
Volume 31. Samuel Weber *Institution and Interpretation*
Volume 30. Gilles Deleuze and Félixe Guattari *Kafka: Toward a Minor Literature*
Volume 29. Peter Szondi *Theory of the Modern Drama*

For other books in the series, see p. 276

Theory and Practice of Sociocriticism

Edmond Cros

Translation by Jerome Schwartz

Foreword by Jürgen Link and Ursula Link-Heer

Theory and History of Literature, Volume 53

University of Minnesota Press, Minneapolis

The University of Minnesota gratefully acknowledges translation and publication assistance provided for this book by the Program for Cultural Cooperation between Spain's Ministry of Culture and North American Universities.

Published by the University of Minnesota Press
2037 University Avenue Southeast, Minneapolis MN 55414.
Published simultaneously in Canada
by Fitzhenry & Whiteside Limited, Markham.
Printed in the United States of America.

Library of Congress Cataloging-in-Publication Data

Cros, Edmond.
   [Théorie et pratique sociocritiques. English]
   Theory and practice of sociocriticism / Edmond Cros ; translation
by Jerome Schwartz ; foreword by Jürgen Link and Ursula Link-Heer.
     p.   cm. − (Theory and history of literature ; v. 53)
   Translation of: Théorie et pratique sociocritiques.
   Bibliography: p.
   Includes index.
   ISBN 0-8166-1579-9   ISBN 0-8166-1580-2 (pbk.)
   1. Criticism. 2. Literature and society. 3. Semiotics.
4. Discourse analysis. 5. Film criticism.   I. Title.
II. Series.
PN98.S6C7413 1987   87-21167
801′.95−dc19   CIP

An earlier version of Chapter 4, "Toward a Semiology of Ideology," appeared in *Littérature*, 36 (Dec. 1979), pp. 71–76.

The University of Minnesota
is an equal-opportunity
educator and employer.

Contents

Foreword *Jürgen Link and Ursula Link-Heer*   vi
Translator's Note   xix

I. Theoretical Questions

1. From Experimental Sociology to Genetic Structuralism   3
2. Literature as Secondary Modeling System and Ideological Form   20
3. Discursive Practices and Formations   34
4. Toward a Semiology of Ideology   45
5. Textual Functions I: Transformational Processes and Codes   59
6. Textual Functions II: Genotext and Phenotexts   75
7. Narrative and Character as Textual Categories   93

II. From Theory to Practice

8. American Films of the Thirties: The Case of Howard Hawks's
   Scarface   119
9. Ideological and Discursive Formations in Contemporary Mexico   153
10. Social Formations and Figurative Discourse in Mateo Alemán's *Guzmán
    de Alfarache*   190
11. Ideology and Textual Genetics   208
    Notes   249
    Index   269

Foreword
Jürgen Link and Ursula Link-Heer

Translated by Brent Peterson

I

One of the most interesting and worthwhile aspects of the Theory and History of Literature series now appearing in Minneapolis is, without a doubt, its already successful effort to bridge the cultural barrier that the Atlantic Ocean has represented for literary theory, and to have done so systematically in both directions. Just how necessary "multiculturalism" within the discipline of literary theory is — and here expanding the "hot line" between North America and Western Europe can be regarded as the first step toward a global network — will be completely visible only when a computer is able to analyze all the works of literary theory and literary history produced in the entire world and then to catalog the earlier publications cited there. Probably the result would confirm to a shocking degree our intuitive feeling that most of these works are the product of linguistic, cultural, national, and, in addition, a kind of school-specific "incest." It is probably also true that the analysis would identify three "levels" of scholarship: "at the bottom," the cyclical reproduction of narrowly regional, if not local works whose citations almost invariably come from the same closed circle and whose dissemination is practically nonexistent; "in the middle," publications that are read nationally or within a particular, linguistically defined culture and that have to be cited, at least in exemplary fashion, in other regional works; and "at the top," a small minority of investigations that are interculturally familiar, frequently cited, and generally translated into a variety of languages. Such a model — assuming that it could be verified in this or a similar manner — naturally raises a number of problems for the sociology of knowledge: What sort of mechanisms control the tripartite division? What kind of "symbolic capital" (Bourdieu) or intellectual authority guarantees works a limited or more general reading, and what are its sources? A simple, marketing model would obviously be much too naive; the whole corpus of literary theory is not simultaneously available to the public as are the products displayed on the shelves in a supermarket, where people's choices, defined by various interests, separate the moneymakers from the losers. In reality a lot of titles have already been "screened out" by language barriers; others are missing under the important keywords of specialized bibliographies; additional titles are not mentioned in research reports or are ignored by reviewers, academics, and editors. Finally, it is in fact true that we really "can't read everything" and that we desperately need some kind of screening mechanism.

It might seem that a sensible selection mechanism is already available in the form of Thomas Kuhn's so-called "paradigm shift": Can't we be satisfied with the hope that existing institutions will, at a minimum, promptly inform us of "new paradigms"? Here, however, skepticism is in order; at least in the field of literary theory, the criteria for determining just what a "paradigm" is—to say nothing of what constitutes a "new" one—are largely absent. Take the obvious example of Jacques Derrida's "breakthrough" in the United States; one would hardly be able to explain Derrida's predominance among the representatives of "new French thought," as John Fekete calls them,[1] by saying that Derrida alone brought about a paradigm shift or that his paradigm is more radical than the others. The case of Derrida is particularly well-suited to examining some of the numerous factors that play a role in any extremely positive selection at the global, intercultural level.

A first necessary, but far from sufficient factor was the ensemble of institutional preconditions for Derrida's "discovery" in the United States: his reception and citation by Paul de Man, his invitation to Montreal (probably the most important "reception channel" between the francophone world and the United States), the proliferation of the term "deconstruction" that emanated from the Johns Hopkins University and from Yale, and finally his symbolic collision with John Searle.[2] As another imaginary computer search would show, any analysis of the necessary, but not sufficient conditions would have to include a comparison of the reception accorded all the literary theorists invited to the United States from Paris and the francophone world who entered through Montreal or other channels. Still the unique phenomenon of the "proliferation" of Derrida/deconstruction must have had other causes as well. It seems to us that a second factor, for which we would suggest the name "theory-political connotation," also played a role. This raises the decisive point that most intercultural receptions are not merely innocent intellectual enrichments, but are rather weapons in intracultural battles. To put it bluntly, Derrida was extraordinarily useful to the Yale School in its struggle against scientist theories of literature with their strict separation of literary language from the metalanguage used to talk about literature, as well as against linguistically inspired analyses with their claim of exactitude. For anyone propagating creative "misreading" (Harold Bloom), Derrida's conscious, playful suspension of the discursive boundaries between poetics, criticism, philosophy, and literary theory must have been extremely welcome. But this is still not sufficient. Every theoretical text connotes a particular response to the intellectual division of labor; a text is closely linked to Marxist political economy, for example, or to existentialist theology or to one variety of psychoanalysis or to sociobiology, etc. — or it polemicizes against all specialized disciplines. One could easily label Derrida's position on the whole system of specialized discourses "deconstructive": He does not recognize their boundaries; he disengages elements from various specialized discourses; and then he redeploys them playfully in his own texts. His initial borrowings seem to come from the discourse of psychoanalysis — at least it provides a positive "point of contact" in the United States. From the standpoint of theory-politics, all this connotes something like an "anarchic" attitude, which is not directed clearly or unequivocally toward political ends (as is the case with Foucault or Deleuze/Guattari). Are we deceiving ourselves if we view this theory-political connotation, which is not political in the ordinary sense of the term,[3] as another important point of departure and contact for the direction taken by "deconstruction" in the United States?

The term "deconstruction" itself signals a third essential factor; paradigms in literary theory probably require extremely simplified and abbreviated guiding models or concepts, which vastly reduce their complexity, without at the same time eliminating their distinctive, polemical, even "libidinous" energy, in order to have any chance of succeeding in the global marketplace. A concept as symbolically and as paradoxically potent as "deconstruction" fulfills these conditions to the utmost.

As a fourth factor, one also has to mention the culturally specific possibilities of association, which are perhaps not even consciously present in recipients' minds. We simply cannot dismiss our suspicion that Marshall McLuhan's theory of the media, most importantly of print media, "had prepared the soil" for the spread of Derrida's theses about "écriture" in the United States (although our friends there have always contradicted us).

There certainly are other factors, including some relevant to this specific case: It was no doubt important for Derrida's reception in the United States that a particular form of the multiplier effect arose when Derrida apparently made a conscious decision not to contradict various types of "misreadings" and "misinterpretations," when he decided to "play" the game, thus producing a kind of "unity of theory and praxis." The paradoxical and novel reseult was that the authority of the "author's role" reinforced Derrida's own position.

This is not, however, an introduction to Jacques Derrida, but to Edmond Cros. We are nevertheless convinced that the ideas expressed above have in no way

caused us to stray from our purpose. If our task is to introduce a French so-
ciocritic, as he calls himself, in a series on the Theory and History of Literature,
we believe that it is absolutely essential to reflect on the conditions and mechanisms involved in the process of intercultural reception. Factors like the institutional channels, the theory-political (and in some instances simply political) connotations, the reduction of complexities with the help of guiding models and
concepts, the culturally-specific associative possibilities, etc. combine to form a
power structure [*Machtdispositiv*] above whose entrance one could inscribe
"Abandon all hope ye who enter here!" Such a structure apparently tends either
to refuse to admit every nonhegemonic form of thought or to subject them to a
"misreading" for hegemonic purposes. We are using the term "hegemonic" here
in the sense advanced by Antonio Gramsci, that is, as a nonjuridical, but nevertheless practically effective network of dominant economic interests, social and
state institutions, and cultural practices of socialization, selection, and recruit-
ment, which never simply prescribe particular theoretical designs (for example,
that the "bourgeoisie produces bourgeois theories"), but which "merely" marginalize "dysfunctional" theories (Talcott Parsons). Defined in this manner, "dysfunctional" refers primarily to beliefs or ideas that attempt to analyze the mechanisms behind the hegemonic network critically, with the intention of destroying
them. In western societies in their present form, these ideas are, in the first instance, efforts to link Marxist suppositions about social and economic antagonisms (class analysis) with an analysis of cultural, discursive, or subject-
forming processes. Sociocriticism is one such effort.

Of course, marginalization does not necessarily mean elimination. Much more
frequently it means that one way of formulating a question is relegated to a marginal position. The treatment of "literary sociology" or "Marxism" by hegemonic
literary theory and literary history in West Germany is a good example of the
process: "Literary sociology" is recognized as a valid "auxiliary discipline" under
the premise that it is unable to get at the heart of literary texts; while "Marxism,"
represented by certain symbolic names (like "Lukács" and "Goldmann"), is accorded a position far from the middle in the pluralistic parliament of literary
theory.

We assume that one of the reasons Edmund Cros suggests the new term "sociocriticism" for his kind of investigations into literary theory and literary history
is to guard against these marginalizing mechanisms at the outset. Also, In France,
Robert Escarpit's school has already appropriated the term "literary sociology"
[sociologie de la littérature] and defined it through its positivistic research into
the literary market, which leaves the structure of texts untouched.[4] In contrast to
this approach, sociocriticism intends to prove that the encounter with "ideological
traces" [traces idéologiques] or "ideological junctures" [tracés idéologiques], and
with the antagonistic tensions between social classes, is central to any "reading"
of texts. Taking a completely different tack from Derrida, Cros therefore de-

velops an analytical and descriptive structure that demands a strict separation of the language of the text from sociocriticism's metalanguage. He also insists on definitions, on the integration of a variety of other specialized discourses, and on operationality. In effect, Cros resists both the reductive mechanisms and the process of hegemonic "misreading" necessary for reception in the global marketplace. His works are scarcely suited to the imaginary museum of postmodernism; they demand an ideal reader's obstinate curiosity about a new solution to an old, unsolved problem (whether and exactly how literary writing per se is a social struggle) as a kind of intellectual "means test." Given the broad spectrum of objects that Cros deals with, ranging from the picaresque novel of Spanish classicism to contemporary Mexican novels (Carlos Fuentes, Octavio Paz), and even to film (*Citizen Kane* by Orson Welles, *Scarface* by Howard Hawks, and *Stolen Kisses* by François Truffaut), readers are presented with ample opportunity to test his ideas.

II

Let us begin by examining why earlier answers to "the social question of literature" led to a dead end. The problem has always been how to correlate society and literature—or more precisely, society and literary texts—in a convincing fashion. Every attempt to correlate them seems necessarily to have operated between two axes of an underlying matrix: one axis uses sociological categories while the other's are literary. The sociological categories are either analytical (e.g., "class," "social strata," etc.) or synthetic (e.g., "feudal," "bourgeois," etc.), while the literary categories include the "author" (production), the "text" (product), and the "public" (reception). The result is correlations of the following type: "Author X is the product of a petit bourgeois background," "his texts express nostalgia for feudalism," "the effect of this text is compensation for the alienation experienced by proletarian readers," etc. Terms like "express" (which, according to Louis Althusser, belongs to the category of "expressive causality") and "effect" (social functionality) are examples of various types of correlations. The most important correlative categories are certainly "ideology" (which has been used in a very different sense since Marx's writings on the subject), "reflection" (Georg Lukács), and "homology" (Lucien Goldmann). Now it is true that both intuition and theoretical reflection have long since cut the ground out from under this whole matrix and its correlations: Lovers of literature have always, quite justifiably, used their intuition to resist the notion that correlations could exist between such complex, and at the same time, individual structures as the mode of literary expression, style, and "tone" on the one hand and crude sociological categories like classes on the other; more principled, however, is the insight that one cannot even posit "expressive causality" without certain metaphysical presuppositions. In fact, when Lukács, and even Goldmann, advance the thesis that literary textuality necessarily imitates constitutive patterns of the socio-economic structure, one has to wonder about the mimetic medium that links the two. To put it somewhat differently, the theoreticians of reflection or homology need something like a substitute for Hegel's world spirit to make the transmission of structures between materially irreducible fields plausible. It is not clear where this ersatz spirit might come from. Symptomatic of this aporia is the fact that, in spite of every intention of establishing homologies between socio-economic structures and literary *forms*, the analyses, even Goldmann's, either revert to purely *thematic* correlations (Brecht referred sarcastically to Lukács's "contentism instead of formalism")—or, at best, they attempt to correlate *images and symbols* (for example, "reification") from the two levels.

Cros logically begins his attempt to find a new answer with a rejection of Goldmann's "genetic structuralism." As the development of his arguments illustrates, this rejection is primarily related to the axis of literary categories, which foreground the text as such. Cros's sociocritical readings no longer conceive of texts as "expressions of structure" but rather as complex and contradictory examples of materiality in their own right, which means that their textuality is both linguistic and semiotic. Any analysis therefore has to include a lexical and syntactic examination, as well as aspects of "microsemiotics." At first glance, the axis of sociological categories appears to have undergone a few modifications. "Collective subjects" are still identified with units like "classes" or, if need be, with "groups" (for example, various "generations of immigrants" in the United States), and the analysis continues to make use of synthetic concepts such as "bourgeois." Whether equally radical innovations were also necessary here is something we can only wonder at this point.[5] By comparison, the third dimension of the matrix, namely that of the correlation between social and literary categories, has been significantly modified and differentiated. To be sure, Cros still uses the metaphor of "mediation," but the term gains an operative profile in his usage because Cros conceives of it empirically as an *ensemble of "discursive practices" with a synchronic social system*. As examples of "discursive practices" in sixteenth- and seventeenth-century Spain he cites "sermons, pastoral letters, synods, catechisms, Hospitalers' statutes, instructions to the police, and wills." In addition, Cros speaks of the "discourses of collective subjects"; he refers, for example, to "the discourse of merchants," the "plebian discourse," the "discourse of the bourgeoisie," and he also includes the "ideological discourse," the "discourse of morality," the "ethical-religious discourse," the "pre-physiocratic discourse," etc.

This poses the question of the coherence of Cros's terminology. Apparently there are discourses that can be attributed to particular social strata. Yet to avoid misunderstandings, it should be pointed out that this usage, which Cros takes from Michel Pêcheux and Régine Robin, differs significantly from Michel Foucault's. Foucault's theory of "discursive formations" (abbreviated to "discourses") starts from the *axis of the division of labor*, not from the *axis of stratification*. For

Foucault the division of society into specialized, nondiscursive disciplines at the intellectual level corresponds to specialized fields of knowledge, which he calls "discursive formations." For its effectiveness in forming societal "objects," as well as in according competence to selected speakers, any historical ensemble of discursive formations (and here Foucault sometimes speaks of "interdiscursive configurations") is an extremely important factor in the *disposition of power*. Foucault is obviously aware of the functional importance of these discursive power networks (in his final phase he spoke of the instruments of power) within the overall system of social reproduction in a society, including its economy. Foucault nevertheless avoided any ordering into classes and the term "ideology." The question is whether one should view this as an attack on Marxism or as his reluctance to propose quick, possibly false answers in a field of research that is still open.

Michel Pêcheux has, at any rate, attempted to confront Foucault's more tentative and strongly empirical models with a systematic and coherent model, which is primarily theoretical and which is oriented around Althuser's theory of "ideological state apparatuses"; it is Pêcheux's model that Cros adopts. Althusser translated the Marxist notion of state apparatuses, which enforce the interests of the ruling class while claiming to represent the interests of all classes with the result that those ruled are accorded subordinate and marginal "positions," into the sphere of ideology. An "ideological state apparatus," like the medieval or early modern church, accordingly guaranteed the formation of subjects who functioned within the system of feudal reproduction, which meant that sermons for peasants or town-dwellers were different from those for the court.[6] The difference is that the sermons for the peasants and town-dwellers also spoke to the interests and spontaneous ideologemes of the dominated classes, if only in an always subordinate position. These class-specific "rituals" (Althusser) reappear in Pêcheux, Robin, and Cros as "discursive" or "ritual" practices. Cros therefore examines the picaresque novel of sixteenth- and seventeenth-century Spain for traces of the Inquisition and the carnival.

The result is that one encounters in Pêcheux (and also in Cros) first the ensemble of the relations of production and classes, second the ensemble of "ideological state apparatuses," and third (related directly to the former) the ensemble of socially stratified "discourses," which is also called the "interdiscourse."[7] As coherent as Pêcheux's model is, it nevertheless raises a variety of questions. To begin, it simply ignores Foucault's implicit question about the relationship between the discourses generated by the specialization of labor and knowledge and those generated "directly" by society. In Cros the dilemma is reflected in the confrontation of terms like the "discourse of merchants" with an "ethical-religious discourse" or a "moral discourse." More important, however, it keeps any correlation of the three ensembles, and the constitution of class-specific discourses, vague.

In a series of remarkably complex and penetrating analyses Cros attempts to

answer the questions left open by Pêcheux. He insists on the fundamental difference between the "semiological" and the "ideological" components of texts. One
could term the first set of components "integral," while the second refer to a culture's "differential" elements. Examples of the first are universal topoi, collective
symbols, and the categories, beliefs, etc. that are generally accepted (often with
the aura of tradition) throughout the culture. On the other hand, those semiotic
and linguistic elements that bear the clear "mark" of class-specific "discursive formations" are "ideological." The minimal unit of the first type is called a "seme";
the second is an "ideoseme." (As enlightening as this differentiation is, one could
still criticize the choice of terminology because both components are "ideological" in the usage of socially functional semantics or semiotics.)

Using a method analogous to the model of generative grammar (Noam Chomsky), Cros works out the specific chain of "transformations" that begins with the
"semiotic" and "ideological" elements and ends with concrete texts. "Seme" and
"ideoseme" combine to form "microsemiotic" units, which are typically *ambiguous*. An example that Cros frequently employs is Mateo Alemám's phrase
"piedras de precio," which is a defamiliarized version of the topos "piedras
preciosas" (precious stones/costly stones). The seme is therefore linked to an
ideoseme from the "discourse of commerce," i.e., with a connotation from the
world of commodities and inflation. The example is characteristic first of the
microscopic exactitude of Cros's analyses and second it allows us to comprehend
how an analysis of semes and ideosemes can be coupled with a theory of intertextuality derived from Bakhtin: Cros views Bakhtin's social "polyphony" as the
necessary result of his own model of the generative process.

III

The question of how a reconstruction of such "microsemiotic" units is related to
the reconstruction of whole texts naturally arises here. In contrast to the assumption of "totality," at least for literary texts, made by Lukács and Goldmann, complete texts now appear to be made up of a contradictory series of relatively disparate microsemiotic units. A sociocritical reading "deconstructs" this montage,
and Cros uses Derrida's term consciously while at the same time redefining it in
a sociological direction. This form of deconstruction demonstrates that texts are
the result of the *combination* of "semiotic" and "ideological" elements, whereby
the effect of the "semiotic" components is to integrate, for example, by generating
closed series of symbols or ingenious chains of motifs, whereas the "ideological"
components evoke junctures and polyphonies, which are not easily integrated.
The "semiotic" fields therefore appear to be ordered, but at the same time torn
and ruptured by "ideological junctures" [tracés idéologiques]. A sociocritical
reading attempts to reconstruct these ordered/disordered fields as minutely as

possible in order to interpret them (in effect by reversing the generative process "in the direction of the source") as "traces" of social antagonisms.

How Cros proceeds concretely can be seen in his detailed, monographic studies of the novels and films. In *Citizen Kane*, for example, he analyzes the "semiotic" component minutely as a topical network of collective symbols (the rose, the crystal ball, various natural elements, building the Tower of Babel, etc.), which represent the underlying cultural oppositions nature/culture and chaos/order semiotically. The "ideological" faultline in this symbolic network appears in the previews and flashbacks that constitute the narrative's chronological structure, in which Cros sees what is effectively a quasi-Calvinistic ideology of predestination. Whether this thesis is defensible need not be discussed here. For our purposes it is more important to note that these monographic studies tend to omit or at least suspend a precise class analysis of the "ideological" component. Have Cros's concrete historical analyses led him to a position similar to Foucault's skepticism? Furthermore, it is remarkable that the "semiotic" analysis of the textual and cinematic material culminates in an analysis of a "series" or "network" of symbols (in which "symbol" is understood as "image"/"imagery"). In fact, such symbols are "microsemiotic" elements par excellence, in which cultural topology and social polyphony in Bakhtin's sense are particularly closely connected. They function as strategic points of cultural integration. The beauty, fragility, and transitory nature of the rose as a symbol of human existence (*Citizen Kane*) is certainly not class specific. Cros convincingly demonstrates its religious, specifically Christian character, and even its individual components fit: the "bud" is identical to the "virgin snow of childhood innocence." There is, according to Cros, a complex connection between the accumulation of "religious" symbols in the opening sequence and the symbolic "figuration" of the second sequence, "The news on the march." Cros sees a thematic evocation of large-scale capitalism and modernism in the latter sequence, although with the same religious or Christian symbolism (the creation myth, the myth of the construction of the Tower of Babel), which serves to denounce Kane's undertaking as blasphemous hybris. The double reference to Calvinism and large-scale capitalism is thus a sociological indication of the ambivalent coexistence of the petit and haute bourgeoisie.

For Cros, however, the point of this argumentation is to emphasize the ideological semanticization of filmic syntax and the medium itself: the techniques of flashback and insert are themselves treated as symbols of predestination. The result is that Cros's sociocritical reading has progressed beyond elements of content or semantics to the analysis of apparently "contentless" aesthetic forms — which, as has already been pointed out, correspond, when viewed with a great deal of caution, to his sociological assessments. This really raises the question of whether his choice of Pêcheux over Foucault as the source of his concept of "interdiscourse" does not demand a reappraisal. As long as polyphony, for example in collective symbols, is simply conceived of as stratified *social* polyphony (i.e., as the polyphony of various classes or social strata), a fundamental element is missing. This component is nothing less than the *social integration of the "schizo-praxis" brought about by the division of labor and knowledge*. In *Citizen Kane* it means that the traditional Christian interdiscourse (in the sense of the integration of economy and sexuality in the nuclear family) is confronted by the modern, irreligious interdiscourse of the technological mass media. Orson Welles's point— which Cros has worked out brilliantly— is that the technological mass medium film is itself used symbolically, just as religious ideology is. Still the question naturally remains, who ultimately "sublates" whom in this synthesis?: Is the predestination implied in filmic syntax not itself marked by an "ideological" faultline, which reflects the discrepancy between this modern medium's obvious sovereignty over time and the underlying symbols of vanity? Would a complementary hypothesis, one wholly inspired by Cros's sociocritical reading, allow for a more exact sociological classification? Certainly not in the sense of a class analysis. But a classification using "*socio-historical blocks*" and "*hegemonies*" in Antonio Gramsci's sense probably is possible. In this particular case the result would be an analysis of the specific form of tension between the petit and the haut bourgeoisie, who are part of the same block, which is nevertheless dominated by the haut bourgeoisie through a *hegemonic process*: *Citizen Kane* tells the story of a failed attempt to build a gigantic capitalist enterprise in order to recapture the happiness of the little house in the snow—but the aesthetic sovereignty is that of the camera, which not only did not exist at the same time as the little house, it could not have existed then. Cros does not attempt to explain the ambivalence of this sovereignty: On the one hand, it functions as a fateful technological process; on the other hand, as the desire for the union of technological perfection and childlike innocence. It would be a mistake to correlate one aspect with large-scale industry and the other with the petit bourgeoisie, and Cros is completely correct in rejecting such a classification. In principle, however, it seems to us that the ambivalence and contradictions could be correlated with the contradictory *hegemonic processes* that operate between the two sectors of the bourgeoisie. Gramsci at least reflects on the process in his notes on "Americanism and Fordism" in the *Prison Notebooks*. Cros's extremely detailed and convincing analysis of Howard Hawks's *Scarface*, which we are unable to deal with in the space of this introduction, points in this direction.

One could elaborate our implicit argument that Cros's sociocriticism be expanded to include Gramci's concept of the socio-historical block and its corresponding hegemony—or what is generally more important for literature, the *project* of a socio-historical block and a hegemony—using as an example Cros's own central text corpus, namely the picaresque novel of the Spanish Golden Age. First and foremost, however, the example seems well-suited to illustrate the innovative differences and advantages of Cros's sociocriticism over other forms of literary sociology. The picaresque novel is after all the *classic* paradigm of a

fictional text that even established academic literary criticism attempts to correlate with social conditions. The "compulsion" behind this *sociological* form of
literary criticism rests on the belief that the picaresque novel is somehow "realistic" (in contrast to pastoral and chivalric novels, which are generally thought to
be "idealizations"), in that it is the product of a highly complex form of
referentiality—namely the integration of various types of "real references" in
Searle's sense. In addition, the challenge seems to be a result of the anonymity
of the author of the first picaresque novel (*Lazzrillo de Tormes*): Since there could
be no recourse to the notion of the author as an individual genius, solving the riddle he presented, especially because *Lazzrillo de Tormes* confronts the interpreter
with an apparently *autobiographical form*, involved turning to the ideological and
social sphere. Besides, because of its autobiographical form the picaresque novel
always awakened a particular interest in the genesis of "modern subjectivity."

The voluminous secondary literature on the picaresque novel is therefore
characterized by its fundamental *socio-historical* impetus, and it is filled with excursions into the cause and extent of beggary in imperial Spain (the age of Charles
V and Phillip II) and the repressive measures employed to limit it, with accounts
of the Spanish notion of honor (the "limpieza de sangre"), with discussions of the
degree of poverty experienced by the old Christian nobility ("hidalgos"), and so
on. If we speak here somewhat polemically of "excursions," the reason is that
these thoroughly valuable investigations do not actually come to grips with the
textual structure of the picaresque novel; they simply assume referentiality on the
part of the novel and hope that ideological and historical explanations of supposed
"real equivalences" will help clarify the novel itself. In the best of circumstances
these more or less intuitive assumptions approach the theoretical status of the
ideas of the Russian Formalist Jurij Tynjanov, who imagined a correlation (in his
theses "On literary evolution") between occurrences within literature and extra-
literary social phenomena using the formation of series as a model.

That Cros proceeds differently is obvious at first glance. He completely omits
the sort of excursions into the extra-literary "series" mentioned above, which are
supposedly closely connected with the picaresque novel; he also does not attempt
to derive the ideosemiotic features of the picaresque text from knowledge about
the instance of the author (the "converso" or newly Christian Mateo Alemán in
the case of *Guzmán de Alfarache*, and Don Francisco de Quevedo, who is generally considered to have been a representative of—Tridentine—orthodoxy, in the
case of *Buscón*). Instead he focuses his socio-critical examination on textual
structure—and on it alone. Specifically Cros presents a number of suggestive and
brilliant analyses of the semiotic and ideological function of a fictional, polyphonic discourse in which one and the same "I" unites such heterogeneous, self-
denying, and camouflaging voices as those of a marginalized criminal aktant, a
penitent sinner making a general confession, and a moral guardian with his claims
of universal validity (*Guzmán de Alfarache*), which parallels the extraordinary

artistry and linguistic gymnastics used to stage a discourse that mystifies and demystifies at the same time (*Buscón*). Cros's description of the contradictory relationship of these voices to one another, including the cultural and social norms and values that they both proclaim and deny, can be summed up with the categories of *simulation, assimilation*, and *dissimulation*. Building on research carried out by Antonio Gómez-Moriana[8] and L. Cardaillac, Cros is able to demonstrate convincingly that these complex—textual-semiotic—mechanisms of simulation, assimilation, and dissimulation are linked to the ensemble of discursive and ritual practices generated by the constitution of the Inquisition's tribunals—an example of a repressive, ideological state apparatus par excellence. Just as the assimilation of the "converso" into Christianity always encountered the suspicion that it was merely a simulation, which fundamentally relegated the notion of "truth" to the realm of dissimulation, so too do the structural laws of the picaresque novel seem to be based completely on double or multiple codifications, which are the result of constant friction between an orthodox and a heterodox discourse. The carnival, when viewed in Bakhtin's sense, offers a paradigm case of the coexistence of orthodoxy and heterodoxy. In a similar fashion, Cros can plausibly argue that the ideo-semiotic structure of repression is articulated in the code of the festival, and conversely that the Inquisition and carnival function as complimentary interpretative frameworks.

One could therefore describe Cros's sociocritical praxis as the discovery of a series of "transformations" that occur between social practices and the narrowly defined, semiotic structure of texts. The distance from Cros to Goldmann is clear: Whereas in Goldmann the correspondence between a social collective's vision of the world and the vision expressed in any given text, or by its genial author, always remains mysterious, not matter how many parameters from intellectual history are arranged around the text, Cros is able to explain in a plausible fashion how a text—independent of the author's "will" and even of his supposed "personal" ideology—is related to an "ideological formation" ["formation idéologique"], which transforms textual semiotics into ideosemiotics. However, as suggestive as Cros's analyses of the picaresque novel within the framework of a discursive formation are, how he makes the step from the semiotics of ideology to the correlation with a "social formation" nevertheless remains vague. He postulates the correlation theoretically, for example, when he writes: "Every act of speech sets in motion an interdiscourse that marks in the text the discursive traces of an ideological formation and, in this way, refers us to a social formation." (p. 84). In practice Cros limits himself on the one hand to an extremely detailed linguistic and semiotic analysis of the complex of signs related to "wool" and "cloth" in order to associate them with the dominant sector of the Spanish economy, namely the cloth industry and the cloth trade; on the other hand, he restricts himself to decidedly global statements about class analysis. For example, when speaking of the class antagonism between an aristocracy that was losing its economic power and a bourgeoisie that was prevented from acquiring political power, Cros neglects to explain the specific, concrete details of this antagonism in Spain. In our opinion, it is precisely the possibility for such specification and differentiation that is opened up theoretically by Gramsci's concept of the social-historical block, especially because it does not refer to the union of various classes and social strata solely for the purpose of obtaining or stabilizing their hegemony but rather to the ensemble of forms and realms of social praxis, which are necessary to make "cementing" a particular social-historical block seem advantageous, and which eliminate and marginalize dysfunctional forms of praxis. It is this simultaneous conceptualization of a (more or less "vertical") social stratification and a (more or less "horizontal") division of labor that could make it possible to integrate the work of Américo Castro—which Cros barely touches on (or for an analysis of Spanish social formations, the important debate between Castro and Claudio Sánchez-Albornoz), and which stresses the extremely "horizontal" division between the old Spanish Christians and the "conversos" and "morisocos"—into an approach that does not neglect the categories of class analysis.

It is precisely in his analysis of the contradictory nature (if you will, the polyphony) of the first person pronoun as a sign of the contradictory, polyphonic *subject* that Cros succeeds de facto in correlating instances of discursive and ideological practices with hegemonic *processes* (i.e., with block-forming *relationships*) instead of with substantial classes. The carnivalesque masking of the subject and the dictation of the subject by the Inquisition are the two poles of the hegemonic magnet between which the picaresque subject carries out his meandering journey. Not the least of Cros's achievements is that his reading of the picaresque ego provides a sociocritical decoding of an extremely important prototype for the modern subject.

Translator's Note

I should like to acknowledge my debt to two colleagues at the University of Pittsburgh: Keith McDuffie, of the Department of Hispanic Languages and Literatures, who gave of his time to check over and in some cases correct my translations from the Spanish; and Dana Polan, of the Film Studies Program in the Department of English, who allowed me to make use of his translation of part of Chapter 8. In addition, I take this opportunity to thank the editorial staff of the University of Minnesota Press for the care they took in preparing the manuscript for publication.

Part I
Theoretical Questions

Chapter 1
From Experimental Sociology to Genetic Structuralism

I

"The sociology of literature suffers from an obvious and excessive backwardness; its foundations are practically still to be laid. We hesitate over methodological perspectives: we are certain neither of the manner of posing the problems, nor of their hierarchical ordering; nor are we sure of the exact scope of the discipline: hence its frequent wallowing in the sociology of art or in the sociology of knowledge; we do not differentiate vigorously enough between problems specific to the discipline and those common to other disciplines.[1]"

Albert Memmi, who wrote these lines in 1960, justified this backwardness by a "refusal of sociology" based on two fundamental reasons that, it seems to me, still hold true: on the one hand an "evident revulsion on the part of writers themselves to see themselves in sociological terms"; on the other "the very resistance of society to the development of this sociology." The fact is that we are dealing here with an ideological conception of the literary act, which should serve precisely to reveal the nature and function of literature in our societies: surrounded by the same respect as religion, cultural "creation" perceived as a privileged means of access to universal categories, with exceptional minds leading the way, would be, through the mystery of inspiration, incomprehensible in its genesis, unforeseeable in its destiny." Thus conceived, it would reconstruct the social consensus insofar as it ensures the constant reproduction of unanimously recognized values. "It is a fact that, to the bourgeois mind, culture and art are completely

3

independent of social forms—a vision of the world that is dehistoricized, depoliticized, and desocialized. For the bourgeois mind, art develops as a specific history no longer contained within social history.[2]"

There is nothing surprising, then, in the fact that the precursors of the sociological approach are to be sought in materialist milieus. Let me call to mind the fact that Taine's determinist position has survived in the form of a schematic neopositivism which tends to explain every literary text on the basis of a single, unmediated social phenomenon. This reductive methodology, which, as A. Memmi further explains, ends up destroying the very object of the scientific enterprise— namely, the specificity of the literary act—has, until now, done a considerable disservice to sociological criticism.

Other factors, however, are involved in this supposed backwardness, in particular the absence of any delimitation of the object of theoretical focus. Certain currents of opinion are interested above all in extratextual elements: the economic and professional status of authors, the problem of literary generations, the book trade, audiences, the evolution of printing techniques, and so on. Such is the case of the "experimental" method of R. Escarpit, who is interested as much in the "locus of reading, consumption, and reception" as in the "locus of incubation," claiming that the "reality" of a text can only appear through its utilization by successive audiences. When he attaches the historical value of a work to the necessity of "thoroughly studying the makeup of the audience that has received it, its different social categories, the life-styles of these diverse social categories," or when he differentiates, among these several publics, the public *qua* support, the public *qua* interlocutor, the public the artist has in mind when he or she writes, the publisher's theoretical public, and the real public, Escarpit has us measure exactly certain incontestably important facts, only to the degree, however, that these extrinsic facts are invested in the text in one form or another.[3] For this reason, one can justly appreciate the relationship he establishes between the invention in 1800 of the steam-driven printing press—responsible for the appearance of mass culture—and the rise of certain phenomena termed "aesthetic":

> From this time forward, there is a break between artist and audience;
> the artist, the producer, can no longer know his public, have a sense of
> it; the numbers are too great. A system appears which makes the author
> a producer for a market; and this system of mass communications is en-
> tirely new. There is a mutual breakdown between author and au-
> dience. . . . From this state of affairs, a great number of aesthetic
> phenomena arise: the isolation of the Romantic poet, the impression
> that his voice is stuck in his throat because he cannot see his audience,
> etc.[4]

We may reproach him, however, for separating "aesthetic criticism" from the sociological approach and for setting his sights on the elucidation of problems of literary history by means of sociological methods.[5] This valorization of the quantifiable and of the intersubjective level at the expense of intrinsic textual criticism is shared—despite the differences separating them—by A. Silbermann ("Goldmann and Sanguineti seek what they call the 'structure' of literary works, a word I find most inappropriate: it would be better to speak of their 'value.' This seems to me a purely aesthetic pursuit which can, of course, be accomplished from the psychological point of view as well as from the sociological point of view. . . . For an empirical sociologist concerned with cultural sociology the aesthetic value of the work of art, the distinction between noble and vulgar literature, are facts of no importance"),[6] H. A. Fügen ("By considering the literary work not as an artistic . . . but as a social phenomenon, the sociology of literature foregoes aesthetic evaluation"),[7] and K. E. Rosengren.[8] For each of them, the fictional text is conceived only as a catalyst capable of setting processes in motion. According to Silbermann, "the sociological fact exists only from the point when there is social action, a relation between two persons, between an individual and a group, among groups or societies. A literary fact can also be a sociological fact but the literary act itself is not sociological. A musical score sleeping in a drawer does not exist in a sociological sense. It must be played and listened to. Only the musical event—the performance and the hearing of the work—is sociological. The same goes for literature."[9] This position reminds us of that of Jean-Paul Sartre in *What Is Literature?*: "The literary object is a strange top which exists only in movement. In order to make it appear, a concrete act called reading is required. It lasts only as long as this reading can last. Outside of that, there are only black marks on paper. . . ."[10]

At first glance, the sociology of content, according to which the literary work is a historical document bearing direct witness to the societies involved, seems to be opposed to the exclusion of fictional texts from the domain of empirical research. Several options will be described here. The most important one is represented by North American content analysis, which is particularly interested in the way in which so-called trivial literary texts, the short stories of popular magazines, reflect social values and behaviors. Thus B. Berelson and J. P. Salter have established that ethnic minorities, underrepresented in fictional texts, most often play devalued roles.[11] For his part, Miltos Albrecht, finding in a corpus of similar texts a broad reproduction of ten social values previously identified by reference to nonliterary sources, observes that the degree of autonomy of the texts with respect to this system of values is all the greater as one climbs the sociocultural ladder.[12] In France, Henri Zalamansky has taken the same path, proposing in this way to complete the studies of Escarpit. He writes,

> Our intention is to gather the most complete data possible, and by making an inventory of the contents of contemporary works, see what conclusions we can draw from this classification. Every author responds

to a problematic of his time: by examining the content of contemporary works, we shall see how the problems of our time are approached and what solution they receive. The whole set of answers which each author proposes will acquaint us with the ideological models presented to the imagination of readers and designed to act upon their consciousness.

To illustrate this program, Zalamansky, after having chosen to examine three problems—the city, colonialism, and the couple— poses the following questions:

(1) What do they contain, that is, how can we classify their themes?
(2) What information can they give us about the particular problems we are studying?
(3) What conclusions can be drawn from our readings? What is the nature of the suggested responses? Do they achieve a coherence that would enable us to speak of them as "models"? What are these models?[13]

Undoubtedly the argument stating that this method is more appropriate for the more delicate problems posed by contemporary works is not lacking in force, but we can see immediately the reservations that arise from such an approach. Indeed, Umberto Eco teaches us, after Lukács and Goldmann, that the reproduction of social models operates not at the level of contents but at the level of structures: "Fleming is not reactionary because he puts a Russian or a Jew in the slot marked 'evil' in his schema; he is reactionary because he proceeds by schemas; Manichean role distribution is always dogmatic and intolerant."[14] Other objections can be raised. The investigation of texts proceeds from questions external to the corpus being examined, posing the problem of their choice. P. Henry and S. Moscovici answered that objection by proposing to identify

> words or fragments of texts grouped by thematic categories or classified by likeness. These words and textual fragments are significant insofar as they denote something pertinent from the point of view of the attitude under consideration, that is, as a function of the possibility of relating them to one of the components or subcomponents of this attitude. Components and directions define thematic categories. The enumeration of the elements in each category should in principle describe the intensity of the attitude according to this or that component and in this or that direction.[15]

In that case, however, the meaning of the observed frequencies depends upon the comparison that can be made between them and the frequencies of the same elements noted in other texts, whether literary or nonliterary, or in reality itself. Nonetheless, other reservations remain: in what way, for example, does such a criticism differ from traditional thematic criticism? Did not Zalamansky himself, using the classification proposed by Memmi, see in the sociology of contents a sociology of themes? We note, moreover, that the conception of literature under-lying such approaches makes a historical document of the fictional text:

> Such a study seems to us incontestably rich for the understanding of our own period, for it analyzes the intellectual and psychological nourish-ment of a whole sector of the population. . . . If, in other respects, we speak of information, it is because we think that, in many cases, a book is truly an act of knowledge, and that it is false to claim that the writer cannot contribute any information of value, on an equal footing with the journalist or the historian: the writer's talent permits him to convey the atmosphere of an event or of a period, to seize hold of a reality which escapes the cold flatness of objective reporting.[16]

It is a question not of denying the fictional text an informative function, but rather of giving it its specificity and of situating it elsewhere than in those superficial zones of the literary work where content analysis places it. Zalamansky relegates to a footnote a significant remark of Hemingway's in *For Whom the Bell Tolls*: "Even if you read twenty newspapers you will never get a complete image of the situation."[17] It happens that the literary work accomplishes what the newspaper cannot claim to attain, thanks precisely to fiction's capacity to accumulate infor-mation. This prompts Yuri Lotman to say that "art is the most economical and the most dense means of preserving and transmitting information."[18] But the qual-ity of this information cannot be perceived in an anthology of isolated reflections, selected according to criteria extrinsic to the work. "We must have people," writes Tolstoy, "who display that aberrant quest for isolated ideas in an artistic work, who keep guiding readers inside the infinite labyrinth of connections in which the essence of art consists, according to the laws which serve as the basis of these connections."[19] "And if myopic critics think I have only wanted to de-scribe what pleased me—what Oblonski eats for lunch or the shoulders of Anna Karenina—they are mistaken. In everything, or almost everything, I have writ-ten, I have been guided by the need to gather ideas that express themselves in con-nection with one another. But each idea set forth in words taken separately loses its meaning; it is dreadfully degraded when it is taken in isolation and outside the sequence in which it appears."[20] Using this remark of Tolstoy's as support, Lot-man synthesizes with remarkable clarity the objections that can be made to con-tent analysis on this point.[21]

P. Zima writes,

> A sociology of literature, in which dramatic or novelistic representa-tions of social groups are immediately used at the level of explication, that is, wrenched out of the total fictional context constituted by con-notative writing, loses its raison d'être. It is based on the naive preju-dice according to which literary texts refer immediately to "reality" (to referents); in other words, that they have a denotative character as

"semiologic facts" (Mukarovsky). At the same time it ignores connotative procedures without which literature is inconceivable as fiction, as a second "connoted" reality, whose signs do not immediately designate elements of common sense reality.[22]

Are literary texts the only ones in question? Analyzing two recent works by French historians whose merits she discusses in detail, Régine Robin regrets that only thematic categories have been implemented:

> The thematic method, as we have already said, goes through the linguistic structure of the text, its own materiality, constituted of selected words and combinations, thereby neglecting the syntactical structure of the text, its specific lexicon, and the semantic network that ties all the words together.
>
> In the same way, the very level of discourse itself, its structure, its strategy of argumentation, its rhetoric, the mechanisms of enunciation by which the speaker participates in discourse—all are eluded. In short, texts are used only for their content, with the initial and implicit axiom that the content is univocal, rendered in its plenitude by the mere act of reading.[23]

This remark of Régine Robin's leads us to nuance the preceding judgments by Lotman and Zima. Undoubtedly there exists a specificity of the fictional text, but it is really a question of distinguishing the specificity of one discursive practice from the other discursive practices operating within the framework of a given society: sermons, bishops' summonses, synods, catechisms, rituals, official orders, hospital statutes, police rules, testaments, and so forth, must equally be examined apart from their denotative function.

Is it right to pile up these objections, and in doing so, are we not passing over in silence a number of established facts? The preceding approaches do have certain merits: the exploration of the conditions of existence of the literary act, the extrinsic spotlighting of certain socialized elements in the message, the sensitivity to mass culture (magazines, songs, detective novels, children's stories, advertising slogans, newspaper reporting, etc.). By broadening the scope of our studies, they can give the impression of clearing away certain barriers and enlarging the scope of literature, thus playing a liberating role. One may wonder, however, if, by including in one and the same undiversified approach such heterogeneous categories each of which thereby loses the specificity of its function and its modeling form, one does not end up revalorizing "classical" literature all the more.

The problem seems to me to be epistemological. Experimental sociology (Escarpit, Bordeaux) and empirical sociology (Silbermann), as well as North American content analysis, are interested in the sociological phenomena represented by literary phenomena and not in literature in itself, which explains why they do not take into consideration the specificity of the fictional text. The polemics that have arisen between empiricists and Goldmannians are, at a certain level, meaningless, since they are applied to different theoretical objects. Is this confusion maintained by an absence of tradition, which, according to A. Memmi, characterizes the present state of the sociology of literature? If so, one needs to make some distinctions. Indeed, Memmi made this judgment at the beginning of the 1960s, which saw the onset in France of a radical change in this domain, with the studies of Lucien Goldmann, the discovery, thanks again to Goldmann and the *Arguments* group, of the work of Lukács, and, especially, that of the work of the Social Research Institute of Frankfurt whose members (Max Horkheimer, T. W. Adorno, Herbert Marcuse, Erich Fromm, Walter Benjamin) would henceforth serve as "principal reference," according to Gérard Delfau and Anne Roche.[24] Zima remarks, however, that the empirical sociology of literature must be linked with certain traditions in sociology, and that the theories of those who quote the authority of these traditions draw their inspiration from the criterion of *Wertfreiheit* (scientific objectivity) defined by Max Weber. "In the sociology of literature," writes Zima, "which conceives itself as an empirical and 'exact' science, Weber's attempt to trace a line of demarcation between ideology and science repeats itself each time theoreticians motivated by neopositivist ideals seek to substitute quantifiable empirical knowledge for 'subjective' value judgments."[25] It is this axiom, he asserts, that leads to that peculiar concept of the literary text "as a pure object, so that the social events responsible for its genesis as well as the ideological changes that it does or does not produce at the level of reception remain *external* to it," as if it were a pretext for the study of social communication or a mirror of social customs and values.[26] Declaring that the specificity of the literary text does not concern sociological analysis, empirical sociology excludes the possibility of displaying the sociohistorical setting as it may appear in structure or in writing practice. Moreover, it furnishes "immanent philological interpretation with 'scientific' arguments to support the official theory according to which 'literary works of art' are autonomous entities born of general inspiration."[27] In both cases it reveals the ideological foundations of its theory.

However this may be, the reader will understand, at the conclusion of this rapid survey, the need for propounding a theory based on the prior definition of a specific object of study different from the one that the sociology of literature has considered thus far. This implies the establishment of a new discipline and, to avoid any confusion, the creation of a new terminology.

2

With respect to the traditional sociology of literature, genetic structuralism seems to me to represent a radically new approach to literature. It is well known that in Lucien Goldmann's own view his principal discoveries were the *trans-*

individual subject and the *structured* character of this subject's intellectual, emotional, and practical behavior.[28]

> With the appearance of Man, that is, of a being endowed with *language, social life and the division of labor* appear. One must henceforth distinguish individual behaviors (libido) from transindividual behaviors (collective or plural). When John and Peter lift a heavy object there are neither *two* actions nor *two* autonomous consciousnesses for which each partner would perform the function, respectively, of *object* for the other, but one single action whose *subject* is *John and Peter*. The consciousness of each one of these two persons is understandable only with respect to this transindividual subject.[29]

Every individual, at a given moment of his existence, is part of a great number of different collective subjects, and passes through many more in the course of his life. This perspective leads Goldmann to distinguish three levels of consciousness: to the first two—the unconcious and the alert consciousness—already mentioned, he adds the nonconscious (*le non conscient*) "formed by the intellectual, emotional, and imaginary structures and practices of individual consciousnesses. The nonconscious is a creation of transindividual subjects, and on the psychic level, it has a status analogous to that of the nervous and muscular structures on the physiological level. It is distinctly different from the Freudian unconscious (*l'inconscient*) in that it is not repressed and need not overcome any resistance in order to become conscious but has only to be brought to light by scientific analysis."[30]

In fact, every human behavior transcribes both a libidinal structure and a structure in which the nonconscious has been invested. As different as they are, these two structures intermingle such that "each of the two meanings assumes, in a concrete case, a greater or lesser importance with respect to the other."[31] In this context, Goldmann imagines two extremes, "on the one hand, cases in which the libidinal meaning is predominant to the point of totally disorganizing the socialized meaning—the case of the mentally deranged—and, on the other hand, those in which, on the contrary, in a certain zone of the individual's activity, the collective meaning is carried to its ultimate coherence, and without undergoing any distortion, totally assimilates the socialized meaning. This is the case of the great creative minds. Between these two extremes are ordinary people—myself, you, all the others."[32] This statement allows us to understand better what makes up the world vision of transindividual subjects. It can be defined as the totality of aspirations, feelings, and ideas that unites the members of a group and opposes them to other groups. The world vision of a collective subject is an abstraction. It can be defined only by extrapolating from an actual tendency in the members of a group "who all attain this class consciousness in a more or less coherent manner. Individuals have a *relative* awareness of the orientation of their feelings; rarely do they attain complete coherence. To the extent that they succeed in expressing it on the conceptual or imaginative level, they are philosophers or writers, and their work is all the more important as it comes close to the schematic coherence of a world vision, that is to say, to the *maximum potential consciousness* of the social group they express."[33] *Real consciousness* is indeed the result of the obstacles and deviations that different factors of empirical reality oppose to the achievement of this potential consciousness.[34] It is, in particular, the actions of other social groups that are opposed to possible consciousness. *Possible consciousness* is in turn an abstraction that defines, on the basis of definite historical circumstances, what ought to be the consciousness of a social group involved in these circumstances. This hypothesis presupposes that awareness varies from one individual to another and that only exceptional individuals (great artists, in particular) are capable of giving coherent expression to the collective consciousness of their group. World vision, when it is embodied in a literary structure, would somehow reveal the totality – unachieved in reality – of the feelings, the aspirations and ideas of the members of a specific class, organized in a coherent and perfectly rational system. To wonder if Pascal was a Jansenist would be to wonder, Goldmann asserts, "to what extent his thought was similar or analogous to Arnauld's or to Nicole's." He proposes a reversal of the problem "by first establishing what Jansenism was as a social and ideological phenomenon and then what an entirely consistent Jansenism would be";[35] it is this rationally consistent Jansenism that constitutes a world vision.

At the heart of Goldmann's theoretical apparatus appear connections between genetic structuralism and

(1) Goldmann's reading of Lukács's work, in which the "category of totality (*History and Class Consciousness*)" is presented "as a historical, materialist version of the concept of form (*The Soul and Forms*),"[36] whereas, if we accept Zima's analysis in *Pour une sociologie du texte littéraire:* "By considering the conceptual discourse of the young Lukács as a continuity marked solely by the transition from an ahistorical idealism to a historical materialism, Goldmann gives greater importance to Lukács's Hegelianism and neglects the Kantian phase of his thought (dualist, hostile to the principle of identity). His *genetic structuralism*, which he himself conceives as a development of the methodological approach of the young Lukács, is thus a logical continuation of the Hegelian aesthetic."[37]

(2) The thought of Max Weber, from which Goldmann incorporates certain concepts: (a) The data of *comprehensive analysis*, which aims at reaching the internal, subjective meanings of human behavior. (Cf. "One of the principal merits of phenomenology and, in psychology, of the school of Form, has been to remind us of the importance of this consciousness and of the meanings that acts and events have for it. In a sense, to study history is first to try to *understand* the actions of men, their motives, the goals they pursued, the meaning that their behaviors and their actions had *for them*.")[38] (b) The notion of *ideal type*, already an abstract

construction, whose elaboration strove to surpass the empirical, descriptive approach in order to arrive at the essentials. In this sense, Weber's puritanism has been viewed as having no real existence, but rather, as an operative concept uniting the essential, typical features of that religion, while eliminating all the empirical data not essential to the definition of the phenomenon. The notion of ideal type is itself to be related to that of *objective possibility*, which consists in imagining an academic hypothesis according to which history is reconstructed as a function of the consequences that would have been brought about by a historic event that, in fact, did not occur. (What would the United States have become had the South won the Civil War? What would Europe have become had Hitler not been defeated?)

Such, in its essential features, is the contribution of a line of inquiry that its author, just before his death, deemed it useful to pursue and to complete in two directions: "The most important gaps in our research, it seems to me—and I insist on emphasizing it here—concern the reception of literary works, which could and should also be studied with genetic structuralist methods, and the element I have called the 'richness' of the work, which presents an important sociological dimension."[39]

The polemics arising from genetic structuralism are well known: in its time it was reproached for being an illustration of "a pseudo-Marxism," for conceiving art only as imitation, for making the artistic work fit preestablished sociological hypotheses, for developing a new theory of reflection, or for establishing in too mechanical and too schematic a way "direct dependencies, beyond the ideas and the ideology of a period, between the social and economic structures of a society, on the one hand, and the structure of literary creation, on the other." In his lifetime, Goldmann made short work of most of these accusations, certain of which reflected bad faith and were based on hasty, biased reading.[40] On the other hand, we should keep in mind Zima's analyses of the principle of homology between aesthetic structure and social structure,[41] taking as his point of departure Goldmann's thesis on Kant.[42] Zima summarizes the thesis in these terms:

> Goldmann distinguishes three stages in bourgeois philosophical thought: the individualist stage, during which empiricism and Enlightenment rationalism were born; the tragic stage, whose reversals mark the philosophies of Kant and Pascal; and finally the dialectical stage, characterized by the theories of Hegel, Marx, and Lukács. . . . According to Goldmann, the principal reason for the abstract, "reified" character of the Kantian and Pascalian categories is the inability of tragic thought to go beyond individualism and the concept of the "individual subject," to discover that concrete knowledge is possible only from the point of view of a *collective* ("transindividual") *subject* positioned within the historical process.[43]

Along with Zima, the reader can, in this philosophy of history, readily recognize the general outlines of Goldmann's critical approach to the theater of Racine, to the dramas of Gombrowicz (in *Operette*, "reproduced in simplified form, is the schema of Racinian tragedy: the individualist ahistoric consciousness [in Racine, tragic consciousness; here existentialist consciousness] is dialectically transcended by a revolutionary concept of the world, the isolated 'self' moves toward human community"[44]), to the theater of Jean Genêt, or to the novels of André Malraux.[45] The reader will likewise notice, with Zima, the different perspectives in which homologies between literary structures and social structures are defined, as a function of the works studied. Indeed, it is only in relation to Racine and Pascal that the basic concept of genetic structuralism will be applied, namely, mediatization by a world vision; this concept disappears, in particular, when the analysis of a contemporary novel is taken up: "Fiction, perhaps like modern poetry and painting, is an authentic form of cultural creation that it is impossible to connect even to the potential consciousness of a particular social group."[46] One last reservation remains, concerning two interrelated questions: Is the content of a fictional text reducible to a monosemic conceptual discourse? Is it permissible to attribute a coherent organization to textual structures and to world visions which reorganize in this way the chaos of actual experience? On the first point, at the very least, one might plead that, had Goldmann lived, he probably would have been led to question his early conclusions in order to take into account the results of the research he intended to carry out on "the richness of the work." Let us be content with the observation that in acknowledging the "lacunae" of his theory, he was clearly conscious himself of the pertinence of this objection. On the second point, it is obvious that he is a prisoner of his own premise, since world vision, the keystone of genetic structuralism, can be defined only within the framework of a *rational* reconstitution of the data. Indeed, what separates this concept from the concept of real consciousness is, of course, the way in which the investigator constructs a *coherent* extrapolation from a specific thought system in order to build the mediating structure.

The problem, however, remains intact and deserves our undivided attention. In a first phase of analysis, we shall be careful not to confuse the coherence of a hypothetical vision of the world with the equally hypothetical coherence of the text. Concerning the latter, one cannot but subscribe to the affirmation in *The Hidden God* that the "sense of one element depends upon the coherence of the whole work in its entirety."[47] This is certainly the way in which the text, "semanticizing" the totality of the work, is organized. (We shall return later to this question; see pp. 80–84.) We shall make the following assumptions:

(1) There exists for each text a combinatory system of genetic elements responsible for the global production of meanings, which does not mean that these elements have a monosemic character. On the contrary, since they have appeared to me, in the course of my analyses, as vectors of conflict, I have been led to con-

sider that every textual element inserted at the heart of the production of meaning can be functioning only in a pluriaccentuated form.

(2) This specific textual system renders the text autonomous with respect to referential reality, a theoretical position that is radically different from genetic structuralism, and that rests, in turn, upon an observation I have made, allowing me to affirm that every ideological trace invested in a textual structure seems to disconnect itself from the ideological set upon which it depends in order to enter a new combination to which it transfers its own capacity to produce meaning.

Allowing for these reservations, certain of genetic structuralism's conclusions seem to me incontestable and will form part of my own critical approach. These are the concepts of the transindividual subject and the nonconscious. This last point, however, calls for further precision insofar as it seems to operate for Goldmann only at the level of the implicit values of a literary work. I have sought to describe its effects in a more precise way, taking as my point of departure the pertinent remark of Tynianov's that "social life enters into correlation with literature through, above all, its verbal aspect."[48] Proceeding from the principle that every collectivity inscribes in its discourse the indexes of its spatial, social, and historical insertion, and consequently generates specific microsemiotics, I have endeavored to describe the levels where these indexes may be found. It has seemed to me that the most obvious traces are located on the paradigmatic axes, in readymade expressions, stilted phrases and *lexies* [taken in the sense given to the term by Roland Barthes in *S/Z* (Paris: Seuil, 1970, p. 20: "a unit of reading"]. The way the last named become lexicalized actually appears to me to transcribe, in a much more immediately noticeable way, social value systems and the changes that modify them, modes of living and of socioeconomic insertion of the milieus producing them, as well as the evolution of mental structures. Let us take a few particularly striking examples: the progressive disappearance, or, more carefully put, the diminution of the frequency of use of such expressions as *vieux garçon, vieille fille* (the usage of which tends to be reserved for description of character and no longer for designation of civil status), or *fille-mère*, which transcribes the evolution of the French conception of marriage or virginity as social values. Likewise, the events of May 1968, which put principles of authority and hierarchy in question, spontaneously produced lexicalizations connected with the differentiation of functions (*enseignants/enseignés*), rejecting signs that, until then, had described social relations now appearing to have ideological significance (*professeurs, maîtres, étudiants, élèves*). This lexical pattern was extended to other domains (*soignants/soignés; pénétrant/pénétré . . .*), but we shall note, with interest, that the sectors concerned were those in which the problematizing of subjection remained the most acute. Like all social movements, May 1968 produced meaning, and it would be interesting to study how the fluctuations of these lexicalizations translated the appropriation by the dominant ideology of values that had been, for a time, contested. Similarly, we shall investigate the relations that may have existed between the crisis of colonialism and the expression "*à part entière*," which, born in a famous political speech, was spontaneously applied to domains other than the one from which it came. Let us take other periods and other structures: the expression *piso principal*, which is not found in Covarrubias but is, however, found in the *Diccionario de autoridades*, seems to correspond to a first stage of urban expansion in Spain, where, entrenched inside the old boundaries of the city, the "bourgeois," before exploring the possibilities of horizontal social segregation, opted for vertical segregation. *Piso principal* (etymologically, the *noble story*), just as it contributes to describing a type of architecture, bears witness even today to a specific phase in the history of modern urbanism, and beyond that history, through a chain of cause and effect, to certain upheavals in the socioeconomic structures of the time.

To this first interest one may add that the way in which these expressions are often delexicalized only to be relexicalized in new forms inside a text (and this happens under the evident effect of the deep structures of the text) makes more apparent the criteria of choice effected by the message on the paradigmatic axes at the time it is instituted.

For the sake of greater clarity, I shall take a very brief example from *Guzmán de Alfarache*. When in a given text (that I analyze elsewhere) I observe that the stock phrase "*piedras preciosas*" is delexicalized as "piedras de *precio*," I believe I may safely say that this alteration, by blurring the virtual metaphorical meanings of the first expression, gives back to *precio* all its semic plenitude and places the concept of exchange value in relief. Then, if one inquires into the deep causes of such a transformation, one can make convergent remarks on a few lines, observing that on the paradigmatic axes examined, the text has used a similar solution over and over again. These similar solutions reveal the functioning of a criterion of selection imposed by a certain type of discourse which refers to the mental structure of the merchant class (*Estar por escrito, ser contados, guardar en fiel depósito . . .*). Consequently, I would readily say that by applying principles of analysis that might be said to belong to a transformational semantics, the fundamental structures of a text may be grasped through the alterations affecting lexicalizations.

There exists another category of ready-made expressions, however, those revolving around a pattern that itself includes a variable. Sociocriticism's interest in the study of these variables originates in the fact that, by means of these variables, different social groups adapt a linguistic schema as a function of the modes of social insertion peculiar to them and thereby confer upon it the status of discourse. I see an example of this in the following passage drawn from the *Buscón*: "No hay para mi [*perdiz*] que se le iguale." One can well imagine that transindividual subjects who have no immediate contact with rural life would choose different signs, better fitted to the diverse fields of experience that constitute their specific environments, to describe in comparative terms the excellence of an object. One can make the same observations about popular expressions used to describe a person who does not know how to find something perfectly obvious: "Not to find pebbles in the Adour" (from the region of Pau); "Not to find water in the Rhone" (from Ardèche-Drôme); "Not to find water in the sea" (from the coast of Languedoc). Spanish remains more dependent on its rural memory ("Not to see a donkey four steps away").

Thus, mental structures, landscapes, and life-styles are inscribed in the discourse of collective subjects (generations, employment and trades, family, social classes, regional collectivities, etc.). The reader will find applications of this approach in the ensuing study of *Guzmán de Alfarache* (Chapter 10).

It is not a question, however, of our relating directly and systematically these discursive traces to what would be a genetic instance of the text. We shall be content to reconstitute the indexes that will permit us to speak of paths of meaning or ideological traces. We shall allow, as well, that these discursive traces may be spotted in ideological loci or in enunciations that come into contradiction with their point of origin. They will be considered in relation to the total set of correlations established by writing, as referring, in the same way as the microsemiotics that would be opposable to them, to the complexity of the social formation concerned, by means of ideological formations. Thus, commercial discourse in the text of Alemán generates zones of conflict when it butts up against the resistance of paths of meaning encoded in the *topos* of the Golden Age and in which physiocratic or, more precisely, prephysiocratic, preoccupations are inscribed.

Thus one can see that while I place my own critical reflections in the wake of genetic structuralism, I have progressively diverged more and more vigorously from it, favoring other elements in textuality, posing problems concerning discursive practices in other terms, centering my analyses more on the "literariness" of works of fiction, attempting finally to give pride of place to the practices of the written word.

This brief introduction explains why genetic structuralism has occupied, and still occupies, such an important place in the sociology of contemporary literature. Indeed, on two points, it considerably renews the approach to fundamental problems posed by the analysis of the relationships between literary works and society: namely, the scope of writers' fields of social visibility and their modalities of transcription. How can producers of texts grasp a reality external to them, and in which they are, nevertheless, immersed, other than by expressing the immediacy of their own experience or by the roundabout way of reflection and analysis? Even by assuming the existence of a project in an author who commits himself or herself to describing his or her own identification with a certain social class, and by assuming as well that we accept the posing of the problem in these terms, can we, on this first point, confuse what an individual thinks at a given time with real consciousness of class, which we have every right to consider as the maximal field of a certain level of perception? And what does this first divergence presuppose? Lucien Goldmann replies to this question by exchanging the notion of *author* for that of *collective subject*, a notion which, in order to be functional, must imply either that the collective consciousness is superior to the individual consciousness—but then how does that collective consciousness function in textual production?—or that deep within this individual consciousness there functions a collective level which eludes the lucid consciousness. Goldmann's concept of the nonconscious has the merit of covering both of these possibilities, since, in some fashion, relations with the world that are neither perceived nor perceivable at the level of immediate experience are objectivized in it. As Pierre Bourdieu has demonstrated, subjects are not in possession of their behaviors as immediate data of consciousness and . . . their behaviors always hold more meaning than they know or wish.[49] Thus, beyond the field of social visibility, properly speaking, extends an interiorized but nonconscious projection of the relations external to the speaking subject, inscribed in experience in the form of linguistic, gestural, and, broadly speaking, social practices. This second zone of phenomena, which causes the horizon, not of perception but of transcription, to recede—and this is what affects every linguistic practice and every practice of writing—shows that every critical procedure that invokes genetic structuralism, either closely or distantly, cannot allow itself to pose problems of textual analysis in terms of intention or project. By making semiotic systems—vectors of these objective, nonconscious relations structuring experience—work in writing, the writer (*le scripteur*) always says more than he or she understands and more than he or she grasps.

Whatever the extent of this double capacity to seize hold of reality, however, this perspective can be partial and distorting only to the degree that it seems to correspond to that of an ideology: "Let us add *hypothetically* that one can perhaps base the distinction between *ideologies* and *world visions* precisely on the *partial*, and therefore, distorting character of the former, and the *totalizing* character of the latter."[50] This quotation from *Sciences humaines et philosophie* is useful because, on the one hand, it gives a definition, however fuzzy and hypothetical, of what Goldmann means by ideology, and on the other, it clearly marks a second divergence, separating Goldmannian world vision from ideology, with which it is sometimes confused. It appears with no less clarity that, linked itself to precise social interests, a world vision can be neither objective nor totalizing. Following Lukács, who in *History and Class Consciousness* asserts that the maximal knowledge of reality in our time is represented by the potential consciousness of the revolutionary proletariat, Goldmann explains that different world visions do not have an equal capacity to grasp reality and that certain of them are epistemologically superior, in particular, the world vision of the proletariat: "by its social position, although much less cultivated and having less knowledge than bourgeois intellectuals, the proletariat, alone in classical capitalist society, is in a global situation that allows it to refuse reification and to give back to every spiritual problem its true human character."[51]

We know that Goldmann retracted this last position, asserting the integration of the proletariat into consumer society: "The old Marxist thesis that saw in the proletariat the only social group able to constitute the foundations of a new culture, due to the fact that it was not integrated with reified society, was based on the traditional sociological model which assumed that every cultural creation . . . could only be born of a fundamental agreement between the mental structure of the creator and that of a more or less important social group that, although partial, had universal ambitions."[52] As Jacques Leenhardt explains, "having disappointed the hopes of intellectual Marxists, the integrated proletariat talked about in the early 1960s apparently nullifies the theory of cultural creation defended until then by Marxist writers like Goldmann."[53] This statement may explain the abandonment of the concept of world vision as mediating structure in *Toward a Sociology of the Novel*: "The absence of mediation, that is to say, the absence of the political and cultural mediation the proletariat was supposed to be, will exert an effect in turn on the history of the genre of the novel itself,"[54] justifying a recourse to the hypothesis of a *homological* relationship between two radically dichotomous structures. In this sense, the concept of mediation contained in the notion of world vision functioning in *The Hidden God* cannot be confused with that of mediatization borrowed from René Girard, and upon which Goldmann bases his analysis of the modern novel. Indeed, Goldmann's new approach eliminates the role of mental structures in favor of the single mediatization represented by the market economy, which involves the fact that social values can henceforth operate only implicitly. In the sense in which the term was understood in *The Hidden God*, it is no longer possible to discover mediations "between the textual structures of ideological or political entities and social groups."[55] This affirmation was to be convincingly contested by Jacques Leenhardt, who links Robbe-Grillet's *Jealousy* and, in a broad sense, the New Novel, to an ideology "that would have the same function as that of the technocratic subclass at the level of production, namely, that of transcending class antagonisms, symbolized by socialist thought, as well as individualism, to which traditional novel production and right-wing political ideology are connected."[56] Leenhardt's brilliant essay is, nevertheless, undoubtedly situated within the context of genetic structuralism, insofar as its methodology obeys the pattern of explaining the signifying structure of a work by successive insertions in structures ever more vast. It seems to me, however, that he gives importance—and this is his chief merit—to mediations other than that of the Goldmannian world vision, by situating, for example, *Jealousy* in relation to the history of the colonialist novel—and through it, colonial life and the history of the Third and Fourth Republics—as well as in relation to the myths produced by a bourgeois ideology in the process of disintegration.

Thus we come back to the problem posed by the notion of world vision as mediating structure, whose functioning and whose validity must be questioned with respect to other possible mediations. We have seen that such a notion involves taking into account value judgments and transcends the question of the scope of social visibility in order to deal with the question of objectivity of vision. It implies, moreover, an attitude toward the world and a point of view, which has the dual disadvantage of attributing too much to the text by assuming it capable of transcribing a global and coherent vision and of reducing the capacity for transcription to a single perspective. On the contrary, I hypothesize that there is no point of view in a fictional text, in the sense that there is no point from which a more or less broad social vision would develop, but rather a series of focal points constantly constructed and deconstructed by writing. Working, moreover, with preconstructed linguistic material, the fictional text brings into view new relationships to the world—producing meaning—thus doubling the scope of its transcription of society with the creation of a second, no doubt much deeper, broader, more complex field of transcription in which the totality of a social formation is inscribed in its discursive practices and formations. In like manner, we should not forget that, at a certain level and from a certain point of view, this transcription is, at least in appearance, as chaotic as experience.

Chapter 2
Literature As Secondary Modeling System And Ideological Form

Writing As Autonomous Space

Our point of departure here is the work of Pierre Bourdieu on the organization of the market of symbolic goods in a relatively autonomous field,[1] according to a process that would be

> correlated to the appearance of a socially distinct category of artists or professional intellectuals more and more inclined to know no other rules than those of the properly intellectual or artistic tradition they received from their predecessors, furnishing them with a point of departure or a point of rupture, and more and more able to liberate their production and their products from any external servitude, whether it be the moral censorship and aesthetic programs of a Church concerned with proselytizing, or whether it be academic controls and the orders of a political power inclined to see in art an instrument of propaganda.[2]

In the nineteenth century, with the coming to power of the bourgeoisie, the autonomy of this field may have thus been acquired through its liberation from the instances of external legitimacy and from the ethical and aesthetic claims of the supervisory authorities (Church and aristocracy) to which it had been subservient. The term chosen by Bourdieu—autonomy—might be questionable if one did not immediately add that a certain type of dependency is substituted for a primary dependency, under the influence of institutionalization and the development of a "true cultural industry due, among other factors, to the mass production of works that are made according to quasi-industrial methods, such as the serial (or, in other domains, the melodrama and vaudeville)" or to the growth of the audience and the spread of elementary education. To speak of autonomy, even in a relative sense, is thus only conceivable if one grants to the cultural object a double value—symbolic and commercial. This duality explains the parallel institution of two fields of production: the first—limited—in which the work of art is irreducible to the status of mere merchandise; the second—mass produced—"which obeys the law of competition for the conquest of as vast a market as possible." Evidently, whereas the latter is firmly dependent on economic laws, the former tends to "produce its own norms of production and the criteria for the evaluation of its products."[3] Principles of evaluation in this field are not reducible to the commercial criteria that characterize the second field, hence the rejection of commercializing cultural practices by every writer in the sphere of limited production. In spite of their required interrelations, these two domains remain mutually antagonistic.

Bourdieu's analysis is fundamental in more than one respect. First, to the extent that it justifies the hypothesis of the cultural object's release from variations in the infrastructure, a hypothesis on which my own reflection rests, it confirms the pertinence of Adorno's arguments when, in *Theory of Aesthetics*, he pleads that the specific nature of art must be taken into account:

> Art is social neither because of its mode of production in which the dialectic of productive forces and of relations of production is concentrated, nor by the social origin of its thematic content. It becomes social much more through the antagonistic position it adopts vis-à-vis society if it occupies this position only as autonomous art. By crystallizing itself as specific in itself instead of opposing existing social norms and instead of qualifying itself as "socially useful," it criticizes society by the mere fact that it exists, which puritans of every obedience disapprove of.[4]

The second merit of this thesis is that, by posing the problem of principles of differentiation appropriate to each of these two spheres, it permits us to identify more accurately the criterion for legitimacy of the first field of production, which, contrary to what Bourdieu affirms, is not to be sought, in my view, in a heightening of distinctiveness and the quest for originality. I shall return to this second point.

Basing his arguments on Bourdieu's work, but equally, though to a lesser extent, on Sartre's *What Is Literature?* and Roland Barthes's *Writing Degree Zero*, Jacques Dubois propounds a theory of the institution of literature, inquiring particularly into the functioning of instances of production and of legitimization as well as the status of the writer.[5] Dubois, in my opinion, skews Bourdieu's perspective, giving excessive importance to the criterion of controlled originality as a criterion of emergence, in the struggle of writers for access to symbolic power. Indeed, this position leads him to stress rivalries of schools:

> We conceive the field of letters as a theater of bitter struggle among writers and groups of writers desiring to assert their authority and become the representatives of literary legitimacy. These struggles are expressed in a well-known historical form, the competition among schools (or movements). This rivalry generally occurs in two directions: on the one hand, a new group emerges only by asserting itself against other new groups, but on the other hand, this emergence finds its real springboard in its opposition to the legitimacy in place, that is to say, the School, which by that time has accumulated sufficient symbolic capital for the exercise of a temporary domination. Thus we see that the reproduction of the established system is ensured by the rivalry of schools and by their succession.[6]

He also emphasizes the writer's strategy: "In the first place, we shall not forget that the writer entering the literary field and its play of rivalries is forced to make his strategy of emergence depend on the relation established between his sociocultural capital and the whole structured set of positions in the field appropriate to agents, genres, and instances of consecration, such that these positions refer to a hierarchy of legitimacy."[7] It is not surprising, then, to see Dubois's thought sometimes leaning toward problems of literary history, sometimes merging with theories that have more to do with a sociology of the writer, when he broaches, in particular, the problem of the status of authors. Such a skewing appears quite clearly, moreover, when he puts his principles to the test by applying them to three examples: Zola's *Le Docteur Pascal*, Mallarmé's poetry, and Beckett's *Waiting for Godot*. In each, the analysis is based on a series of elements corresponding to "facts about the life and career of the writer, about the situation of the literary field to which he belongs, about his emergence and that of his group."[8] The temptation to establish too strict a relationship between the biography and the work seems to me to contradict Bourdieu's own explicit statements:

> The degree of autonomy of a field of limited production is gauged by its power . . . to *retranslate and reinterpret all external determinations* in conformity with its own principles: in other words, the more the field is capable of functioning as the chosen field of a rivalry for cultural legitimacy and for the properly cultural power of conferring it, the more the principles according to which internal demarcation lines operate will appear irreducible to all the external principles of division, such factors of economic, social, or political differentiation as birth, fortune, power . . . or even political attitudes.[9]

It is true, however, that to pose the problem, as Dubois does, in terms of an establishment leads us further astray by envisaging the facts as a function of a history of an institution, which would only be another transformation of the history of literature, hiding the fact that the cultural object is really, in the last analysis, linked to the infrastructure.

As useful as it is, does Bourdieu's thesis not need to be reformulated? The notion of autonomy, or autonomization, is indeed a factor of ambiguity. Would it not be preferable to state precisely that the sphere of limited production, if it is not independent of economic laws — and how could it be? — is at least characterized by the fact that within this sphere the subject *experiences* and *demands* his or her status as autonomous? In this sense, the representation of this social practice, the practice of literature, manifestly becomes an ideological effect. What bothers me more in Bourdieu's theory is the "voluntarist" aspect of the writer, who is described as essentially driven by the achievement of recognition through the claim of originality. Doubtless the argument employed is seductive: to the extent that what is in question corresponds to a legitimacy granted inside the field by a public of *peers/rivals* who would be invited to co-opt or recognize the newcomer, the criteria of appreciation are thus defined by "connoisseurs," thus leading the whole field to seek more and more refined technical principles, in the context, moreover, of the two terms of communication (production vs. consuming and specialized criticism).[10] The way the problem is posed, however, has the double drawback of reintroducing the notion of author and of reducing the subject bearing this notion to an excessively schematic level in that the sole criterion of the author's attitude would be the quest for originality. This is why I wish to extend Bourdieu's ideas in another way. Indeed, it seems to me to reduce considerably the interest of the distinctions between the two fields of production Bourdieu introduces, to propose the refinement of technique as the unique consequence of the process studied. Once we have acknowledged "the almost perfect circularity and reversibility of the relations of cultural production and consumption that result from the closure of the field of limited production,"[11] we shall better understand why, inside this sphere, attention is not drawn to *what* is being said but to the *way* it is being said, which far surpasses mere problems of technique or stylistics and refers us back to the problematics of writing. We understand, therefore, more clearly that what separates these two fields from each other is the specificity of their respective discourse, more than any possible thematic variations, which is tantamount to supposing that, in passing from one to the other, the sign changes status. Each of these two spheres of production thus gives a particular stamp to the utterance expressed in it. In this sense we can speak of each of these codes of communication as distinct, secondary modeling systems.

If we go back for a moment to the sphere of limited production, we note that the written word, for the reasons I have just put forward, is properly the locus of autonomy, the only such locus, we might say, because it is no longer determined by what it has to say but is preoccupied by its manner of saying it, liberated from the preoccupation of making itself understood because it believes or knows that it is external to any economic circuit. It is a locus of autonomy but also of dependency, as we shall see. But in shifting the problematic, formulated first by Bourdieu and then by Dubois, away from the writer and the institution of literature and back toward writing and consequently to a social practice, we are not quarreling over terminology. Quite the contrary, I think we are removing certain ambiguities, at the same time rendering more general the range of possible applications of the thesis set forth in *Le Marché des biens symboliques*, limited thus far to French literature from the mid-nineteenth century to the present day. Such a displacement also permits us to establish particularly enlightening relationships among a number of other contemporary studies in neighboring fields. Reformulated in this way, the theory of the double sphere of cultural production provides a rational and convincing basis for the hypothesis I am proposing, after Zima and Adorno among others, concerning the specificity of the fictional text.

Writing Well-Defined

As Robert Escarpit remarks, literature as an apparatus "comprises production, market, consumption. . . . The literary product is the result of a series of selections effected by various social, economic, and cultural filters, in the projects that writers have brought as far as the stage of *écriture*."[12] In this sense, literature constitutes a social practice. It is, however, quite another aspect of the problem that interests Etienne Balibar and Pierre Macherey when they define literature as *an ideological form* actualized through certain Ideological State Apparatuses in the form of well-defined practices. No doubt, in a general way, a linguistic practice is involved, but they demonstrate, using the research of Renée Balibar and Dominique Laporte,[13] that this linguistic practice is inseparable, in France, from practices in the school system during the bourgeois democratic revolution, a period which saw the formation of a national language. The establishment of the economic, political, and ideological domination of the bourgeoisie led, indeed, to a radical transformation of the superstructure, which means that the new ideology, as a dominant ideology, is actualized in new Ideological State Apparatuses and leads to "a total alteration of the relations among the different ISA."[14] In this case, it is the scholastic apparatus—which teaches two different practices of the same language, elementary French and literary French, a bipartition transcribing social contradictions—that prevails. Renée Balibar shows, in several modern texts, that the utterances of literary discourse "always diverge by one or more pertinent features from those exchanged in practice, outside literary discourse, even if they are all syntactically 'correct': because they are linguistic 'compromise formations' between usages that are socially contradictory in practice, and thus, in a tendentious way, mutually exclusive."[15] Balibar and Macherey see in these analyses a confirmation of Macherey's theses, according to which the literary text is produced by the efficacy of several ideological contradictions expressed in it "in a form that represents, at the same time, their imaginary solution, or better, that displaces them, substituting for them contradictions in the religious, political, moral, aesthetic, or psychological ideology that are reconcilable in the realm of the imaginary."[16] This is why, in light of R. Balibar's work, they can assert that literary discourse, constituted by the effects of an ideological class contradiction, "is not itself external to ideological conflicts, like an article of clothing, a neutral and neutralizing veil covering its terms after the event. With respect to these conflicts, it is not secondary, but always constitutive, implied in their production."[17]

Thus the literary text, just like the discursive practice upon which it is based, would be enacting the fiction of an imaginary solution of irreconcilable ideological contradictions. The function of literature would consist, then, in giving to a class domination the image of a unitary, universal form.

Etienne Balibar and Pierre Macherey deduce consequences from these givens which might seem irrelevent to our present purpose, but which we shall briefly call to mind, for we shall have occasion to come back to them, either explicitly or as background to our own reflections:

(1) If literature cannot be reduced to a mere reproduction of images and, consequently, cannot be defined either as fiction or as a function of its realism — both of which concepts imply the idea of a model or a reference external to discourse — it produces, on the contrary, *effects of reality* or *effects of fiction* by the intermediary of utterances "which seem objective: it is these which constitute *in* the text itself the hallucinatory reference to a 'reality' we come closer to, or from which we move farther away."[18]

(2) Every text produces *effects* in the sense that it is itself an effect of material causes in a circuit of consumption and in the framework of a cultural practice that recognizes it as literary, but also because it becomes an agent of a reproduction of ideology in the aggregate. Indeed, all the commentaries arising from it constitute its "tendential prolongation." It provokes ideological discourse drawn from its own content by offering it "to interpretation, to selective variation, and, finally, to the personal, subjective appropriation by individuals. It is a privileged agent of ideological subjugation in the 'critical' and democratic form of 'freedom of thought.' "[19]

No doubt the case studied by Renée Balibar is not transposable as such and is thus not directly generalizable, owing to the historical peculiarities it reflects upon and to the evolution of the notion of *literature*, which does not begin to take on its present meaning until the mid-eighteenth century.[20] When the word imposes itself between 1770 and 1800, first in Germany, then in France and England,[21] it sanctions, it seems, "the promotion of not only the novel, but also all the prose genres born of journalism and the theater."[22] *Literature* is then substituted for the old generic concepts of History and Poetry, transcribing the upheavals affecting cultural production and consumption (1) by a kind of, at least apparent, ideological homogenization, inside which a new redistribution of the typology of genres is carried out (in this manner comedy and tragedy will hence-forth be considered "theater" and no longer "dramatic poetry");[23] and (2) by a freeing and an equal homogenization of literature's audiences. (The old categories of "Ilustre Senado" [theater], "discreto lector," 'vulgo," which, in Spain, de-scribed the limits of an intellectual aristocracy, are abolished in favor of a single term, *the public*, now revalorized so much the more.) Is it excessive, in these cir-cumstances, to speak of a new ideological form whose emergence is connected to the whole set of changes affecting other forms of the superstructure?

The preceding remarks will be useful in our investigation of the deconstruction of earlier forms. We have seen, indeed, that the definition of literature as ideolog-ical practice is, in contemporary France, grounded in the fact that it is joined to a dominant Ideological State Apparatus that determines the specificity of its dis-course.

First we shall define what is meant by the notion of Ideological State Apparatus (ISA). The power of the State, according to classic Marxist analyses, is composed of various bodies and authorities: the central power—the administrative, military, police, and judicial apparatus (tribunals, prisons)—and, on the other hand, specialized institutions not subject to any apparent constraints (Church, Univer-sity), which Louis Althusser proposes to call Ideological State Apparatuses. They do not spread the dominant ideology without difficulty and must be conceived as relatively autonomous with respect to the power of the State, as the loci of con-tradictions which run through the whole social formation.[24] They have a time and a history of their own,[25] which explains why they may appear *dislocated* in rela-tion to the power of the State. Régine Robin, in this connection, cites the example of eighteenth-century France, when the "discursive ruptures" described by J. P. Gutton and M. Volvelle[26] concerning poverty and death bear witness to a ten-dency toward dechristianization. Is not this tendency, she inquires, "the index, the trace, the result of the fact that the Church is losing its position as dominant ISA (typical of social formations in which the dominant mode of production is feudal), a position that, in its day, the Reformation in Europe and in France *had threatened*, and that the Counter-Reformation and Gallicanism had allowed it to regain in the seventeenth century?" This would mean, in that case, that "the level of ISA is dislocated with respect to *the power of the State in crisis*. The State has not changed *its* nature, and, seeking readjustments in order to erase this disloca-tion, is caught between multiple contradictions which accelerate or block the readjustment mechanisms required by this upheaval of the dominant ISA."[27] The ISAs are subject to changes brought about by the fact that they are linked to the *Whole*; this dependency may thus explain the appearance of certain transitional ISAs, as seems to be the case for academies and Masonic lodges in the eighteenth century, "insofar as practices and discourses developed within these institutions (as a general rule despite some important exceptions) which tended, in a con-fused, unconscious, and often contradictory manner, toward an identification of position between the bourgeoisie and the nobility: the status of academies which allowed their meetings to be presided over by anyone regardless of social position; Masonic discourse on equality in the lodge and on the equivalence between noble birth and talent."[28] Robin's examples can be compared with the eighteenth-century Spanish example of the *Sociedades de Amigos del País*, created by royal authorization to examine proposals for reform submitted to them, where nobles, clergymen, and government officials met as equals.

Undoubtedly, this very dependency also explains why certain Apparatuses that are separate today were perhaps not so distinctly differentiated in earlier social formations. Such may be the case of the Church and the University, at least as far as Spain of the Golden Age is concerned, a social formation dominated by the feudal mode of production. It is an obvious fact, though all too often forgotten, that the literature of the period, considered as an ideological practice, was linked to the dominant ISA, through the various institutions that the State controlled (Church, School). Several key concepts of the classical period—chosen from many others and seen in this perspective— will suffice to remind us of this fact, whether it is a question of literature's announced purpose to "ensenar deleytando," its explicit didactic and exemplary concerns, or its valorization of the category of the Universal through the glorification of Poetry as opposed to History, the realm of particulars ("The poet, singing of the exploits of Hercules, depicts his valor by giving his attention not to Hercules but to the excellence of a courageous man").[29]

This language of the Universal is not innocent:

> Class contradictions require that a State power represent the fundamental interests of the dominant class in the sense in which classical Marxism asserts that the State is like a *digest* of economic life, the *unity* of the social formation. The State presents itself as if above classes. Its existence assumes as axiomatic the existence of ideological processes of rationalization/autonomization that make it seem to speak *the language of the universal*. This language of the universal is diffused by the ISA, and in particular the dominant ISA of a social formation, which are the means by which classes represent for themselves their interrelationships in ideology.[30]

The reading of *La hora de todos* of Quevedo that I have proposed[31] is an obvious example of this, to the extent that we can observe the seemingly decentered ethicoreligious discourse of Jupiter obliterate in the epilogue the display of class relations characterizing certain of the preceding episodes. Jupiter's discourse is not content to play "a functional role of unification";[32] it reveals itself as an essential vector of ideological practice in itself.

In texts of the Spanish Golden Age, readers are interpellated as ideological subjects, summoned to define themselves vis-à-vis Good and Evil, but in spite of what we have just said, readers are also invited to represent themselves in the social position they occupy in relation to others, in the hierarchy enacted by notions of *decoro* and stylistic categories. The characters with whom the reader is supposed to identify, must they not be obliged, in theory, to live, act, love, talk, or make us laugh in ways consistent with their condition? Whether they conform to this Aristotelian law or whether they transgress it, the texts imply a reader capable of recognizing the play of these trangressions or their perfect application, which entails in every case a faithful reproduction of ideological discourse in the subject/reader. This ideological practice serves as a model of the very forms and structures of literary discourse: thus picaresque writing (in *Lazarillo de Tormes*, the *Buscón*, and *Guzmán de Alfarache*) reproduces an ideological trace corresponding to the phenomena of diffraction of individual and collective consciousnesses produced by the Institution itself (the Church) as a guilt-inducing system, as well as by the practices of the judicial and religious Apparatuses (Inquisition) which force ideological subjects to humiliate and defile themselves.

Is the expression "ideological trace" apposite? Would it not be more precise to consider the various examples I have just mentioned (didacticism, glorification of Poetry and the Universal, ascendancy of *decoro*, the play of identification and distancing in picaresque writing) as so many traces by which literature, as ideological form and practice, marks in both multiple and convergent ways the messages it proposes and imposes upon the *subject-support?* Indeed, it would seem that in every case these elements, which I shall term *vectors of writing*, are part of a system that constructs a level of generalization capable of erasing spaces in the text where contradictory ideological traces are confronted. Consequently, we can already distinguish these traces from the totality of textual phenomena through which literature impresses upon the text the constraints of a specific ideological practice, and which show that it is establishing itself as a secondary modeling system.

The same is true if, for the same period, we consider that other stage of the ISA, the school system. This determinant in our modern societies is, no doubt, a central fact. Pierre Bourdieu, in his analysis of the system of instances of cultural preservation and consecration that regulates the field of limited production, justifiably sees it functioning like a Church, which, in Max Weber's terms, must "lay the foundations and systematically delimit the victorious new doctrine or defend the old against the attacks of prophets, establish what has and what does not have sacred value, and make it penetrate the faith of the laity."[33] Higher education and the teaching profession play a determining role in this system, from a triple point of view, as Jacques Dubois reminds us, to the extent that we must add to the educational determinant analyzed by Renée Balibar two other functions assumed by the teaching of literature: on the one hand, the latter "inculcates in the pupil a normative behavior which will be efficacious for any subsequent cultural practice, and which consists principally in the ability to apply a reading code (or indeed a writing code) in the form of stylistic and thematic categories"; on the other hand, this teaching introduces works of the past "into the logic of a system which necessarily projects its principles and its categories onto the productions of the present,"[34] thus orienting production toward a set of norms. This dependency remains clearly discernible in texts of the Spanish Golden Age, even if the modalities of this determination overlap the effects of religious dependency too closely for them to appear clearly in their own right. Thus, I have shown elsewhere how the modern novel was born in Spain, at the end of the sixteenth century, by integrating a schoolbook "savoir-faire," or, more precisely, how the different elements of the text (general textual fabric, description of landscapes and characters, montage of digressions, typology of characters, etc.) developed from mechanisms learned at the University in those notorious courses in Latin grammar and rhetoric, and how the novel itself inherited, at other levels, that parascholastic literature constituted by the miscellanea.[35] This characteristic is not limited to the production of meaning. A text's first readers comment upon it starting from the same criteria; translators bring to view the ideological matrix of the new and brilliant exercise submitted to them, either by marginal annotations in which they recognize the exercises in question, or else by restoring to Latin literature the original expression which was diluted in its Spanish version. Just as Alemán's text redistributes knowledge and rewrites an art of writing, they in turn refer this production back to its point of origin, in a sort of closed and autarkic circuit of communication. Authors and readers/critics reproduce at successive levels one and the same discourse—an ideological discourse, if ever there was one, to the extent that it is fundamentally didactic, interposing between itself and the *vulgo* to whom Mateo Alemán addresses himself in his preface the limits of its specificity and fictitiousness.

Certainly, it is as difficult to take the measure of this fictitiousness of discourse, of this gap that separates it from daily speech, as it is to evaluate the elements composing its specificity. When R. Balibar speaks of the specificity and, especially, of the fictitiousness of "literary language," she thereby demonstrates that it is not reducible to any discourse. This entails certain consequences and is opposed in particular to a monosemic conception of fictional texts. On the other hand, however, this "language" is thus established as a system of communication outside, above, or beside discourse. This leads me to make the following distinction between macrosemiotics and microsemiotics:

(1) "Macrosemiotics" correspond to natural languages (French, Spanish, English, etc.), that break up the continuum of the "real" world, thus defining referents. In this sense, they "categorize" the world of experience, inform it, and determine an initial world vision.

(2) These "macrosemiotics" are made up of a set of "microsemiotics," just as natural, which slice and categorize, in their own way, experiences that are perforce multiple, diverse, and often contradictory.[36] Each of them is dependent

upon a transindividual or collective subject. I shall call them *discourses*. These discourses inscribe in "macrosemiotics" conflictive situations in that they inform different referents and are capable of giving contradictory views of one and the same "reality." (What is *work*, for example, for the peasant, the agricultural worker, the merchant, the intellectual, the laborer, or the corporate chief executive officer, each of whom is a collective subject?) We shall note that the only reality in which the *subject* is steeped is the microsemiotic. From the point of view of the speaking subject's experience, the language (*la langue*), as a macrosemiotic Whole, is an abstraction. Microsemiotics are effectively preexistent to this Whole.

(3) In opposition to these semiotics termed "natural," we shall consider that literature, as a constructed "language" irreducible to any discourse, is a secondary modeling system. This phrase, which we have borrowed from Soviet semioticians, is especially eloquent. It means, in effect, that every word uttered within this system undergoes the effects of formal constraints and thus that its original virtual utterance is, as it were, transformed. Considered as a discursive matrix which informs/deforms the supposed content of the initial message, this system, for that very reason, asks to be examined in relation to the different and contradictory world visions we have just discerned.

It is not a question of being content to oppose the written language to the spoken, even if we recognize, with Barthes, that the writing subject is fundamentally different from the speaking subject. What is important is to know within what institutional framework one writes or speaks. From this point of view, for example, a lecture given by an established writer, which is, at first glance, an instance of the spoken language, belongs to the same secondary modeling system as the written texts of his or her work. This specificity of "literary language," which makes it an autonomous modeling system, is, quite apart from the facts noted by R. Balibar, particularly in seventeenth-century France, which saw the establishment of "a literary language and art" produced by assimilation in an identical social group, that of "the Court and the Town," that is, a defeudalized aristocracy and a newly rich bourgeoisie, a group whose essential values were transcribed into the ideal of the "honnête homme."[37] This social group renewed itself very rapidly; soon it was the Town alone, the bourgeoisie, consolidating and extending its economic and political hegemony, which *conditioned literary language*, that is, shaped it as a *modeling system*. This does not mean, as we have seen with R. Balibar, that this system be confused with a bourgeois microsemiotic, a bourgeois discourse.

These limits are not always easy to define, however. I refer the reader to what Erich Auerbach tells us about late Roman antiquity, in which the spiritual unity of the people was founded upon the existence of a common language, that is to say, of a specific code of communication that conditioned both the formation of an audience and the emergence of the literature this public required. This public, which came from the ruling classes, spoke a language that was scarcely accessible to the average person. "One has the impression (a mere impression)," he writes, "that in the fifth century the senatorial aristocracy and the social groups close to it spoke a uniformly elevated Latin that was understood only with great difficulty by the man in the street." Auerbach here assimilates this elevated Latin to the *literary* language of the cultivated public, which he opposes to colloquial Latin, while observing that with respect to colloquial Latin, literary Latin remained relatively stable, evolving only very slowly. This remark leads him to propose the retention of three characteristics for defining "literary language": *selection, uniformity*, and *preservation*. Actually, Auerbach's observations are somewhat confused in that he presents literary language as including "the colloquial language of cultivated people," which implies both the discourse of a collective subject (the ruling classes) and a sphere of application (the field of culture).[38]

The problem is of a different sort: we have to understand the nature and origin of this discursive matrix, and on this point Auerbach's work is useful, despite the above-stated reservations. Underpinning this modeling system are two essential elements: on the one hand, a written Latin that, as a result of the Carolingian reform of education, definitively broke away from the spoken language and was transformed into "an international vehicle of intellectual life, as it were, a linguistic organ to which no popular idiom corresponded"; and, on the other hand, briefly stated, the Augustinian discursive modality of the *sermo humilis* operating throughout the Middle Ages and afterward.[39] The Church, which was early on responsible for education, was caretaker of classical culture, at the same time giving it a new content and a particular stylistic nuance. Thus Christian preaching used the rhetorical tradition in which the classical world was steeped to convey its own doctrine, and whereas traditional rhetoric exhausted itself in formalism, Christian thought gave new life to it, subduing yet bending it to its own didactic project.

This remodeling of the modeling system was organized around a certain type of discursive practice founded in biblical style—in total variance with classical taste—and which can be understood only in the context of the fundamental antithesis of Christian doctrine, itself born of the dogma of the Incarnation (*man/God—humilis/sublimis*). It is from this principle that Saint Augustine redefined traditional stylistic levels, a consequence of which was the matrix synthesized by Auerbach in the phrase *sermo humilis*, which he finds in every Christian literary text from low Latinity to the *Divine Comedy*. The characteristic features of this new form (confusion of stylistic levels, reinstatement of vulgarisms and graphic terms to which the thematic context confers a new dignity, bringing together on the human level the I and the unknown Thou in the elevated style of classical antiquity, awareness of a communal body—all of us *hic et nunc*, etc.) are still perfectly readable in late sixteenth-century Spanish texts such as *Guzmán de Alfarache*. Within the secondary modeling system we are studying, they have contributed to inscribing trajectories of meaning, formal constraints of every sort in which the messages of fictional texts are encoded and ultimately twisted out of shape.

We can see, then, from Auerbach to R. Balibar to Bourdieu, how a number of analyses, conducted in terms of quite divergent objectives, lead to several convergent conclusions:

(1) "Literary language" is a fictive and specific language, a conclusion which is tantamount to positing the existence of a double dislocation both with respect to different discourses and to a referential universe, declaring the nonpertinence of any positivistic or neopositivistic approach to literature.

(2) This specificity and fictitiousness are linked to a dominant ISA (the School in R. Balibar's studies, the Church in the *sermo humilis* of Auerbach, School and Church in my own analyses of the Spanish Golden Age). When one has taken into account this dependency and the variations in the instances of domination at the very heart of the system of ISA in terms of the evolution of socioeconomic structures, the elements defining this specificity and this fictitiousness inscribe the text in historical periods of long duration.

(3) The very same elements contribute to the establishment of a discursive matrix shaping literature at a first level, like a kind of generic marker which does not fundamentally bind the discourse uttered within it, yet which that same utterance cannot possibly escape. We are dealing here with a necessary mediation which analysis must take into account so as not to confuse its effects with what is truly at stake in any given text.

(4) Through the attention it pays to ways of enunciating things, writing opens up diversified semiotic stratifications in textuality. When they are not channeled in the direction of predetermined trajectories of meaning, these stratifications give textuality the means of its freedom.

Thus far I have neglected the field of mass production, to which certain contemporary sociological schools of thought have justifiably called attention. Insofar as it obeys, above all, economic laws of competition, as Bourdieu reminds us, it delivers "an undifferentiated message, produced for a socially undifferentiated public, at the cost of a methodical self-censorship leading to the abolition of every sign, every factor of differentiation." This explains the most characteristic features of this *middlebrow art* "as a recourse to technical devices and immediately accessible aesthetic effects, or the exclusion of every theme that might prove controversial or shocking to a particular sector of the public, in favor of optimistic and stereotyped characters and symbols, 'common places' in which the most different classes of the populace may project themselves."[40] Then again, however, the same middlebrow culture can define itself only with respect to the culture developed by the field of limited production: "Thus middlebrow art can only renew its techniques and its thematics by borrowing from highbrow culture and, even more frequently, from 'bourgeois art' the most widely disseminated devices among those it employed one or two generations earlier, and by 'adapting' the most hallowed themes or subjects, or those easiest to restructure according to the traditional laws of composition in the folk arts (e.g., the Manichean division of roles)."[41] The sphere of mass production thus can be viewed as closely dependent upon the sphere of limited production. It is to the latter alone that the character of legitimacy may be attached, and in relation to which the former offers itself to the reading public, redistributing the latter's criteria and values.

This rapid review of Bourdieu's analyses is not altogether useless, for it permits us to understand why we find ourselves confronting an ideological form that, in both cases, remains the same in its main outlines. For all that, it will nevertheless be appropriate, when we undertake the examination of a product of middlebrow art, to introduce parameters that take into account the effects of a possible quest for uniformity; these will at once be attributed to "genre," defined as specific modalities of a particular secondary modeling system. The preceding remarks illuminate *a posteriori* the methods of North American content analysis and experimental sociology, at least insofar as the investigations of both are especially concerned, it seems, with the effects produced by the situation of dependency characteristic of the mass production of symbolic goods, without having first posed the problem of its existence, nor, *a fortiori*, its functioning. Thus we must conclude that the results they have reached are more directly useful to sociologists than to literary critics. This last statement makes explicit, on another level, in what sense my project differs from theirs.

Chapter 3
Discursive Practices And Formations

At the outset, I should like to stress the fundamental importance of Michel Foucault's work, in particular the *Archaeology of Knowledge*, in which, from a new perspective, he redevelops certain analyses of *Madness and Civilization, Birth of the Clinic*, and *The Order of Things*. As is well known, this perspective is an investigation of the rules of the formation of discourse, that is, a search for units of discursive events that are formed in a population and that are free from all earlier forms of continuity:

> We must grasp the statement in the exact specificity of its occurrence; determine its conditions of existence, fix at least its limits, establish its correlations with other statements that may be connected with it, and show what other forms of statement it excludes. We do not seek below what is manifest the half silent murmur of another discourse; we must show why it could not be other than it was, in what respect it is exclusive of any other, how it assumes, in the midst of others and in relation to them, a place that no other could occupy. The question proper to such an analysis might be formulated in this way: what is this specific existence that emerges from what is said and nowhere else?[1]

After having initially emphasized the discourses defining the sciences of man, while stressing, however, that this mapping is neither definitive nor necessarily valid, Foucault undertakes to describe the relations discernible within great families of statements—grammar and medicine, for example. This leads him to observe that each one's unity is founded not on a hypothetical field of objects, nor on a definite type of enunciation, nor on a well-defined set of notions, nor on the permanence of a thematics.

> Hence the idea of describing these dispersions themselves; of discovering whether, between these elements which are certainly not organized as a progressively deductive structure, nor as an enormous book that is being gradually and continuously written, nor as the *oeuvre* of a collective subject, one cannot discern a regularity: an order in their successive appearance, correlations in their simultaneity, assignable positions in a common space, a reciprocal functioning, linked and hierarchized transformations.[2]

Thus, I shall speak of *discursive formation* when I can discern and define a regularity among objects, types of enunciation, concepts, and thematic choices; and of *rules of formation* to designate the conditions of existence of these various elements. Let us take, for example, the case of psychiatric discourse in the nineteenth century. It is characterized not by its objects but by the manner in which it forms them, that is, by establishing relations among old instances of *emergence* (family, close social group, workplace, religious community) and new ones (art, sensuality, legal punishment); instances of *delimitation* (medicine, justice, religious authority, literary and art criticism); *grids of specification* (systems "according to which the different 'kinds of madness' are divided, contrasted . . . , classified, derived from one another as objects of psychiatric discourse").[3] It is precisely insofar as discourse establishes relations among social institutions, economic and social processes, behavior patterns, systems of norms, techniques, types of classification, and modes of description[4] that it is perceived as a social practice. It is by establishing discursive relations among all these elements that discourse forms the object of which it speaks, and that it itself accedes to the status of a discursive *practice*, this "place in which a tangled plurality—at once superposed and incomplete—of objects is formed and deformed, appears and disappears." This is why discourse is not "a mere intersection of things and words" nor a "slender surface of contact, or confrontation, between a reality and a language (*langue*), the intrication of a lexicon and an experience."[5] It is irreducible to language and to speech, and it cannot translate verbally a preexisting synthesis effected elsewhere.

Understood in this sense, the concept of discursive practice, which, as we have just seen, always implies the sociality of the speech act and a profound relationship to history, is at the center of Foucault's reflections; that is, the enunciative modalities of clinical discourse do not refer to the unifying function of a subject, for if the levels from which the subject speaks are linked by a system of relations, "this system is not established by the synthetic activity of a consciousness identical with itself, dumb and anterior to all speech, but by the specificity of a discursive practice. The same is true in the analysis of the formation of concepts and of the enunciative field in which rules of formation reflect not mentalities or the consciousness of individuals but the discourse itself; these rules "operate, therefore, according to a sort of uniform anonymity, on all individuals who undertake to speak in this discursive field."[6]

Discursive relations do not bear upon the chain of ideas, concepts and words inside discourse; they determine, rather, "the group of relations that discourse must establish in order to speak of this or that object, in order to deal with them, name them, analyze them, classify them, explain them." Nor is it a question of writing "the history of the referent." ("In the example chosen, we are not trying to find out who was mad at a particular period, or in what his madness consisted, or whether his disturbances were identical with those known to us today.")[7]

On the contrary, of fundamental interest to Foucault are the historical conditions that make possible the emergence of the object of discourse. "One cannot speak of anything at any time whatever."[8] Fields of perception are reorganized according to alterations affecting institutions and social practices. In posing the problem of relationships between discursive and nondiscursive practices, Foucault was bound to encounter historical materialism. Thus, Régine Robin, while recognizing the "immeasurable debt that historians of the discursive field owe to M. Foucault" and while calling attention to the interest of his opposition to such notions as the anthropological subject, history as continuity, the history of ideas, and the hermeneutics of meaning, regrets that "the relationship between discursive and nondiscursive practices [is] thought of in terms of *juxtaposition* without hierarchy, without dominance, without the discursive level ever being related to the articulated whole of a social formation, to its complex play of instances and dominances."[9] Is such an objection tenable? Does not Foucault present his reflections as a set of observations intended to outline problems and open avenues of exploration? In a first approach, only the instant in which discourse is instituted, and which, by that very fact, institutes its object, holds his interest. Finally, and especially, does he not refer implicitly to this complex play of instances when he differentiates the system of primary or real relations, which are not always congruent with the relations that form objects of discourse ("the relations of dependence that may be assigned to this primary level are not necessarily expressed in the formation of relations that makes discursive objects possible"),[10] from the system of *secondary* or *reflexive relations* and from the system of relations that properly can be called *discursive?*

This debate leads me to restate the Marxist concept of social formation, both from the standpoint of its relation in Foucault's mind to the new concept of discursive formation he proposes, and because such a relation has been explicitly posed by other critics. We recall, with Régine Robin, that the multiple contradictions of a social formation "cause the functions of the ideological state apparatuses to jam, to veer off track, to deviate, to be transformed"[11] and, with Pierre Macherey, that the same contradictions are invested in the literary text. This leads us to another basic concept of historical materialism, that of social formation. Every society presents a number of classes and social groups engendered by a specific straddling of several modes of production; this complexity of economic structures, interacting with a complexity of superstructures, is called *social formation*, a notion that must be considered as corresponding to a concrete, historically determined, social totality: "The concept of mode of production characterized by an opposition of two antagonistic classes never exists in the original state," affirms N. Polantzas. "In fact, there exists solely a historically determined social formation, that is, a social whole, in the broadest sense of the word, at one moment of its historical existence. . . . Thus, Bismarck's Germany is characterized by a specific combination of capitalist, feudal, and patriarchal modes of production. Only the combination exists in the strict sense of the term."[12] This means that "if the State is thought of as the expression of the dominant class, as an economic digest, as the official expression of society, the State is, however, analyzed by classical Marxism in an equally complex manner, with every sort of displacement and dislocation with respect to class domination, and to the domination of a mode of production."[13]

This brief summary allows me to address two controversies concerning Spanish literature of the Golden Age.

(1) In contrast to those who describe sixteenth-century Spain as, above all, a caste society (Christians of long standing, *moriscos, conversos*), I believe that this distinction does not eliminate the problematic of class. To those who accept the validity of his analyses for the modern world but not "for the Middle Ages, in which Catholicism, nor for Athens and Rome, where politics, reigned supreme," Karl Marx replies:

> In the first place it strikes one as an odd thing for anyone to suppose
> that these well-worn phrases about the Middle Ages and the Ancient
> World are unknown to anyone else. This much, however, is clear, that
> the Middle Ages could not live on Catholicism, nor the Ancient World
> on politics. On the contrary, it is the mode in which they gained a live-
> lihood that explains why here politics, and there Catholicism, played
> the chief part. For the rest, it requires but a slight acquaintance with
> the history of the Roman Republic, for example, to be aware that its se-
> cret history is the history of its landed property. On the other hand,
> Don Quixote long ago paid the penalty for wrongly imagining that
> knight errantry was compatible with all economic forms of society.[14]

(2) Undoubtedly, the corresponding social formation is dominated by the feudal mode of production, but this domination operates within the framework of a specific combination of other modes of production (patriarchal, crafts, precapitalist). The existence of a bourgeois mode of production, in particular, is confirmed by a large body of historical research. I shall not hesitate, then, to

speak of a bourgeoisie (a rural bourgeoisie giving evidence of the onset of the peasantry's disintegration, an industrial bourgeoisie, and a mercantile bourgeoisie) even though, in the corresponding period, it had not yet been *constituted as a class*, and I shall refer here to what Marx said about the small-holding French peasantry of the 1850s:

> Insofar as millions of families live under economic conditions of existence that separate their mode of life, their interests, and their culture from those of the other classes, and put them in hostile opposition to the latter, they form a class. Insofar as there is merely a local interconnection among these small-holding peasants, and the identity of their interests begets no community, no national bond, and no political organization among them, they do not form a class.[15]

Michel Pêcheux uses the notion of *discursive formation* in an appreciably different sense from that proposed by Foucault. For Pêcheux, the ideological state apparatuses (ISAs) simultaneously and contradictorily constitute both the site and the means of domination of the dominant class and the site and the ideological conditions of transformation of the relations of production. Moreover, they do not consist in a mere list of juxtaposed elements but are organized in a complex set, to the degree that their regional properties ("their specialization in religion, knowledge, politics, etc., 'goes without saying' ") situate them hierarchically. Hence his notion of *ideological formation*, which implies both a regional character and a position of class. "We shall speak of ideological formation in order to characterize an element likely to intervene, as a force confronting other forces, in the ideological conjuncture characteristic of a social formation, at any given time; thus each ideological formation constitutes a complex set of attitudes and representations that are neither 'individual' nor 'universal' but are more or less related to positions of class in conflict with one another."[16] These ideological formations are organized in the form of a "complex whole in dominance" by a structure of inequality/subordination which reproduces that of the ISAs.

Pêcheux poses, moreover, as one of his theses that the meaning of a word does not exist in itself but is "determined by the ideological positions set in play in the historical social process in which words, phrases, and propositions are produced (that is, reproduced)." In other words, a word changes meaning according to the position of the person who uses it. "Consequently we shall call *discursive formation*, in a given ideological formation, that is, from a given position in a given conjuncture determined by the state of the class struggle, that which determines 'what can and must be said (articulated in the form of a harangue, a sermon, a pamphlet, an exposé, a program, etc.).' " Discursive formations thus represent "in language" the ideological formations that correspond to them. The latter "necessarily include as one of their components one or several interrelated discursive formations."[17] Discursive formation is the locus, the matrix, of the constitution of meaning. What is interesting about Pêcheux's work is the manner in which he links this latter concept of meaning to the constitution of the subject through Louis Althusser's notion of ideological interpellation.

Althusser's well-known thesis is synthesized in a now-famous phrase: "Ideology interpellates individuals as subjects." Pêcheux rightly insists on the displacement of the formula "individual/subject" and on the paradox that it presupposes of a "subject called to existence." He remarks with great acuity that this paradox consists in the fact that by a *retroactive effect* every individual is already a subject. "The subject has always been an individual interpellated as subject," doubtless because "all individuals receive as self-evident the meaning of what they hear and say, read and write . . . as speaking subjects,"[18] that is, to yield to Althusser's suggestions again, as *subject-forms*. ("No human, that is, social individual, can be the agent of a practice without assuming the form of the subject. The 'subject-form' is indeed the form of historical existence of every individual, the agent of social practices."[19]) How are individuals constituted as subjects of their discourse? To this question Pêcheux replies: by forgetting what determines them, by the fact that they identify themselves as subject-forms with the discursive formation which dominates them, and that they identify themselves with the latter by reproducing in their own discourse the traces of what determines them.

In order to understand Pêcheux's position, we must now parenthetically recall Paul Henry's work on "the preconstructed," a term that refers to a prior external construction, independent of what is "constructed" by the utterance. From the following example, "He who saved the world by dying upon the Cross has never existed," Pêcheux observes that "the discourse of militant atheism denies in the 'total proposition' the very existence of what is being assumed in the subordinate clause."[20] This utterance apparently stripped of meaning has the merit of placing in relief a lack of correspondence between "what is thought before, elsewhere, or independently, and what is contained in the global affirmation of the sentence." Hence the distinction he proposes between two "fields of thought," one overflowing the other.

The preconstructed is the vehicle for utterances produced by the "complex whole in dominance" of the *discursive formations* (which are themselves part of the "complex whole in dominance" of ideological formations), a complex that Pêcheux terms *interdiscourse*. The preconstructed interpellates the individual as subject, but subjects create for themselves an illusion of autonomy by taking responsibility for this "elsewhere," by integrating into their own discourse this "always already there," which interpellates them. In other words, it is by identifying oneself with this "elsewhere" that one identifies with oneself. It is in this preconstructed matter that speaking subjects constitute themselves. Pêcheux distinguishes interdiscourse from *intradiscourse*, the functioning of discourse with respect to itself. Intradiscourse redistributes interdiscourse; in this sense it appears as the thread of the discourse of the subject as "an effect of the interdiscourse upon itself, an 'interiority' entirely determined as such from the 'exterior.' "[21] I do not think I am betraying Pêcheux's thought when I say that in reproducing itself in the speaking subject in the form of an allegedly interiorized specularity, the Subject hides this congruence within himself in the illusory effect of the autonomy of the speaking subject.[22]

Pêcheux continues his reflections by showing how self-identification is equal to identification with others in the framework of a given discursive formation

> in which the subjects that it dominates recognize one another as mirrors of each other: that is, that the coincidence (which is also a connivance, indeed a complicity) between the Subject and oneself is established by the same movement among the subjects, according to the modality of the "as if" (as if I who am speaking were there where I am listened to), a modality in which "the embodiment" of the interdiscursive elements (preconstructed and articulation/support) can go as far as mingling them so that there would no longer be any demarcation between what is said and that about which it is said.

He illustrates his observation with a brief analysis of the following sentence: "The white cross that the demonstrators had attached to a lamp post was not touched by the police" (*Le Monde*, report on Ireland), showing that the "poetic" effect of the *mise en scène* rests upon a discrepancy between "present and past, coupled with a lack of that correspondence of a subject to other subjects which constitutes identification ('Ireland as though you were there,' 'If you had been there, you would have seen that cross and you would know what I am talking about')."[23]

Pêcheux's work is obviously of great interest. Unfortunately, however, his observations remain at the level of enunciation, and they isolate discursive formations from social practices, even though the former are presented generally as if they were part of the infrastructure. It is on this question that the contribution of Michel Foucault is essential, for his perspective permits us to understand how, within a specific ideological formation, the latent utterances of the Subject are actualized by means of a *discursive practice*. Let us take an example to clarify this: I have shown elsewhere[24] how, in sixteenth- and seventeenth-century Spain, in civil law as well as in inquisitorial practice, the dominant ideology interpellated its victim as subject at the very moment it condemned him precisely for having eluded it. Indeed, at the foot of the stake or the gallows, where the dominant ideology obliges the victim to acknowledge his "errors" and the justice of his torture, it obliges him for that very reason to reproduce it and, in doing so, fugitively becomes incarnate in him one last time, the better to survive him.

In this case, to identify oneself with the Subject is no longer to identify with oneself but, quite the contrary, to exorcise and forswear the self. The enunciative level alone is not, therefore, a pertinent unit of analysis for sociocriticism. On the other hand, these rites of self-profanation and self-humiliation produce consciousness-diffracting phenomena which, invested in the picaresque novel, make it an essentially conflictive text that, in its own way, renders problematic the ideological interpellation in question. The latent utterances of the Subject reach the discourse stage only to the extent that a writing or a discursive practice relates these social practices to other practices, such as the organization of charity, to the play of the ISAs (religion, family, etc.), to economic and social processes (development of arterial roads, organization of trade routes and corresponding development of mule transport, inns, towns, etc.; phenomena of currency inflation, economic crises, bankruptcies of individuals and of the State, intervention of foreign banks, etc.), to conflictive situations (rise of the merchant and rural bourgeoisie, tensions within the nobility), to behavior patterns and to normative systems (money, honor, chastity, opulence, poverty, asceticism, distinction between licit and illicit love, etc.), to debates which themselves transcribe the evolution of the infrastructure (reform of begging, reform of highways, luxury, idleness, etc.), to modes of characterization (typology of beggars, pages, nobles, priests, princes of the Church, women, nationalities, etc.), or to an ideological practice that offers a specific matrix (literary tradition with its clichés, rules, techniques, etc.).

By taking into account the *nondiscursive*, or rather the *prediscursive*, we shall avoid confusing ideological formation with discursive formation, that is, what determines with what is determined.

I have another reservation to make that, this time, bears upon the functioning of this "complex whole in dominance" termed *interdiscourse*. I should like to emphasize that interdiscourse is itself a space of conflict, made up of contradictory "discursive formations," and that, though referring in the last instance to a dominant formation, it is nonetheless articulated in a ceaselessly fluid combinatory form capable of organizing itself, if only fleetingly, around another domination. Here, the choice of terms is problematic: whereas in good Marxist orthodoxy the notion of *formation* implies a complex of contradictory economic structures, the same term in Pêcheux designates both the totality and each one of the elements in combination. This is why it is preferable to apply it only in order to define the "complex whole in dominance" that would, in this case, be constituted by discourses in each one of which divergent and contradictory social interests are invested. It is clear, then, that the identification of the speaking subject may be an identification with the discursive formation (in the sense in which I shall henceforth take it), or with a discourse that is itself defined by its relationship to a class—and to a region (for example, the bourgeoisie's discourse on the family at a specific period).

We may next pose the problem of *the asserted*, whose relation to discursive formation is not very clear in Pêcheux. If *the preconstructed* refers to a discursive formation or to a discourse, to what does *the constructed* refer? Régine Robin replies, "To the individuality of the subject, a situated point of view, as support;

to what is placed within a system of gestures and speech, to something functioning in subjectivity, that is, still functioning in ideology."[25] In this case, Robin is clearly making use of the hypotheses of T. Herbert, who distinguishes two forms of ideology: an *empiricist* form, referring to the process of production, and a *speculative* form, referring to the social relations of production.[26] Each one fulfills a distinct function: in the first "the law of economics that assigns agents of production their *position* in the production process is *repressed* and *disguised* in other signifying chains which have the effect both of signifying an inescapable position to subjects/agents of production and of hiding from them the fact that this position has been assigned." The "speculative" guarantee of the second "permits ideology to be mirrored by the support of the other as a reflected discourse. Here are set in motion the mechanisms of communicated belief, the 'quasi-factualness' of testimony and of narrative—the evidence that identifies subjects with the discourse they utter or that are uttered in them."[27] The first of these forms is organized, according to Herbert, around a system of signals that mark out behaviors, gestures, and speech.

Robin is thus able to relate *the preconstructed*, as reflected discourse, to the speculative form, and *the asserted* (or *the constructed*) to the empirical form. The asserted or constructed corresponds to a set of traces "situated at the level of explicit judgments, rationalizations, interiorized norms, values, models, assertions and complex phenomena that cause the subject to interject . . . pejorative or meliorative features, such as 'fortunately,' 'unfortunately,' etc., into his own discourse." At this level, Robin writes, "there is never total obliteration of the place of the enunciating subject and of the conditions of production."[28]

Let us consider an analysis of a text from Mateo Alemán's *Guzmán de Alfarache* (1604).[29] The preconstructed elements here are several, and noticeable at different levels, showing that this notion does not merely involve enunciation: in this case, the preconstructed elements are related at the mythical and topical levels (Golden Age, generosity of the Earth), as well as at the level of didactic thematics (theme of friendship). From this second point of view, we observe that the first part of the text develops from an "already said," "before, elsewhere and independently," namely, that the true friend is essentially faithful and capable of self-abnegation. This implies a whole sedimentation of commonplaces remaining implicit or *not said* because presumed to be included in the preceding definition (frequency of false friendship, harmfulness of appearances, sense of authenticity, condemnation of selfishness and selfish motives, etc.), of values (fidelity, generosity, friendship), that is, a whole system of latent utterances accompanying this schematic textual enunciation ("it has always been considered difficult to find a true and faithful friend"). By reproducing this affirmation, Guzmán, the narrator, presents himself to the reader as the *receiving/emitting* consciousness of a discourse that, by means of universal categories, aims at erasing the emplacement of class relations: at the same time that he reproduces this discourse, he, in fact, asserts his adhesion to this "already said," takes responsibility for it, thus creating the illusion of his autonomy. Thus, he is presenting himself as *subject-form*, as *agent* of a social practice; this enunciation belongs to the domain of discursive formation, that is, it belongs to the *dominant discourse* (in the framework of a complex whole in dominance). It is for that reason one of those traces that provides evidence of the manner in which literature, as an ideological form, marks its messages. I am more interested, however, in what is asserted, that is, in the enunciation that joins the preconstructed to the text and establishes the Earth as a paradigm of Friendship. But here a new *preasserted* appears, conveyed by *topoi*: the motif of the Earth's generosity, which allows us to pass from one preconstructed to another, so that the asserted attributes to the Earth an almost "new" quality, namely, its stability, its fidelity.

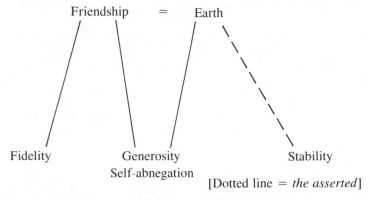

If this asserted is placed within Mateo Alemán's whole text, we observe that it fits inside a complex dialectical system (stability vs. instability), organized around monetary themes. Everything contaminated by money bears the sign of the inauthentic, the ephemeral, the unstable. In the chain of semiotic equivalencies, money becomes the metonymical sign of the unstable, such that it is possible to establish the following contradictory equations: *money* (= instability) vs. *Earth* (= stability). We cannot help comparing this symbolism with the phenomena of monetary inflation characterizing the Spanish sixteenth century, especially its last decade, and which, in the context of social and economic life, brought a quest for investment hedges such as the purchase of *land*.

To what must the asserted be related? At first, we might be tempted to relate it directly to a specific socioeconomic conjuncture, at least if we were to isolate it from its context. If, on the contrary, we try to link it to the chain of meanings, our perception changes somewhat. In that case, we observe that this enunciation is but one of the textual markers by which a prephysiocratic discourse, bearer of specific social interests, is invested in the text. These interests are opposed to other social interests conveyed by another discourse—mercantilist discourse—

equally invested in the same text, such that in these few lines I can discern, as a background to the production of meaning, an entire social formation, a complex and contradictory totality. How, in these circumstances, can one pose the problem of the speaking subject? It is clear, upon reflection, that the analyses of Pêcheux and Robin do not take the specificity of the literary text into account. Indeed, to do so would require that the production of meaning be analyzed also in relation to the practice of writing and not merely from the perspective of subject-supports.

Chapter 4
Toward a Semiology of Ideology

At this stage in our reflections, we may question the apparently contradictory character of a position that, on the one hand, claims to discern in a text the possible markers of the discourses of transindividual subjects linked in a discursive formation and, on the other hand, asserts that literature as constructed language is irreducible to any discourse. I have already answered this objection in part by suggesting that one distinguish between two levels of ideological marking that do not function according to the same modes: whereas Level 1 imprints upon the text the constraints of a secondary modeling system, Level 2 inscribes in the same text contradictory social interests that correspond to an entire social formation. These two levels work upon each other, however, and as we have seen in the example of *La hora de todos* of Quevedo, the elements of the modeling system that I have termed *vectors* of writing construct a level of generalization that erases the textual spaces of social confrontation. In this sense, we may say that the discursive matrix that forms and deforms the text of fiction somehow transforms an original utterance itself referring directly, however, to the specific discourse of a particular transindividual subject. Thus an identical textual phenomenon can be read simultaneously in its primary meaning and in the framework of a fictional system in which it acquires a new meaning.

However, in stating this first point, we are, for the moment, only displacing the problem, for no text is reducible to what I have termed the matrix of literary discourse. We must, then, assume that Level 2 is joined *equally* to another system that, this time, is specific to the text being studied. Consequently, I shall approach the problems posed both by the analysis of Level 2 and by the ideological meanings produced by the fictional text from this primary material. What we have already said in Chapter 1 implies the elimination of every reference to content. The autonomy with respect to referential reality that the text acquires by establishing a figurative language appropriate to it denies it any possibility of coincidence, other than accidental and ambiguous, with an organized, argued thought expressing itself in ideological terms. This type of thought may, at the very most, appear in the form of traces and residues that are insignificant in themselves. This is, moreover, the trap into which Lucien Goldmann fell when he was led, because of the excessive attention he paid to content, to give prominence to the organization of a referential universe rendered, at this level, autonomous, and in which any immediate sociohistorical anchoring is nullified by writing. A methodological impasse follows from this, from which Goldmann can escape only by recourse to the dubious concept of homology. If we define content as the signified of figurative language, we shall readily understand why sociocriticism gives preeminence both to the analysis of the signifier and to everything that is said—or not said—at the point of articulation of the signifier and the signified (see the analysis below of *Citizen Kane*). On this point I shall refer the reader to what I wrote in Chapter 1 concerning the modalities of direct intervention in writing of the nonconscious of transindividual subjects. At the heart of the written word there thus appear indications of the *problematized* investment of certain social interests; problematized, I maintain, for Level 2 is rarely perceived as an autonomous functioning, since it most often appears in the form of a deconstruction effected by textual structures. The textual phenomena to which these interventions give rise thus form totalities that are not *necessarily* meaningful in themselves, points of evenness along trajectories of meaning, and that, at first, do not *necessarily* put structures into play. The same goes for what I shall call the textual enactment of certain manifestly ideological social practices.

For an approach to this problem, let us recall Louis Althusser's definition of the notion of materialized ideology: "The ideas or representations, etc. . . . . which seem to comprise ideology have no ideal, ideational, spiritual existence, but a material one. . . . An ideology always exists within an apparatus and its practice or practices. Its existence is material." We experience this ideology on a daily basis through a series of acts "inserted within practices" that are themselves "regulated by rituals, in which these practices are inscribed at the heart of the material existence of an ideological apparatus, even if it were just a tiny part of that apparatus: a little Mass in a little church, a funeral, a little game in a sports club, a school day, a meeting or rally of a political party."[1] These ideological practices are, however, but one of the possible ways of actualizing the materialized ideology infiltrating every level of social life. This is how every society produces behavioral models through which it materializes the evolution of appropriate values (son, mother, daughter, father, well-brought-up young lady, *femme fatale*, liberated woman, secretary, boss, student, playboy, sportsman, immigrant, etc.) and which constitute *social roles* in terms of which each individual defines himself or herself. These behavioral models, which subsume individual subjects under the category of sameness, also create certain behavioral expectations; it is, of course, because I know a certain attitude is expected of me that I adopt it, and in so doing I am the victim of what might be termed an "ideological interpellation." The decoding and the reproduction of these social roles are ensured by a whole syntax of signs that permit their transmission to the nonconscious level, and that program the whole of our social life.

Every materialized ideology, then, produces microsemiotic systems of ideosemes that ensure its reproduction. This ideology effectively exists to the degree that it is recognized by a *receiving/emitting* consciousness, before being reproduced by the practice of a *receiving/emitting* subject; it exists only through the way it functions and in the forms of its functioning. Nevertheless, it is appropriate to define what we mean by a *recognized* ideology. This form of recognition, obviously, does not consist in exposing an ideology in a behavior or in a discourse, but rather, at the *nonconscious* level, it either consists in receiving a discourse as an incontestable truth (such is the case of *sententia*) or, when an attitude is involved, it consists in projecting oneself on a behavior of reference, and in identifying oneself with an image of the individual established and conveyed by a collective consciousness that, through these forms of reference, materializes those values appropriate to it.

Thus, the task of the semiologist is to reconstitute these types of sign networks in order to uncover the ideological practices that have produced them. Nevertheless, it is appropriate to state that an ideological practice is an ideology *experienced and represented* by a collectivity. In this sense, homiletic rhetoric, whose impact on the textual structures of the Spanish picaresque novel I propose to analyze, becomes an ideological practice only when it comes to life and creates a type of social relationship between speaker and listeners. Here we must define, from both a semiological and an ideological point of view, the distinctions between these two levels. The first system refers to a fabric of textual references and norms; this discursive practice, transhistoric in nature, is embedded within different ritual practices representing as many different ideological practices; thus a sermon delivered in the presence of the Court cannot function ideologically in the same way as a sermon on the same theme given in a country church. The same will be true, *a fortiori*, for a sermon delivered in a prison. On a common ground of obligatory commonplaces forming the first level, a second network is operating, consisting of an intermittent series of signposts recalling the specific nature of the relationship created in the situation of communication, and upon which, at a certain level, the essence of ideological production is based.

To clarify my critical objective, at the risk of a brief digression from the problematics of the sermon, I shall take the case of *Lazarillo de Tormes*, in connection with an extremely seductive hypothesis advanced by Antonio Gómez-Moriana, who notes that at the time of *Lazarillo* there existed in Spain a type of oral or written confession delivered before the tribunal of the Inquisition or addressed to a father confessor. Such confessions are attested by Theresa of Avila's autobiography, which was written at the request of her confessor, as well as by many other seventeenth- and eighteenth-century spiritual autobiographies. Gómez-Moriana's hypothesis is supported by his research on the Acts of the Inquisition and on archival documents concerning different religious orders, which reveal a dual autobiographical practice observable as early as the fourteenth or fifteenth century:

> On the one hand, we find the "soliloquio," a form of confessional prayer addressed to God, following, more or less, the model of Saint Augustine's confessions. On the other hand, we find a practice imposed by the tribunals of the Inquisition: the accused had either to write his autobiography to justify the crime of heresy or the amoral position of which he was accused, or to do so orally in front of the tribunal of the Inquisition. The tribunal's notaries transcribed these autobiographies verbatim, using the first-person pronoun, the third person being used only for the epigraphs which divide the accused's narrative into fragments. We find precisely the same structure of these oral confessions in *Lazarillo*. . . . We discover . . . besides the interrelation "Lazaro-Vuestra Merced," another interrelation between the presenter and the virtual reader. Indeed, at the heading of each treatise or chapter, seven in all, of the narrative of *Lazarillo* is an epigraph in the third person summarizing the fragment's content.[2]

This discovery is of great importance, for it throws new light on two textual problems that have given rise, in recent years, to brilliant commentaries. The first relates to A. Marasso's interpretation, often repeated, of the formula in the prologue *Your Lordship*. Marasso's interpretation allows us to grasp more clearly the indirect characterization of the personage hiding behind the title as well as the play of relations established between him and the speaker. The passage is well known: "And since Your Lordship writes me to write him and tell him the case in all its details. . . . " Calling attention to the frequent use of the introductory formula "writes me to write him" in the *Epístolas familiares* of Antonio de Guevara, Marasso led us to think that what was involved was a pure rhetorical formula devoid of any immediately perceptible ideological articulation, and justified Claudio Guillén's use of the term "spoken epistle" in reference to *Lazarillo*. For his part, Francisco Rico saw in the *caso*, apparently quite rightly, an allusion to the dubious relations between the wife of the public crier and the archpriest of San Salvador. In the context of the seventh treatise, it is difficult not to follow his reading, but only in the seventh treatise. Indeed, *caso* is, semantically, an empty form of designation in which only the immediate context is invested. Another passage from *Lazarillo* reminds us of this: "In order that Your Lordship may know the extent of the intelligence of this shrewd blind man, I shall tell you a *caso* among many others that happened to me when I was in his company. . . . " The semantic availability of this sign allows it to enter into every semiologic convergence governed by different ideological practices, and it is not certain that the *caso* of the last treatise, whose polyvalence is provisionally dissolved, is invested with the same content as the *caso* of the prologue, which remains open to many possible reductions of meaning. The research of Antonio Gómez-Moriana precisely suggests, in a particularly convincing way, a context capable of investing this semantic void: he sees in this *caso* a "cas de conscience," a problem of conscience, thus linking in an identical response two fundamental questions posed by the text.

In this new reading, we see that a number of phrases and linguistic schemas from a discursive practice that is itself produced by ideological practices mark the text of *Lazarillo*: in particular, the apparently innocent formula "Your Lordship," behind which the mediator (the confessor) of repressive social structures (the Inquisition) is hiding. This is also true, in a general way, of the epigraphs in the third person. Clearly, an ideological practice is participating in the structuring of a literary product and, through it, is participating in the establishment of a genre, by means of a microsemiotics of ideosemes.

Moving ahead in this new perspective, let us take the case of the picaresque novel that comes after *Lazarillo*: *Guzmán de Alfarache*. What has always been a stumbling block of criticism regarding this work is the supposedly "monstrous" character of a text in which the autobiographical narration is constantly interrupted by general reflections presented as so many homiletic statements, and is, as it were, transferred to a tissue of feelings (*affectus*) against which the expression of sincere contrition and the appeal to a divine mercy alone capable of tempering the rigor of a justice presented nevertheless as necessary stand out with particular clarity. Most of the attempts at explication either concern themselves with the individual aspect of creation or explain each of the major components of the text by another. I have suggested that we see in the mediation of rhetoric the common origin of these two elements, which are only apparently contradictory, thus insisting for the first time on the existence of a collective practice.[3] Although I deem this last point established, today I consider this analysis only partially satisfactory since it takes into account only what I shall call a writing practice, which, even if it bears ideological markings admitting of more precise definition, corresponds to a transhistorical support of the production of meaning. A more precise study of the phenomena on this transhistorical axis should permit us to discern different categories of collective practices, certain of which seem to have a more direct impact.

In Spain, at least in the sixteenth century, preaching was directly linked to social repression. Thus in a great number of cases, the execution of the condemned was preceded or followed by a sermon whose aim was to strike the mind all the more keenly because the enactment of a living drama and the horror of the scaffold were being shown to a generally large audience as the concrete and tragically present consequences of an individual's presumably deviant acts. On this point, we have a precious piece of evidence, the Second Appendix (*Subjects of the Talks Addressed for Their Profit to the Public Who Came to Witness the Execution of Evildoers*) of the "Summary of some experiences in the course of ministries exercised by the Company of Jesus in which the success with which they are exercised appears concretely, through several events and documents,"[4] written by the man who was chaplain of the Royal Prison of Seville from 1578 to 1616. A reading of this work by the Jesuit father Pedro de León gives us, moreover, a better idea of what these spectacles conceived for the edification of the mob were like, and whose centerpiece was often a sermon, which, it seems, followed the execution and could affect a relatively large audience. Some twenty thousand people were present at the executions of Pedro Roldán, Pedro Salinas, and Manuel Morales, and of Don Alonso Giron. Over the heads of the spectators, the preacher addressed all the participants he imagined guilty of the same sins and deserving of the punishment inflicted on the day's victims: "How many have remained to contemplate how justice struck the heads of other individuals who did not deserve it as much as they did themselves and how many times have I told them so in the course of the sermon itself."[5] Thus the sermon aims at two different audiences: it functions for some as a mere warning, whereas for others it is an explicit threat. In both cases, the conditions of its functioning transform it into a ritualistic, concrete act of social repression, in which Christian morality takes on the appearance of a gallows, thus taking upon itself all the rigor of human justice and transforming all the ethical and abstract considerations with which it unceasingly nourished itself into ideosemes carried over into a new code. This means that the relation maintained by the homiletic act with the world of marginality has radically changed its meaning. I find it difficult not to see this new relation inscribed in transposed form in *Guzmán de Alfarache*, especially the different projections in the text of various faces of the addressee—the *Thou* so often apostrophized by the speaker—recalling that these interpellations follow one another against an immutable background of warnings and threats in which the shadow of the convict ships has replaced the sight of the gallows.

Every element in the text related to the discourse of preaching (*sententia*, divine authorities, interpellations, commonplaces of sermon practice, *exempla*, etc.) does not refer the reader any longer to a set of abstract principles making up what is generally termed Christian morality, but *reproduces this relation* in terms of its metonymical virtualities. *I shall call every textual phenomenon that produces this effect an ideoseme contingent on an ideological practice.*

Preaching is an integral part of organized religious life in the prisons. According to Pedro Herrera Pug, two or three sermons were delivered each week, permitting the abundant development of a very limited choice of broad themes: resignation, divine Providence, and mercy.[6] We shall come back to the last two; let us say, for the moment, that a logical link is established between the theme of resignation and that of divine Providence and mercy, which raises the prisoner from the human to the spiritual level and to a level of reasoning whose aim is to justify, by means of theological hairsplitting, the circumstances of both his life and his punishment. Indeed, God displays his mercy only through the rigor of his justice. Prison is a regal dwelling-place compared with hell: "For if those who are condemned to hell were given this prison for all eternity, as long as God were God, they would deem it a garden and take it for an abode of kings," and human justice is but the instrument of a God who, by obliging the condemned of every condition to expiate their transgressions on earth, redeems them from eternal damnation. This truth is ceaselessly presented to the future torture victims to the point where, under the force of this constant emotional incitement, they themselves take it up: "for God wanted to save me from the hell beyond by making me pay the price down here in my body," concludes Hernando de Gelves, a highway bandit executed on April 28, 1615,[7] who sees the accomplishment of the hidden designs of Providence in the chain of events that have marked his life.

It is an explicative discourse that, proceeding from a sociologically defined place (the prison, but it could just as well be the gallows or the galley), selects autobiographical events in the past that are now integrated into the preconceived schema of a trajectory brutally illuminated by them and which illuminates them in return, the inverted face of a path of perfection in which the destiny of the creature-object is inscribed. Such seems to me the import of Hernando de Gelves's reflections on his life, but far from being spontaneous, this meditation *only reproduces* the image it has been offered. It is this very type of discursive practice that Guzmán de Alfarache reproduces in his turn: "to those whom God has predestined, after sin he sends them penitence"; "Even if it is true that it is your sins that have brought you here, invest them in a place where they will pay you dividends. Act in such a way that you may buy Paradise"; "What has God known? What has God loved? What has God borne? Suffering. So when he has you share it, it is because he loves you so, you are his favorite, he receives you with open arms"; "Let me live, for God has been willing to prolong my life so that I might chastize myself and has given me time to mend my ways"; "But when he who inflicts [suffering] on us proves in this manner the mercy that he has placed in such suffering, and when we see it for what it really is, we shall consider it pleasure."[8] It is important to take careful note of the difference, on the one hand, between the suffering the virtuous man may offer to God and, on the other hand, the suffering society *imposes on the criminal* and which it *forces him to take upon himself as the instrument of his redemption*. It is through this ideological grid that we must reread Alemán's novel. Thus it is that Guzmán can see in his present circumstances as galley-slave the most glaring proof of his predestination, and can reconstruct the apparently uncertain trajectory of his dissolute life as a mysterious progress toward his eternal salvation. As we have just seen, such a justification by the subject of his own execution only *reproduces* an ideological element imposed upon him by the society that inflicts it upon him. Every interpretation of these facts that poses the problem at the individual level—character, narrator, author— fails to recognize that a collective practice is involved and must be definitively rejected as irrelevant. Our perception of things changes, on the contrary, if we come back to the ideological underpinnings spread by preachers inside the prisons: whereas the exaltation of resignation appropriates the horror of incarceration and the gallows in order to propose its transcendence, the portrayal of God's mercifulness, with all that it implies, transforms this repulsive object into a miraculous sign of the accomplishment of his destiny, thus passing beyond this primal horror, turning its meaning around in a contradictory, transcendent vision. In their own manner, and by addressing different areas of affectivity, both elements of this vision transcribe the same preoccupation, the need of the double repressive system to oppose, for religious as well as social reasons, every individual or collective attempt at revolt. Objectively, they are actually instruments for keeping order in the prisons and, in a much broader perspective, for maintaining a theocratic order.

Since he organizes his semipublic confession around the leading idea of the prison sermon, namely the merciful implacability of God, Hernando de Gelves's case is exemplary: he effectively shows us that the boundaries apparently separating the acts of preaching and confession must really be erased: the latter is but the interiorized reproduction of a sort of ideological matrix from which it is distinguished only by a change of perspective. The self-humiliation of the future victim repeats in another mode, as it were, from the inside, and in the framework of a dramatic enactment, the preacher's abstract warnings to which it, in turn, gives an incontestable force of truth and which it *materializes* in the strongest sense of the word. These two acts are thus as interdependent as the wrong side and right side or, more precisely, as inside and outside of one and the same vision of the facts. This double aspect of an identical collective practice is organized around a play of crossed perspectives, between an external point of view— required by didacticism—situated at the level of the "ideal reality of the must be" and that other, contradictory requirement—indispensable to its efficacy—that imposes an internal vision of the problematic reality of existence. This play of perspectives, which is the basis of the integration of didacticism in fiction[9] and, on the formal level, structures the organization of the autobiographical narrative in *Guzmán de Alfarache*, thus seems to be an ideological production, *which, once again, is evidence of the inscription of an ideological marker in the formal structures of texts.*

Logically, confession leads finally to contrition and penitence, whose forms of expression we must now examine. The latter cannot be perceived in the absolute; they must be analyzed only with respect to the ritual acts that accompany them. What is at first striking in the expression of this repentence, as it is reported by the Jesuit father Pedro de León, is the excess with which the subject abandons himself to a kind of defilement of his own image, of his *imago*: "Is there any possible way for a man as *perverse* and as *wicked* as I to be saved? Father, take care of this vile traitor, enemy of God."[10] Guzmán de Alfarache submits in his turn to this practice of self-humiliation: "Then I saw my hideousness" (p. 559); "I had sunk into the swamp of vice as far as my very eyes. . . . I shall never forget my evil life . . . my evil condition, the lack of honor, the lack of respect of which I rendered myself guilty toward God all the time I pursued such an evil path" (p. 845); "What vile deeds and deceptions I have committed!" (p. 430). No doubt it would be possible to find in these different expressions of repentence an entire rhetoric with its turns of phrase, its lexicon, its specific constructions. The richness of such a study is suggested by the reading of a very brief but, in more than one respect, extremely curious text; it concerns the prayer said by the prisoner a few minutes before his execution, of which certain stock phrases are found in the spontaneous act of contrition expressed under other conditions by Don Lope Ponce to his confessor: "My God, how great is my [unawareness]! How great is my [madness]! (cf. official prayer's "How great my [abuse]!"). "Do not take my sins into consideration" (cf. official prayer's "Take not my sins into consideration," p. 231). But one might find equal resemblances between Don Lope Ponce's expression of repentence and that of a Turk condemned for pederasty: "Ah, how late I came to know you, my God!" ("Ah, Lord, how late I came to know you!" p. 231). In the case of the Turk Hamete, his expression of regret is valuable both for his recent conversion to Christianity and, as with the other prisoners, for his awareness of his deviant conduct. But his case is all the more interesting because one may doubt (in view of the very recentness of his conversion) the spontaneity, perhaps not of his regret, but at the very least, of the discursive form in which he expresses it. We divine in his discourse the discourse of another, whether it be his confessor (p. 201) or, what is more likely, a collective discursive practice. But, obviously, does not the same hold true for all the others, including Alemán's protagonist? In view of the emotional disturbance provoked in them by the perspective of their execution, how can one doubt that prisoners tend to *reproduce* formulas which cannot authentically be engendered by the poverty of their discursive capacity or, in all probability, by their true state of mind? All we have to do is to follow attentively Pedro de León's strategy, when the prisoners condemned to death express to him, with their last request, preoccupations that seem to him quite frivolous but in which we find a touching legitimacy: a concern with dignity ("let them be taken down promptly from the gallows and be buried in the presence of many priests," p.245), anguish at the prospect of death and, even more so, of an unimaginable suffering ("let the executioner not let them suffer too much, and at the end let them not be left loathsome, their tongues protruding, but on the contrary, let their mouths be shut so that the tongues remain inside," ibid.). To these desires and fears the Jesuit opposes Christ's suffering, which justifies and invokes our own, or rather *theirs*, to the point of making them not merely accept this suffering which they rejected until then, but, more precisely, invoke it in their prayers: "Those who had asked to be taken down from the gallows promptly now desired to be left there until they fell to pieces. And those who had asked to be buried with great pomp asked to be thrown on a dung-heap. . . . And those who had asked that they not be made to suffer too much, then begged to be put to death in such a way as to suffer for a long while, and to be left in the most repulsive state imaginable so that everyone would flee them" (p. 246). No doubt today we would see in this mad, exaggerated wish to be devoured by what one fears the pathetic testimony of a terror of staggering proportions. However this may be, it is clear that, in the profoundly emotional form that explains the very excesses of their reactions, these people about to be executed send back to their interlocutor the reflection of his own arguments. This type of evidence may be compared to the prayer recited by the condemned at the moment of their execution. The text needs to be quoted in its entirety:

> Oh, my God! How I regret having irritated you. I would not have offended you for anything in the world. What an error was mine, and where was I, Lord, when I offended thee. Oh, merciful Father, take not into consideration my sins or the offenses of my youth. I am the unknown prodigal son who wasted all the goods Thou gavest me. What has become of so much error, so much folly, so much profligacy? What is left to me? Pain and confusion, these are the fruit of my pitiful pleasures! Alas, my God, thou supportest me because thou lovest me. Now it is sufficient, O Lord, I must sin no more. Never more, O Lord, for there was no other way for me to mend my ways and renounce my criminal life than to see myself upon the gallows. Happy rope, happy gibbet, you are the instrument that will now end my sinning! (p.194)

We find here, *in fine*, the leading idea of the prison sermon we described earlier, namely the collapse, in one and the same axiomatic truth, of two traditionally opposite concepts, justice and mercy, linked here in a relationship that, at first glance, is quite exceptional in nature. If, indeed, in the context of serene social relations developing within normal limits, one may conceive of a divine mercy capable of tempering the implacability of divine justice, on the contrary, once the limits of marginalization have been crossed, as with criminals who have been made to forget love and the possibility of pardon, the conceptual frontiers are, in turn, abolished, since God's mercy is measured by his justice. This adaptation to a particular sociological context demonstrates the marvelous plasticity of ideology that permits it to adapt to contradictory sociological realities.

The important fact here is not that the condemned bless their torment, but rather that, through this formula, society *compels them to do so*, obliges them, at the threshold of death, to offer themselves in sacrifice at a ritual which takes on, as ritual, a social function that we must question. The link that joins this ritual prayer for the mutilation of one's own body to that other rite, the profanation of one's *imago*, is too obvious to require emphasis: both enact the self-exorcism of the subject, who, as a sinner, assumes responsibility for his past, and who, as a repentent sinner, rejects it. Thus, from a concrete point in their existence, defined by the convergence of a criminal trajectory whose path has been preconceived by Providence, and a spiritual evolution programmed by a series of rituals, the condemned are invited to project an *ideal Self* who pronounces judgment upon the one who has dreamed it up. But this ideal distance is abolished, at other levels, by the way one's punishment is experienced, since, whatever one's perception of oneself may be, what is also involved, above all, is a condemned person's perception. In this confrontation of two characters (repressive/repressed) within the same consciousness, two discourses are established of which the first relates to the true subject, as we shall see, and the second to a repressive ideal Self. This second discourse is, in fact, the discourse of an Other.

We should therefore no longer be astonished by the extraordinarily repressive remarks of the galley-convict Guzmán de Alfarache, who specifically speaks with this voice of the Other: "on the contrary, for petty theft heavy penalties should be inflicted on them. Throw them, throw them to the galleys, shut them up in prisons or inflict other punishments on them more or less according to their crimes. . . . *That* is justice" (p. 576). "And thus, His Divine Majesty permits it as consolation for the righteous, for those who lead a life of sin and debauchery, committing public outrages and unjust actions, must be punished publicly so that they may praise His justice and find consolation in His mercy, for to punish the wicked is equally to exercise mercy" (p. 270). "He expresses himself justly when he says that those who draw no profit from good works and are not touched by soft speech must be bruised by severe admonishments accompanied by hard and rigorous punishment" (p. 433); "Rewards and punishments are necessary. If everyone were just, laws would be useless, and if everyone were wise, writers would pass for fools. Medicine is for the sick, honor for honest folk, and the gallows for the wicked" (p. 486).

The narrator thus condemns the *actant* for, in the logic of fiction, by thus condemning criminals of every kind, he repeats a discourse that also condemns him and reproduces this "praise of God's Justice" whose ritualistic character we have observed in daily practice. Modern criticism has certainly been right to make a sharp differentiation in *Guzmán de Alfarache* between the narrator and the actant, but one must add that this formal distinction, while convenient and productive for critical analysis, consists merely of a fictional separation between the two characters. Indeed, this distinction functions only at the level of composition and narrative structure, but it does not take into account certain other facts, in particular the fact that the narrator is writing his memoirs "*from the galleys* to which he has been condemned for offenses committed," that is, he sees the punishment of the *actant, which he never ceases being*, and completes his criminal trajectory not only by expiating his errors but also by surrendering himself to this ritual practice of self-debasement and self-punishment. The narrator thus remains *actant/criminal* even in his very narration, and it seems more exact to speak of the coexistence of two (repressive/repressed) discourses within one identical consciousness. This means, then, that the structural function of the I, which we had recognized earlier in Alemán's text, is equally linked to the reproduction of an ideological marker by means of the ritualistic practices imposed upon the convicts.

Beyond any problematizing in terms of narrative or psychological verisimilitude, we shall find this very same *collective practice* reproduced in the *Buscón*, in which, emerging from an identical writing practice, the mystifying discourse of the *repressed actant* stumbles against the demystifying discourse of a *repressive narrator* reflecting the discourse of an Other. The demystifying discourse reproduces an entire ritualistic system of the subject's self-debasement. It is true that the way in which these two discourses are combined varies enormously from one work to another; indeed, these combinations employ fundamentally different mediating structures (rhetoric in *Guzmán de Alfarache*, carnivalesque literature in the *Buscón*), but what connects these two picaresque narratives most strongly is the discourse of self-punishment superimposed from the outside upon the discourse of the authentic subject.

We find an identical play of discourses in another act of the religious life in prison, the practice of confession. Indeed, with a few rare exceptions, the prisoners have not the slightest idea of what a confession might be; they do not use the appropriate terms, and they narrate their sins more than they confess them, heightening their accounts with a verve that their confessors judge inappropriate: "These are creatures who have lost all sense of decency, and they start talking to you about their sins just as they committed them; they fill your head with their boasting and insolence, their tales and their foolishness; this is why one has to be very careful" (p. 198).

To avoid this nuisance, the confessor chooses to teach them God's commandments and how they must speak about their sins. This strategy of Pedro de León's confirms (1) that confession, as noted earlier, is the reproduction, the materializing, of an indoctrination; and (2) the confrontation of these two discourses and their contradictory nature: the first is authentically rooted in a past that has truly been appropriated, whereas the second is superimposed and must be felt by the "criminal" as if no longer precisely his own. This play of distancing is more complex than it seems at first glance; the didactic discourse imposed by the ideal Self is the reversed reflection of the authentic and spontaneous discourse of the subject, who feels closer to the censured representation of his past than to the one he is being asked to reproduce.

Finally, we see emerging in the practice of confession the importance of the ritualistic formula already observed in the convicts' prayers. Thus, criminal discourse, or, more broadly speaking, marginal discourse, is cast in an ideological mold we may term *ritualistic practice*. This mold transforms the material shaping it and confers upon it an eminently specific marker. What is involved in both cases is a discourse *about oneself* whose peculiarity is that it is not a discourse *of the self*. Society makes individuals adopt an image of themselves that society offers to them, so that, by accepting it and adopting it effectively as their own, they *reproduce*, from within their marginalization, the values threatened by their very existence. In the mirror it offers to the prisoner, society has inscribed beforehand the contours of its own projection.

In conclusion, we may say that double picaresque discourse, as analyzed in this chapter, reproduces a ritualistic practice in the form of a textual practice. Consequently, every ideoseme in the text reproduces the trace of an ideological practice inscribed within it, in the sense that it materializes, in terms of its metonymical value, the whole set of these two (ritual and textual) practices. The meaning of this set of signs is perceptible, however, only if we bring to light the functioning, both in daily practice and in textual practice, of signs, which, outside these two contexts, are located at a much less immediate ideological level and whose meaning and function are consequently different. Such is the case of many passages like the one quoted earlier: "He expresses himself rightly when he says that those who draw no profit from good works . . . must be bruised" (p. 433). An abstract idea whose immediate impact is not discernible, this *sententia* is transformed, through a social practice, into an ideoseme. To the extent that there exists in the text of *Guzmán de Alfarache* a transposition of this everyday practice into a textual practice, this sign will be perceived as referring to an ideological practice.

The importance of the analysis of ideologies and their modes of functioning in the fictional text needs no justification. Whatever one's critical standpoint, the need for it is self-evident. Ideology, modeling experience and all the individual and collective phenomena of consciousness, effectively intervenes, as we have seen, in every stage of the production of meaning, and in a general way in all circuits of cultural communication—hence the advantage to be derived from elucidating the complexity of these networks of ideosemes in which a whole discursive formation is concretized in the text. In this sense, the semiotics of ideological factors must be considered a basic discipline of sociocriticism. One cannot, however, limit oneself to this methodological step, for reasons no less obvious. On the one hand, the ideology that is visible must not make us forget the ideology residing in the unconscious of the text whose categories and structures it manipulates. On this point, I intend to compare the way philosophic and religious thought operates in *Citizen Kane* with the way the same (?) thinking operates in Carlos Fuentes's novel *La muerte de Artemio Cruz*. On the other hand, recall that I isolated the various constituent microsemiotics only for the convenience of exposition and analysis. We have just seen how, in *Guzmán de Alfarache*, these sets of ideosemes are related to various textual strata, and how they act upon forms at the same time the latter act upon them. Governing writing, ideology is also governed by it, operated upon, and redistributed by mechanisms that produce meaning; hence the need for our concern with the functioning of textuality.

Chapter 5
Textual Functions I
Transformational Processes and Codes

A Materialist Philosophy of Discourse

Every literary text is the product of a phenomenon of consciousness or, rather, a series of phenomena of consciousness. Consciousness does not constitute a preexisting immanent reality but, on the contrary, as Mikhail Bakhtin writes, "a socioideological fact" that "can only arise and assert itself as a reality through material embodiment in signs."[1] It is inseparable from the whole set of semiotic markers configuring it and causing it to exist. There is no consciousness apart from the sign understood in the broad sense, since semiotic material also comprises "every gesture or process of the organism: breathing, the circulation of the blood, the movements of the body, articulate speech, interior discourse, mimicry, reactions to external stimuli (light, for example), in short, *everything that takes place in the organism can become material for the expression of psychic activity, given the fact that anything may acquire semiotic value, may become expressive.*"[2] The word, however, is the privileged material of inner life: "For a psychism which is to any extent developed and differentiated a subtle and flexible semiotic material is indispensable, and it is essential, moreover, that this material lend itself to formalization and differentiation in the social context, in the process of exteriorized expression."[3] Whether or not at any given time the semiotic operation concretizing mental activity is organized around the word, this expression arises, in any event, outside consciousness, and without this external contribution of the sign no psychic activity is possible. The sign is essentially social; it can be exchanged only by individuals belonging to a particular community possessing specific structures; it materializes a communication, and investing consciousness, it consequently traces within it the markers of a certain type of sociality.[4]

Using this hypothesis, and limiting the discussion to the problem of language, I assume, for a start, three levels of consciousness (the clear consciousness, the nonconscious, the subconscious),[5] structured essentially by and around *acquired* signs, which means that not each one of these signs has thus transferred its valence intact, but that, on the contrary, the valence has been redistributed inside and by this new system. In this sense, semiotic expressions form a system only through the modalities of their assimilation.

Consistent with what I said earlier, but quite apart from Goldmann, I shall add that the transindividual subject invests the individual consciousness of each individual participating in it by means of specific microsemiotics. These microsemiotics transcribe in signs the totality of aspirations, frustrations, and vital problems of each of the groups involved. They provide a kind of "readout" of the ways each group is immersed in history. Each of us belongs, at any given moment of our lives, to a series of collective subjects (generation, family, geographic origin, profession, etc.); we pass through many of them in the course of our existence, even though we may be marked more specifically by the one that, in the last analysis, conditions the whole of our activities, namely our social class. These different collective subjects, when we pass through them, offer us their values and world visions through the materialization of the semiotic, gestural, or verbal expressions characterizing them (social roles, set phrases, hierarchical organization of paradigmatic axes, etc.). On the one hand, the whole set of these materializations is available to organize our inner life every bit as much as our external circuits of communication, and on the other hand, the expression of every phenomenon of consciousness organizes certain of these signs around a specific configuration corresponding to a particular situation. An initial conclusion may be drawn that, though obvious, deserves to be emphasized, if we are to base a critical approach to the cultural artifact upon a materialist philosophy of language: the text selects its signs not within language but within the totality of semiotic expressions acquired/proposed by collective subjects. (We shall see that other centers of selection must be specified.) Thus we may refute Saussure's distinction between language (*langue*) and speech (*parole*) or, more precisely, the criteria advanced in order to establish this distinction:

> By separating language from speech, one separates in one stroke: first, *what is social from what is individual*; second, what is essential from what is accessory and more or less accidental. *Language* is not a function of the speaking subject; it is *a product* that the individual *passively records*. . . . *Speech* is, on the contrary, an individual act of will and intelligence in which one should distinguish, first, the combinations through which the speaking subject uses the code of the language with a

view to expressing his personal thought, and second, the psychophysical mechanisms which permit him to exteriorize these combinations.[6]

The concept of *langue* is an abstraction that exists only for the historian. The individual passively records not a language but a multiplicity of discourses, which are essentially *assimilated* within enunciative contexts along with their potential variations. These variations are closely *dependent on the situation of communication conveying them* and thereby conferring upon them their social and ideological valence. The sign is *acquired* "in a situation" and remains a bearer of sociality and interaction: it keeps in its memory the *dialogic space* from which it arose.

The act of speech is an individual response to a given circumstance, but speech itself is essentially a product derived from a collective subject (the *Nous*). This does not mean that one may isolate a proletarian discourse from a bourgeois discourse, or that there are class languages and grammars, which would contradict the definition of social classes[7] and the concept of discourse to which we have just referred. Discourse, whatever the collective subject whose aspirations, frustrations, or values it expresses, transcribes with these aspirations, frustrations, or values, and through their very mediation contradictory elements that are contiguous or complementary to other transindividual subjects. In our sense of the term, there is no ideologically pure discourse, but more specifically, there are discursive traces capable of reconstituting themselves in meaningful microsemiotic systems that mark an utterance more or less strongly, and these traces are sometimes capable of giving it a sociohistorical meaning. Within the spaces of contradiction that discourse, whichever one it may be, enacts, it reconstructs at its own level, and according to modalities appropriate to it, the contradictions in the social formation upon which the corresponding collective subject depends. I have given several examples elsewhere of these semiotic systems organized contradictorily within the same utterance;[8] here I shall cite the example of *taqiyya* ("a term that designates the act by which a Muslim isolated in a hostile group refrains from practicing his own religion, pretending to adopt externally the religion imposed upon him"), concerning which L. Cardaillac quotes an *aljamiado* text reporting the reply of a mufti of Oran to the *moriscos* of Grenada, who are questioning him about the practice of their religion: "What must the morisco do when he is obliged to renounce his faith . . . ? If, for example, the Christians force the Muslims to blaspheme the prophet, they will then have to pronounce his name *Hamed*, as the Christians do. . . . As far as prayers are concerned, when the *morisco* finds that he is obliged to go to Church at the very moment when he should be saying his Muslim prayer, he will be dispensed from doing so. . . . In like fashion, if he cannot say his prayer during the day, let him do it at night."[9] This casuistry is part of the countercasuistry of the *Manual of the Inquisitors*, which warns judges against the dissimulation in the replies of the accused ("the heretics have ten ways of deceiving inquisitors who interrogate them . . . as when we speak to them of the true body of Christ and they respond: *of his mystical body*; or if we ask them *if this is the body of Christ*, they answer yes, meaning by that their own body, a nearby stone, in the sense in which all the bodies on Earth are of God").[10] These two intertwined discourses show how a dominant ideology integrates into its own system of representations the spaces that the dominated ideology attempts to infiltrate, and in the case of the *taqiyya*, how the dominated ideology allows the dominating structure to show through. Thus, each of the discourses, in turn, invests the discursive space confronting it and envelops its principal components.

The Word's Plurality of Accent and the Spaces of Dialogue

When we undertake a more precise analysis of the word, as Bakhtin does, we find a space fraught with conflicts. Bakhtin speaks, in this connection, of the pluriaccentuation of the word, "which makes it a living thing":

> The possible contexts of one and the same word are often in opposition with each other. The replies in a dialogue are a classic example. Here, the same word figures in two contexts struggling against each other. It is true that the dialogue constitutes a particularly glaring example of contexts that are oriented differently. It may be said, however, that every real utterance, whatever its form, always contains a more or less clear indication of agreement with something or refusal of something. Contexts are not merely juxtaposed, as though they were indifferent to each other, but are in a situation of interaction and of intense, uninterrupted struggle. The shift in a word's value accent from one context to another is totally ignored by linguistics. . . . Although value accents are lacking in substance, it is the plurality of a word's accents that makes it come alive. The problem of pluriaccentuation must be closely linked to that of polysemy.[11]

What is problematic in this case is the univocality of the word, which, when it enters into the enunciation of a textual message, undergoes the effects of semantic reduction. How then can it restore its original plurality of accent while inserted in only one context? One might expect, in fact, two levels: on the one hand, by the elaboration of semiotic systems;[12] on the other hand, by the reconstitution of the microsemiotic systems acquired by the speaking subject.[13] To clarify the problem, I refer the reader to two texts.

In the example of *Scarface*, what is involved is not a word but a sign[14] – the St. Andrew's cross – that is related to a sensationalist type of journalistic writing whose objective is to expose the facts, and that represents one of the modes of transcription of a new, urban, immigrant culture turned toward collective action and mass communication. At the same time, however, it is a sign of interdiction belonging to a "rhetoric of silence and concealment" that materializes within the film the presence of the Hays Code, that repressive code of censorship weighing heavily against the film industry, a product of the mental structures of an older rural, conservative, and Protestant America. These contradictory connotations of the same sign can be restored only as the sign is put back into the context of the two chains of meaning functioning in the film's text. We are at an intersection of two voices testifying to a situation of conflict, speaking within the text through two contiguous semiotic systems.

The case of *Guzmán de Alfarache* is more complex.[15] In this text, the glorification of the Earth's generosity begins with the mention of a series of products it offers spontaneously ("It gives us precious stones, gold, silver, and other metals which we need so much and for which we *thirst*"). The term *thirst* enters into a microsemiotic that transcribes within textuality the mark of one of the traditional topics of the Golden Age, namely the description of the first human beings, who have only elementary needs to satisfy and who live in a world that generously provided for them. Within this microsemiotic, *thirst* relates to other signs such as "necessity, herbs, fruit, water, drink, sheep, milk, wool," and so on. But it also belongs to a second microsemiotic of exchange and mercantilism (gold, silver, commerce, etc.), of products of a second order of need (cloth for decoration, etc.); in this context, the accent is placed on another value of *sed*, namely avidity. In this term two thoughts intersect, which, to borrow Pierre Vilar's words, "have coexisted and fought one another" over the role of gold and precious metals in the prosperity of a State. Is gold the "sole sign . . . of the greatness of States," or on the contrary, is it the "seed of dissolution of true wealth that consists only in the production of goods necessary for life"?[16] In a first reading, apparently set within a semantic reduction that makes it a sign of cupidity and the textual index of a moral discourse on mercantilism, the word is here somehow destabilized in the framework of textual semantics, and also says something else—namely the opposite of its first meaning. In this sense, it represents a crossing of voices, a space of conflict.

What I have just said about the word remains valid at the level of the broader units that enter into the combinatorial structure of the genotext. I refer here to the *Buscón*, in which, as we shall see, the representation of sociopolitical reality takes place through the inscription in the text of the two social practices: the feast of Carnival and the repressive actions of the Inquisition. These practices are invested in the text by means of semiotic systems resting in turn upon contradictory value systems that we may consider as phantasmal projections of social *Destructuration* and *Restructuration*. When we investigate the mechanisms that permit the system to swing from one semiotic system to another and, consequently, from one space to an opposite space, we observe that the point of coincidence is the polyvalent concept of mask, the tragic mask behind which forbidden rites, especially, hide and which the inquisitorial procedure strives to remove, or the festive disguises that permit marginal people to express themselves. The fact that, in a burlesque context, these masks reproduce the features of the established authorities, as is frequently the case at Carnival time, or that in the dramatic masquerades of the autos da fé, they reproduce, because they are obliged to do so, the ritual practices of the dominant society, shows how the discursive spaces of marginality coincide with the structures producing situations of exclusion.[17]

The comparison between this analysis and the preceding analyses of the sign in *Scarface* and the word in *Guzmán de Alfarache* suggests a generalization: every textual element inserted at the heart of the production of meaning can function only in a polyvalent form.

Returning to our central problem, we see that it is impossible to conceive of discourses of transindividual subjects *functioning* autonomously. Every act of speech sets in motion an interdiscourse that marks in the text the discursive traces of an ideological formation and, in this way, refers us to a social formation. That is why this utterance must be considered in turn as polyvalent, which requires reconstituting often contradictory vectors of meaning that transcribe the social interests of the different transindividual subjects involved. These different vectors of meaning carve up one and the same reality in myriad ways and create polysemic spaces of reading.

To say implicitly that the phenomena of consciousness that generate texts are not reducible to the category of the individual does not mean that we have rejected the notion of a text's originality, for speech always redistributes these different voices in particular ways. These voices have themselves shaped consciousness in a unique mode by giving it a specific configuration.

Processes of Transformation and Codes of Mediation

Textual production itself is not reducible to phenomena of consciousness. Indeed, it sets off complex processes of semantic transformation: in the first place, an already elaborated linguistic material, an "already said" that supports meaning, in which it simultaneously deconstructs itself, at every level:

(1) First at the discursive level (which refers us back to the preceding point) of the preasserted, set syntagmatic groups and lexies in which every human community materializes the particular modalities of its historic, spatial, and social insertion.

(2) Then at the textual level, as in the well-known thesis of intertextuality.[18] Contrary to other critics, such as R. Barthes[19] or Michael Riffaterre, who conceive of the intertext from the reader's point of view,[20] we place it within the context of the work of writing. Taking up, though from a different point of view, a suggestion of Riffaterre's — who himself borrows the term from Charles S. Peirce[21] — I emphasize that it is not the intertext that is deconstructed, but more precisely its interpretant, that is, a certain idea

of this intertext; it is not a previous textuality that is deconstructed within the new one, but in some way a certain manner of reading this earlier text. This decoding is provided, in the context of a grammar of reception, by the same semiotic apparatus that informs interdiscourse in another sense, unless one assumes — which would probably be more precise — that this decoding, none other than the interpretant, is but an effect of meaning produced by the genotext.

(3) At the level of myth (see the analysis below of a text from *Guzmán de Alfarache* that rewrites the different components of the Golden Age myth), traditions of gesture and language in folklore (see the studies in Chapter 11 on the *Buscón* and *La hora de todos*), that is, a broader domain of "social imagery."

(4) At the level of archaic schemas deeply embedded within a cultural context and redistributed under the effect of particular historical circumstances (see Chapter 11, pp. 225–30).

With respect to interdiscourse (speech), in which we see a primary modeling system, we see that these preconstructeds — or rather preconstraints — represent a number of secondary modeling systems.

However, it is not only the *media* that intervene in the process of transforming observable reality, and it is necessary to conceive, on another level, of the existence of new intermediary structures that somehow are capable of displacing signs and homogenizing them within an identical code.

Let us take the case of the first sequence of *Citizen Kane*, the representation of the character's death. The camera, after showing the sign forbidding entrance to the palace, travels the length of the gate and enters a garden of exotic plants; the silhouette of the castle stands out in the background; a light in a window — the only one that is lit — suddenly goes out, at the same time that the musical accompaniment falls silent. Now inside the house, we perceive a recumbent body, then a snow-covered house inside a glass globe, held in a hand that drops the object; it rolls down some steps and breaks. In a closeup, two lips pronounce the word *Rosebud*; in a distorted vision, a nurse coming to cover the face of the dead man is seen walking through a doorway.

If we try to go beyond the anecdotal level, we observe, throughout this series of frames, the functioning of the concept of passage, crossing, or transgression: first, in the crossing of the surrounding enclosure, followed by the invasive entry into the room in which Kane has just died, but also, in a subtler, more meaningful way, as our gaze, at first fixed upon this microcosm of the glass ball, leaves it and then gives us an external view of it; finally, in the discourse on time, punctuated by two flashbacks, so that the precise moment of the character's death is signified three times (interruption of light and music — shattering of glass — veiling of the face). The image of death is thus linked to the reversal of the flow of time, which is linear during the camera's progress toward the castle and is then, as it were, refracted and regresses to the precise instant when consciousness expires. Insofar as this recurrence is perceived within the context of an analogical series, the flashback hides its syntactic function (which is to coordinate frames) to its own advantage. No doubt it reverses the events, but it tells us above all that it is reversing them; it draws attention to its nature from a double point of view, both metalinguistic and poetic. Here the concept of crossing is effected by the evocation of a sort of barrier against which temporal linearity stumbles and breaks, and can now only bend back toward the past. In this sense, the flashback is integrated into a semiotic text that, apparently semanticized by the anecdotal, represents death as a *transitus mortis*.

This first observation is an index of a key to the decoding of the text and with respect to which other facts emerge. Thus, the entrance to Xanadu is shown as a sudden irruption into a haunted universe, devoid of any human presence, inhabited only by a light, which will soon go out. Emphasizing the temporal closure I have just described, the nesting of these closed spaces (property lines, high walls of the castle, the bedroom of the dying man, the crystal globe) betrays, at the same time, their emptiness and represents a theater abandoned by its actors, a shell definitively emptied of all content since the reign of darkness. It is in this context of emptiness that we perceive the central image of the rosebud, a dense focus of abundance rich with promise. We readily recognize in these phenomena a religious symbolism all the more clear since, at another level, *Rosebud* inscribes the theme of transience, fragility, and ephemerality, a message reinforced by the silhouette of the unfinished and ridiculous palace, signifying that, perceived from this point of closure, all is vanity. The shattering of the glass ball after a brief run down the stairs says it also, an evident symbol of the rapidity with which we reach the end of our existence, evoking the classical metaphor of the road of life. This first sequence is thus a meditation on death governed completely by Christian *topoi*. They will be noted in later frames that evoke a demiurge whose proud accomplishments (economic and journalistic empires, residences, etc.) are threatened by destruction. In the second sequence, *The News on the March*, this *topos* is expressed especially through the myths of Genesis and the Tower of Babel, which are there only to be deconstructed. These myths are not precisely what is in question in the first sequence, where, indeed, an entire cultural stratum seems to be filtering, generating, or displacing the images. This *topos* filters down into the hollows of the anecdotal pretext whose logic and programming it rejects for its own benefit. Thus emerges what will be one of the cinematic text's major codes of transformation.

What is at issue will appear more clearly if I reduce the global signified of the set of images we have studied to the following schematic formulation: "Death came to X at home." I have not been specific about the nature of this residence on purpose; indeed, I would be led, in the contrary case, to consider the narrative in terms of a puzzle and to mortgage, as it were, my analysis by introducing circumstantial aspects that relate either to the narrative or to the text, I am not sure which (X apparently dies alone, in a sumptuous castle: is this solitude connected with the religious text informing the film, or does it correspond, in the fictional context, to the authenticity of the character's experience?). Reducing the first sequence to this formula, I bring out the arrangement of the visual material used to signify death: thus, on the first point, a series of symbols (interrupted light and music, shattering of the globe, veiling of the corpse's face), but these first symbols themselves, whose neutral, banal, and somehow "secular" character is obvious, describe two points of view, by evoking not only contemplated death (recumbent body, dead man's face covered by a sheet) but also *experienced* death, as the invasion of consciousness by silence and darkness. By this evident appeal to a process of identification, the text, going beyond the mere anecdotal pretext, interpellates me, insofar as this first signifier (the series of symbols mentioned above) acquires its autonomy: this death is henceforth no longer that of X but mine, ours. Textuality opens onto another dimension. The imaginary element brought into play to lend support to the narrative calls attention to itself and afterward develops, through an effect of contiguity, its own universe and its own text. The images chosen to signify the death of Kane are transformed by signifying a philosophical and religious conception of life, which is exteriorized in the iconic forms of the rose and the racing of the globe, a functioning that can be schematically represented as in the accompanying diagram. [Note that Se denotes *Signifié* (signified) and Sa denotes *Signifiant* (signifier).]

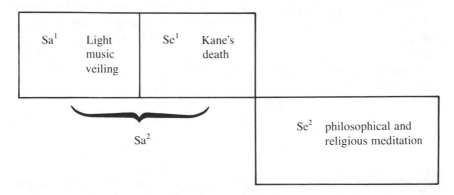

Between Se^1 and Se^2 an ideological function is operating for which the fact of death is the occasion for a meditation on human existence and for setting rules for living. The transformational code I mentioned earlier corresponds to the ways this ideological instance intervenes in the production of meaning.

This ideological instance is expressed not only at elementary linguistic and visual levels. It also commands the syntagmatic ordering of signs and controls the narrative's points of focalization, that is, the points of reference with which writing provides itself in order to organize the architecture of its signs. Thus, as we have also seen, the approach to Xanadu, exactly like the functioning of insert and flashback, concretizes at the phenotextual level the concept of crossing, which is semanticized in turn by the point of anecdotal focalization, as a modulation of the thematics of *transitus mortis*.

Beyond the framework of this first sequence the same voice is operating through interventions of a perceptibly different nature. The reconstruction furnished by the newsreel (*The News on the March*) is effectively organized around the growth of Kane's power (its display, its extent, its origin) through a significant figurative language articulated, as we have said, essentially around two myths — Genesis and the Tower of Babel. The first of these myths, which is explicitly invested in the cinematic text by a landscape in which the boundaries between water and earth appear indistinct, develops as the background of a thematics dealing with the artificial construction of a second universe characterized by the accumulation of resources, economic means, and wealth. This sacred text, originally presented as the basis for a certain type of spirituality, functions here as the index of a point of reference in relation to which we are being invited to form a judgment on Kane's undertaking. The presence of this text and the modalities of its deconstruction denounce, in the organization of this new Noah's ark, the absence of any reference to God. The spiritual dimension inscribed in the text of Genesis reveals what is to be condemned in this project of reification; it points up, by a countermovement, precisely what was involved in the concept of vacancy in the initial frames. The textualization of the building of Xanadu, reconstructed in three stages (the creation of a mountain in a geographical environment — the flat stretches of Florida — which makes it appear as the work of a madman, the silhouette of a multistoried tower, the castle itself), contributes to a similar condemnation. A new series of indexes reinforces the preceding one: the symbolic nature of the mountain, a sacred site; the systematic use of low-angle shots, which are then semanticized by the whole semiotic text, and which organize its frames; the enumeration of the different titles — in every language — of the newspapers on the planet; the unfinished look of Xanadu, which, however, is already developing cracks; the fact that this castle has twice been likened to a tomb, the first time explicitly, the second time by analogy to the pyramids. The myth of the Tower of Babel is functioning, in that case, as the reverse of the myth of Genesis: contrary to Genesis, which acts as a foil, by analogy, Babel fits Kane's project perfectly. It reveals the other side of the myth of Genesis, resolving its possible ambiguities. Thus the ideological authority reinforces its message through both of them.

Once these initial phenomena have been clarified, they, in turn, throw light on the role of the newsreel commentator's voice — the exaggeration in which he cloaks himself, his way of distancing himself from his subject, his critical attitude. We should not attribute any merit to the journalist who presumably presents this obituary, remembering that all Kane's projects, whether political or sentimental, have fallen into ruin, and that his predictions have proven false (on the Second World War, for example). All of Kane's creations bear in them, at the same time, the mark of their nonconformist character with respect to ideological criteria and, as a consequence, the premonitory sign of the annihilation toward which they are heading. We see, then, how the ideological instance intervenes in the production of meaning through the mediation of a transformational code.

Thus far we have been grouping together phenomena that do not belong to the same category. The first refer to an obviously figurative language already recognized as such, as in the case of the mythical elements we have recognized, which are bearers of diegesis, according to the accompanying schema:

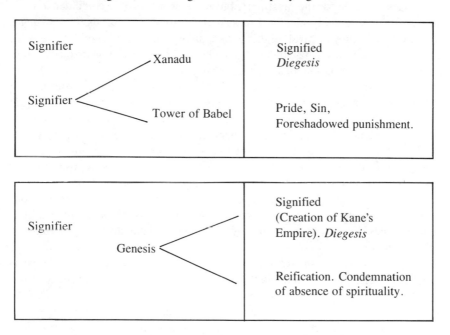

Clearly, figurative language feeds two strata of textuality, allowing us to clarify the functioning of the deconstruction in both cases. At the same time the text is being constructed, it is organizing the ideological reference points permitting it to be read.

However, as we have seen, this figurative language also controls the text in the form of a kind of secondary symbolization especially apparent in the first sequence, and that coincides only with the first level of symbolization by means of an internal focus of semanticization. This is true of the fall of the glass globe or the words spoken by the dying man. It is a question here no longer of the mere reproduction of a symbolic code repeated verbatim in the text but of a new con-cretization of the same code. This refers us to a textual instance that manipulates this first code but cannot be confused with it. It is this instance that semanticizes the syntactic axis and enters the combinatory genetics it creates, among other things, by systematically reproducing the category of the *crossing*, the implicit bearer of the vision of the *transitus mortis*. Consequently, I shall distinguish be-tween the deconstructed symbolic material (Genesis, Tower of Babel) and the ac-tive principle of its deconstruction (the textual instance in question). We thus op-pose the *code of symbolization*, understood as a figurative language conveying the signified, to the *code of transformation* that manipulates it and that is the active center of meaning.

If this distinction is problematic in the case of *Citizen Kane*, it is because the two codes coincide for the most part, but the reasons for this coincidence must be investigated. It will be clearer if we take the example of *Guzmán de Alfarache*. The text I shall study in Part II of this book employs, in order to signify the Earth's generosity, the myth of the Golden Age and of a Nature that spontaneously offers Man its products. This classical figurative language, conveying a nostalgic vision of the past, especially condemns commercial agitation and activity. After having fragmented the elements of this nostalgic vision, which now claim autonomy, the text of Mateo Alemán, under the probable effect of a code of transformation that remains to be described and defined, perverts this code of symbolization by in-scribing in it themes of modernity (the overseas adventure, for example) and by transgressing the interdiction that, in all preceding texts, was imposed against trade; the latter thus comes to occupy the whole textual space.

In the case of the *Buscón*, the codes of transformation of semiosis are con-stituted by two social practices (Carnival/Inquisition) invested in the form of tex-tual practices. From that point on, any element of mental structure that may be related either to interdiscourse or, when materialized in a text, to intertextuality, any linguistic material, any referent will undergo this double work of transforma-tion before it is finally encoded in textual structures. Let us take the reality from which the *word* originates, namely the existence of an *hacedor de paño* (cloth maker), who represents an economic power in Castile at the beginning of the seventeenth century and whose sociopolitical integration is being rendered problematic. The object (*el hacedor de paño*) is apprehended by a mental struc-ture in the framework of an enunciative and interactive context associating him with a community that is outcast because it is linked to a religious heterodoxy (converted Jews or new Christians) and is threatening on both religious and politi-cal grounds, since it is perceived as aiming to supplant the hegemony of the domi-nant group (manifested by interdiscourse). Such, at least, is the *interpretant* that the rest of our analysis leads us to reconstitute. The disappearance of the interpre-tant as such is already a problem in itself, and which would deserve further in-quiry. (Why this refusal to designate the adversary other than indirectly?) The interpretant itself generates (or is generated by) a series of associated meanings: as a converted Jew, the *hacedor de paño* is supposed to hide himself and his condemnable religious practices; because he has economic power, he imitates the ostentation of the nobility.

These two elements, the *already said (hacedor de paño)*, and the interpretant, pass, at the intertextual level, through a first *medium*, which is conceptist rhetoric: a lexicalized phrase is cunningly assimilated by the narrative instance to these enigmatic circumlocutions whose fashion, as Jean Molino remarks, extended at the time to all of Europe under the names of *agudeza, wit, concetto*.[22] Behind this practice, we recognize the norm of the Ciceronian *ornatus* destined to enrich the noble style and functioning as an index of the locutor's selection of a certain level of language. It is thus a question of valorizing one signified through the intermediary of *translatio verbi*, substituting for the first signifier a second that in some way transfigures the referent.

It so happens in this case that, on the one hand, this *translatio verbi* is applied to an incongruous referent, the object *barber*, which cannot enter the gravitational field of the elevated style, and, on the other hand, the substitute signifiers (*shearer* of cheeks and *tailor* of beards) correspond as well to pejorative signs. Clearly, we are seeing the reverse effect of the use of conceptist circumlocution, which catches the character at his most degraded and ridiculous: his desire to present an appearance and his inability to manipulate a certain type of discourse. The threat to social status inscribed in referential reality (the wool manufacturer aspiring to political hegemony) is out of place in parody, but this displacement presupposes a double encoding: an initial semiotic operation, assuming a will to disguise (Carnival/first code of transformation); a second semiotic operation that implies a demystification (Inquisition/second code of transformation). Thus in this way observable reality undergoes successive mutations that add to it a "semantic surplus value."

Our sociocritical reading would be incomplete, however, if we did not investigate the nature and origin of these codes of transformation. The reader will have observed that they are the very creations of the text, and that, for this reason, it hardly seems possible to set up their typologies. I have shown elsewhere how these codes, in the text of Quevedo, are part of the immediate context of the object at the source of the production of the text. This was self-evident in the case of descriptions of the Inquisition, which still remained closely linked to the persecution of the new Christians in Spain, but what about festive practice? Research on contemporary documents provides an answer. In early seventeenth-century Segovia the urban bourgeoisie represented by the cloth manufacturers turned the rural folkloric traditions of Carnival to their profit, as was the case elsewhere in Europe. Thus the sociohistorical situation that generated a series of phenomena of consciousness carried in its wake modalities that were destined to preside over its "textual enactment" and determined the foundations of writing. Another question emerges: did these two mediating structures have a relationship between them other than the one linking them directly to the *Buscón* as pretexted object? Yes, for the Carnival functions in the *Buscón* as the interpretant of the Inquisition, and the Inquisition functions as the interpretant of the Carnival. If these social practices are operating in textual production, the text, in return, gives voice to them, forces them to actualize their latent potentialities in the practice of writing.

These observations have been confirmed by my analysis of *Scarface* (see Chapter 8), since journalistic writing, which enters the production of meaning in its role as mediating structure, is as much a part of the immediate context of sociohistorical and sociopolitical facts transcribed in the film (namely the questioning of the cultural model characterizing the new wave of immigration to the United States, the struggle of the dominant groups of white, Anglo-Saxon, Protestants for what they believe to be their survival) as the background of the economic crisis and the impact of its fluctuations on political life. At the heart of the new culture that is supposed to be menacing the old, the domination of the media, mass communications and especially the great power of journalism are beginning to be felt.

My demonstration and definition of the codes of mediation in the cultural object furnish a response to the irritating question that is endlessly asked by "sociological" literary criticism, yet never resolved, at least if we refuse to accept as satisfactory the hypotheses advanced by Lucien Goldmann (recourse to the notion of world vision and the concept of homology). Indeed, it appears that mediations in the text present themselves through a set of concrete and discernible semiotic traces whose modes of presence vary from the mere transposition of ideosemes to the investment by ideology and interdiscourse of textual semantics and structures.

The structures of mediation that intervene between societal structures and textual structures are thus discursive in nature, whether involving cultural texts (the gestural and linguistic traditions of carnivalesque festivals or the codes of symbolization of social practices, for example) or the specific discourses of transindividual subjects. These structures of mediation always present themselves in the form of semiotic traces, signifying sets and paths of meaning that we may term *intratextual microsemiotics*. The following analyses, however, as well as the theoretical generalizations we have drawn from them, demonstrate how these microsemiotics function at the different levels of the text. One must, indeed, consider them as essentially dynamic sets generating deconstructions deep inside the centers of textual production. These deconstructions themselves are powerful semantic loci, to the extent that the intratextual microsemiotics reveal themselves and their ideological origin. To illustrate this process I shall group a certain number of phenomena, several of which will be developed further in Part II of this study. I have often cited the case of the deconstructions affecting the conceptist metaphor in Quevedo's *Buscón*. The diffraction around which the deconstructions are organized, and which requires me to simultaneously decode, behind the bur-

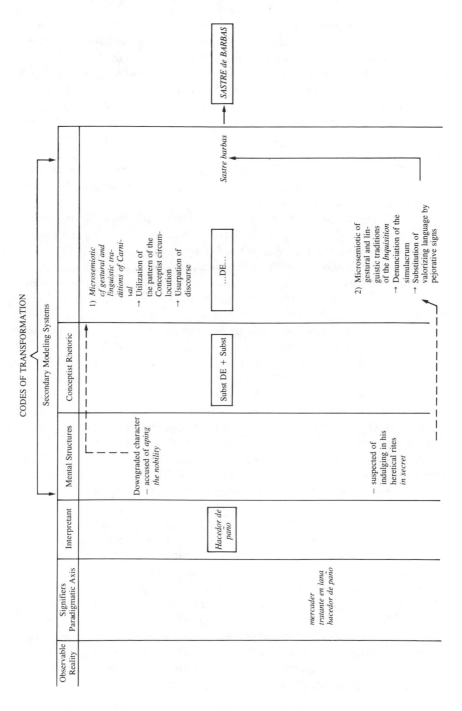

lesque phrase "shearer of beards," the traces and the rhetorical mold of noble speech, signifies both the latter's existence and its misappropriation by a subject incapable of mastering it, that is, by an individual who, in the last analysis, intends to hide his social position by identifying himself with a social group he deems superior to his own; but this misappropriation is visible as such by the discrepancy between referenced reality (barber) and the phrase he uses to describe it. The subject unmasks himself by the very way he tries to hide himself. In this way we grasp the double function (masking vs. unmasking) of discourse in the whole text. I have attempted to show, above, concerning codes of transformation, how within these phenomena of deconstruction the effects of two social practices (festive practice and repressive practice), themselves understood in the context of their respective cultural texts, coincide.

We shall also see in the reading of a passage from *Guzmán de Alfarache* how an intratextual microsemiotic, which inscribes in the text the traces of a mercantile discourse, remodels the myth of the Golden Age.

The opening lines of *La región más transparente* attest a similar functioning. There the Christ-like image of the "crown of thorns" is deconstructed into a "crown of *nopales*," in which two iconic traditions connected to different religious cultural texts coincide (Christian religion/Aztec religion). The syncretism emerging from this coincidence appears to be produced by the operation in Fuentes's novel of a microsemiotic transcribing in the last instance the fundamental lines of force of bourgeois ideology in postrevolutionary Mexico.

We may apply the same methodology of concrete modes of intratextual representation of mediations to cultural objects other than literature. Take the case of Litin's *Viva el presidente*, a film version of Alejo Carpentier's novel *El recurso del método*. On the transhistorical axis, a number of ideological tracings, among them positivism, are being deconstructed. At the very moment the President, in a train heading for the front, puts on his official uniform, we see behind him what seems to be his motto or his country's motto: "God, Fatherland, Order," suggesting in the background Comte's "Order and Progress." The gap between the original motto and what it has become is extremely significant in that the new formulation inscribes values absolutely contradictory to those of Comte and Comtism. Indeed, not only was positivism atheist, at least in its initial phase, and preached the love of humanity, but in a certain number of cultural texts God and Fatherland are contradictory to the notion of Progress. Thus, in this new figuration, Comtism is being shown in a profoundly disfigured form. This principle of falsification, of inadequacy, of perversion, turns round and round in the text, and we can compare it with the thought of Marti, itself contained within Castroism, which Carpentier claims as his authority and according to which every system of centrist thought is inadequate in Latin America. But Castroist thought is presented in the film, as it is in the novel, through a set of discursive traces and paths of meaning that organize an intratextual microsemiotic producing meaning.

Chapter 6
Textual Functions II
Genotext and Phenotexts

The discussion in Chapter 5 demonstrates how a problem may be approached *seriatim* only for convenience of exposition, for obviously the textual phenomenon is the product of a complex of elements operating simultaneously. But how, precisely, does this complex of elements function and from what point in the text?

Using a spatial metaphor, we may imagine the point of intersection of two axes, a vertical and a horizontal. On the first axis is *interdiscourse*, which materializes both mental structures and ideological formations produced by a social formation. The discourse of time upon itself is read on this axis, or, in other words, interdiscourse translates into semiotic operations, through multiple ideological traces, the sociohistorical conditions in which a speaker is immersed. On the horizontal axis is the *intertext* — the preasserted, the preconstructed, the preconstrained, that is, all the linguistic material destined to materialize and give shape to meaning (see the accompanying diagram). On the horizontal axis, as on the vertical, are preestablished paths of meaning offering a more or less strong resistance to textual modeling, inside which they maintain semiotic pockets, microspaces of reading capable of producing zones of conflict under the effect of the narrative instance's possible monosemic project. It is at this intersection that we must imagine the process of transformation of observable reality under the effect of codes of mediation: the complexity of the elements in play proves at once the necessary polysemy of the fictional text, the importance of its distancing with respect to referential reality, as well as the resistance it offers to critical examination. Within this crucible, however, arise lines of force, centers of meaning around which new semiotic operations and semantic models are organized, that

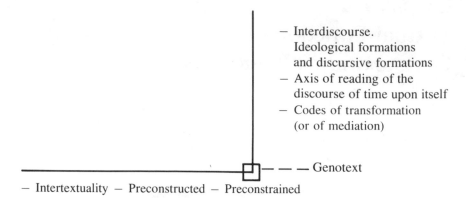

— Interdiscourse.
Ideological formations
and discursive formations
— Axis of reading of the
discourse of time upon itself
— Codes of transformation
(or of mediation)

— — — Genotext

— Intertextuality — Preconstructed — Preconstrained

— Axis of the modeling system

— Symbolic codes

is, a whole complex of elements that thrust textuality into a state of becoming; the conceptual framework is thus put into place that will ensure the autonomy of the text/sign with respect both to the consciousness that is supposed to produce it and to the originally invested reality.

To borrow a term from Julia Kristeva, I shall call this focal point of meaning a *genotext*. The work of writing is a constant deconstruction of this composite in the form of *phenotexts* destined to actualize at every textual level the syntax of previously programmed messages, depending upon their specificity.

The use of these terms can be problematic, to the extent that my use of them does not correspond to Kristeva's,[1] who borrows them herself from the generative theories of the Soviet linguist Saumjan-Soboleva.[2] Kristeva introduces these notions in the context of a theory of meaning, conceived as a germination process related to *semanalysis*, a discipline distinct from semiotics, and confined to "gathering . . . . signifying truth." Kristeva is concerned with distinguishing a state from its production, a signified structure from the process of generation of the same signified. If the term *phenotext* is clear insofar as it refers to the printed text, conceived as one of the possible actualizations of language (in the Saussurian sense of *langue*), the term *genotext* demonstrates something more complex if not more ambiguous. Indeed, it refers in Kristeva both to a linguistic *process* at work in language, at an abstract level of linguistic functioning, and to a *state*: "the genotext is the infinite signifier which cannot 'be' a 'this' for it is not in the singular; it would be denoted more accurately as plural and infinitely differentiated 'signifiers,' with respect to which the *signifier* that is present here, the signifier of the present-formula-of . . . -the-said-subject, is only a milestone, a named-place, an ac=cidence (that is, an approach, an approximation added to signifiers while its own position is abandoned)" (p. 283). Kristeva's concept of genotext, conse-quently, situates textual actualization within a broad and undifferentiated whole to the extent that "the genotext can be presented as the *mechanism* (*dispositif*) of the history of the language and of the signifying practices that textual actualization is capable of knowing: the potentialities of every existing and future concrete lan-guage are 'given' in the genotext before falling back, masked or censored, into the phenotext" (p. 284). As for printed texts, or phenotexts, these "are to be en-visaged as formulas of significance in the natural language, as modifications or successive revisions of the fabric of language; formulas that would occupy a par-allel position as important, if not more so, for the constitution and transformation of monumental history as discoveries in mathematics and logic" (p. 286). Thus, we can better understand why it may be claimed that "semanalysis protects itself from psychological thematics as well as from the aestheticizing idealism currently competing for the monopoly of what has been called *écriture* (Derrida)" (p. 279).

Everything Kristeva writes on this point is extremely suggestive, but, as we have seen, it is not at this level that I intend to pose the problem. I intend to use these notions to establish a rigorous parallelism between two states of the enuncia-tion characteristic of *a* text; the first functions with conceptual categories and cor-responds to an ungrammaticalized enunciation, in the sense that this enunciation is not yet formulated. It is not a structure, but it is to become a structure by struc-turing itself within the different phenotextual actualizations of the same text. In-deed, the text opens onto different levels (narrativity; the multiple signifying wholes that are, among other things, characters and codes of symbolization; the chain of meanings of signifiers; etc.), in which linguistic categories and those ap-propriate to these levels are both operating in the framework of a signifying proc-ess tending to actualize in an apparently incoherent and fragmented way the semantic latencies of the same utterance: the genotext. This genotext exists only in these multiple and concrete actualizations—phenotexts—and it corresponds to an abstraction reconstituted by the analyst.

Between these two *states* of the utterance (*énoncé*) is the functioning of the var-ious codes of transformation, that is, the process by which the signifying system is generated, what Kristeva (by another displacement of terms) means, in part, by the notion of genotext. This conception of textual functioning, moreover, must not be confused with the distinction generative grammar introduces between deep structure and surface structure. Indeed, for Chomsky, deep structure is postulated as the archetypal reflection of performance, as Kristeva pertinently notes: "The components of depth are structurally the same as those of surface, and no trans-formational process, no passage from one type of component to another, from one type of logic to another, is observable in the Chomskyan model. Thus, gener-ative grammar does not, properly speaking, generate anything at all: it is only posing the principle of generation by postulating a deep structure that is only the archetypal reflection of performance" (p. 282).

In order to illustrate the type of relation I am proposing to establish between genotext and phenotext, let us return to *Citizen Kane* to isolate a series of phenomena to be considered as forms of reference.

(1) The first corresponds to a sentence written on a card that appears in the newsreel sequence devoted to Kane's death: "Last week the largest and most extraordinary funeral of 1941 took place at Xanadu." In order to understand how this inscription is functioning, let us recall that the shooting of the film was finished on October 23, 1940, its editing was completed at the beginning of February 1941, and its first performance was scheduled for some time in mid-February. (The first performance did not take place until April 9, owing to the scandal caused by William Randolph Hearst, who claimed the film was a caricature of his own life.) The film's first audience was thus being offered, in the framework of a newsreel, a reconstruction of Kane's past projected into the audience's own future (the end of 1941, implicit in the formula "the most important of the year"). We might, no doubt, observe that the film is presented to us as a pure fiction, were it not for the fact that this formula, in which the past and the future are being confused with the present time of performance, is discernible elsewhere in the film.

(2) The sequence that, in Bernstein's account, describes the move of a team of reporters from the *Chronicle* to Kane's *Inquirer* can be reduced to a similar schema. The reporters are shown lined up in a double row in a photograph displayed in the window of the *Chronicle* as Leland, Kane, and Bernstein pass by. Suddenly, this photograph is taken apart, each man freeing himself from the pose he had assumed. Kane's arrival on the scene makes us understand that what is involved this time is a photo taken at the offices of the *Inquirer*. Six years have elapsed between the two instances of diegesis which have been evoked. In reality, what has happened, no doubt fleetingly, is that an effect of reading has been constituted to take us back to a time prior to the first photograph. This reading effect has us pass from the instant when photo 1 is perceived as already taken to the instant when it is being taken, that is, from moment 2 to moment 1, before canceling itself in a new effect which makes us understand that this anteriority is but a false anteriority insofar as this moment 1 is actually linked to photo 2. The first effect of reading corresponds, in common with photo 1, to an image of the past bearing an already accomplished future at the very moment it is perceived. Thus past and future are colliding, as it were, in a point that implies the present time of viewing. Inscribed in the past, the future presents itself as an "already there."

(3) This coincidence of the future and the past in one point, which has been semantically focused in its category of the present, will be actualized again and again in the dialogue. I shall quote only two examples: the first is readable only in the context of the analogical series which we are in the process of reconstructing: "I am, I have always been, I shall never be anything but an ordinary American citizen." The second, on the contrary, hardly needs to be made explicit; it con-

cerns the words spoken by the voice-over of the newsreel journalist to describe Kane's last years spent at Xanadu: "Alone in his never-to-be-completed [*future*], and already [*present*] cracked [*past*], palace, withdrawn from the world, receiving only infrequent visitors."

Three forms of reference, we have said, but also three levels of the filmic text, if we accept the distinction between the editing (case number 1) and the use *in situ* of the syntax of images (here, the series of lap dissolves of case number 2), each of which has its own signifying system and rules of functioning, and which, in the very same text, do not play the same role. However, these forms of reference are all saying the same thing, and this same thing they are saying corresponds to an utterance (*énoncé*) of the genotext. This utterance is being deconstructed and redistributed by the specific components of each of the three levels that, in their fashion, structure phenotextual modeling.

In the case of *Citizen Kane*, this statement, in its own schematic form, repeats—as we have just seen in these three cases—that "what will happen is already there," a concept actualized on the level of that other textual category—narrativity—by the system of prolepses and all the premonitory signs of Kane's destiny (his failures in love and politics, his lack of political insight, etc.). The same might be said about the codes of symbolization that have been chosen (Tower of Babel, Pygmalion, etc.), in which the signs of the future failure of Kane's projects are inscribed at the very moment he undertakes them. Does the plot itself not tell us, by an effect of reversal, that the answer to our eventual query and, at any rate, to the problem that the film poses as its objective—to solve the question, Who or what is *Rosebud?*—was present from the very first sequences?

However, the most interesting case to consider is that of the figurative language enacted in the very first frames. Indeed, we remember how the evocation of Kane's death is reconstructed in the perspective of a *transitus mortis*, which is itself concretized by recourse to the thematics of the mirror, envisaged as the dual poetic locus of transgression and diffraction; this thematic constitutes the figurative support shaping the filmic text and thus generating a systematic fragmentation. Here the mirror functions contradictorily, as a symbol of a threshold to cross and as a reflecting surface, a sort of buffer against which temporal linearity is shattered and can, henceforth, only develop in reverse. In this way, past and future merge with one another. Thus, by multiple paths, we are constantly brought back to the first statement (*énoncé*), the genotext.

The genotext can be considered, in turn, as an ideological product. In the case of *Citizen Kane* we shall compare this first state of enunciation ("what will happen is already there") with the theories of predestination ("what must happen is already there") of a Puritanical society. We shall also reexamine from this perspective (relations between the ideological element and the genotext) the sociocritical reading of *Scarface* I am proposing.

On Textual Semantics

It is important to keep in mind, as the basis of our reflections, Yuri Lotman's definition of the text: "the text is an accomplished sign, and all the isolated signs of the broadly conceived linguistic text have been reduced to the level of elements of the sign." This concept is based on the fact that in an artistic text "a semanticization of the extrasemantic (syntactic) elements of the natural language is produced. Instead of a clear separation of semantic elements, a complex interlacing is produced: a syntagmatic element at one hierarchical level of the artistic text becomes a semantic element at another level." This disappearance of an opposition between the semantic and the syntactical transforms the limits of the sign, since it is the syntagmatic elements that mark these limits and "segment the text into semantic unities."[3] This argumentation entails a first consequence, namely that the text generates its own semantics, displacing and homogenizing the meaning of every element inscribed within it.

To illustrate this remark of Lotman's, I shall return to the initial frames of *Citizen Kane*, in which, when we approach the window at which Kane has just died, a flashback reconstructs the last moments of his agony. The last word he utters refers, we learn later, to the sled he used as a boy and to the name given it, while the snow-covered hut alludes to the second-rate guest house run by his parents when Thatcher comes to get him to give him an education worthy of his new wealth. Thus, both of these frames exteriorize the interiorized discourse of the dying man; in this context, the flashback, which must be considered as a syntactical element in the film because it organizes the composition of shots, plays a role in the constitution of a discourse on memory and time. But a more nuanced approach to the film informs us that the myths of Genesis and the Tower of Babel are invested in it: the thematics of confusion and chaos are connected to these other centers of semanticization. They are perceived in the landscapes preceding the construction of Xanadu, in which water and earth are mingled, or in the superimposing of the various foreign-language periodicals, as much as in the unfinished nature of this demiurge's arrogant construction projects. In the second part of the film, however (*The News on the March*), the opposite concept—construction, order, classification (of cultural objects, of animal species), capitalist organization—comes to the fore.

Curiously, three other technical devices, also related to the syntax of images, function here in a contradictory manner. The first, *lap dissolve*, in which, from the very first sequences, the landscape and its reflection merge, generates whole sets of superimposed, blurred, and jumbled signs in which objects lose their definition. *Insert*, the technique of shooting that enlarges to the point of distortion and makes it impossible to identify the objects being filmed, helps to create the same effect; the insert is used in the presentation of the crystal ball in which the reality being referred to is not immediately perceptible to the eye, which can focus on it only when the lens moves back to a close-up. Consequently, one can understand how the insert and the lap dissolve, as elements converging toward the same center of meaning that they are themselves helping to establish, can have the same semantic value as other related signs (Genesis landscapes, confusion of elements, thematics of incompletion, disordered accumulation of matter, the primitive, etc.). In the allusions to the building of the palace, we see, quite the contrary, a will engaged in a creative effort, assembling and ordering this wealth in an architecture of synthesis, separating the animal species from one another, labeling them and bringing them back to life again in the secondary universe of culture, cataloging its objects, and defining itself as zoo or museum. In this latter case, the succession of frames is done by means of the *wipe off*, a device generally employed in newsreels at the time the film was made in order to arrange subjects in a series and thus punctuate the presentation of the news. These wipe offs inscribe the category of order and a certain type of rationality, in the sense that they are the markers of thematic differentiation, of the separation of shots and frames. For that very reason, they are presented in *Citizen Kane* as semanticized in turn by the semiotic text, which I described earlier as expressing construction, order, classification, and capitalist organization. The opposed pair of terms (chaos vs. creation) is thus actualized at the level of filmic syntax. Although, at first glance, this syntax consists of extrasemantic elements, it is apparently being semanticized by the two centers of polarization of meaning that have been brought to light.

Another example is provided by the initial frames of *Scarface*. They are organized as a single sequence shot, which would not be significant in itself if it did not include, in succession, an exterior shot followed by an interior shot, a sequence that is generally a function of editing: without stopping the motor during the shooting, the camera, which at the start of the scene is in the street, ostensibly passes through the wall of the cabaret to get into the interior, revealing the thickness of this wall as it moves along. This is tantamount to saying that it causes a visual obstacle to appear at the very moment when it is, nevertheless, crossing and piercing it. Filmic syntax, that is, the syntagmatic chain of images and focal planes, is thus integrated into a semiotic text that problematizes the concepts of transparency and opacity, a text that is prolonged in the following sequence (the interior of the newspaper office) by means of a reversal of the givens: the glassed-in cubicles, easily discernible as so many indexes of a sort of visual continuum, are being invested as markers of a closed space, presented as such by painted letters, which, seen in reverse, are interpretable as designating spaces forbidden to the public.

As far as the literary text is concerned, I shall refer to the following explication of a text from the *Buscón* of Quevedo, in which the grammatical actualization of aspect (that is, the contrastive use of the imperfect and the simple past, or of the imperfect and the pluperfect) obeys the laws governing the deep structures of the text and is being semanticized by them. It thus combines them, as constitutive elements, with a semiotic text reproducing the image of a caste society in which the individual is defined as a function of his or her social origin, and group/individual relations are problematized in terms of social exclusion or assimilation. We shall see as well, in the same passage from the *Buscón*, a syntactic systematics of inversion (*aunque, sino que, sólo diz que*, etc.) entering, as an element semanticized by the corresponding center of meaning, a semiotic network signaling the modalities of investment of the language practices of Carnival within the textual fabric.

Our last example is *La muerte de Artemio Cruz*, by Carlos Fuentes. Here the reality at the origin of the fiction is of an exemplary simplicity: a dying old man, in front of a mirror, remembers his life. This element, the mirror, focuses and semanticizes the entire production of meaning: the splitting into two of the narrator, who projects himself as the object of his own gaze; the systematic division of all the characters; the breakup of time into present, past, and future; the correlative play of personal pronouns (I, you, he); the dislocated, contradictory, or complementary images of the facts; the fragmentation of the narrative; the modulations of the thematics of reflection by means of those other mirrors—tape recordings of the voice, memory or even writing itself. These various elements all pass through the same point—the focal point of the mirror, as it were—the consciousness of the narrator at that tragic moment of truth when Time stands still and, in standing still, loses its linearity. The mirror is, in this context, the iconic sign of consciousness, but also the metaphor of the narrative pretext, of the concept of the threshold of the beyond, of the inversion of Time, which can now only flow backward. The extrasemantic elements are effectively being semanticized here, not by the theme directly, but by its figurative treatment. It is not the idea of death that entails textual production (nor, moreover, a hypothetical project that is autobiographical in style), but one of its iconic reproductions. Death is seen in the perspective of *tránsito de la muerte*, a mental representation that, in turn, is given material form in the plastic image of the mirror, as a poetic locus of crossing. At that point, every textual phenomenon creating effects of diffraction, at any level, reproduces the iconic image of agony. We shall observe in passing that referential reality (the death of Artemio Cruz) enters a transformational process governed by structures of mediation (didactic literature; a surrealist vision of the world supported textually by the metaphorical use of the mirror) that, inside textual structures, encode this same reality in the form of figurative language.

I shall approach from this direction the problem of the establishment by fictional writing of the system that, to use Pierre Zima's terms, "suspends the conventional (social) value of verbal signs"[4] and weakens the referential dimension of language. We have just followed one of the processes that shows Lotman's critical acuity when he writes that "signs in art do not have a conventional character, as they do in language, but an iconic, figurative character."[5] Let us reread from this point of view the text of *Guzmán de Alfarache*. The theme of the passage is the praise of true friendship, but this theme is treated as an apparently coherent chain of allegories; when it is read more attentively, all is not so simple. The Earth embodies friendship, we see first, only to find next that, at our death, the Earth alone will receive in its bosom our putrid corpse "while no one, not wife, not father, not son, *nor friend* can stand us." Is the Earth, then, a friend or not, or something more than a friend? It would be wrong to denounce here the inconsistency or the negligence of the narrator; what has happened is that the signified has been displaced; the characteristic common to both the Earth and true friendship — stability — has now become the object of discourse. It is, thus, a new signified that selects another signifying vector, that of the Mother, whose dominant feature, abnegation, will in turn be metaphorized by the figure of the sheep. This last detour precedes a return to the maternal image in which is inscribed the desire of the subject tempted by regression to the fetal state.

Signified Friendship
Signifier Earth　 → Signified Stability
　　　　　　　　　　Signifier Mother → Signified Mother
　　　　　　　　　　　　　　　　　　Signifier Lamb// 　Signified Mother
　　　　　　　　　　　　　　　　　　　　　　　　　　Signifier Earth

Like the mirror in *La muerte de Artemio Cruz*, which is the vehicle of the surrealist concept of the passage toward the beyond, the figurative image is embedded, as it were, in textuality, where it develops centers of semanticization. The slippage from one signified to another creates strata of signification that overlap and give rise to zones of conflict. Let us pause to consider them. If we accept the interpretation of the nostalgia of a fetal state bearing the promise of a rebirth ("to bring us to a new and eternal life") as the textual expression of an infratext in which a profound feeling of insecurity is inscribed, this would mean that the "surface" text says the same thing in inverted form, or rather, in displaced form, since we have seen the value of stability foregrounded in it. Thus the Earth is opposed to the unstable. But *Guzmán de Alfarache*, as we shall see, establishes an identity between money and instability, which, by turns, can be signifier and signified of each other. Textual semantics tells us that the Earth is to money as stability is to instability (Earth vs. money // stability vs. instability). There is all the more reason to see in this figurative language the signifier of a socioeconomic signified since the beginning of the text makes an obvious apology for mercantilism. In other words, figurative discourse is ordered according to a chain of meanings which problematizes the more denotative discourse of the beginning ("The Earth gives us precious stones, gold, silver, and other metals"). It follows, on the one hand, that "the language of art" — at least as far as the fictional text is concerned — is not uniformly figurative, contrary to what Lotman and, to a lesser extent, Zima, give us to understand; on the other hand — and this remark seems much more important — if it is true that "the connotative devices of literature tend to weaken the conceptual (and referential) dimension of language,"[6] they cannot entail even a relative autonomy with respect to the socioideological structure that has engendered the fictional text. On the contrary, we have just seen that the figurative image (the symbolic in this case) becomes the signifier, the vector of ideological traces.

Textual semantics is inscribed not in signs but in the relations among them, outside, beyond, or above syntagmatic sequences. Even if it is true that syntagmatic elements are semanticized at a second level, they nevertheless perform their conventional function at the first level such that this textual semantics is a duplication of conventional semantics and cannot in any way nullify it. On the contrary, it is this "complex interlacing" that permits the play of the polyvalence of the word against the background of its univocality.

Thus, the fictional text encodes a first syntax of messages within its relational system: in this framework, the sign institutes its meaning in a zone of coincidence marked out by oppositions and contiguities that multiply its expressive possibilities. From this perspective, in an analysis of two poems in Pablo Neruda's *Residencia*, I bring out a number of analogical series that are then organized in a contradictory system: on the one hand, signs transcribing emptiness, but also a color (green) signifying death; on the other hand, the color red, the idea of plenitude, which, by investing the sign "coffin," undermines the sign's conventional semantics and makes it mean the opposite of what it means in language, that is, transforms it into a figure of life.[7] On this point, one may also read the study of the *Continuous* and the *Discontinuous* in the work of Octavio Paz, observing that again this textual semantics, although founded on connotative devices, unfailingly retraces the contours of a socioideological reality.[8] I thus agree totally with Zima's remark opposing scientific discourse, "which creates a particular convention in order to *avoid* the polysemousness of spoken language, in order to render discourse univocal," to the fictional text, in which "every word *can* acquire a different meaning from the one attributed to it by social convention"[9] in order, on the contrary, to *achieve* polysemousness.

The Textual Semiotic System and the Structure of the Substance of the Signifier

To consider that the concept of text and the concept of sign are identical entails an equally important secondary inference. Indeed, this hypothesis leads us to split the text/sign into a signifier and a signified. It is not a question of differentiating a form that would model a content and of repeating the axiom stating that, in every masterpiece, form "admirably serves content." On the contrary, we shall consider that, in the case of language, the signifier selected by the text is arbitrary, *from a certain point of view*, and that, *in a certain way*, meaning might well have had a very different linguistic material as its vehicle. We shall add to this a second observation, namely, as Tolstoy noted, that "people are needed who carry out the aberrant quest for isolated ideas in a work of art, who tirelessly guide readers in the infinite labyrinth of the sequences in which the essence of art consists, according to the laws that serve as a foundation for these sequences."[10] We have just shown, moreover, concerning textual semantics, that there is no meaning that can be discerned in "isolated ideas," and that it is *the structure of the work that semanticizes the text*. In the preceding cases, we were more interested in the *structure of the signified* that we reconstructed by exposing the chains of meaning it organizes. Consequently, we should bear in mind that there exists a *structure of the signifier* that is autonomous with respect to the structure of the signified and that carries meaning in its own right.

If we grant with Lotman that the same text "can be read . . . as a succession of signs that are larger than the words of which it is composed, to the point of transforming it into a single sign"[11] or else as a chain of signs organized according to the rules of natural language, we will be led to assume that all these signs must be organized autonomously, at a level other than syntagmatic, with respect both to conventions and to the signified, in the form of sequences of specific meaning.

Thus, the metaphor of a three-dimensional figure most aptly accounts for the status and functioning of the text. On the front we shall place all the pathways of meaning, that "infinite labyrinth of sequences" that Tolstoy wished to see explored in the "work of art," and that are governed by textual semantics. But beyond and in the background of this signified, other chains of meaning are present that are established in a dual contradictory relation of dependency and autonomy with respect to the former. Between these two systems—that is, between, on the one hand, the system of linguistic material that, *among other things*, produces the immediately perceptible signified, and, on the other hand, the system of this very signified—lies the whole density of textuality, whose complex meaningfulness proceeds from the interaction of the two faces, from a continual movement back and forth between the two signifying systems.

In order to perceive what the signifier *also* says, apart from any relation with the utterance, we must destroy contextual semantics, atomize the *text/sign* by reducing it to its minimal constituent parts, which implies that it may be perceived no longer as a *succession* but as a *juxtaposition* of *words/signs*. In this way, words/signs must cover all of their expressive potentialities, that is, the totality of their respective semantic fields, which had been temporarily neutralized by contextual semantics. In the logic of our method, this decomposition will be carried to the point of splitting each acceptation into its sememic components, to use Bernard Pottier's terminology.

The sign corresponds, however, to an arbitrariness codified by a semiologic community, which, in our reconstruction of its expressive capabilities, justifies our taking into account the many codes of representation and symbolization upon which it depends. To explore this hidden face of the text, I propose that we use the semiotic concepts of *text* and *system*, which seem to be the structures of understanding that are the most apt to account for both the autonomy of the signifier and its cultural dependency. Before specifying what I mean, however, several observations must be made.

Methodological Assumptions

The setting up of a semiotic system aims at establishing the network of sign convergencies, not at the level of what they express but at the level of what they are; it is not interested in the participation of the sign in the utterance, but in what it signifies in connection with other signs, independently of what the text says.

Thus the system has a finality in itself, and the domain to which it applies is specific; it does not tend to give a first approximation of the text which would have to be examined more thoroughly in later stages of the analysis; furthermore, it does not have to confirm earlier conclusions.

Provisionally, it resolves the semantic polyvalence of the signs involved. This semantic reduction is a function not of the content of the message, as with the utterance, but of the concordance the different signs establish among themselves. Every confrontation of one sign with another reactivates certain meanings of both but neutralizes most of them. The multiplication of these confrontations gives to the whole system a coherence of meaning that must not be confused with the utterance's coherence of meaning.

We shall take into account, in the examination of these confrontations, the eventual evolution of the semantic fields involved, and only historically pertinent acceptations will be retained. This requirement means that one must define beforehand the historical connotations, or points of anchoring, of the text. These points are of several kinds: historical, socioeconomic, sociopolitical, sociocultural references, levels of discourse, and so on. They may be more or less immediately perceived according to what the reader knows or does not know, but they always lend themselves to the establishment of tables of concordance. In a passage of the *Buscón* the phrase *cristiana vieja* is one of these points of anchoring, orienting the semantic reduction of signs such as *caballo* or *trabajos*, for example. These two cases demonstrate with particular clarity, moreover, how these changes in social structures affect semantic fields and, through them, paradigmatic axes. For Covarrubias, the *caballo* is essentially the instrument of the nobility, in relation to the practice of war, in contrast to the *rocin*, "o cavallo viejo y cansado quales suelen ser los de los molineros y los demas de servicio que no son para cavalleria de gente noble ni para la guerra" ("or old worn-out horse used by millers and servants and not by the nobility or in war"). His definition of *trabajo* is even more interesting; obviously, for him the term denotes neither a product nor a function, nor the human effort applied to the production of wealth as opposed to capital (the first meanings in the Dictionary of the Royal Spanish

Academy), but on the contrary, he defines it as "el *cuydado y diligencia* que ponemos en obrar alguna cosa"[12] ("the care and diligence we take in doing something"), in which we find wonderfully transcribed a concept of human effort oriented toward the production of the object, a concept based on usage value.

The importance of calling attention to these connotations beforehand may not be obvious in the case of a signed text of the Golden Age, in which all is apparently clear. In fact, it is a question not of a problem of signature or of the authentification of the author, but rather of knowing whether the semiotic text ought to be established within synchrony or within diachrony. This imperative is especially necessary when we approach contemporary literary production, particularly Spanish-American literature, in which the problems become doubly complicated to the extent that notions related to cultural syncretism are added to those of time and historical period. In a poem of Octavio Paz such as "Himno entre ruinas" (*La estación violenta*), for example, the detection of several systems of connotation—the first of which refers the reader to the Golden Age by means of explicit references to Góngora, the second to the pre-Hispanic cultural context, the third to the contemporary period—controls the establishment of the lexical map by orienting the semantic reductions in various ways. It is in the framework of these diverse sociocultural contexts that I must decode a *lexie* such as "*agua de vida*" (precious water, sacrificial blood, in Aztec thought), which, as a result, establishes various concordances on the levels of both pre-Hispanic and Christian rites and beliefs (for example, the antinomy of water and wine).

This method is equally indispensable in defining levels of discourse, the appreciation of which may have, in certain cases, a direct influence on the establishment of semiotic systems. For example, a text of Vasconcelos, "Un llamado cordial," is marked by a short series of mexicanisms: the author, addressing his readers in the familiar form, uses the form *vosotros*, when, as we know, the plural of *tu* in Mexico is expressed by *Ustedes*. In Mexican Spanish, the passage from *Ustedes* to *vosotros* is an index of an extremely lofty level of language. This connotation (level of discourse), derived from the disclosure of a first connotation (the Spanish spoken in Mexico), serves to orient semantic reductions in a certain direction.

One might object to the validity of this system as we have just defined it (the reconstitution of a set of signs stripped of any sign/sense relation to the utterance) by noting that it does not signify in time and that it is an exercise in pure formalism. This stage of the analysis regains a diachronic perspective, however, if one accepts the methodological assumptions I am proposing.

The Substance of the Signifier

We must first define what we mean by *substance of the signifier*, as well as the way this research fits into a sociocritical perspective, by considering two examples.

(1) I may call for help by shouting "Help!" by setting off a flare, or by sending an SOS: three different utterances of the same message. Although an SOS may be transmitted in different ways—by means of light signals, by radio, by semaphore, and so forth—it will always be the same message and the same utterance. However, the fact that this message reaches me by light signals gives me a series of interesting bits of information about the sender or, more precisely, about the collectivity to which the sender belongs. Thus I may observe that I am dealing with a human group accustomed to work or act at night in dangerous conditions, which have led it to create a system allowing its members to communicate with each other, and that this code presupposes that they are not able or do not wish to be heard; I deduce the existence either of an enemy presence or of an obstacle (wind, distance) that makes any direct acoustical system inefficient or even dangerous; this obstacle must not, however, be material since it allows light to pass, and so on. Compared with this code, radio broadcasting expresses a more advanced state of the technique of transmission, even though it transcribes some of the facts involved in the preceding system. This type of information is *also* what interests the sociocritical perspective and is, among other things, what it seeks through semiotic analysis, which we shall consider homologous to forms of communication.

In the examples from the *Buscón* in this volume, the burlesque metaphors *shearer of cheeks, tailor of beards, mender of pleasures* have an obvious first level of meaning (barber, procuress), to which, in the context of textual semantics, may be added the suggestion of ridiculous pretentiousness, which is perceptible only in the form of the conceptist type of metaphorical circumlocution. But beyond these meanings, which they, however, nourish and render meaningful, the signs, chosen and organized in their semiological autonomy, institute another sort of discourse presented to us as a new field of research to the extent that they seem to make the *semic form* (a ridiculous pretentiousness evoking a threat to disrupt social order) coincide with the *substance of the signifier* (a specific zone of activity in Castilian society defined by the convergence of the lexical field implying the cottage textile industry and, through this industry, probably the cottage-craft sector of the economy.

(2) The cursory study of certain uniforms and professional attire furnishes a second example. I can distinguish a lawyer from a judge, a canon from a parish priest, a professor of the faculty of letters from his or her colleagues in law, pharmacy, or medicine; their functions and respective specialties are described by a characteristic element of their official dress (the color of the hood). We may liken these signs (semic forms of the signifier) to the level of meaning represented by the utterance. What attracts our attention, however, is that all these professionals wear black robes—an identical signal that must be investigated in turn and that I call the *substance* of the signifier. In a first approach, I observe that this black robe seems to be reserved for the representatives of the Ideological State Appara-

tuses; consequently, I would be inclined to establish a relationship between the frequency of use of this dress and the power of the ideological function of the state apparatus implied by it.[13]

The preceding points permit us to establish the correspondences shown in the accompanying table.

	Semic Form	Substance of the Signifier
Example 1	*"Help" Information of facts	*Modalities of transmission of the message Socioeconomic information
Example 2	*Color of the hood Information designating a profession	*Robe Information transcribing an ideological content
Textual levels	*Metaphor: "tailor of beards" Information designating laughable pretentious- ness, foregrounding the inadequacy of discourse	*Lexical field of cloth trade Information transcribing a social dynamic and the vision of a threatened break in social status

Semiotic Texts

We attempt here to discover the criteria for the selection of signs that permit us to determine either the specific characteristics of the discourse of a collective subject or the possible inscription of ideological traces. The semiotic text will be defined by the existence of a coreferential relation brought into focus by successive semiological reductions. Although it may, in theory, be organized around a lexical or semantic field, this relation consists in each case, however, of a polarity transcending these categories to the extent that it may include indirect signs whose connotations it reactivates (as in the semiotic texts from the *Buscón* discussed in Chapter 11). This coreferential relation will be translated insofar as possible in terms of conceptual oppositions or convergencies. We shall consider that it homogeneously semanticizes in return all the signs that have produced it. Since each point of coreference around which the semiotic text is organized has been formulated in this way, it will be considered, in a second stage of regrouping, as a pertinent sign capable, in turn, of entering a second process of semiological reduction, marking out a new field of coincidence.

The accompanying schema clarifies this process. In the first stage of semiotic regrouping is a series of coreferential relations, defined by the letters [a] through [x] (primary relation) ([ ] defines a zone of semantic coincidence corresponding to a coreferential relation and will be translated in conceptual terms).

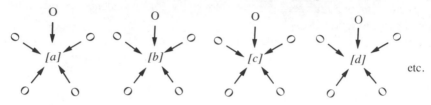

Semiotic texts

The second stage is a regrouping, insofar as possible, of these different zones of coincidence around an eventual secondary relation. In this second stage, each zone of coincidence is, in turn, treated as a sign (see the accompanying diagram, in which a' defines a zone of secondary coincidence). The preceding hypotheses are verified in the case of two Golden Age texts (the *Buscón* and *Guzmán de Alfarache*; see Chapters 11 and 10, respectively), a contemporary Mexican literary text (*La región más transparente* of Carlos Fuentes; see Chapter 9), as well as the initial sequences of a 1932 American film (*Scarface*; see Chapter 8). Thus we have a sufficiently broad sampling to generalize our observations.

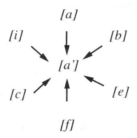

Semiotic system

In each case, we see the establishment of chains of signs that pinpoint a concept, a value, or a discourse, whose organization is presented to the reader as a configuration of conceptual oppositions, as in textual semantics. Meanings emerge that derive their signifying capabilities from the *relations* established among the elements, and not from the elements themselves. In other words, it is the system, once again, that brings the meaning into focus and that, in return, semanticizes in a certain way each of its constituent elements. Inside the whole system, however, subsystems (which have been presented either as subsets or as semiotic texts) set up, at their own levels, centers of meaning that can function autonomously with respect to the total system.

Let us take the case, in the first sequences of *Scarface*, of the polarity between night and day, in which we had seen a representation of the old and the new. We see it operating in the reorganization of the gangsters' syndicate; in the mimetic rivalry opposing Lovo to Camonte, both on the "professional" level and on the level of love interest; in the enthusiasm aroused in the gangsters by the discovery of a new weapon—the machine gun—more murderous than the old ones; and in a general way in the confrontation between two generations of gangsters. Each of these textual phenomena *actualizes* one of the basic elements of the *genotext*. Most often, however, these textual actualizations—or *phenotexts*—transcribe the interactions of various elements of the genetic combinatory principle. This is, in particular, the case of the St. Andrew's cross, which, as I said, was related both to journalistic writing and to a rhetoric of hiding—and which actualizes on the textual level the genetic coincidence of several conceptual polarities previously described. This is latent, on the one hand, in the opposition *dissimulation/display* and, on the other hand, less direct in the opposition *new/old*, since, in this case these two codes (journalistic writing vs. the Hays Code) transcribe the ideological confrontation opposing white, Anglo-Saxon Protestants to the new generation of immigrants. Basing our conclusions on these two examples, chosen from among many others, we shall see that the dialectical conceptual axes emerging from the reading of the semiotic system we have reconstructed correspond to socioideological traces that are thus directly responsible for the genesis of the text and the production of meaning. Let us consider the old and the new with respect to the problem of generational conflict. We have just rapidly reminded the reader how the text deals with it. In the sociohistorical reality upon which this text is based— according to North American historian Norman H. Clark—it seems that, in the 1930s, it was in the dominant white, Anglo-Saxon, Protestant group that the new generation was terrorizing the old. Thus we see that the ideological instance that undergoes this social dynamic "projects it outside of itself by assimilating it to all the evils it intends to exorcise," since it is to its class enemy that it is attributed. To emerge from the collective unconscious of the dominant group, assent must undergo a displacement. This observation led me to state that "it is in a chaotic form and as an effect of displacement (in the Freudian sense) that ideological traces are invested in structures. Each of these traces seems to be disconnected from the ideological totality to which it belongs, and to enter into a new configuration to which it transfers its own capacity to produce meaning."[14] This observation should be kept in mind in the ensuing textual analyses. These are ideological traces in the pure state, which, in abstract form, enter the genetic combinations that the description of textual semiotic systems permits us to reconstruct.

The problem being posed, then, is that of the relations between textual semantics and the semiotic system. In a general way, these two chains of meaning play against each other in a complex manner according to processes specific to each text. But this interplay is in turn productive of meaning. The case of *Guzmán de Alfarache* is once again exemplary: whereas, in a first reading, the passage I have analyzed is characterized, at the thematic level, by the praise of generosity and abnegation and somehow glorifies the gratuitous gift, the second chain of meaning, that of the semiotic system, superimposes on this first reading a set of values in which the universe of exchange, merchandise, and money is inscribed. Thus this second chain of meaning reveals both the internal contradictions of the Golden Age *topos* that have been deconstructed and the contradictory feelings of the speaking subject caught in conflictive socioeconomic circumstances. The example from *La región más transparente* illustrates the same tendency of this play of relations. Indeed, the semiotic system transcribes, on the one hand, the existence of a relation between structures of dependency and, on the other hand, interrelations established between a problematic of integrity and a problematic of independence; from another standpoint, textual semantics displays the functioning of a repressed discourse remaining below the surface in the "not said." In other words, to put it briefly, the semiotic system reveals the point of fixation hidden in explicit discourse—namely, a sociopolitical and socioeconomic position of dependency threatening national identity. The critical perspective I am proposing thus permits us to better explore the complexity, the density, as it were, of textuality, and to reveal the breadth of its expressive capabilities.

Chapter 7
Narrative and Character as Textual Categories

One might object that the critical method proposed in the last chapter destroys the textual constructs of narrative and character. This objection raises two questions: (1) Does the sociocritical objective eliminate the problem of narratology, and supposing it does not, how would sociocriticism include it in its analysis? (2) What is the relationship between the two concepts of narrative instance and ideological instance that we have used (or that we shall use in the approaches to specific cases)? Do they overlap or must they be differentiated, and, if so, at what level?

On Narratology

Considerable progress has been made in this field and certain definitions are now firmly established. Our point of departure here is the distinction made by the Russian formalists between *fabula*, "which is only material," and *subject*, which corresponds to the organization and the working out of this material ("The notion of subject is often confused with the description of events, with what I have proposed to call by convention *the fable*. In fact, the fable is but a material serving to form the subject").[1] From these two notions, Todorov proposes the terms *histoire* and *discours*, which he borrows from Benveniste but uses to mean something quite different.[2] This division of the narrative into two levels is not fundamentally questioned by Barthes,[3] who, however, substitutes for *discours* the term *narration*, a notion picked up by Gérard Genette in *Figures III* in which three levels are discerned: (1) the narrative (*récit*), that is, "the narrative utterance, the oral or written discourse that undertakes the report of an event or a series of events"; (2) the story (*histoire*), namely, the succession of events, real or fictive, that are the object of this discourse, and their various relationships of sequence, opposition, repetition, and so on; and (3) the act of narrating itself.[4]

Genette's merit is to have brought out an instance of enunciation that itself produces a narrative (*récit*) supporting a *story*, thus perceptibly modifying the propositions advanced by the Russian formalists. However, the disadvantage of this formulation is that it excessively valorizes the notion of narrator and, especially, can cause confusion to the extent that it attributes to the narrator a project, a coherent and totalizing vision. In the view of certain contemporary critics, it seems, the narrator is but the direct projection, the surrogate of the author, even though the narrator is supposed to be relatively autonomous. The notion of narrator, at first glance, destroys the notion of text. The question being posed is whether the narrative text is the product of the narrator or, on the contrary, the narrator is the product of the text. In *Problèmes du nouveau roman*[5] Jean Ricardou implicitly posed the same problem in different terms: while in turn opposing fiction to narration, he observed that narration cannot be reduced to the mere organization of a set of preexisting narrative materials, but that the act of narrating in itself creates fiction. While valorizing in this manner a textualizing of the event that, in his view, would be capable of perceptibly modifying the course of its unfolding, his perspective eliminates what had seemed implicitly established thus far, namely, the preexistence (to writing) of the story (the fable or the fiction) to be told. Indeed, in his demonstration the narrative text does not reproduce a previous model or schema; both the narrative material and its organization are being instituted at the same time by the work of writing. The scriptor is substituted for the narrator, which is tantamount to saying that the problems concerning the analysis of narrative are not capable of being isolated and must be dealt with in the framework of a broader semiotics. Milke Bal invites us to take this step when she writes in *Narratologie*:

> According to the semiotic point of view, the narrative text is considered to be a sign. The sender of this sign is the author, the receiver is the reader. Inside this sign, another sender, the speaking subject or narrator, sends a sign to a receiver, the narratee. The sign transmitted by the narrator is not the story . . . the latter is not told as such by the narrator. It is true that the story is a signified. There must be another level of communication, an intermediary between the text and the story, a level in which the signified of the text and the signifier of the story are situated at the same time. The narrator emits the sign-narrative inside which the sign-story is transmitted . . . the narrative is the signified of a linguistic signification but it itself signifies by nonlinguistic means.[6]

We must still reach a consensus on what the narrator is and is not. The narrator is certainly one of the internal reference centers of discourse, defined by a series of textual markers, but not the only one, and it is always quite artificial to attribute to the narrator the responsibility for those elements foreign to diegesis such as description or digression. Attributing them to the narrator leads criticism to use a revealing vocabulary that assumes in the narrator a will, an intentionality or a strategy, which amounts in the end to hypostatizing a real character. In that case, such a notion reinstates the entire heritage of that sovereign creator dethroned by modern criticism. The narrator does not know what he or she is telling and still less what he or she is going to tell. This is why it is preferable to speak of the text's narrative instance or narrative function, which is itself translated by a series of points of focalization of the voice that are not necessarily coherent. This is an essentially mobile narrative voice whose displacements bring about the various focalizations of the narrative and which can itself be invested or traversed by potentially contradictory discourses. Thus, in *Scarface* we saw within the narrative instance two microsemiotics operating face to face. We should not forget, therefore, that the notion of the narrator is but an operative notion, an effect of reading, which is produced and governed essentially by writing. In this way, we are led to reverse the terms of causality as they were used by the Russian formalists: the "fable" is not the *material* serving to form the "subject," but its *product*. The prime reality is that of the text, which does not reproduce a model that might be fictive or real, but which, more precisely, *produces* a *narrative*. The narrative itself does not organize a *story*, which would be prior to what it says, but on the contrary, it allows itself to be reduced to the story.

The answer to the second question I posed earlier is now evident: the ideological instance cannot be confused with the narrative instance since it operates upon writing and can intervene only at the level of points of vocal focalization through the narrative instance.

If the narrative has no existence prior to the text, it does not have any more meaning outside of it. Abstracted from the textual fabric, it would be but a chain of events stripped of profound, authentic meaning. The center of narrative programmation is not in the narrative but in the text. This can be briefly demonstrated in an analysis of a film, Truffaut's *Stolen Kisses*, by differentiating the microsemantics that establish the film as a *text* from the elements that establish it as a *narrative*.

At the thematic level, *Stolen Kisses* describes the confused itinerary pursued by Doinel before he is united wtih Christine. This quest is developed by means of a double narrative vehicle: on the one hand, a discontinuous series of the protagonist's adventures with prostitutes and, on the other hand, the narrative of his ups and downs in his job as a private detective. The latter represents the essential part of the narration with, here and there, two brief episodes: the first (the brief function as night watchman), which really permits the narrative to get started; the second (the job as television repairman), which initiates the denouement. Before and after these two episodes two scenes are placed: (1) at the beginning of the narrative, a scene that takes place first in a military prison, then in the office of the chief warrant officer; and (2) at the end, Doinel and Christine, reunited at last, take a walk and are approached by a curious character who has been following Christine all through the film and who claims that his own destiny is to live with her permanently, Doinel being only a temporary lover. From the point of view of macrostructure, the syntagmatic sequence of the narrative may be represented as in the accompanying diagram:

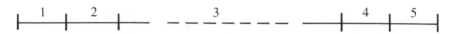

1: Scene in the military prison   4: Doinel as TV repairman
2: Doinel as nightwatchman   5: Stroll − denouement
3: Private detective agency

From the same point of view, as soon as the narrative is initiated, it establishes a "matrix of expectation" (What is Doinel's destiny? Will he end up, as the chief warrant officer predicts, as a necktie salesman in the Paris metro?) to which an answer, at the end, is both given (Doinel has finally been united with Christine) and not given (this is only a temporary ending). This double horizon of expectation is dramatized in both cases by a puzzle: how does it happen that a volunteer has refused induction? (beginning). Where does this mysterious character come from? Who is he? (end). Upon reflection, we observe that it is to this structure of the puzzle that most (if not all) of the episodes of the narrative, the narrative in its entirety, and the filmic text itself can be reduced, which would tend to prove once again that the narrative is but one of many phenotextual actualizations and has the same nature as the textual fabric. Let us attempt to demonstrate this through a closer study of the narrative and the text.

The Narrative. In this context, it is obvious that all the clients of the private detective agency ask the director receiving them a question for him to solve, so that the whole narrative sequence 3 decomposes into so many similar units; what is more, inside these units, a derivative question is inscribed several times that seems to place "en abyme" the enigmatic nature of the first question (Does the boss have his salesgirl shadowed because he is in love with her or because he suspects her of theft?). The case of Mr. Tabar is the most significant in this respect, since at first, at least, his problem is that he has no problems, as if at first glance the structure of the narrative was idling and producing meaning in a perfectly autonomous fashion, "enigma for enigma." Similarly, the text weaves narrative threads that traverse the principal narrative. We do not know where they come from or what will become of them (Why does Christine have her mother tell Doinel that she is out of town? Why does she come out of a basement that looks out on a garden, and where is she going? What is the meaning of the fact that Doinel is walking in the street alongside a prostitute disproportionately taller than he is? etc.). Matrices of expectation are thus constructed that, contrary to the implicit contract between the fictional text and its narratee, will never be satisfied.

The Text. At this level, the facts are even more significant, owing to their repetitive character. Thus the characters, on several occasions, play guessing games: Christine's father has her guess Doinel's new employment; meeting by chance in the street, the protagonist's girlfriend, who has a baby with her, exclaims: "I'll bet you're wondering if it's a girl or a boy" (without giving any answer). The magician, at the same time that he does his customary tricks, tells an enigmatic tale to the cabaret audience. One could add to this series of signs the uncertainty about the precise way in which the victim of the Ministry of Culture committed suicide (did he hang himself or shoot himself?), the game of the seven errors that relieves the boredom of Doinel's colleague, the content of the telephone call received by the old detective before he has a heart attack, the reason why the first prostitute refuses to get undressed, and why Doinel refuses to let another prostitute undress, and so on. This last parallel is revealing: one certainly would be wrong in seeing in this successive play of relationships just another demonstration of Doinel's "unstable character," whereas these two episodes, taken in the context of the series just described, draw a *second* meaning from the system in which they are inserted and which gives them meaning.

Indeed, the text interpellates us in the same manner, directly asking us new questions: What does the image of the closed Cinémathèque mean? Why is the text of a song, in which Charles Trenet nostalgically recalls his village steeple, plastered over a panoramic view of Paris? How can we explain the minesweeping lesson given by the chief warrant officer before freeing Doinel?

A closer study of the last scene allows us, however, to see in it the outlines of the textual structure's matrix, since we find there as well: (a) an awareness of hiding (we know that a mine is hidden); (b) the working out of a strategy of unveiling (how to go about defusing it); and (c) a context of danger that makes both the unveiling and the total mastery of the problem indispensable (one false move makes it explode)—all are elements capable of being lexematized as follows:

(a') The exposé of a problem
(b') How to deal with it
(c') The danger of the wrong response
In other words:
    Problem
    Response or lack of response
    Danger of the response

Doubtless, it would be easy to reduce the various series of enigmas we have observed to this narrative schema, since certain of them are resolved and others are not, and since certain responses bring about more or less serious catastrophes (the magician's marriage sets off a fit of hysterics in his former lover; Tabar's curiosity brings about his wife's infidelity; a piece of information unknown to us provokes the old detective's heart attack, etc.). The presence of this third element (c), which is pointedly stressed from the very beginning of the film, radically transforms the nature of the enigma, which, at that point, refers us back to the myth of the Sphinx and its *dangerous* questions, with which Oedipus is confronted. By reducing the narrative episode to abstract sequences, we see a semiotic system appearing, organized in a signifying configuration. The mine-sweeping lesson itself is the direct figurative vector of a second signified, namely, the erotic display which precedes coitus ("tourner autour [d'une femme]," to hang around a woman; "mettre la main au panier," bayonet/penis). These various elements cause, in turn, the emergence of an explicit psychoanalytic discourse punctuating the text: the "unstable character" of Doinel, the psychoses of the agency's clientele, as well as the symbolic value of the images: the phallic allusions represented, among others, by Montmartre and the Eiffel Tower are opposed to padlocked, gaping orifices, symbols of a forbidden female sex organ (the entrance of the Cinémathèque, the military prison, etc.). Thus, from the very first frames, the film reveals its deep meaning by giving us the key to its symbolic decoding. Doinel's strange behavior becomes clear at the surface diegetic level, as well as, in particular, that enigmatic image of an ill-matched couple in which the protagonist is crushed by the corpulent silhouette of his partner, which becomes the transparent symbol of the mother. The role played by Mrs. Tabar in the initiatory journey of the hero both drawn to and paralyzed by the forbidden maternal image becomes clearer still. Let us recall his earlier behavior in front of women: among all his encounters with prostitutes are only two allusions to the beginning of intimacy linked by the theme of undressing (refused by the partner – refused by Doinel), which cast doubt on the consummation of sexual relations. From that point they will be linked to the young man's apparent panic when he sees the shoe salesman's wife burst into his room. It is, seemingly, by losing his virginity with her, that is, by transgressing the interdiction against the mother, that Doinel can have access to Christine. This explains the mirror scene confronting the three actants of this triangular drama, which functions as the symbolic space of transgression and mediation.

If one accepts this reading of *Stolen Kisses*, one observes that, when the course of the narrative gets lost in subterranean ellipses, it is the textual fabric that permits us to fill the gaps, tending to prove that narrative programmation is inscribed and governed by the text, and that narrative is consequently only a textual category.

If we take this semantic focalization as a point of departure, certain sequences of the film become clear. The curious description of the functioning of the pneumatic letter service, for example, at first glance may appear to be a documentary digression stripped of any connection with the narrative and of little interest. If we read it symbolically, as the Oedipal enigma of the mine-sweeping lesson invites us to do, we see in it, on the contrary, one of the strongest points of articulation in the film, in which the implacably determined subterranean life of the unconscious, from which only symptoms/messages emerge, is being enacted (the metal box in which the letter is enclosed follows a precise course from intersection to intersection). This is how Mrs. Tabar understands it; she superimposes on what she knows of Doinel's feelings for her the slip of the tongue committed by her husband's young clerk and thus reads it transparently. The anecdote in which she clothes her own letter presupposes that an interdiction hangs over the young woman whose privacy has been violated, the transgression of this interdiction (*Pardon, madame!*) or the refusal to accept this transgression (*Pardon, monsieur!*) on the part of the unintentional voyeur. Thus in Doinel's slip of the tongue (*Oui, monsieur*), Mrs. Tabar reads the fantasized projection of transgression and the consciousness of an interdiction. We see, therefore, in the sequence describing the subterranean itinerary of the pneumatic letter, genetic markers that repeat in the symbolism of the textual fabric what the narrative has just enunciated; similarly, we see in the oblong shape of the metal box emerging from subterranean ducts the iconic image of the slip of the tongue. In this context, which enacts textually the transference mechanisms affecting the maternal image, the anecdote the magician tells, about the sailor whose knots move from one rope to another, takes on all its meaning.

If this is so, a final layer of meaning remains that, at first glance, is not reducible to this explicative schema: I am thinking of the image of the Cinémathèque, whose entrance is barred by iron gates and to which I believe I can relate all the signs permitting the film, and through it, cinema itself, to be read as gaze. The way the filmic sign presents itself as visual sign is not original in itself, and we shall see it operating in *Scarface*. However, like other elements of textuality, it cannot say anything by itself: it derives its authentic meaning only from the system it helps, as textual element, to establish. Here, the case is exemplary; let us rapidly explain how and why. The answer is to be found once again in the parable imagined by Mrs. Tabar in her letter, a parable which explicitly links the interdiction to voyeurism and, consequently, which we shall take as the center of polarization of a new microsemantics, in which the following form an integral part: Doinel's stage business when he "goes upstairs" with the prostitutes, the way in which the theme of undressing is inscribed in these scenes, the camera movements that ostensibly unveil what is hidden in the depths, the very image of the "periscope"; and, on the narrative level, the activities of the detective agency, particularly the scene in which the adulterous lovers are caught in bed. From this point of view, the many allusions to the *shadower* that the protagonist has become are also allusions to the *voyeur*; it is thus in this aspect that Doinel is almost naturally perceived. One may wonder, in that case, if the behavior and the use and function of the character do not refer to the film medium as the signified for which the narrative is in some sense the figurative vehicle, an interpretation that implies a dual center of semanticization (Oedipal message; reflections on the media).

The two elements brought out by this analysis as centers of the organization of meaning (Oedipal enigma and movies) establish a point of coincidence, for the concept of voyeurism belongs equally to both. Whereas it is obvious in the case of the movies, in the case of the Oedipal myth this observation calls for an explanation. It may be found in the new reading of the myth by Géza Róheim in *The Gates of the Dream* or in *The Riddle of the Sphinx*,[7] in which he interprets the hybrid body of the monster (lion's body and woman's bust) as the plastic transposition of the primal scene ("The Sphinx herself then is the being with the indefinite number of legs, the father and mother in one person, and a representative of the two fundamental tendencies of the Oedipus situation, which are awakened in the child when he observes the primal scene"[8]). The riddle posed by the Sphinx only repeats this first message (the four legs of the "beast with two backs," the two open legs of the mother, the single leg/penis) in referring to parental coitus. The "guilty assimilation" of the hero, the murder of the father and the possession of the mother are based on this "primitive voyeurism." The original interdict does indeed hang over the gaze, and from this point of view, the symbolic image of the padlocked door of the Cinémathèque superimposes the two dimensions of the Oedipal enigma in which the female sex organ (the gaping mouth of the entrance) and voyeurism (the cinema as gaze) are equally forbidden to us. (The barred windows of the military prison, however, are crossed by the camera.) Thus the structural matrix of the film is established from the very first scenes by the superimposition on this last image of the mine-sweeping lesson previously analyzed. The enigmatic denouement of the narrative ties all these threads by predicting to Doinel that, as with Oedipus, his victory is only temporary.

All the preceding remarks refer to the semiotic system set in place at the very first sequences: high/low; surface/depth; hidden/revealed; interdiction/transgression; and which is actualized at the phenotextual level by means of a transformational code—namely the Oedipus myth or, to be more precise, a psychoanalytic reading of the riddle of Oedipus. It is this structure of mediation that, deconstructing the semiotic system according to its specificity, generates the textual fabric that, in turn, is the vector of the narrative and through it the vector of the story.

Let us return now to the narrative to follow the two intertwined threads. The first one begins within the matrix of expectation defined by the chief warrant officer's prediction ("You have no certificate of good conduct, so you won't be able to work," is the gist of what he says to Doinel). In this perspective, which is firmly established from the start, the different narrative sequences are perceived as a series of countertests reducible in this case to the following functional sequences.[9]

(1) *Doinel as night watchman.* Initial situation: Doinel is without a job [α]; Christine's father finds him work, thus putting him to the test [D1]. Intervention of the old private detective [intention to deceive the victim η1]; Doinel is deceived by his explanations [θ3]; transgression of an implicit interdiction, that of the night watchman's code [δ1]. Doinel is fired. Taking of a test with negative result [E1neg.]. Return to the initial situation [α].

(2) *Doinel as private detective.* Initial situation [α], the private detective finds him work, the exaggressor is transformed into a donor, thus putting him to the test [D1]. Here, several sequences are intercalated:

(2.1) *Shadowing a young lady in the street.* Putting him to the test [D1]; Doinel draws attention to himself, thus transgressing the code of the private detective [δ1] [E1neg.].

(2.2) *Shadowing the nanny.* Putting him to the test [D1]; test passed [E1pos.].

(2.3) *The affair of the magician.* Doinel, aided by the old detective, picks up his trail [D]. Test passed [E1pos.]. Doinel shadows the magician, is put to the test [D1]. He telephones Christine in the course of his surveillance, thus once again transgressing the code of his profession [δ1]. A truck blocks the way between Doinel and the man he is shadowing [loss of sight, blindness A6].

(2.4) *The Tabar affair.* Doinel takes a fictive test before being hired; he loses but is hired anyway and helped by Tabar [D]. Doinel put to the test as "periscope" [D]. He falls in love with Mrs. Tabar in the course of his work; transgression of an interdiction [δ1]. He is fired. Test with negative result [E1neg.]; return to the initial situation [α].

(3) *Doinel as TV repairman.* Initial situation [α]; put to the test [D1]. Doinel forgets his work, giving in to the temptations of Christine. Transgression [δ1]. He will probably be fired [E1neg.].

This functional sequence may be represented as in the accompanying diagram.

αD^1 η1 θ^3 δ1neg. αD   E1 neg.αD1 δ1 E1neg.

D1δ1E1neg.D1 E1pos.D1 E1pos.D1 δ1 A6 E1neg.D1 δ1

With respect to the matrix of expectation at the beginning of the film, if we include the whole set of givens at the initial situation of the text, insofar as Doinel has been punished (denial of his certificate of good conduct) for having transgressed military discipline (unsubjugated), the sequence may be represented as in the accompanying schema.

This functional sequence demonstrates, in the first place, the unimpeachable nature of all predictions. That the prediction seems to come out wrong twice

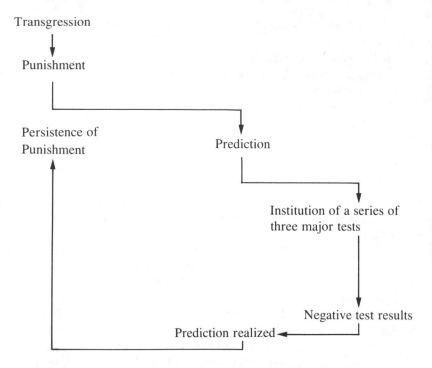

[E1pos.] would tend to prove precisely once again that it is the prophetic function of the chief warrant officer's discourse that is being rendered problematic and textualized. From that point on, the wanderings of the protagonist, who is seen running in the streets of Paris without any apparent objective, attest to the implacability of destiny. In this sense, the functional sequence weighs heavily on the denouement and answers by itself the question raised by the prophecy of Christine's strange lover. Contrary to what we might think at first, the film really closes upon itself, since it begins a second loop whose end we know in advance. This second prophecy, like the first, is condemned to be realized. Contrary to the chief warrant officer's explanation, however, Doinel's failures are due not to the fact that he has been deprived of a certificate of good conduct, but essentially to a series of transgressions. This functional sequence links the accomplishment of a prediction to transgressions of interdictions, whose paradigmatic axis is significant, since all of them imply, in one way or another, the gaze. Doubtless the hotel episode, in which Doinel, his face turned to the wall, seems somehow to be hiding his face at the very moment the adulterous couple is caught in bed, remains the most revealing in this respect; but the same is true when Doinel is unmasked as shadower or voyeur [2.1]. It is not a surprise, therefore, to see him struck "blind" when, after he transgresses the code of his profession, a truck hides the magician from his view [2.3]. Similarly, Mrs. Tabar uses a voyeurist metaphor to speak of the transgression to which she is an accomplice (on the theme: "What does a polite or tactful gentleman say when he accidentally surprises a lady in her bath?") [2.4]. In this semantic context, the spare parts of the television set, which function as so many ideograms of voyeurism, inscribe the indexes of a new transgression [3] when they mark the route leading to Christine's bedroom.

We thereby come to the second narrative thread, which, from a specific initial situation (the couple's separation), takes us to the union of the two lovers. Here, moreover, several sequences may be discerned (Doinel's first visit to Christine's parents; Christine's visit to the hotel; dinner at Christine's; the evening at the cabaret; Christine's visit to the shoestore; Christine's staged provocation of a meeting with Doinel). All the scenes involving prostitutes are related to this series. Let us take these scenes as our point of departure. If we consider that the refusal of the kiss and the refusal to undress are transgressions of the erotic code, in the first scene we see the following functional sequence: Seductive behavior → Transgression of the erotic code → Failure → Withdrawal → Seductive behavior (second prostitute) → Situation opening up a possibility. If, in brief, we are concerned only with the couple (Transgression of the erotic code/failure), we find it repeated in a number of Doinel/Christine sequences. The most obvious ones are the cabaret episodes, Christine's visit to the shoestore, and the television-repair scene. In two of these three cases, I discern a link between professional activity and the separation of the couple (Doinel, absorbed in his spying mission, abandons Christine; when she visits him at the Tabars', he reproaches her for it). In the last episode, on the contrary, it is because desire takes precedence over Doinel's professional concerns that union is accomplished. This new systematic can be formulated as follows: Seductive behavior → Transgression of the erotic code → Failure/Seductive behavior → Transgression of the professional code → Success.

When Doinel puts his relations with Christine above a mission that has been entrusted to him (the shadowing of the magician), that is, when, within the scope of his activities as a detective, he breaks an implicit professional code, he is metaphorically struck by blindness; in other words, the preceding functional sequence is working in a manner contradictory to the one operating elsewhere (Professional activity → Transgression of the professional code → Failure). Love and work are countervalues: thus in the case of prostitutes, the professional code appears as a perversion of the code of love ("never with clients"); thus, moreover, Christine's strange lover stresses the fact that he does not need to work and can devote his life to loving her.

The concept of transgression governs not only the development of these two narrative threads, but also the systematics of their coincidence. Articulated almost exclusively around three significant elements (prediction – voyeurism – transgression), the narrative is thus seen once again as the actualization, at its own level, of a genetic programming, and as a textual category.

Clearly, a sociocritical extension of this critical reflection would relate *Stolen Kisses* to what may be considered the ideology of the movement of May 1968. Approaching the problem from another direction, bearing in mind the suggestions of Claude Bremond,[10] we observe three types of elementary sequence.

(1) *Doinel/Christine Plot*

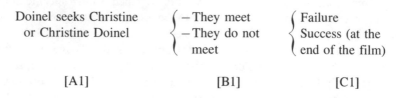

[A1]	[B1]	[C1]

(2) *Adventures with the Prostitutes or with Mrs. Tabar*

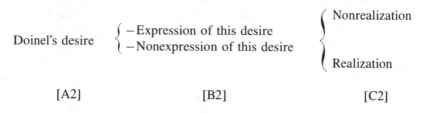

[A2]	[B2]	[C2]

(3) *Professional Ups and Downs*

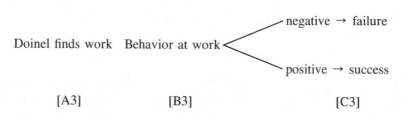

[A3]	[B3]	[C3]

These sequences combine with one another in various ways: either they are linked (Doinel's different jobs) or they are nested, the enclosing sequence remaining, at the end, that of the Doinel/Christine plot. Sequence 2 is a more specific form of sequence 1, for it corresponds to the transferral of Doinel's first desire. The same is true for sequence 3, since, as we saw earlier, the character's inadequacy in the situation opening up the possibility of success in love is due to a certain kind of work behavior (the evening at the cabaret, for example). In that case, the corresponding elementary sequence is the following: [A1] [B3] [C1]; in the context of sequence 3 we have a positive behavior [Bpos.3]. This formulation— we put it in another way above—is reversible (Doinel loses the person he is shadowing because he telephones Christine during his work hours), which entails the following formulation: [A3] [B1pos.] [C3]. Thus the narrative draws its first meaning not from its morphological *organization* but rather from the way in which the elementary sequences *function* with respect to one another.

We reach a similar conclusion if we examine "the narrative possibilities" (*les possibles narratifs*) in sequences 1 and 3: they do not *operate* in the same way. In the case of the Doinel-Christine plot, the spectator follows its course with interest; each new encounter gives way to an alternative, and we do not know, at the outset, which solution will be chosen. Will Doinel find Christine at home when he visits her parents? Will the interview provoked by Christine have a positive result? Does the presence of the couple, hand in hand, during the evening at the cabaret mean that they have resolved their apparent differences? Will the visit Christine pays to Doinel at the very moment he is having an amorous tête-à-tête with Mrs. Tabar have a sensational ending? and so on. Now the two come closer, now they draw apart. When I see them advance toward each other I cannot predict what their conduct will be. The narrative constantly reestablishes in this way the same horizon of expectation.

This is not the case of the series of elementary sequences 3. The night watchman episode eliminates this interest and this type of narrative logic. From now on, we know that Doinel's behavior is a behavior of failure. The unfolding of the narrative, on this point, is henceforth encumbered, and the outcome of each corresponding elementary sequence is known to us in advance. In this case, can we speak of the narrative as having a dual center of programming?

To answer this question, we need to go back toward what the analysis of the textual fabric has allowed us to glimpse of the role played by the chief warrant officer's words. Perceived solely at the diegetic level, they scarcely have any meaning, in the sense that they seem at first to be only a spontaneous reflection devoid of any importance. They are somehow *banalized* by the context. If, however, they are grasped in the context of the mythical structure operating in the film, they take on quite another meaning. They are thereby the object of a sanctification through myth, and these words, originally banal, are henceforth understood as expressing the implacability of destiny, thus attaining the status of prediction and prevision. From that point on, they loom over the whole narrative. Thus they program the narrative only to the degree that they are themselves semanticized by the textual fabric. They are but the path taken by programmation, not its source.

The analysis of elementary sequence 1 leads to a similar conclusion. Here, the narrative is content with transcribing unexpected behaviors in the apparent context — as we have seen — of a classic narrative logic, but it says nothing about the causes of this *unexpectedness*. These causes, at first glance, may be understood as the category that governs diegesis and, in turn, *programs* its course, since, without it, no alternative would be possible, and temporality would be transformed from linear to cyclical. It is the way in which the cyclical operates on the linear that produces diegesis and gives it a first meaning. However, when a text's centers of focalization have been marked out, this unexpectedness does not have a programming effect, but, on the contrary, it is itself programmed by what may be called an *infranarrative*. When we link these unexpected behaviors of Doinel to the existence of an obstacle arising between him and Christine, but which is never expressed as such at the explicit level, it is clear that it is the obstacle and not its perceptible *effect* in diegesis (namely, the behavior) that is programmatic. The infranarrative makes explicit and qualifies this obstacle by presenting it as linked to a text of interdiction weighing heavily on the image of the mother and on voyeurism, so that in the infranarrative this unexpectedness is transformed into its opposite, and the linear reverts to the cyclical. As in the case of the chief warrant officer's words, the textual fabric sacralizes the obstacle and semanticizes it by presenting it as *interdict*. It is indeed this element that governs the unfolding of the other narrative thread since the transgression of this interdict (the love scene with Mrs. Tabar) lifts the weight hanging over the narrative and permits the typical narrative logic to operate, in the sense that from now on an authentic alternative is established proposing to diegesis a "free" choice between two "narrative possibilities," namely, the couple's union or their definitive rupture. Everything in the narrative is then suspended at this nodal point and problematic resolution, both of which depend on the text and not on the narrative. It follows that only the analysis of the textual fabric permits one to define the true functions of the narrative, and it is this textual fabric that semanticizes them.

At this point in our analysis, the distinction between text and narrative may blur, since we may be tempted to confuse the text with the infranarrative. Why not see, then, in the latter a sort of gloss of the story? To clarify the problem, we shall consider Todorov's analysis of *La Quête du Saint Graal*, in which he observes, following Albert Pauphilet, that the "text contains . . . its own gloss":

> No sooner is an adventure completed than its hero meets some hermit who informs him that what he has experienced is no mere adventure but the sign of something else. For example, at the outset, Galahad sees several wonders but fails to understand them until he has encountered a sage. "Sire," the sage replies, "you have asked me the meaning of your adventure, here it is. The adventure consisted of three dreadful ordeals: the stone which was so heavy to lift, the body of the knight which had to be flung outside, and the voice you heard which made you lose consciousness and memory. Of these three things, here is the meaning. . . . " And the sage will conclude: "Now you know the meaning of the adventure." Galahad declares that it has "much more meaning than he supposed."[11]

One can easily perceive where the difference of perspective lies: in the lines I have just quoted we have not left the narrative and entered the text. The hermit who is being asked to give the meaning of this adventure is part of a narrative whole that is broader than the first narrative of the adventure, and the glossed repetition of the events is but a diffraction of the facts he recounts. Upon further reflection, the term *infranarrative* is not very felicitous, to the extent that a mythical functional sequence does not correspond point by point in any way to the complex sequence of the diegesis. There is no true mythical discourse but, more precisely, an intratextual semiotic system semanticized by a mythical discourse. I mean by this that systems are functioning here in a way that is not necessarily organized or coherent. Strictly speaking, the question of whether they are functioning in a way rigorously identical to what they establish in the architecture of the mythical narrative (*narré*) does not arise.

Thus far I have eliminated the question of the essential need to differentiate, in a narrative text, between those elements related to the text and those related to the narrative. The problem may seem all the more difficult to solve since, in the very hypothesis I am putting forward, namely, that the narrative is only a phenotextual category, analysis will initially grasp, along with the deconstructed elements of this composite — the genotext — the specific effects and the characteristics of this level performing the deconstruction in question. I have answered it both implicitly and explicitly: implicitly, at the beginning of my study of *Stolen Kisses*, when I separated the respective elements of these two levels by applying a first criterion consisting of considering irrelevant to the narrative those phenomena that cannot be related to any elementary sequence (the question about the baby's sex, the game of the seven errors, for example). In this case, I have approached the film from this angle solely for the convenience of exposition, but from a general point of view, I shall refer to what I said earlier about textual semantics and semiotics.

Character as Textual Category

The ensuing remarks are based on the assumption that several aspects of the complex and confused notion of character have been distinguished at the outset. First I shall reject the referential illusion that would make of character something other than a product of writing and, apart from interpretations of its status, would lead us into psychological perspectives and presuppose the hypostatization of a real person.

The term *character* covers several textual categories:[12]

(1) As actant, a functional element of the narrative, an agent of the diegetic program, taking on functions in the narrative text's macrostructure. In this context, it is defined by its functioning and its narrative position.

(2) Its configuration is part of a semiotic whole defined by multiple, discontinuous textual markers and is only complete with the last of these textual markers. Here, Philippe Hamon's definition of character as "a discontinu-

ous signifier of a discontinuous signified,"[13] inviting us to consider it as a sign among other signs, comes to mind.

(3) A product of writing, it is worked on as such in the same linguistic material as the other constitutive elements of fiction. In that case, it shall be considered as a sample of the textual fabric.

These are undoubtedly convenient analytical categories; nevertheless, they do not account for the coherence of textual genetics.

The same ideological traces run through all three of these categories. Of these ideological traces, each of which is infinitely complex, I shall deal with only one for the moment, using Foucault's notion of *episteme* to try to follow, along the line of rupture that turned the organization of knowledge upsidedown in the sixteenth century, the radical changes affecting the status of the sign in the great debate that took place between Being and Naming.[14]

I shall, therefore, set aside the specific problems of the different worldviews implied by the two texts I have chosen—that of the merchant in *Guzmán de Alfarache*, that of the nobility of Segovia in the *Buscón*—and shall deal with only the two following questions: (1) In what way does the status of the sign in these two texts coincide with an ideological trace? (2) How is this ideological trace found in the configuration of character—this illusion of reading?

I shall approach this problem indirectly by first examining a "preconstructed element" of *Guzmán de Alfarache*, an *exemplum* whose source goes back to Eusebius of Caesarea and that is deconstructed in the text in order to produce meaning. We shall analyze how this element, which we shall find again in the configuration of character, is being integrated and homogenized within a textual fabric. It is the well-known description of the monster of Ravenna with which the narrative opens at the end of Chapter 1, Book 1, Part I:

> But if there be any discharge or satisfaction in a thing that is evil, I will tell thee one curiosity, because it falls out pat for this place, and did succeed all, as it were about one and the selfsame time. To thee it will serve for counsel; to me, for comfort, as a common evil, that goes not without its fellows.
>
> In the year 1512 (a little before Ravenna was sacked), there were cruel wars in Italy. And in this very city (I mean Ravenna), there was born a strange monster, which did strike the beholders into great admirations and caused much wonder. He had from the girdle upward, all his whole body, face, and head, like unto a man, saving that he had one horn in his forehead: he wanted his arms, but instead thereof, Nature had given him two wings like a bat: he had figured in his breast the Pythagorical Y, and in his stomach down to his belly, a well-formed cross or crucifix. He was an Hermaphrodite, both those two natural sexes, being in a very proportionable manner well and truly formed: he had no more but one thigh, and to it one leg with its foot like a kite's,

and the talons answerable thereunto. In the knotty part, or locking joint of the knee, he had one only eye. These monstrosities and unnatural shapes possessed men's minds with extraordinary admiration; and those that were learned men, and great scholars, considering with themelves, that such monsters in nature were usually prodigious, and did foretoken some strange effects, did beat their brains and exercise the strength of their wit, in the speculation and search of the signification thereof, and what this strange monster might portend. And amongst many other that were given, only this that followeth, was well received amongst them: That the horn did signify Pride and Ambition; the wings, Inconstancy and Lightness; want of arms, want of good works; the foot, of that bird of rapine, Theft, Usury, and Avarice: the eye in the knee, affection to vanities and worldly things: the two sexes, Sodomy and beastly filthiness; in all which vices, all Italy did then abound. For the which, God did scourge them with that his whip of wars and dissensions. But the cross and the Y were good and fortunate signs; for the Y in the breast did signify Virtue: and the cross on the belly, that if men, suppressing their dishonest lusts of the flesh, should embrace virtue in their breasts, God would give them peace, sweeten his displeasure, and abate his wrath.

You see here (in a case prohibited), that when the whole current ran with a troubled water, my father followed along with the stream, and did as others did, and was not the sole and only offender. And therefore more worthy shalt thou be of blame, if thou shalt offend, having been brought up in a school of Christianity, and taught by example what to avoid. God lend us his helping hand, that we may not fall into other the like miseries: for all of us, even the best of us, we are but men.[15]

The monster of Ravenna introduces us to a universe that is marked, covered with signs disseminated on the surface of the Earth so that human beings may decipher them; it illustrates, as we shall see, a conception of knowledge and of the organization of knowledge at a period when knowing the universe consisted not in analyzing experiments, but in interpreting signs. No doubt the case of the omen or prodigy is somewhat special, since it is a message from God intended to *predict* the future: "Prodigio: the same as *praedicare*, to foretell. Prodigies that God has wanted to send us as premonitory signs and messengers of important things and events have frequently appeared at all times. We well know that when Christ our Redeemer died there were wondrous signs and portents. . . . Thus it is equally true that before his glorious birth three suns of equal size appeared, soon becoming one . . . which meant the distinction and the equality of the three divine persons and the unity of their nature" (*Dictionary of Covarrubias*, 1612).[16]

The passage about the monster is interesting because it offers an absolutely complete semiological system consisting of both a coded message and its decoding, providing the means of studying the relations between the object and its representation, and thus of analyzing the status of the sign in the text. I shall group these relations around the following series.

(1) A series of *icons*: the wings (symbols of wantonness), the absence of arms (symbol of the absence of good works), the claw of the bird of prey (symbol of theft and usury), the eye (symbol of desire), the two sex organs (symbol of sodomy). The icons refer to these referents only as a result of a semantic reduction performed by the way this code coincides with an ideological axis: the wings are not liveliness but inconstancy; the claws are a symbol not of strength but of theft; the nature of desire is seen as the interdiction of vanity; the absence of arms corresponds not to an absence of criminal acts, but to that of good works; the male/female equivalence, signified by the juxtaposition of the two sex organs, is a symbol not of unity but of perversion. As we have seen, such a code is the language of God, and God can only mean Good and Evil, Order and Interdiction.

It remains to emphasize how these icons signify, and from this point of view, one is struck by the naive character of the representation, the absolute transparency of the signified, as it were, its compulsory character. The relation between the signifier and the signified is essentially analogical: the object is already in the sign; the icon is both sign and object. Drawing the graphic outlines of the iconic symbol is tantamount to reproducing the outlines of the object itself. What is generally recognized as one of the fundamental characteristics of any code of communication—its arbitrariness—does not appear at all.

(2) The horn, referring to pride and ambition, is iconic only in appearance. Actually, its meaning comes from another place and another code. Let us go back to Covarrubias:

> By that is meant the power of one who governs by delegation of authority and mandate from God, such as the prelate and the preacher, the prophet in the Old Testament . . . *Cornu tuum ponam ferreum et ungues tuos ponam aereos.* And in Psalm 3: *Cornu ejus exaltabitur in gloria*, concerning the power of Christ and his apostles. . . . The psalmist uses the verb *exaltare* in the sense of raising and growing, using the similarity to the horn not only because of its hardness but also because of where it is situated on the animal, namely, the top of the head. This is why, although in another sense, it means the arrogance of the haughty in Psalm 74: *Nolite extollere in altum cornu vestrum, nolite loqui adversus Deum iniquitatem.* And among the profane authors, Horace, lib. 3 *Carminum, oda 21*, speaking of Bacchus, or, in his name, of wine: *Tu spem reducis mentibus onxiisque viresque et addis cornuu pauperi.* Dehorning and breaking the horns signifies humbling the pride of those who have exalted themselves.[17]

The insertion of this meaning superimposes two worlds, the world of the reality of a universe in which God has disseminated the visible marks of his language and the world of writing, itself covered by a series of signs decoded by exegetes.

The horn image belongs to these two worlds of reality and of scripture. God repeats in the figure of the Ravenna monster what he says in the sacred texts; the monster of Ravenna is an actualized and living sign of scripture. The whole perceptible universe is in scripture. They are both supports and vectors of God's language. Scripture glosses the world and permits it to be glossed; the world glosses scripture and permits it to be glossed.

(3) We find the same transparency in the case of the cross and the Y. They are insignificant in themselves but derive their meaning from their localization, which is in the last instance a new form of analogy, as Foucault points out.[18]

In other words, the sign derives its meaning from its resemblance to the object. To decode a sign is to rediscover in and through it the object to which it is similar; knowing the secrets God has left in the universe comes down to establishing analogic relationships between reality and the language that describes it, between language and what this language describes. This reversibility of paths of knowledge is inscribed in the formula cited by Claude-Gilbert Dubois: *Nomen, Lumen*.[19] By means of resemblance, we go back from the sign to the object, and from the object to the sign. The way in which the virtue of aconite (monkshood), that plant used to treat certain ailments of the eyes, is interpreted is a perfect example of the manner in which the secrets of nature are encoded, since it is sufficient to observe that the aconite seed resembles an eye, thus justifying the foundation of medical science, as well as every other science, on the search for and observation of similitudes in things. As Foucault has observed, the category organizing knowledge is that of resemblance; *knowing* is picking up markings in the sensible universe and, beyond impressions, organizing resemblances. Such is the basis for the *episteme* that defines the possibilities of knowledge until the end of the sixteenth century. As a probable effect of the progress accomplished in the medical field, as Dubois has shown,[20] this *episteme* is challenged at the beginning of the seventeenth century by the *episteme* that will be characteristic of the Classical Age. Henceforth, resemblance will disappear from the horizon of knowledge and with it will disappear the fundamental agreement of language and the world.

Don Quixote transcribes perfectly this line of rupture at a period when

writing has ceased to be the prose of the world; resemblances and signs have become deceptive and verge upon the visionary or madness; things still remain stubbornly within their ironic identity: they are no longer anything but what they are; words wander off on their own, without content, without resemblance to fill their emptiness; they are no longer the marks of things; they lie sleeping between the pages of books and covered in dust. Magic, which permitted the deciperment of the world by revealing the secret resemblances beneath its signs, is no longer of any use except as an explanation, in terms of madness, of why analogies are always proved false. The erudition that once read nature and books alike as parts of a single text has been relegated to the same category as its own chimeras: . . . The written word and things no longer resemble one another.[21]

Similitude no longer represents the road to knowledge; it has become the instrument of bewilderment. People will apply themselves no longer to bringing things together, but to seeking out what differentiates them: "This being so, the written word ceases to be included among the signs and forms of truth; language is no longer one of the figurations of the world, or a signature stamped upon things since the beginning of time. The manifestation of and sign of truth are to be found in evident and distinct perception. It is the task of words to translate that truth if they can; but they no longer have the right to be considered a mark of it."[22]

As a consequence, the status of the sign changes radically: from now on, it cannot derive its significance from its resemblance to the signified. It no longer "sticks" to the object it designates. Henceforth, codes of communication will no longer be considered as "figurative codes." Gaps are established between words and things, which the thematics of a book like *Don Quixote* illustrates. In this gap all of baroque art is engulfed.[23]

I propose to follow this line of the rupture of the *episteme* by attempting to reconstruct these contradictory ideological traces in two picaresque works. The text that served as our point of departure functions in *Guzmán de Alfarache* as a veritable *exemplum* intended to illustrate a truth that is repeated throughout the book and upon which is based the rhetorical argument aiming at enlisting the reader's sympathy, namely, that we are all sinners and that by virtue of this truth one can condemn neither him nor his father. Turning points in the text frame this preconstructed element: *before*: "But if there can be some excuse for evil, assuming that my father was in some way guilty, I wish to tell you a curious story. . . . It will serve as a warning to you, and to me as consolation by means of someone else's misfortune"; *after*: "You see that . . . my father was not the only one to sin. You would be much worthier of blame, if you were to sin, you who had better examples."

Thus a first analogical series is developed at the beginning of the narrative. From the marvelous monster of Ravenna, this chain goes back to the reader through the protagonist and his father, expressing in this way a common nature and destiny; an analogical chain present throughout the book in the apostrophes to the reader, who is constantly reminded that "you are not any more a man than I." The architecture of *Guzmán de Alfarache*, both didactic and narrative, is itself centered on a whole network of *exempla* and represents another actualization of this "demon of analogy" that superimposes at a distance a past event on a present narrative situation, thus giving to autobiography all its potential for generalization. Set in a textual fabric enriched and diversified by similes and other rhetorical devices, the picaresque fable is transformed into a parable of human life, a mirror held up to readers so that they may contemplate themselves; thus the *I* and the *Thou* become interchangeable, and the individual trajectory of Guzmán's destiny acquires a value as warning.

We shall better understand how *Guzmán de Alfarache* and *Don Quixote*, for example, depend upon two different *epistemes* if we bear in mind the protean nature of the character (which I have had occasion to study elsewhere[24]): whereas Cervantes's character learns at his own expense that similitude and appearances are the instruments of aberration, Guzmán teaches us that it is *differences*, in their myriad surface metamorphoses, that lead us astray. Thus, we see clearly how an identical conceptual category is invested at every level of the text, whether it be the way in which the sequences of episodes are organized, the insertion of preconstructed elements, the digressive character of the diegesis, or — what concerns us here — the different systems of textual markers that lend substance to the illusion created by the character. If, from these brief observations, we try to rise to a more general level capable of providing an understanding of the status of the sign in the whole work, approaching the problem of language as it functions at all levels of the text, we are led to generalize these first conclusions, observing the sanctification of language accomplished by Mateo Alemán in the work. Writing, in *Guzmán*, revolves around a prodigious anthology of quotations in which it continually seeks support in order to base its affirmations on truth, and makes of the fable a new commentary on these texts that are already commentaries on texts,[25] thus adding language to language.[26] Radiating from this galaxy of indexes referring to a sacred conception of language, the narrative fiction becomes part of this great, unique text in which the universe speaks, hides, and reveals itself, justifying the work's subtitles (*Atalaya de la vida humana, Comedia de la vida humana*). In this context, the incontestable and continual mediation of rhetoric in the production of meaning bears witness to the world vision of a collective subject that still believes in the strength and the authenticity of the word. Such a status of the sign, conceived as trustworthy, stable, ontological, gives autobiographical writing a manifestly strong note of sincerity: the character *Guzmán*, himself defined by a mobile configuration of signs, "sticks" to his language, is identical with it, takes it on as his own. As a character, in the history of ideas and, simply, in history, Guzmán thus appears to us as one of the last textual creations produced by the mythical conception of language. Indeed, such seem to be the philosophical foundations of the *episteme* described by Foucault. The dominance of analogy as a category of thought derives from the presumed adequacy of the sign to its object, of words to things, in short, of a conception of language "that does not make of words mere signs separate from what they designate, but truly the signature of things, their very essence perceived in graphic or auditory form 'in correspondence' with their nature."[27]

We know well enough that such is not the case of the *Buscón* in which the sign is constantly being displaced with respect to referential reality. In *L'Aristocrate* and *Ideología y genética textual*[28] I studied the interplay of discourses, the mystifying word and the "acrobatics" of Quevedo's language, which cause the appearance of a semantic void, a chasm immediately filled by the demystifying phrase that provisionally reestablishes the adequacy of the referential universe and of the sign. Thus, the writing of the *Buscón* unfolds with respect to the two poles of naming and of being, in a systematic confrontation made perfectly perceptible by the analysis of the text's semiotic system. A product of this writing, the character is constantly being diffracted, a mask without a face, an illusion projected by disembodied and inadequate signs, hence this impression of psychological void, of the absence of any inner life, stressed by traditional criticism.

Seen from this point of view, Quevedo's text expresses with particular violence the nostalgia of the myth of the word, that is, of a system of communication in which the sign coincides with the object and in which the word is a bearer of authentic and stable meaning. In the framework of this argument, when we go beyond the case of the *Buscón*, Quevedo's verbal acrobatics, his brilliant manipulations of language, are perceived as phenomena deriving from this rupture of the *episteme*.

Is it so astonishing, then, that we should find the effects of this rupture in the behavior of the autobiographical narrative? In a system in which the sign is essentially hollow, how can the speaking subjects take responsibility for their own discourse and speak authentically about themselves? For this to happen, the union of reality and discourse would have to be reconstructed around the I, in itself and by itself.

This distancing of the narrative from the presumed point of emergence of discourse, which in fact reproduces phenomena of sign displacement, is certainly perceptible in a first reading. It can be assessed more precisely, however, on the basis of a quantitative analysis of occurrences of the notional, the nonpersonal, and the imperfective, which can then be compared to occurrences of the same forms in an autobiographical narrative considered *a priori* as free from the problematics we are analyzing here—the *Lazarillo de Tormes*.

In the *Buscón* the *I* is not an authentic *I*, but a *he*. It is a question not of asking whether or not the narrator refers to the author, but of inquiring solely into the semiological status of the speaking subject, defined by a configuration of textual markers. This analysis reveals another abyss in which the narrator is involved, and thus another evasion of the sign with respect to what it is supposed to signify.

Not only is this distancing perceptible at first reading, but the *I* presents itself openly as a *Non-I*. Here let me repeat the observations, which were pertinent in the context of the old psychological study of character, of those who thought they discovered cynicism in the way Pablos flaunts his dishonor. The same facts are used in my own argument, but in an entirely different way.

No doubt Pablos speaks of his parents' dishonor with an almost cynical levity, as if he were not involved; this comes down to saying in another way that the *I* narrates itself as though a *he* were involved. In other words, the *yo* is presented as a distanced sign in relation to its object. As we raise this question of the status of the sign in the *Buscón*, let us consider two phenomena I have studied — from another point of view — in *L'Aristocrate*: the functioning of the diminutive and the parodic conceptist metaphor. I maintained that the former plays a role as an index of decoding, that is, that every time it is used, it is a marker of the falsity of the sign to which it is joined. As regards the latter, I stated that it is structured by an internal contradiction, an elevated, preconstructed discursive form that is invested by a semantic context referring to a plebeian discourse. This contradiction is, in turn, an explicit marker of the inadequacy of discourse, of the widening gap between the universe of the sign and that of the object. In other words, in these two cases, as in that of the *yo* which is presented as a *Non-I*, the sign carries within itself what I shall call the negative mark of the sign, that is, that at the same time it asserts itself, it is denouncing the illusory character of its function and its semantic emptiness.

From these rapid observations, a few conclusions may be drawn. Two contradictory conceptions of the sign operate in every textual category, whether it be the sign/character or any other semiotic element in the text. Consequently, the character has no specificity with respect to the textual fabric. Whereas in *Guzmán de Alfarache* the sign/character is what it asserts itself to be, in the *Buscón* it denounces the emptiness of its signified and is shown as not being what it claims to be. Such modifications are bound to be noticeable in the macrostructure of the narrative text in which the functioning of the actant I, and its narrative position, in Alemán's text are reversed in Quevedo's text, since the *I/subject* is transformed into an explicit mask of a *nonperson/object*.

Part II
From Theory to Practice

Chapter 8
American Films of the Thirties
The Case of Howard Hawks's *Scarface*

Exorcism and Economic Crises:
Toward a Semiological Reading of Film

Study of Sequences

SCARFACE
(dialogue and shooting script)*

Street scene at night

Medium close-up of the globe of a lighted lamp-post, in a low-angle shot; beneath the globe, a sign indicating "22nd Street." The camera moves back, and a horse-drawn delivery van comes into view, stopped in a dark, deserted street; then the camera goes around the vehicle. Next we see that the delivery van is stopped in front of a nightclub with its windows still lit up; the driver is loading crates of bottles. The camera comes closer so that it just frames the façade of the nightclub. On the doorstep, a man wearing an apron is waving, and we hear offscreen the sound of the wagon going away. Then the man removes from in front of the door a large poster announcing the pleasures of the evening and goes inside to put it away.

---

*Text taken from Eliane Le Grivès, *Scarface, L'Avant Scène*, 132 (Jan. 1973). Because the original Howard Hawks/Ben Hecht script no longer existed, Eliane Le Grivès viewed the film frame by frame, translating the dialogue.

Nightclub—interior at night

In a wide-angle shot, we see the man put away the poster in a corner of the room cluttered with green plants from which streamers are hanging, and which are also strewn all over the floor. The man takes a broom and starts to clear away a tangle of streamers and party hats, in which he finds a brassiere, while he moves toward the center of the room from which light and muffled sounds of a conversation are coming. The camera follows him a moment, then passes him and reveals the empty room where only three revelers are left seated around a table laden with bottles. It comes close to them and frames them in a knee shot, while their voices become audible. A fat bald man, seated between his two guests, is telling them a story in a heavy Italian accent.

BIG LOUIS: I told him: what would we do with it? Let the others have their share . . . I have everything I want . . .

His neighbor on the right, a thin, serious-looking man, interrupts him.

THE NEIGHBOR: Johnny Lovo is talking about tackling a job.

BIG LOUIS: Yeah! He's looking for trouble? Johnny's a damn fool. Look at me: I have everything a man could want. I'm rich, I have a house, I have a car, I have the prettiest girls . . . (*he hiccups*) . . . I also have a rotten stomach . . . (*he laughs*).

THE NEIGHBOR: Well, I'm going to bed. (*He gets up and walks around the table.*)

BIG LOUIS: OK. (*He gets up too, imitated by the third man who has remained silent, and joins his companion. He seems very satisfied with himself.*) Well, it was quite an evening, wasn't it? (*he laughs*). Next week, I'll give one like you've never seen yet. We'll have lots more music, lots more girls, lots more of everything . . . (*bombastically*). Everybody's gonna say: That Big Louis, he got the world at his feet! . . . (*he laughs*).

THE NEIGHBOR: Buona sera!

He leaves, followed by the other man. Big Louis, left alone, watches them go.

BIG LOUIS: Buona sera, fellas, take good care of yourselves!

He remains motionless for a minute, then, followed by the camera, he crosses the room to go to the telephone at the rear of the room, near a glass door. Behind the glass, we make out the silhouette of a man wearing a hat. The camera comes closer to Big Louis, who has picked up the telephone.

BIG LOUIS: Hello, give me Lakeside 4173.

While he continues to ask for this number, the camera leaves him and sweeps the room, framing in the foreground the green plants near the entrance. The shadow wearing the hat passes in front of them while whistling softly, the camera follows his progress, then lets him disappear in the darkness, and frames a glass door through which the light from the room is passing. The shadow is then seen in profile behind the lit-up glass, a revolver sticks out from the end of his arm, and the soft whistling stops. *

THE SHADOW: Buon giorno, Louis!

Two shots are fired, then the man takes out a handkerchief from his pocket, wraps the weapon up in it, and throws it on the floor. He runs away whistling. The camera leaves the glass door and reveals the corner of the room where Big Louis's body is lying. Offscreen, the whistling can still be heard when the nightclub employee arrives calmly and suddenly stops in front of the body stretched out on the floor in front of a closet door. The employee quickly takes off his cap and apron and tosses them into the closet, from which he takes his jacket and hat, hastily slipping them on as he crosses the room. He runs away.

Editorial room of the *Daily Herald*—interior daylight

General view of the room, full of activity. A man enters, holding a printed sheet with a headline in big letters, shouting in the midst of the hubbub: "Here are the proofs, here are the proofs!" He gives the paper to a reporter sitting in the foreground, who takes it and gets up immediately. The camera accompanies him: he crosses the room and goes into the office of the editor-in-chief, who is seated at a large desk and is busy writing.

• • • • • • • • • • • • • • • • • • • •

Medium, frontal shot of the editor taking the paper, glancing rapidly at it, crumpling it furiously, and throwing it on the floor.

EDITOR: That's no good! (*accentuating each syllable*). "Costello Murder To Start Gang War": that's what I want!

Medium shot on the reporter, from behind.

---

*The shadows form a sort of cross, a graphic leitmotif appearing at each violent death. This cross resembles the scar Toni has on his cheek.

REPORTER: I'm giving it priority. I have four men on the story.

Medium shot on the editor.

EDITOR: Four? You'll need forty men on this story for five years to come. You know what's happening? They're going to struggle for control of this town, you understand? Look: Costello was the last old-style gang leader. A new team is taking over. Any little guy with enough money to buy a revolver is going to try to take the place of the others. They'll shoot each other down like rabbits. To improve their business! . . . It'll be war. That's it, war. Put that on the front page: War . . . Gang War.

Barbershop—interior daylight

Lap dissolve. The front page of the Daily Herald. *The headline reads: "Costello Murder To Start Gang War." The camera moves back and shows the whole newspaper, lying folded on a chair in a barbershop. All the barber chairs are covered with white sheets; a man's legs are protruding from one of them. The barber, dressed in a white smock, crosses the room holding a glass in his hand. In the background, seated on a bench in front of the shop window, a man wearing a fedora is reading a newspaper. The sound of an approaching car is heard. The man gets up with a start.*

THE MAN: The cops!

But he sits back down immediately, while through the windows we see a car stopping in front of the shop and men getting out. A hand holding a revolver emerges from the sheet with the legs protruding from it. The barber grabs it and throws it into a chest full of towels. Close-up of the revolver lying on the towels. Master shot of the room. The man sitting in front of the window is absorbed in reading the newspaper. A policeman is seen approaching the door and entering. Medium shot of the policeman on the doorstep.

THE POLICEMAN: Hello, Rinaldo!

Medium close-up from behind of the seated man, who raises his eyes placidly.

THE POLICEMAN (*offscreen*): You coming?

Rinaldo lowers his eyes to his newspaper again, then gets up as if resigned. Medium shot of Rinaldo and the policeman face to face.

THE POLICEMAN: Where's Camonte?

Rinaldo gestures with his thumb toward the occupied barber chair, then takes out of his pocket a piece of change that he negligently tosses in his hand.* The camera moves back to frame the barber chair and the policeman walking toward it. Camonte takes off the sheet and reveals himself. Medium close-up frontal shot of Camonte. He has a scar on his left cheek.

CAMONTE: Hello, Guarino.

THE POLICEMAN (*offscreen*): Come along.

CAMONTE: You're sure in a hurry. I'm also having a massage.

Medium shot of Guarino.

GUARINO (*impatient*): You'll finish that at the police station. Put on your coat.

Medium shot of Camonte from the rear. He sits up slowly, staring at Guarino.

CAMONTE: I've got plenty of time.

He takes off the smock that was covering him, gets up and goes to take a cigarette from a dresser, turning his back to Guarino, who has come closer to him and is standing behind him at knee shot distance.

CAMONTE: Who wants to see me?

GUARINO: The boss.

CAMONTE: That idiot!

He turns toward Guarino.

GUARINO: Have your laugh . . . Come on, let's go.

CAMONTE (*to the barber*): I'd like to see how it looks in the back.

He takes a mirror from the dresser and shifts it, turning his head to try to see his haircut better.

---

*This mannerism of the character made the actor George Raft famous. In fact, Howard Hawks liked this gesture so much because in Chicago, hired killers used to put a nickel in the dead man's hand as a sign of disrespect. And the character is a killer who is always ready to kill.

BARBER (*offscreen*): You look real good.

Camonte grunts with satisfaction. He puts the mirror down, puts a cigarette to his lips, takes a match from the dresser and brings it up close to the star shining on Guarino's chest. Close-up of the hand striking the match on the star; the flame leaps out. Medium shot of Camonte and Guarino face to face. Camonte peacefully lights his cigarette and blows the smoke in Guarino's face. Medium three-quarter frontal close-up of Guarino punching Camonte, turning into a three-quarter back shot. Medium shot of Camonte, from the front, falling backward near the linen chest. Flash on Rinaldo, in the middle distance near the door, who starts to move forward. Medium shot of Camonte getting up. Guarino approaches him and grabs his collar.

GUARINO: Come on, you bastard!

Camonte frees himself and straightens his shirt. The barber appears, looking stupefied, holding out Camonte's jacket and hat. Camonte puts on his hat and takes his jacket. Guarino grabs his arm.

GUARINO: Come on, let's go.

They cross the shop, the barber takes several steps after them. Rinaldo, still in front of the door, is the first to leave. We see through the window that a crowd has been forming. Scarcely have the three men left when they disappear behind the crowd of curiosity seekers. We hear the car's motor starting up. Dissolve out.

Methodological Principles

(1) We shall consider that every element of the various levels of the filmic message (visual, linguistic, auditory) is part of one semiotic system and plays an equal role in the production of meaning.[1]

(2) This system is itself composed of a set of texts, each of which is defined by a coreferential relation existing among the various signs involved.

(3) Every element selected by analysis as being pertinent[2] will be separated from the visual or linguistic context that had given it a contingent primary meaning, and will be placed in a different network in which it occupies an autonomous position with respect to this primary context.

(4) Within this new network, reductions of meaning are effected by the concordance established among themselves by the various signs, regardless of their nature or level. Every confrontation of a sign with another sign effectively reactivates certain meanings of both, but neutralizes most of them. The multiplication of these confrontations gives the whole system a coherence of meaning that must not be confused with that of the contingent or opposite meaning of each of the different levels. These successive confrontations have the result of producing increasingly narrow semiological reductions, leading, in theory, to the discovery of a coreferential relation, which will be translated, as far as possible, in terms of bipolar concepts.

(5) When each point of coreference, around which the semiotic text is ordered, has thus been formulated, it will be considered in turn, in a second phase of grouping, as a pertinent sign capable of entering a second process of semiological reduction, marking off a new field of coincidence.

(6) It has been posed as a hypothesis: (a) that the results of these various operations should permit us to discern the principal components of the filmic *genotext*; (b) that this composite is deconstructed by each of the different levels, according to its specificity, in the form of diverse actualizations—*phenotexts*—that a subsequent analysis should permit us to verify.

1. Interior/Exterior

Camera outside in the street → camera moves: cabaret interior; doors, successive entrances and exits of characters (first sequence); camera: → interior newspaper office, transparent cubicles, entrances and exits of characters, voices and sounds offscreen (third sequence).

We pass successively from exterior → interior (first sequence); to: ————— interior → interior (second sequence); then to: ————— interior → exterior (third sequence).

The systematic aspect of this back and forth movement makes it a pertinent element around which two specific spaces are arranged, governed by distinct laws and, ultimately, by different codes of communication.

If we study the modalities of functioning that permit us to pass between these two spaces, we observe several phenomena of reversal: in the first sequence the camera, which is outside in the street, ostensibly passes through a wall (Ph. 5)[3] to enter the interior of a cabaret, thus placing in relief a visual obstacle shown as unsurmountable at the very moment it is nevertheless surmounted. On the contrary, the series of glassed-in cubicles (Ph. 13 and 14), which are easily perceptible as so many indexes of a sort of visual continuum, become masks of a closed space, a space presented as such by the lettering on the door, seen in reverse that is, from a space that has already been crossed and that can be interpreted as describing spaces forbidden to the public. A system of obstacles standing out against transparency consequently establishes a perfect correspondence, though now with a negative sign, to the camera movement noted above. Opacity and transparency thus appear, within a coreferential relation, as signs signifying the opposite of what they are supposed to signify. This ambiguity of the sign designates it as a locus of problematization capable of opening up two areas of possible subsequent semiotic correspondence: no doubt what is involved is *passage*, but it is a questioning of the visual realm and suggests a reversal of the concepts of the *visible* and the *invisible*.

2. Night/Day

→ Lamp going out (Ph. 2 and 3), hour of the milkman and the streetcleaner (Ph. 6), end of a night of revelry, poster announcing the evening brought inside (Ph.

5, 6, and 17), "Well, I'm going to bed," "It was a great evening," shadows of artificial light, empty room, vestiges of the party (first sequence) (Ph. 6).
← Production of the early edition of the paper (previewing the proofs) (second sequence) (Ph. 14 and 15). Close-up shot of the headline of that edition of the paper in the barbershop (third sequence) (Ph. 20).

We are thus at the *dividing line* between day and night (Ph. 2 and 3). Contrary to what one might think at first, this boundary does not separate the first sequence from the subsequent ones but is inscribed deep within each sign from the very first frames. It is a part not of the temporal organization of the episodes, but rather of a thematic whole. A comparison of the leave-taking formula Big Louis uses with his friends (*Buona sera*) with the one the killer uses a few seconds later (*Buon giorno*) demonstrates this. Significantly, then, the first character is part of a semiotic set connoting night and the past, whereas the second looms up from a pale dawn connoting an ambiguous future (Ph. 7, 8, 10, and 11).

In this way, the opposition *night/day* is, at a second level, a symbolic representation of the *old* and the *new* explicitly expressed by the words of the editor in chief (old ways vs. new team). Thus, hinging upon this text, a new space of reading opens up marked by a brief lexical field (next week, start, [five years] to come, changing of the guard, takeover).

3. Work/Festivity
→ Milkman, streetcleaner, wagon, "I'm working," team, smock, barber, barbershop, policeman, towel, sheets (Ph. 5, 6, 16, 17 . . .).
← Revellers, dancing, party hat (→ exotic plant), brassiere, champagne, whiskey, glasses (Ph. 6, 7, 8, 9, . . .).

It is a question here not of a mere confrontation of two worlds, but rather of the overlapping of the first inside the second, as if the *reverse* of the images were systematically being seen through their transparent *obverse*.

4. Hiding/Displaying
→ Hiding by the janitor of a brassiere and an unidentified object (Ph. 6), killer in hiding (Ph. 10), hiding of fingerprints, hidden revolver (Ph. 18, 19), towel as mask, newspaper as mask (Ph. 20).
← Gestures of pointing (Ph. 19), revealing of the headline (Ph. 20), the newspaper perceived as the instrument of unveiling (Ph. 20).

This list does not take into account a number of phenomena that are difficult to formulate in terms of signs. Such is the case of the two scenes in which Camonte hides behind pretexts to *avoid* police action: having a massage and examining his haircut in the mirror (Ph. 25 and 26). The mirror renders this scene metaphorical: at the same time it is being used to make the back of the neck visible, it is also presented as one of the expedients used by the gangster in a game of *hide-and-seek* and provocation. This is tantamount to saying that the mirror functions as an instrument both of hiding and of revealing. We shall find an identical problematization of this sign in the dual role assigned to the newspaper. Added to its function of denouncing scandal and crime, emphasized in American film tradition, particularly in so-called gangster films, are the orders of the editor-in-chief (*Put this across*) (Ph. 15). On the other hand, however, in the barbershop, Rinaldo twice hides behind his newspaper (Ph. 20). This is certainly a stereotype, but it must be linked with what I have said about the mirror, in that the meanings of both are being reversed in parallel fashion and, consequently, as I have said about transparency, are being problematized. This is all the more true since these reversals occur several times in the text. Thus the camera, which must be seen in the context of the analogical series (camera - newspaper - mirror), by describing the gesture of the barber throwing the revolver into a chest full of towels (Ph. 18 and 19) in order to hide it, conspicuously unveils this will to hide.

5. Power/Submission

→ Let the others take their share. I have all I want. I have all that a man can want. I am rich. I have . . . I have . . . I have . . . I have. . . . He has the world at his feet, gang leaders, boss, series of coercive orders of the policeman (You coming? Come on! Come on, you bastard!) Big Louis's gestures of power (Ph. 7 and 8), those of the editor (Ph. 15), and the policeman (Ph. 22). Displays of power (punch) (Ph. 23), typology of the leader (gang boss, editor-in-chief, police chief).

← Fellas (as index of subordination), *I've got plenty of time*, stage business of Camonte's resisting police power, his final capitulation (Ph. 22 and 23).

When these signs are put back in their respective textual contexts, we observe that several instances of power are playing against one another. In other words, power and domination are definitively perceived less with respect to submission than with respect to various struggles that allow them to be won or preserved. This is as valid for Big Louis's liberal strategy (We must let the others take *their share*) as for the leaders of the new team aiming at taking the *place* (thus the *share*) of the others, or for Camonte's attempting to dominate the policeman (Ph. 27). We are thus witnessing multiple power confrontations. This manifold repetition of confrontations prevents us from setting the place of confrontation at one level or another (among the gangs, between the police and the gangs) and leads us to generalize this problematic. Camonte's gesture of striking the match on Guarino's badge—a sign of social order—is an obvious challenge to power, and the most spectacular actualization of this problematic.

6. Distance/Assimilation

Several convergent phenomena are grouped under this rubric.

(a) At the level of dialogue, the opposition *I/others* (in Big Louis's discourse), *we/others* (in the editor-in-chief's discourse). We observe in this connection that discourse about oneself can be distanced: thus Big Louis refers to himself in the third person (Everyone will say: Big Louis, he has the world at his feet!), whereas the reporters and newspaper editors are presented, initially, as readers of their own text beside the editor-in-chief, who is being informed of it.

(b) Group frames systematically organized around one individual:

Big Louis ← vs. → his two guests (Ph. 7)
Editor-in-chief ← vs. → reporters (Ph. 14)
Camonte ← vs. → the other characters in the barbershop. (Ph. 18)

(c) *Problematization of social integration*. From the very first frame, we know what to think: the camera puts us on "22nd Street," that is, at the edge of the Italian neighborhood (Ph. 2 and 3). The majority of the characters belong to this minority even if they are defined by distinctive textual markers: some (Big Louis) have an Italian accent, whereas the origin of the others is revealed by either their occupations (the barber) or their names (Guarino, Camonte, Rinaldo). The diversity of these markers seems to reveal another barrier, that of generations: the young gangsters, unlike the old, speak English with a perfect American accent, an obvious index of their integration into American society. But this new generation, at the same time that it is inscribed within the new national collectivity, is, in turn, undergoing a process of diffraction. The individuals who make up this new generation are divided on both sides of the ideological inclusion, a division that cannot be more clearly marked than by the typology of the characters (policeman/gangster).

Once again, we are led to deduce from the repetition of this phenomenon that it must be generalized. Consequently, we shall see in this generalization the transcription of a recurrent opposition of inclusion and exclusion, an opposition that the French version of the film placed in extraordinary relief (Ph. 1) by presenting the facts narrated in *Scarface* as the expression of an "implacable struggle among these men, *scum* [exclusion] of *society* [inclusion]."

By limiting myself to a *microtext*, I cannot judge *a priori* the pertinence of certain signs that are isolated and apart from my groupings. Thus, when the killer is silhouetted in profile behind the glass door, a revolver in his hand, the shadows form a cross (Ph. 11). This cross is found again in the gash on Camonte's left cheek when he unmasks himself in the barbershop scene (Ph. 24). From that point, it is a veritable "plastic leitmotif." But there is no need to anticipate the ensuing frames. The title (*Scarface*) is there to program, at least on an elementary level, the explicit production of meaning and to synthesize the message by focusing not only on an actant, but also on physical (mark on the face) and symbolic (marked with a cross) characteristics. In fact, when this phenomenon is perceived as a preconstructed element belonging to a long series of antecedents, it is marked with a destiny that transcends the individual level. Even though it may be isolated in this microtext, this sign, which refers to a point external to the narrative but internal to the film and explicitly given as center of focalization of meaning, is thus linked to a zone of coreference.

This zone of coreference will be clearer if we approach the second process of semiologic reduction, which is capable of marking out a new field of coincidence and which takes into account the first coreferential relations. The latter, it seems to me, need to be grouped around certain points for which I propose the following formulations:

(A) Problematization of the crossing (edge; frontier; transition; old vs. new) (Texts 1, 2, 6c)

(B) Hiding vs. unmasking (Texts 1 and 4)

(C) Inclusion vs. exclusion (Text 6)

(D) Reverse vs. obverse (Text 3)

We shall link the center of polarization to the specific status of the signs identified as being the most pertinent and that constantly reverse their respective primary meanings (transparency/opacity; instruments of revelation/instruments of masking, etc.).

In such a semiotic context, an isolated sign that we have deliberately neglected until now orders these apparently unconnected elements and gives them all their meaning. I refer to the party hat Big Louis is wearing (Ph. 8 and 9), a paper crown or ridiculous monarch's hat designating him as the comic king of carnivalesque celebrations, dooming him to being dethroned. That this dethroning is in turn presented as the result of a generational conflict is another index of the social practice invested in the textual circumstances of the film. Whether it be the role traditionally played by age groups in the organization of these festivities, or the rites of the passage of power shaping certain carnivalesque festivals (festival of the king of roosters, or of the king of crossbowmen), it is certainly a social practice that is involved. In light of this fact, the various structural elements we have uncovered clearly appear for what they are—namely, specific actualizations, each of which deconstructs, at the various levels of the filmic message, that composite, the genotext: time flowing backward, systematics of reversal, problematics of crossing (of life and death, winter and spring), overturning of phenomena of inclusion and exclusion—all are components of carnivalesque rites. In that case, we shall give to the symbol of the cross the full symbolic meaning conferred upon it by its insertion in the carnivalesque world, which entails a displacement of the signified, since, situated as well in such a point of convergence, it is no longer the premonitory sign of atonement and redemption but functions as an index signaling the latent presence of a dynamics of exorcism.

It is here that hypotheses of a sociocritical reading open up perspectives to us that broader studies (extended to the entire film) and more complex studies (examination of the articulations linking textual structuring to social structures) should allow us to confirm, to nuance, and to describe in detail. At this point, however, how can I not compare, on the one hand, what I have presented as the possible outline of a genotext in which is invested a state of serious economic and social crisis running through the society implicit in *Scarface* with, on the other hand, what I have said about the thematics of exclusion, which designates as scapegoat not merely a group defined as morally and socially marginal, but an entire unintegrated ethnic minority? Has not history taught that every society confronted with real or imaginary threats attempts to exorcise them by seeking in its own heart or, more precisely, at the periphery of its unitary structures, victims chosen to appease destiny?[4]

Far from being limited to the message alone, my analysis is concerned with the history of film as consumer product. Indeed, this initial discourse on power structures, which, however, seems to cast a critical gaze on the marginal universe and, thus, to reproduce the revelatory function of the press in a successive nesting of discursive structures, has had, in turn, to submit itself to the laws of another repressive space, the Hays Code. The Code surrounds the first message, a possible vector of evil threatening the collectivity, with a second message whose function is essentially *redressive*,[5] by imposing a subtitle ("A Nation's Shame") as well as an ideological interpellation addressed to the spectator and designed to reconstitute an ideological inclusiveness.[6]

A Sociocritical Reading

In a first approach to *Scarface* I had reconstructed the semiotic system of the initial sequences of the film before proposing the outlines of a sociocritical reading. The problematics that have emerged may now be submitted to new analyses conducted from perceptibly different and, for that very reason, complementary points of view. Our point of departure is the major semiotic text that emerged from our analysis, namely, the polarity of hiding and unmasking, which seems to run through the whole system.

As the film unfolds, this dialectic is explicitly articulated at the denotative level by a scene that the Hays Code censors required from the producer and the director: the interview that takes place in the offices of the *Evening Record*, opposing the apparent editor of the newspaper, Mr. Garston, to people who seem to be representatives of a pressure group. The latter reproach Mr. Garston for giving *publicity* to gangsters, for "keeping their activities *spread all over the front page*," for thinking that "our children must be saturated with violence and murder." The editor tries to convince his interlocutors that one cannot "get rid of gangsters by *ignoring* them; *by removing them from the front page*," and he draws their attention to the danger involved in "*hiding the facts*." "We must arrest them, *unmask* them, and rid this country of them. That is how they will disappear from the front page."[7]

This coincidence between the formulations of the ideological instance and the interplay of textual structures is extremely interesting to follow. From my methodological point of view, I can deduce a series of remarks. For those who have followed my semiological analysis, the remark of the editor will seem only a redundancy, a gratuitous repetition of what the film is constantly saying. For the Hays Office censors, on the contrary, what was involved was the requirement that something *finally* be said that up to then had not been said. In my view, ideological instances are profoundly invested in the cultural object, which ideology itself refuses to admit and which, by this very refusal, reveals itself for what it is. By entering the film in this form, the ideological instance, paradoxically situates itself as outside cultural production.

I shall not, however, take this coincidence as confirmation of the results of my semiotic approach. That would be to ignore the fact that the two chains of meaning shaping the text—that of the sign and that of the signified—are distinct and autonomous. Seen in the context of their theoretical autonomy, the coincidence that makes the two chains of meaning cross here needs to be investigated.

The scene at the *Evening Record* marks out a zone of ideological conflict, apparently banal and relatively secondary in importance, bearing upon the role generally played by the media: the media are invested in the film in such a way that it may be immediately assumed that the characters assembled around Mr. Garston are making a negative judgment on the film from inside the film itself.

However, the point of view of Mr. Garston's interlocutors is shared by the police commissioner, who sharply reprimands the reporter who has come to interview him about Camonte: "Colorful! What is the color of sewer rats? Listen here, your attitude is that of too many people in this country: they think these criminals are demigods. And what do they do about someone like Camonte? They sentimentalize him, romanticize him, joke about him. It was all right to glorify our bandits of the Old West; they met in the street at high noon and everyone went for the draw. But these creatures sneak around shooting people in the back and running away. . . . When I think about what must be going on in the heads of these people, I want to vomit" (*AS*, p. 24).

This scene, which immediately precedes the *Evening Record* scene, draws our attention to the importance in the text of the little world of newspapermen. Thus, one of the first sequences of the film (the editorial room of the *Daily Herald*) provides a commentary on the brutal images of Big Louis's assassination; the failed attempt on Meeham's life is commented on in the same way (*AS*, p. 16). The gangsters keep close track of newspaper reports and are obviously flattered when they see their photos and accounts of their crimes spread all over the front page ("LOVO: What do the papers say? CAMONTE: I brought them [*medium frontal shot of Camonte holding the newspaper*]. They tell an awful story. There's a picture of you. . . [*he leans forward to give the paper to Lovo*] . . . and one of me, too" [*AS*, p. 16]). They eagerly welcome reporters who want to interview them—as Gaffney does, for example, after the St. Valentine's Day massacre. In their idle moments, they read newspapers (in the barbershop; at the start of the war of reprisal by Camonte against O'Hara's gang: "*A man is reading a newspaper when*

gunfire bursts from an approaching car. . . . He sinks behind his newspaper")
to the point where, in the film at least, the newspaper seems to be part of the
iconography of gangsterism. At least three newspapers are mentioned in the film:
The Daily Herald, *The Evening Record*, and *The Journal*.

From the point of view of narrative technique, moreover, the newspaper has
a remarkable role to play, to the extent that, on several occasions, it takes over
the narration. Thus, it is the newspaper that explains the circumstances of Big
Louis's death ("Do you know what happened? . . . Costello was the last of the
old-style gang leaders. . . . They're going to shoot each other down like rabbits"). The newspaper fills gaps left in the narration, summarizes diegetic ellipses:
it is the newspaper that informs us simultaneously of the attack on Meeham, its
relative and temporary failure, and the fact that it is part of a series ("Another
failed assassination attempt: Meeham, riddled with bullets, escapes death" [*AS*,
p. 16]); it is the newspaper that allows an indirect summary of another action not
witnessed by the spectator, namely, the absence of Tony, who has gone to spend
a month in Florida, and the changes in the criminal underworld during his absence. ("*A newspaper office: In the foreground a seated man. . . . A man approaches him and offers him a newspaper.* THE MAN WITH THE NEWSPAPER: Big
Tony is back from Florida. SEATED MAN [*taking the newspaper*]: Well, he better
be careful [*AS*, p. 30]). The newspaper thus seems linked to the narrative instance, either because it is the means used by the latter to advance the action (as
when Camonte learns through the newspaper that Meeham is only wounded), or
because it takes the place of the narrative function. If the newspaper cannot be
identified with the narrative instance (N), it is, at the very least, a narrator (n);
that is, it plays a role within the narrational level. But the newspaper is a narrative
at the second degree, a mirror of events; elsewhere, it appears only in its status
as mirror. Though what it says precisely may escape us, it is itself commented
upon, and this commentary corresponds to a second *projection* of the event, a
projection that, in turn, will be given visual form in the film (event → reportage
→ commentary → film). This is the case, for example, of the story of Big Louis's
murder and of the announcement of Tony's return. The newspaper loses its informative function in order to become integrated with narratological programming. But in its manner of integration (when it is seen only as a *mirror* of the
event), it presents itself essentially as *observation*, literally as *medium*. In this
role, it most clearly resembles other media inscribed in the text: first, advertising
("*The World Is Yours*"), which metaphorizes Camonte's ambition and his social
ascension and *reflects* in this way the thematic structure; second, the theater,
which reproduces the dual mimetic rivalry whose stake is, or has been, women:
("CAMONTE: I want to know which one of the two guys Sadie chose" [*AS*, p. 25]),
thereby reflecting as well the interplay of the film's two love triangles

(Camonte—Poppy—Lovo; Camonte—Cesca—Rinaldo); and third, the film medium itself, which merits closer study.

The reader will have no doubt noticed the abundance of frames within frames: doors, windows, balconies cutting the depth of the visual field into spaces enclosed within one another: the curtains of Poppy's bedroom defining a forbidden space; the rear window of the car in which Rinaldo and Camonte return after Camonte's interview with Lovo, in which we see passing street scenes, and so on. Two textual phenomena give meaning to this series: (1) the murder of Big Louis at the very moment he goes to the telephone: *behind a window*, we see the silhouette of a man wearing a hat; a few seconds later, the killer's shadow is etched in profile, *behind the lighted window*, and it is through this window that his murderous gestures are seen (the pointed revolver, the cleaning of the weapon, etc.). We do not witness Big Louis's assassination *directly*, that is, we do not see him fall the moment he is hit; we discover his body lying on the floor. Between the action and our seeing it, a window, that is, a screen, a *medium*, has intervened. We have not witnessed an assassination; we have witnessed the *projection* of an assassination. Just as the newspaper is presented as "mirror of the event," the film is being presented here as mirror, reflection, gaze. (2) The first image of *Scarface*, in this context, has a certain *a posteriori* function. This first image bore the mark of a St. Andrew's cross standing out in black against the screen or rather, against a screen that is at the same time that of the movie theater in which we are seated, and a screen that strikes us as such from inside the film, a screen that is signed, marked in its materiality as screen by a sign inscribing in it an idea of projection, and, probably, a message. Thus the film opens with a symbolic reflection of itself. Whether it is a question of sexual rivalry whose stake is first Poppy and then Cesca, or a general thematics of social ascension and world domination, or of the function and nature of the media, or even of narrative processes in general, the film creates systematic reflections of textual phenomena, presented as reflections, shadows, projections.

At this point, I shall discuss a sign that has undoubtedly been misinterpreted thus far: the St. Andrew's cross, which Eliane Le Grivès (in *Avant Scène*), too quickly reads as a Latin cross. Jerome Lawrence, in *The Life and Times of Paul Muni*, cites an interesting comment by Howard Hawks in this connection: "Newspapers at the time always labeled their photographs of killing and accidents with a point of reference. X marks the spot where the body was found. . . . I got the crew together and I said: 'We're having a lot of killings and I want each to be labeled 'X marks the spot' in a cinematic way. So anybody who comes up with a notion we can use will get fifty bucks. No, make that a hundred."[8] The X thus belongs to what I shall call a specific microsemiotic—to that secondary modeling system constituted by journalism. This comment justifies *a posteriori* the observations we have just made and allows us to interpret them. In fact, it is this microsemiotic that is vested in the film and that functions as a code for the transformation of observable reality. This microsemiotic accounts, in particular, for the following:

— The sensationalistic style of the film (the striking series of killings and assassination attempts, the incestuous relationship between Cesca and Tony, the spectacular attack by the police at the end, automobile chases, machine-gun attacks, etc.).

— The status of the narrator, who bases the credibility of his omniscience on the suggestion that he possesses an impressive knowledge of the facts, the kind of knowledge characteristic of any "well-informed" daily newspaper.

— The complicity with the spectator that is established beforehand through the intermediary of journalism. The narrative assumes, in fact, that the spectator already knows a number of facts upon which it is based. These facts are known to us only through the newspapers of the period. (We are explicitly told that the scenario is "based on *Scarface*, by Armitage Trail, *as well as on newspapers of the period*" [*AS*, p. 5].) The film thus situates itself as an extension of written news media, and this gives it a powerful realism. To cite one example, there is the allusion to 22nd Street, notorious in the Chicago of the 1930s for its nightclubs and restaurants, whose "gem" was none other than the cabaret of Big Jim Colosimo, the obvious model for Big Louis in the film. Big Jim was murdered on the doorstep of his restaurant, despite the fact that he had, in 1920, brought from New York two bodyguards, Johnny Torrio and Al Capone.[9] The film's scenario closely follows reality, thus recreating in an obvious manner a reality already known to the spectator through the daily newspapers. The principals of the drama are thinly veiled behind easily readable fictional names: Johnny Torrio becomes Johnny Lovo; Al Capone becomes Camonte; Big Jim becomes Big Louis; and the leader of the Northside gang, O'Bannion, lurks behind O'Hara. However, I shall mention two major differences:

(1) Al Capone is a natural replacement for the Southside gangleader after Torrio leaves for Italy when his life is threatened by the Irish. This enables us to understand better the profound didacticism of the film, which makes "struggle among leaders" into a general law.

(2) Al Capone, at least if we are to believe the eyewitness accounts of the period, especially that of Geo London, was neither foolish nor uncouth ("Outwardly, he was a gentle, sympathetic, articulate man. . . . In addition, he lacked neither a sense of appropriateness nor finesse"[10]). This comment heightens the importance of the carnivalization the protagonist undergoes in *Scarface*, which brings to the fore the way ideological stereotypes function in the film.

While *Scarface* was being filmed, that is, in late spring and early summer of 1931, an investigation was being carried out into the activities of Al Capone, who appeared in court in October of the same year. Finally, let us remember that Ben Hecht was a reporter and that *Scarface* is a reporter's film.

Let us return to the St. Andrew's cross, which I interpreted earlier as the iconogram of interdiction. Clearly, this is *also* its meaning, which is tantamount to saying that the X *also* refers to another microsemiotic opposed to the preceding one on this point: the first has as its objective to reveal, to display the facts on the front page; the second, which we have yet to describe, tends, on the contrary, to hide the facts. An X stamped on a photograph that reconstructs a crime, in fact, marks that photograph with the sign of censorship: it says that the body was *lying there* but that the sight of this body is impossible or forbidden. It signifies the refusal of hypersensationalism, that is, inside a sensationalist form, it inscribes an ideological trace that undermines sensationalism. It is a question no longer of a mere zone of coincidence but rather of a zone of ideological conflict.

Let us provisionally call this new microsemiotic a "rhetoric of silence and hiding." We saw it explicitly operating in the *Evening Record* scene, but it is inscribed as well in each reproduction of the X, that is, in each killing. This rhetoric is also discernible in all the changes the film underwent—in particular the elimination of twelve scenes, including the original ending in which Camonte is shot down by a rival gang and not by the police.

This rhetoric of silence and hiding is also at work in the way killings are generally shown: either the camera momentarily leaves the victim at the precise instant of his death (Big Louis, Gaffney, Johnny Lovo), or it substantially mitigates the brutality of the scene (the anonymous gangster sinking behind his newspaper, the smokescreen masking the bodies of the victims of the St. Valentine's Day massacre). Such veiling contrasts with the din of machine-gun fire and the spectacular scenes of speeding cars.

This "rhetoric of hiding,"[11] which reproduces, in filmic "writing," the interdictions of the Hays Code, is linked to another ideological trace in which repressive social structures are expressed. One cannot miss seeing the connection here between the police commissioner and the editor-in-chief of the *Daily Herald*; seated behind their respective desks, they receive information gathered or written by their fellow workers. Obvious stereotypes, they anonymously embody two types of power. The police, at certain times, take charge of the narration: they add an important element to the reconstruction of the facts preceding and explaining Big Louis's death by recounting Tony's past and by pointing out that at the time of the murder he was both Johnny's friend and the victim's bodyguard (*AS*, p. 8). The police play a role in narratological programming by anticipating events in a way that makes sense of their apparently chaotic presentation ("GUARINO: Take away your gun and you'll fall apart like all these other punks" [*AS*, p. 8]; "GUARINO: Lovo is practically done for; he's scared to death!"; "COMMISSIONER [*to Guarino*]: Good, try to find Gaffney; they'll probably try to get him after they get all the others" [*AS*, p. 24]).

To a lesser extent, certainly, than journalism, the police temporarily take on the function of a narrator (n2), which allows us to assume the coexistence of (n1) and (n2) within the narrative instance (N). We may conclude that this narrative instance, itself representing a space of contradiction, redistributes two ideologically contradictory microsemiotics linked to the bipolar opposition we discussed before: hiding/unmasking.

Now that this zone of conflict has been isolated, we may examine it.

Earlier in this study of *Scarface*, when I brought out other semiotic texts (problematics of crossing; inclusiveness/exclusiveness; wrong side/right side), I suggested that we could see functioning in the film "a thematics of exclusion that designates as scapegoat not merely a group defined as morally and socially marginal, but an entire unintegrated ethnic minority." This direct connection with the economic crisis of 1929 was, I believe, made too hastily, and I should like to propose a more careful study of these phenomena.

I shall start from an obvious fact, namely, that it is the Italian minority that is in question (recall the Italian who is, curiously, one of Garston's interlocutors: "It's true! They [the gangsters] only cast dishonor on my people" [*AS*, p. 24]), but it is a fact whose limits must be defined. "Every incident in this film is based on fact," according to the credits in the French version of the film, and indeed, we have seen how faithful the film's scenario is to the actual facts as reported by the press at the time. In that case, one might wish to object, how, where, and why would ideology be functioning? And yet ideology is operating, but it is true that it operates—as always—in textuality. I have just shown this in part.

Here, we might apply an approach borrowed from the sociology of content, the better to pinpoint just how a true sociocriticism of cultural objects differs from it. Thus, I shall make brief use of a 1946 study by Bernard Berelson and Patricia J. Salter: "Majority and Minority Americans: An Analysis of Magazine Fiction."[12] The corpus analyzed by these two researchers consists of 198 short stories published in eight major magazines between 1937 and 1943 and chosen at regular intervals (first, third, and fifth) for each magazine. The themes generally have to do with love affairs and family and marital problems; we also find a few adventure stories. Almost all the stories are set on the East Coast, most frequently in New York, and practically never in the South. Rapidly summarized, the conclusions reached by these studies are as follows.

(1) *Distribution of characters.* Of 900 identifiable characters, there are only 16 blacks and 10 Jews. While ethnic minorities (Mexican Americans, Italian Americans, Japanese Americans, Irish Americans, Jews, blacks) make up 40 percent of the population at the time, they appear here in a ratio of one to ten.

(2) *Role of the characters.* The important roles are most frequently held by white Americans. "Positive" roles (that is, those that portray likeable, gracious, wise, desirable, respectable, honest characters) are reserved for them. Those roles given to minorities are less positive and are most frequently one-dimensional stereotypes. Certain of these characters are like objects serving to create a specific ambience (thus one American heroine is described as talking politely with an Italian flower-seller).

(3) *Character traits*. Here are a few examples of stereotypes: the ignorant and ridiculous Negro; the Italian gangster with scars on his face; the wicked and wily Jew; the emotional Irishman; the brutish and stupid Pole. The authors of this article note than when stereotypes are applied to ethnic groups such as blacks, Jews or Italian Americans, they function as xenophobic stimuli. The authors add that studies on mass attitudes have shown that people have very set notions about the characteristics and behavior of members of marginal groups, very definite mental images of what people who are *different* from themselves believe and do.

(4) *Status of characters*. White Americans live well and their comfortable lifestyle is shown in descriptions of their clothing, food, and homes. They apparently deserve this level of lifestyle since the source of their wealth is rarely mentioned; this is not the case of members of ethnic groups, about whom, when they are wealthy, the stories think it appropriate to mention how they got their wealth. This seems to mean that it is perfectly normal for white Americans to belong to the highest strata of society, whereas if ethnics do, it calls for an explanation because it is so exceptional. Furthermore, only rarely do white Americans marry nonwhite Americans.

(5) *Characters' goals*. White Americans are idealistic; the others are materialistic.

The best-treated nonwhite American characters are those who come closest to the white, Anglo-Saxon, Protestant type.

Berelson and Salter argue that these stereotypes may be explained by the necessity of creating a style of writing at once fast-paced and conformist, as well as by the needs of a heterogeneous audience that requires the use of well-known and widely recognizable symbols of identification. It is obvious, however, that these stereotypes reactivate the predispositions of a hostile audience only too ready to find in them fuel to feed their xenophobia.

This study has been useful, for it brings out, in fact, all the stereotypes used in the film: apart from the Italian gangsters, there is Epstein, writ of *habeas corpus* in hand, who embodies the wily and wicked Jew. However, the most revealing scenes are the ones devoted to the description of the Italian family: the mother is portrayed through clothing and gesture that marginalize her; she is seen in her folkloric aspect, in a home marked by poverty. This fleeting vision seems to be there only as a point of reference with respect to what Camonte is to become. His rapid rise to wealth is marked by a copious series of indexes (cigars, bundle of money given to his sister, jewelry, cars, apartment, shirts, grotesque self-satisfaction, etc.). As if performing the function of narrator, Poppy cruelly underlines many times the vulgarity of the newly rich: "How elegant you are. . . . I see you're wearing jewelry . . . *an heirloom, of course?* (*AS*, p. 17). Tony's leitmotif: "They don't give them away," incessantly reproduces the view the prevailing ideology has that the marginal person can get rich only by illegal means. What is said about Camonte is equally valid for Big Louis or Lovo ("Look at me . . . I'm rich. I have a house, a car, the prettiest girls" [*AS*, p. 6]).

Thus, filmic writing undergoes a contamination that is all the more insidious since it seems to be perfectly adapted to its subject, and since its scenario seems to produce by itself these iconograms of stereotypical identification that Berelson and Salter's study shows are imposed from the outside and produced by specific mental structures.

The observations of *content analysis* must be distinguished, however, from my own on one important point: whereas my analysis is concerned with modalities of *intratextual* functioning of certain ideological traces that, by their intersection, define zones of conflict, Berelson and Salter's study allows us to connect *Scarface* directly to the entire cultural production of a particular society. Indeed, their work demonstrates how a society is organized by a secondary modeling system whose ideological traces are reproduced in *Scarface*. These traces may be seen in the American novels more or less contemporary with *Scarface–The Great Gatsby* comes especially to mind. Camonte is in some way an exaggerated carica-ture of F. Scott Fitzgerald's hero, who is described by Tom as "Mr. Nobody from Nowhere."[13]

Juxtaposing the two works, we can see explicit echoes of Scott Fitzgerald's 1925 novel in Howard Hawks's film: thus, the illuminated sign *The World Is Yours* can be compared with the gigantic blue eyes of Dr. T. J. Eckleburg, which "look out of no face, but, instead, from a pair of enormous yellow spectacles which pass over a non-existent nose,"[14] concrete markers of the media, with reference to which the narrative seems to unfold in both cases.

One may also recall, in the sumptuous affairs staged every week by James Gatz, alias Jay Gatsby, son of "shiftless and unsuccessful farm people" of the Mid-dle West, the grotesque spectacle of Tony drunk with his newly acquired power and wealth. Gatsby's fortune is the talk of New York high society, and gives rise to all kinds of legends about his past as murderer, adventurer, or *bootlegger*. "Contemporary legends such as 'the underground pipeline to Canada' attached themselves to him and there was one persistent story that he didn't live in a house at all, but in a boat that looked like a house and was moved secretly up and down the Long Island shore" (p. 88).

In the sequence in which Camonte displays to Poppy his piles of shirts in order to seduce her, we see an explicit index of this intertext:

> Recovering himself in a minute he opened for us two hulking patent
> cabinets which held his massed suits and dressing gowns and ties, and
> his shirts, piled like bricks in stacks a dozen high. . . . He took out a
> pile of shirts and began throwing them, one by one, before us, shirts of
> sheer linen and thick silk and fine flannel which lost their folds as they
> fell and covered the table in many-colored disarray" (pp. 83–34)

Behind these two fundamentally different narratives, the same ideological trace is governing the writing process: from the very first lines of the novel, the narrator, Nick Carraway, whose family descends, he claims, from the Dukes of Buccleuch, rejects Gatsby and his world with the scornful remark: "Gatsby . . . represented everything for which I have an unaffected scorn" (p. 8). Fascinated by Gatsby's personality, at the same time he often criticizes him from the standpoint of his own values: "And I was looking at an elegant young roughneck, a year or two over thirty, whose elaborate formality of speech just missed being absurd. Sometime before he introduced himself I'd got a strong impression that he was picking his words with care" (p. 47). Nick's comment on the autobiographical history he hears right out of the protagonist's mouth signals his constant suspicion: "He looked at me sideways, and I knew why Jordan Baker had believed he was lying. . . . And with this doubt, his whole statement fell to pieces, and I wondered if there wasn't something a little sinister about him, after all. . . . For a moment I suspected that he was pulling my leg but a glance at him convinced me otherwise" (pp. 60–61).

By juxtaposing Gatsby's fantasy ("I am the son of some wealthy people in the Middle West. . . . I was brought up in America but educated at Oxford, because all my ancestors have been educated there for many years . . . it is a family tradition" [p. 60]) with the truth about him ("James Gatz, that was really, or at least legally, his name. . . . His parents were shiftless and unsuccessful farm people—his imagination had really never accepted them as his parents at all" [pp. 88–89]), Nick demystifies Gatsby's mask. In doing so, he demystifies the man behind the mask, thus presenting the narrative instance as though itself enslaved to an ideological instance manipulating iconograms of stereotypical identification such as facial characteristics ("The friends looked out at us with the tragic eyes and short upper lips of southeastern Europe," [p. 63]); or by scrupulously conforming to racial or social "models": Gatsby, being who he is, can only be an ignoramus, and the pages of his books covering the shelving of his magnificent "high Gothic library, panelled with carved English oak," have never been cut. One evening one of his guests comments on this fact in particularly scornful terms: "Absolutely real—have pages and everything. I thought they'd be a nice durable cardboard. Matter of fact, they're absolutely real. Pages and—Here! Lemme show you. . . . This fella's a regular Belasco. It's a triumph. What thoroughness! What realism! Knew when to stop, too—didn't cut the pages. But what do you want? What do you expect?" (pp. 44–45).

As for Poppy in *Scarface*, she certainly must be compared with *Daisy*. But what does the choice of such first names mean? We note first of all that in Scott Fitzgerald's novel the narrator insinuates some doubt about the young woman's origins, presenting her as not belonging to the WASP class (" 'The idea is that we're Nordics, I am and you are, and you are and—' after an infinitesimal hesitation he included Daisy with a slight nod" [p. 17]). In a later passage, he describes another character, Benny McClenahan, as always accompanied by four young women, about whom Nick, while having forgotten their first names, remembers that "their last names were either the melodious names of *flowers and months* or the sterner ones of the great American capitalists whose cousins, if pressed, they would confess themselves to be" [p. 59]). Should we conclude that these two first names, Poppy and Daisy, are functioning in the text to indicate Jewishness? I would be inclined all the more to think so, since in the logic of the ideology of *Scarface*, Poppy's blondness, which clashes with the milieu of dark-haired Mediterraneans, cannot be referring us to the Nordic racial type because it is in a compromised position in the universe of Evil. In that case, the name given her would be neutralizing the iconogram of her blond hair. Does Gatsby's refusal of his family background ("his imagination had never accepted them as parents") stem from the same cause? The narrator plants another seed of doubt when he distinguishes between the Gatzes' *real* name (which is never revealed to us), and their *legal* name, consequently synonymous here with inauthenticity and usurpation.

In turn, however, Gatsby in some ways prefigures John Foster Kane insofar as the beginning of his rise in society is indirectly linked to the mining of precious metals. Dan Cody, whom James meets one afternoon on the shore of Lake Superior, and who befriends the boy, is a "product of the Nevada silver fields, of the Yukon, of every rush for metal since seventy-five" (p. 90). But this new paternity is itself presented here as demonic; it is in fact at the side of this "pioneer debauchee, who during one phase of American life brought back to the Eastern seaboard the savage violence of the frontier brothel and saloon," that "the vague contour of Jay Gatsby had filled out to the substantiality of a man" (p. 91). Thus, from *Scarface* to *Citizen Kane*, and including magazine short stories and the novels of Scott Fitzgerald, we may observe, at various levels and organized in different systems, the features of an ideological matrix.

To better understand the interaction of these contradictions in the filmic text, we shall return to the question of minority and majority in America between 1920 and 1930, and examine the whole problem from a certain distance.[15]

At the time the American nation was born, the concept of immigration was based on an enlightenment doctrine that was the product of northern European Protestant culture, according to which the country's greatness resided in the diversity and the multiplicity of its origins. The idea had two corollaries: (1) America was a land of refuge, and (2) every person had the right to leave his native land and move to a place where he might find sustenance and happiness. But the consequences of the application of this doctrine were to come into contradiction with the cultural traditions of an Anglo-Saxon Protestant society—a contradiction that was to be hidden as long as the North American economy needed labor.

Around 1880, another point of view began to be heard: the immigrants were accused of "increasing the rift of classes, complicating the slum problem, causing boss-rule and straining the old moralities. These difficulties, like the immigrants themselves, centered in the recklessly expanding cities."[16] Moreover, with the increasing scarcity of fertile land, people began to realize that America's natural resources had their limits, and the sacred principle of laissez-faire began to be called into question.

The first measures aimed at controlling immigration were put into effect in 1882, just before an economic depression. As this depression became more severe in the 1890s, a movement favoring a restrictive policy spread and led to the first Immigration Act in 1891. At the beginning of the twentieth century, with the return of prosperity and despite the efforts of the Immigration Restriction League founded in Boston in 1894, this policy of control was fought by chambers of commerce and by the National Association of Manufacturers because economic expansion and the simplification of industrial techniques required an unskilled labor force. The immigrant population became larger and larger (more than one million immigrants per year from 1905 to 1914). This lull only delayed the passage of new restrictive laws in 1917, 1921, and especially in 1924, with the passage of the National Act. The war with Germany "stirred public opinion like a cyclone." Americans discovered all at once that they could not remain apart from world conflicts and that inside the country were millions of unassimilated people. This emotional climate affected mental structures; patriotic loyalty was confused with conforming; marginality was suspected of potential treachery.[17]

Thus we see that fluctuations in the mental structures of legislation were directly related to economic crises. Moreover, restrictions were to be even more severe at the time of the Great Depression in 1930.

These economic determinants are, however, not the only ones worth mentioning. Higham notes two other factors that are part of the superstructure.

(1) *The shock of foreign cultural models.* In contrast to the first wave of immigration, which was predominantly Protestant and British, the second wave, extending from 1820 to the National Act of 1924, was much more heterogeneous; it consisted largely of southern European Catholics. This second wave played an important role in the shaping of an urban industrial mentality; increasingly, these new arrivals settled in the cities. (In 1890, 62 percent of foreign-born citizens were city-dwellers, whereas only 26 percent of whites whose parents were born in the U.S. lived in cities.)

In contrast to the individualism of an older America that was not amenable to city life, the immigrant cultures, by nature, impelled the new arrivals toward collective action. Thus the labor unions were dominated by first- or second-generation immigrants; their most effective leaders were Irish, German or Jewish; they did a better job of attracting immigrants than the political parties.

The immigrants succeeded in forging, as well, an urbanized mass culture to replace the traditions they could not transplant intact. It is not surprising that they found the substance of their collective life in the stimuli of mass media. They were the pioneers of the production of a mass culture: in 1835 James Gordon Bennett, a Scotsman, launched the *New York Herald*; a Hungarian, Joseph Pulitzer, presented himself as the immigrants' spokesman in the *New York World*; in the 1850s an Irishman developed advertising techniques in the first high circulation weekly, the *New York Ledger*.

> The prominence of immigrant editors in the creation of mass circulation newspapers and magazines suggests that the need to adjust to a cosmopolitan society and an unfamiliar culture nurtured a burning passion to communicate and an instinctive feeling for what is immediately transmissible to an amorphous public. Americans became a nation of newspaper readers because what they shared was not a common past but rather the immediate events of the present: the news.[18]

(2) *The influence of certain currents of thought.* (a) Social Darwinism, which is responsible for the confusion between natural history and national history, and which justified the theories held by certain Anglo-Saxon thinkers, according to which nations are analogous to species struggling for their survival. (b) "Eugenic" theories resulting from the development of the science of genetics, and which encouraged other thinkers to call for the improvement of society through the preventive elimination of negative traits. (c) A new anthropological vision that, in William Z. Riplay's book *The Races of Europe* (1899), distinguished three European races: the first, Nordic (northern Europe); the second, Alpine (central Europe); and the third, Mediterranean (southern Europe).[19]

The importance of Riplay's theories in America in the 1920s and 1930s can be seen in the American novels more or less contemporary with *Scarface*. It figures importantly, for example, in the following passage from *The Great Gatsby*:

> "Civilization's going to pieces," broke out Tom violently. "I've gotten to be a terrible pessimist about things. Have you read 'The Rise of the Colored Empires' by this man Goddard?"
>
> "Why, no," I answered, rather surprised by his tone.
>
> "Well, it's a fine book, and everybody ought to read it. The idea is if we don't look out the white race will be—will be utterly submerged. It's all scientific stuff; it's been proved." . . .
>
> "Well, these books are all scientific," insisted Tom, glancing at [Daisy] impatiently. "This fellow has worked out the whole thing. It's up to us, who are the dominant race, to watch out or these other races will have control of things." . . .
>
> "The idea is that we're Nordics. I am, and you are, and you are, and—" After an infinitesimal hesitation he included Daisy with a slight nod. . . . "—And we've produced all the things that go to make civilization—oh, science and art, and all that. Do you see?" (p. 17)

In a more or less close connection with this intellectual climate, the partisans of restrictive measures tried to explain that southern and eastern Europeans, who comprised the majority of the new waves of immigration, were not only dangerous but also unassimilable at the racial level; the dangers threatening the nation thus came from a change in the migrants' countries of origin.

I have dwelt for some time on this situation of historical conflict because it generated ideological systems that were, in turn, invested in the textual structures of the film in forms that are interesting to analyze. There is no doubt that observable reality underwent a process of transformation in passing though the two microsemiotic systems we have described, and which encoded them in textual structures. But why these microsemiotics and not others? How can we explain that it is precisely these two codes of transformation that are at work here? Everything I have just said answers such questions. The narrative instance reconstructs the totality of a new urban way of life and a new culture based on collective action. Whatever the reality behind that vision, we cannot help seeing in the organization of the beer racket the transparent caricature of a syndicate whose objectives are being diverted and perverted for the sake of individual self-interest. But perhaps we can even better understand this vision (ecological well before its time) of urban life presented right at the start of the film in its least seductive aspects—a bleak dawn sullied by the city's trash—and that throughout the film gives us only negative images of the city (the sordid atmosphere of bars, streets taken over by gangs). The journalistic writing I have termed a microsemiotic is integrated into a larger system which appropriates everything that is said, everything that is thought about this marginal world of the 1930s. This example, like my study of a text from the Spanish Golden Age, leads me to think that codes of transformation are selected by the cultural object according to their contiguity with respect to observable reality and to the collective vision of it.

In *Scarface*, this vision is organized around the value system of white, Anglo-Saxon, Protestant ideology. The authentic values (in the Goldmannian sense) that are operating most obviously in the film include puritanism, glorification of work and thrift, and family. Let us pause for a moment on this last point and remember that Prohibition was a focus for the fears of the dominant group. The leaders of the Anti-Saloon League delighted in pointing out the correlation they established between the rise of the number of saloons and the rise in the immigrant population in the 1890s. Often it was the newly arrived immigrants who ran them and who frequented them. The ASL saw the saloon as a place of perdition for the worker who wasted his money and his health there, and as a threat to the "Victorian" home. Thus the struggle against alcoholism—which involved a loss of physical and moral control and gave rise to vulgar, blasphemous drunkenness unleashed on the streets—was linked to the struggle against prostitution. It was a matter of protecting the "American family." In this connection, Camonte's mother's home serves as a foil, for it is the setting for a number of countervalues: the inarticulate mother humiliated by her own children ("She told me:'Shut up and mind your own business' just like you told me!" [*AS*, p. 30]), the marked absence of a father (she is presented as Camonte's mother and not as Mrs. Camonte), wine on the table, Cesca described by her mother as an "easy woman" ("I'm always telling her. Come home. . . . She met a man and they both came home together" [*AS*, p.31]). Her home's lack of conformity to the American model makes it a breeding ground for vice.

Thus the image confirms the fears of the Prohibition party, which, in 1870, asked the government to do something about the saloons, white slavery, gambling, and, in general, all the "worthless, dangerous, disorderly, unproductive elements within the United States threatening the purity, the tranquility and happiness of the American home."[20] "The purity of the American home"—that is the leitmotif of the pietists who asked the State to take charge of public morals and protect the essentially pietistic characteristics of the American way of life.[21]

Thus we are touching upon a final aspect of this situation of conflict: the religious component. In the course of the nineteenth century, and probably as a response to the second wave of immigration, generations of Americans were incited to a more or less virulent anti-Catholicism by Protestant preachers such as Lyman Beecher, who, at the same time as he fought alcoholism, predicted a war between Christianity and "popery" for the possession of "the American soul and soil." Even if they did not share this apocalyptic vision, many Protestants nevertheless considered Catholic immigrants to be members of an inferior class, illiterate and vulnerable to the temptations of evil. "They seemed," writes Norman H. Clark, "in need of directions to honor the Sabbath, to resist the liquor traffic, and to assimilate the bourgeois lifestyle. They seemed too much given to an open and public quality of life—they congregated in saloons—than to a private dignity, and too much given to a priestly rather than a bourgeois family discipline."[22]

This last point of conflict as well as all the other elements of the sociopolitical and sociocultural situation we have described were timely again in the presidential campaign of 1928 opposing Alfred E. Smith, the defender of the cultural traditions of the recent immigrants, representing the cities and the abolitionist tendencies, to Herbert Hoover, whose victory represents, in the view of some American historians, "the last major victory of the country over the city, of the old American over the new"; to this Clark replies that Smith lost essentially because he was not born in the United States. In the course of this violent campaign, James Cannon, a Methodist bishop, called Smith "bigoted" and typical of "the Irish Roman Catholic hierarchy of New York City," declaring that Smith's goal was to bring to power "the kind of dirty people that you find today on the sidewalks of New York."[23] Clark summarizes the political atmosphere of the time:

The implication for the older Bryanites was that these men—wet, Catholic, urban, and fabulously wealthy—were about to take over the party and the White House and deliver both to Jews and Catholics who were determined to overwhelm the traditions of the Protestant Republic. During the campaign of 1928, the Reverend Bob Jones was speaking throughout the South to crowds wherever he found them: "I'll tell you, brother, that the big issue we've got to face ain't the liquor question. I'd rather see a saloon on every corner of the South than see the foreigners elect Al Smith President.[24]

Let us look once more at the inscription in *Scarface* of this view of the facts: Angelo stumbling over the word *secretary* and Camonte over the expression *Habeas corpus* reproduce the stereotype of the ignorant immigrant; the theater scene, which is characterized by the stupidity of the gangster's comments and which is only incidental to the story, must be approached from the same point of view. However, it is the incestuous affair between Tony and Cesca that may be problematic from this point of view. Let us note, first of all, that it did not shock the censors for any of the reasons that are generally put forward; in fact, according to Hawks himself (as quoted in Jerome Lawrence, *Actor: The Life and Times of Paul Muni*), the censors felt that the relationship between Camonte and his sister was too beautiful to be attributed to a gangster. Thus, continues Hawks, they did not recognize "the incest of the Borgias." It is true that nothing in the film explicitly refers to the Borgias, but given the anti-Catholic climate I have just described, one cannot help being struck by the fact that this historical connotation was part of the director's *intentions*; in fact, it is to Ben Hecht that we owe the comparison: "The Borgia family is living today in Chicago. And Caesar Borgia is Al Capone."[25] Since, after all, one can treat an incestuous relationship without having in mind a specific historical example, and even if a connotation of this sort were necessary, why make such a specific connection with the Borgias? If, on the other hand, Hawks notes that the "discerning spectator" may perceive this connotation, it is because the character must be treated in a certain way. How and why is it appropriate to see in Camonte the image of a sovereign ("The World Is Yours!") who bases his domination on a perverted doctrine? What is clear in any case — if we leave the film momentarily — is that once again, filmic writing has been ideologically marked, and that the projection of these "precise and specific facts" is being filtered through a mental structure, itself codified by a microsemiotic.

The strong points of this microsemiotic fuse with what I call a discourse of the sacred and the demonic. At its heart is the illuminated sign working at several levels as the symbol of temptation, in the sense, first of all, that it is an invitation to a voyage and solicits desire by its very nature as advertising and by its function; second, by what it says at the mythic level, echoing the diabolic tempter's words in the biblical text: "The world is yours, all its wealth is at your feet," as if this social function revealed itself for what it is, as if it were saying that, as advertising, it is but illusory temptation, illusion, source of sin and evil, in a perfect match of signifier (the medium) and signified; "I am what I say and I say what I am; I give expression to illusions and I am illusion myself." It is an ambivalent sign both of that stretch of the filmic text in which things are hidden, deformed, or perverted, and of that other one in which they denounce themselves as perverse or deformed; marked in this way by the same stigmata that condemn all the media invested in *Scarface* (journalism, film, advertising), a text written in letters of fire, like his own name, which Tony Camonte wishes to write above the city in machine-gun bursts ("I'll write my name over the whole city, and in big letters!" [*AS*, p. 22]). The correlation the filmic text itself establishes between these two phenomena denounces the demonic nature of the protagonist, who, at first fascinated by diabolical messages, later symbolically inscribes them himself in the sky over the city. Let us refer to the levels involved: in the first two cases (*AS*, pp. 19 and 30), the shot shows Tony and Poppy reunited, with the sign in the background, and significantly marks the evolution of their love affair in the context of the gangster's strategy of seduction; the first occurrence precedes the notorious shirt scene); it defines a desire and a dual effect of temptation—direct in Tony's case, indirect in Poppy's case—through the intermediary of a Tony who is both tempter and tempted, and who, because he is a temptor, takes on the diabolical function. But Poppy is the true stake of the contract; she is included in the totality of the world that is coveted: "Some day, I'll look at that sign and I'll say, it's true, it is [you are] mine" (*AS*, p. 19).

The contract is accepted and honored by the two parties (Satan and his instrument). After Lovo's death, Tony reminds Poppy of that implicit commitment: he goes to her place, shows her the illuminated sign, and asks her if she remembers what he told her (*AS*, p. 30). Poppy smiles, and they leave together for Florida. Here one cannot object either that the psychological evolution of the young woman was already broadly outlined (the preceding dancehall scene in which she indicates that she has made a choice), or, *a fortiori*, that no explicit mention of any contract is made. A contract is, in fact, inscribed in the filmic text through the whole mythical text that is invested in it, a mythical text already presented as such in Big Louis's first (and last) words: "Everybody will say: Ah! Big Louis, he has the world at his feet!" (*AS*, p. 7), and which as such denounces the gangster boss, whoever he is, as the chief usurper of the world. This biblical text coincides significantly with the ending of the filmic text; the last shot thereby authenticates its message. In fact, the camera ascends vertically on the policemen and then on the buildings rising up behind them, and frames the illuminated sign. The low-angle shot, obviously signifying here Camonte's Lucifer-like fall, is the penultimate sign of this demonic discourse; it repeats, but at the level of filmic syntax, what was said more explicitly by Camonte's lamentable descent of the stairs, arms open, in a kind of inverted Calvary. But this low-angle shot is itself the support for a final sign: the diabolical phrase, after having flashed, goes out, and only the lighted globe remains visible in the darkness. One cannot better express the idea that Camonte's death liberates the Earth from Satan's power!

Having thrown light on this semantic focalization, we may bring out certain of its semiotic ramifications. We note that in this context the various textual traces which define a character–in particular, the fact that when the killer is about to strike he whistles a well-known tune of the period whose first words evoke a storm ("*Stormy weather* . . . "), a doubly significant phenomenon, first of all, because storms and tempests, in social imagery, establish the habitual contexts in which ghosts or devils make their appearance (in the theater of Shakespeare or Calderón, among others), but also by the very fact that this supernatural object is accompanied or preceded by a sign associated with it which then functions autonomously as a delegated power of the sacred, its threatening force commensurate with its impalpability (in sound or odor). Related to the code of death, which functions here in the narrative only because the successive deaths of Big Louis, Lovo, and Rinaldo have sacralized it, this sign transforms these settlements of account into something more, not valorizing them but, rather, giving them a semantic *surplus value*. Death here surpasses the anecdotal level, not that this sign, at the level of the character's experience of reality, can transform the irruption of the unexpected into an anguished expectancy of its fulfillment, but more simply, because in this way it is the materialization of a force that is beyond us; the concrete and brutal act of crime is transformed into an act programmed by a will superior to the criminal. This semantic modification will be clearer if we relate it to two other phenomena.

(1) Rinaldo's habit of tossing a coin in his hand, which might be alluding to the Chicago killers' practice of placing a nickel in their victim's hand and, more generally, to the ransom the dead have to pay in order to cross the river to the beyond. Thus the same sign can function in a maleficent way, as a foreboding of death, or in a beneficent way, as a propitiatory element; in both cases, it is an index of the beyond.

(2) The series of predictions uttered either by the police commissioner ("Some day you'll make one false move and go downhill . . . and fall to the bottom, you understand, to the very bottom" [*AS*, p. 9]) or by Guarino ("Take away your gun, and you'll fall to pieces just like all the other punks" [ibid.]), or by Camonte's mother ("Some day, when he needs you, he'll use you . . . just like he'd use anybody" [*AS*, p. 12]).

All these textual phenomena consequently define a predetermined text and refer us to the notion of destiny. An obvious index of destiny, the tune Tony the killer habitually whistles makes him subject to forces beyond him. Thus it is that Tony, "inhabited by Satan," bursts out in diabolical laughter at the end of the film, in a blind unleashing of destructive will, at the very instant the floodlights of the authorities bathing the scene in glaring light symbolically represent the struggle of light against darkness. Thus we can see in the background of the narrative the outlines of a Manichean perspective, emphasized even more by the scene the cen-sors had the director add, and which gives an apocalyptic vision of the situation ("The city is full of machine guns . . . Children can't go to school in safety any-more" [*AS*, p. 24]). The values being threatened by this state of affairs (family, school, social order), precisely because they are caught in the orbit of Evil be-come the foundations of Good. Thus, by plunging into the heart of a Manichean struggle between Good and Evil, a specific social group sanctifies the moral cate-gories it honors. The sacred and the demonic define themselves with respect to each other in this manner, as shown by the two following obvious indexes of the functional modalities governing them.

(1) The dancehall where Tony and his gang go in tuxedos and where scenes of violence successively take place (the expulsion of a killer, the threatening rivalry of Tony and Lovo, the expulsion of Cesca by her brother, who teaches a lesson to the dancer with whom he has caught her in the act) bears the name *Paradise*, a paradise where—at least if one accepts my interpretation in which Camonte represents a demonic character—the gangster is flattered and recog-nized as king of the festival. All the elements that tightly weave one scene to an-other (the name of the place, the definition of the gang leader, Big Louis, as mon-arch of the underworld—"he has the world at his feet"; the shape of the streetlamp that reproduces from the very first frames, on the doorstep of the cabaret, the ver-tical and horizontal lines [22nd Street sign] of the Latin cross) establish a relation-ship of identity between the two places. Both are presented in this way as latitudes of perdition, despite (or by the intermediary of) signs that apparently present them as contradictory to what they are.

The gangster himself is escorted by two bodyguards; one of them is named *Angelo* and the other will end up by repenting on the threshold of a new life (Rinaldo). I cannot help seeing in this threesome, *taking account of the semiotic context in which it is functioning*, the distorted projection of Christ surrounded by the two robbers.

(2) This allusion is all the more persuasive since Camonte has a scar on his face in the form of the Latin cross. There is no doubt that this sign echoes the mark of the supernatural that is already inscribed in the killer's tune (*Stormy Weather*), but it is worth noting that it makes it more specific, and that, in con-junction with those I have just mentioned, it illuminates remarkably well the func-tion played by the whole text that has thus been constituted in the course of the film.

Thus we see a discourse of the sacred (*Paradise, Angel, Christ, Cross, cal-vary*), but of a sacred that is subverted—as we have steadily seen—by the demonic. The Latin cross, which seems, curiously, to be related by contiguity or superimposition to the character of Camonte, thereby functions as an index of perversion.

Do these modalities of the functioning of the sacred indicate an investment of dogmatic and theological problems? One might cite in this connection the series of textual marks in which the narrative instance condemns a number of infractions of the fundamental virtues of the Protestant ethic (luxury, lavish spending, idleness, deceit, violence), but it would seem, nevertheless, more correct to see in them only the rejection of a cultural model related to Catholicism, without any deeper matter. Faithful to the nature of the media, *Scarface* avoids the conceptual level and is content to move the viewer by means of a number of *effects* systematically employed.

I turn now to the immediate historical context of *Scarface*. Hoover, the winner of the election, was forced by those who had brought him to power to take restrictive measures against alcoholism; these measures reinforced the provisions of the Volstead Act and became law in March 1929. A wave of arrests took place in 1929 (more than four thousand people were imprisoned for violations of the law), and this repression provoked a violent protest movement. The economic crisis intensified this anti-Prohibitionist feeling: the public became less and less willing to pay federal agents to fight alcohol drinkers; economists noted that the taxes on alcoholic beverages could allow the repayment of the foreign debt in less than fifteen years; the Association Against the Prohibition Amendment, led by several dozen millionaires and a large number of former brewers and distillers, was fundamentally motivated by the realization that a tax on alcohol would greatly reduce the taxes they paid. Thus, after 1926, the Association spent a million dollars a year in its campaign for the repeal of Prohibition. This campaign had the support of the business world and intellectuals. In 1929, a feminist organization was created, the Women's Organization for National Prohibition Reform. In 1931, the Commission on Law Enforcement and Observance, chaired by George Wickersham, submitted its report to the President; it did not propose amendment but did recognize that the situation was difficult and that nothing could be done to improve it.

In the next presidential election, the AAPA financed Roosevelt and the Democrats, favoring the creation of a liberal, anti-Prohibitionist coalition representing urban industrial interests. In 1933 a number of states repealed their dry laws before the Twenty-first Amendment—repealing the Eighteenth—was voted on. A new society was being affirmed. In this battle against Prohibition, the young generation of the middle classes played an important role. Clark writes "that middle-class young people in the United States and in Western Europe were rejecting the social conventions, ideals, and values of their elders."[26] I shall be returning to this question.

Thus we can see that the problems posed by *Scarface* were of burning interest at the time the film was being made; this is why it is presented to us in the form of a space of projected conflicts. For its message cannot be reduced to a single meaning, and we can understand why, despite the difficulties Hawks had with the Hays Office, he published at the time a declaration, reproduced in many newspapers, in which he claimed that the first showings of his film had been delayed by the opponents of Prohibition. We have discerned certain semantic traces in the text of these conflictive zones; but we should particularly note the reflection on the mass media and their social functions, which I link to the polarity revealed by this semiotic analysis (hiding/unmasking), as well as to the intersections of the two microsemiotic systems.

We should also note that it is in a chaotic form and as an effect of displacement (in the Freudian sense) that ideological traces are invested in structures. Each of these traces seems to be disconnected from the ideological system to which it belongs, and to enter into a new configuration to which it transfers its own capacity to produce meaning. It is these ideological traces, in the pure state, which, in abstract form, enter into the combinatory complex of the genotext, and which I believe I have seen in the course of this semiotic analysis.

I shall illustrate this hypothesis by considering the fear the new generation exercised over the old in the 1930s in America. No doubt this social dynamic was transcribed in *Scarface* (as we saw in semiotic text no. 2), but the ideological structure, which undergoes this dynamic, projects it outside of itself by identifying it with all the evils it intends to exorcise. In order to emerge from the collective unconscious, avowal must undergo a displacement. But the problem of the renewal of generations is not the only locus of anguish. The determinants we have passed in review (economic determinants, shock of foreign cultural models, intellectual currents) develop in a certain context; they only illuminate, define, and furnish an intellectual foundation for fears and anxieties that are already widespread.

At a deeper level, what made the restrictionist movement develop in the early decades of the twentieth century was the discovery that immigration was undermining the unity of American culture and threatening WASP dominance.

> The mounting sense of danger—even dispossession—among millions of native-born white Protestants in the period 1910–1930, is not hard to understand. A people whose roots were in the towns and farms of the early republic saw great cities coming more and more under the control of strangers whose speech and values were not their own. A people who unconsciously identified Protestantism with Americanism saw Catholic voters and urban bosses gaining control of the industrialized states. A people whose religion was already badly damaged by modern ideas saw the compensating rigors of their life-style flouted in the saloons and cabarets of a more expressive, hedonistic society.[27]

Clark brings out in his study on Prohibition the profound fear of dispossession experienced by older American Protestants. I see this anguish operating in what I call (to use a concept of René Girard's) the mimetic rivalry enacted in *Scarface*, through a sequence of overthrowal (Big Louis dethroned by Lovo, who will be deposed in turn by Camonte, whose supremacy is threatened upon his return from Florida), systematic repetition at the erotic level (Camonte – Poppy – Lovo; Camonte – Cesca – Rinaldo) as well as at the metaphorical level (advertising billboard *The World Is Yours*; plot of the play the gangsters go to see). On this very point, however, we should refrain from thinking that the ideological instance is content to project these phenomena on the Other, by attributing to the Other those behaviors in which it is not involved itself. On the contrary, it is the ideological instance that seems to generate this sequence, since in every case the provisional victor of these struggles for power seems only to have as objective the imitation of the ideological instance, to be its grotesque parody, and to climb to the social rank it occupies. The conquest of power in the Chicago underworld appears, for that very reason, only as the means of attaining power of a very different nature. Parodic devices, in such a context, are essential to the framework set in place by the narrative instance. On this point, it is useless to dwell on the exaggerated antics of Camonte, whose gestures are magnified by the parodic reflections of Angelo, his double, and which make him a veritable clown. Signs here and there in the filmic text, as well as my semiotic analysis, suggest carnivalization: problematics of crossing; oppositions between inclusiveness and exclusiveness and between right side and wrong side; portrayal of Big Louis as farcical king; latent presence of a dynamic of exorcism. This last secondary modeling system seems to recover and redistribute the microsemiotic systems generated by the mental structures I described earlier. In passing from mental structures to a secondary modeling system, that is, from one level to another, the sign is not abolished in another sign, but it acquires a supplemental meaning, a semantic surplus value resulting from this new phase of the transformational process observable reality undergoes.

At this point in my analysis, it is clear that all the observations we have accumulated confirm René Girard's relation of the *mimesis of appropriation* (mimetic rivalry, Carnival) to the *mimesis of the antagonist*, which "converges two or more individuals on one and the same adversary they all wish to kill" (exorcism represented by Carnival cremation or by the representation of Camonte's death). In Girard's words:

> It is a community's unity that is affirmed in the rite of sacrifice, and this unity rises up in the paroxysm of division when the community claims it is being torn apart by mimetic discord condemned to the endless circularity of vengeful reprisal. The opposition of each against each is brusquely followed by the opposition of all against one. . . . We readily understand what this sacrificial resolution consists in; the community recovers its wholeness altogether, at the expense of a victim not only incapable of defending itself but totally powerless to arouse vengeance.[28]

In my interpretation of Camonte's death, the fantasized reconstruction of the community's unity constitutes the authentic value of the film at the heart of the mechanisms for the generation of meaning. The detours we have taken make this hypothesis perfectly plausible.

One might object that this general conclusion and the description of carnivalization in *Scarface* recall too closely what I have said about Quevedo's *Buscón* to be entirely credible.[29] Far from rejecting this comparison, I think, on the contrary, that it opens up a new debate and a new inquiry: although dependent on quite different determinants, the mental structures generated by the collective anguish of the ruling class in Spain at the beginning of the seventeenth century seem to me strangely similar to those in America during the early decades of the twentieth century. Must we not conclude from this that specific historical facts, both localizable and localized, are capable of reactivating archaic patterns buried deeply in the heart of the cultural context and of being redistributed by the fictional text?[30]

1

2

3

4

5

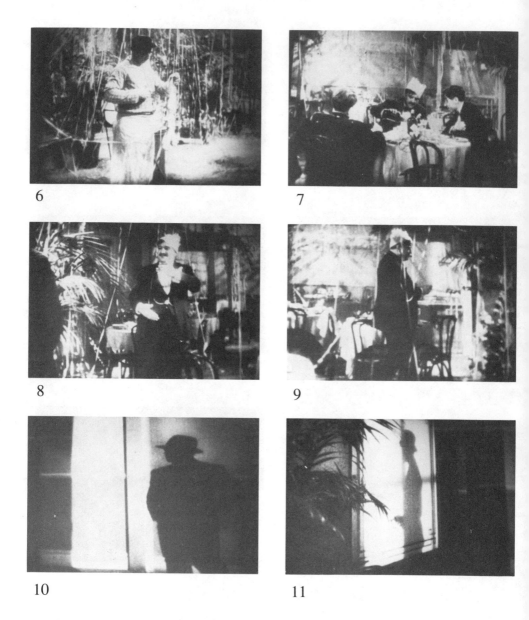

6

7

8

9

10

11

12

13

14

15

18

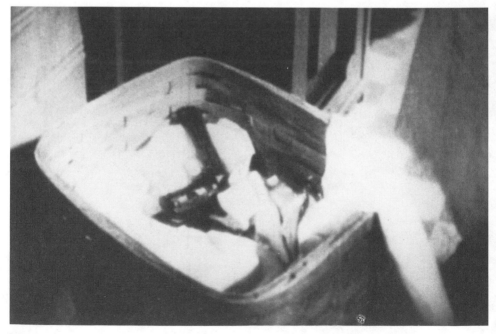

19

20

21

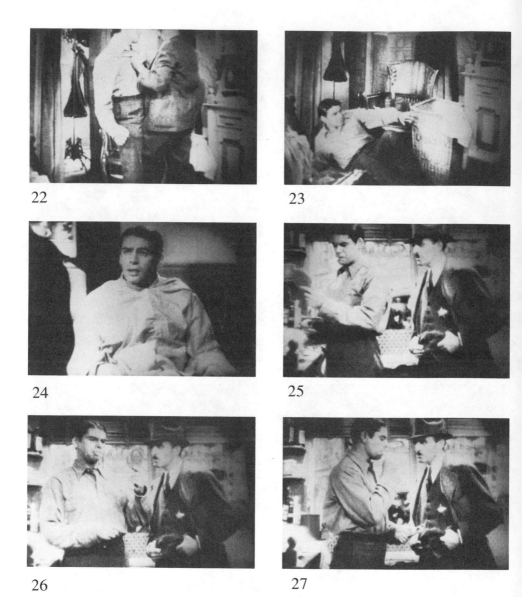

22

23

24

25

26

27

Chapter 9
Ideological and Discursive Formations in Contemporary Mexico

Conscious, Unconscious and Nonconscious: A Sociocritical Approach to Carlos Fuentes's *La región más transparente*

Mi nombre es Ixca Cienfuegos. Nací y vivo en México. D.F. Esto no es grave. En México no hay tragedias todo se vuelve afrenta. Afrenta, esta sangre que me punza como filo de maguey. Afrenta, mi parálisis desenfrenada que todas las auroras tiñe de coágulos. Y mi eterno salto mortal hacia mañana. Juego, acción, fe—día a día, no sólo el día del premio o del castigo: veo mis poros oscuros y sé que me lo vedaron abajo, abajo, en el fondo del lecho del valle. Duende de Anáhuac que no machaca uvas—corazones; que no bebe licor, bálsamo de tierra—su vino, gelatina de osamentas; que no persigue la piel alegre: se caza a sí mismo en una licuación negra de piedras torturadas y ojos de jade opaco. De hinojos, coronado de nopales, flagelado por su propia (por nuestra) mano. Su danza (nuestro baile) suspendida de un asta de plumas, o de la defensa de un camión; muerto en la guerra florida, en la riña de cantina, a la hora de la verdad: la única hora puntual. Poeta sin conmiseración, artista del tormento, lépero cortés, ladino ingenuo, mi plegaria desarticulada se pierde, albur, relajo. Dañarme, a mí siempre más que a los otros;¡ Oh derrota mia, mi derrota, que a nadie sabría comunicar, que me coloca de cara frente a los dioses que no me dispensaron su piedad, que me exigieron apurarla hasta el fin para saber de mí y de mis semejantes!¡ Oh faz de mi derrota, faz inaguantable de oro sangrante y tierra seca, faz de música rajada y colores turbios.

My name is Ixca Cienfuegos. I was born and I live in Mexico City. Which is not so grave: in Mexico City there is never tragedy but only outrage. Outraged, the blood that stings through me like maguey thorns. Outraged, the unchecked paralysis that stains and clots every dawn. Also outraged, my eternal mortal leap toward tomorrow. The game, action, faith, day after day, and not just those days of triumph or defeat; and looking down, I see hidden pores and know that they have held me against the valley's deepest floor. Spirit of Anáhuac, who does not crush grapes but hearts; who drinks no earthly balm . . . your wine is the jelly of your own courage; who does not trap for the flayed pelt of happiness . . . you stalk only yourself, through wet black depths where stone warps and there are jade eyes. Kneeling, crowned with a wreath of cactus, flagellated by your own—by our–hand, your dance adangle from a feather plume and a bus fender. Dead in flowery war, a bar scrap, at the hour of truth, the only timely hour. Poet without compassion, artist of agony, courteous bum who shoots craps with my inarticulate prayer and loses it: condemn me, me always more than others, of my outrage, my downfall never to be known to anyone else, who topples me before unpitying gods and exhorts me on to meetings between my selves only; O face of my destruction, countenance of dry earth and gold blood, tough face of bragging music and mud brown![1]

The Semiotic Texts

First of all, I shall differentiate

(a) function words, among which are
    prepositions: *a* (5 occurrences), *de* (19), *del* (5), *que* (11)

    coordinating conjunctions: *y/o* (7 ← vs. → 2)

(b) determinants, which I shall put in two groups:

    (18 occurrences of *el* (la, lo, los, las) ← vs. → 3 ocurrences of *un* (*una*), noting in passing a clear imbalance to the apparent benefit of the presumed forms.

    Personal pronouns: first person, *me* (5), *mi* (2);
    and third person; *si* (1)
    Possessives: *mi* (6), *mis* (2), *ma* (2), *mis* (1), *nuestro* (2), *su* (4)
    Demonstratives: *esto* (1), *esta* (1)

On this point, we note the preponderance of the first person over the third person (20 ← vs. → 5), as well as the absence of the second person (eventually we shall compare this set to the attributive function of the preposition *de*). This last group of determinants enters into the establishment of our first semiological subset.

1. The *Self/The* Nonself: (31)
   a) → semejantes, como, mismo, propria (→ sin)
      ← otros
   b) determinants 20 ← vs. → 5
2. *Aggression-Torment-Pity*: (23)
   Aggression: (15) defensa, guerra, riña, albur, derrota[3], rajada, afrenta[3], *machaca*, dañar, persigue, (→ caza)
   Torment: (6) torturadas, flagelado, tormento, inaguantable, punza, filo
   Pity: (2) commiseración, piedad
3. *Situational elements*: (20)
   prepositions: en[6], abajo[2]
   concepts of localization: hay, colocar.
   descriptive indexes of the narrative: México D.F., México, Anáhuac, maguey, nopales, lecho, fondo, valle, tierra[2]
4. *Parts of the Body*: (15)
   sangre, sangrante, coágulos, corazones, osamentas, piel, mano, cara, frente, faz[3], ojos (→ veo), poros
5. *Life/Death, Underlain by the Notion of Time*: (14)
   → vivo, nací,

   eterno, mañana, día[3], hora[2], puntual, siempre, fin

   ← muerto, mortal
6. *Movement/Absence of Movement*: (13)
   → salto, hasta, hacia, para, desenfrenada, por[2], camión, comunicar, se pierde, se vuelve
   ← parálisis, suspendida
7. *Festival/Tragedy*: (11)
   → Juego, alegre, danza, baile, plumas, florida, música, relajo, asta
   ← grave, tragedia
8. *Liquid/Solid: (10)*
   → bebe (→ cantina), apurar, licor, vino (→ uvas) licuación, seca

   gelatina

   ← piedras
9. *Light-Colors*: (9)
   Light: auroras, oscuros, opaco, turbios, negra
   Colors: oro, jade, tiñe, colores

10. *Truth-Knowledge*: (8)
    verdad ($\rightarrow$ es^2), ladino, ingenuo
    sé, saber, sabría
11. *Religion-Magic*: (6)
    fe, plegaria, dioses, hinojos, duende ($\leftarrow$ bálsamo)
12. *Whole/Part*: (6)
    todo, todas, nadie, única, *sólo*, desarticulada
13. *Power/Subjection*: (6)
    vedaron, castigo, premio, coronado, exigieron, dispensaron
14. *Identity*: (3)
    nombre, Ixca, Cienfuegos

Remarks on the Formulation and Presentation of These Semiotic Texts

— Ungrouped signs: lépero, cortés, acción, artista, poeta, más, Oh^2
— The texts are presented in descending order of importance, either in the form of dialectical opposites, or as convergent in meaning.
— Certain terms do not seem to be directly related to the groups we are suggesting for them. They may, however, be connected to them by the effect of what I call *derived polarizations*, by means of a sign that is dominant in the field in question. These terms are given in parentheses.
— Terms in italics are those which, in the text, have a negative sign (*no bebe*, for example).
— Every sign in the text has been accounted for, apart from the above-noted exceptions, for a total of 170, if we limit ourselves to the semiotic texts alone. None of them participates in a double or triple grouping.

The Semiotic System

Certain texts, including the following, must be regrouped:

— 1 (*Self/Nonself*) and 14 (*Identity*): 55 occurrences
— 4 *Parts of the Human Body*) and 12 (*Whole/Part*), 21 occurrences, which we shall present in a new dialectical form: *Fragmentation/Wholeness*
— 5 (*Life/Death*) and 6 (*Movement/Absence of Movement*), 27 occurrences

These regroupings display two major semiological polarities. The first is ordered around a transcription of structures of domination, as in the accompanying diagram. This first polarity regroups 75 occurrences, or 40.3 percent of the system.

The second polarity establishes a relation between the problematics of Integrity (*Fragmentation/Wholeness*) and that of Identity (The *Self* and the *Nonself*); it regroups 76 occurrences, or 40.3 percent of the signs.

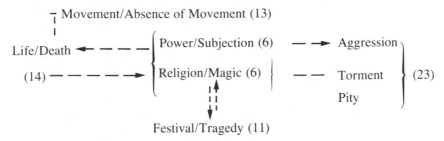

Festival/Tragedy (11)

The formulation of this semiological system transcribes the existence of a relation whose nature and importance must be specified. This entails both structures of dependency and interrelations between a problematic of Integrity and a problematic of Identity.

The Situation of Communication

(1) The first-person singular

The *I* develops a discourse on itself, but the relations it maintains with itself and with its addressee (or addressees) are complex. (See "*flagelado por su propia (por nuestra) mano. Su danza (nuestro baile) suspendida,*" etc.)

First of all a subject, it takes on the oneness of its present (*veo, sé, vivo en México D.F.*) and of its past (*nací, vedaron, exigieron, dispensaron*). The passage from *I* subject to *I* direct object (*me lo vedaron, me lo exigieron*) marks the evolution of a point of view and the somewhat incoherent dynamic of the narrator's vision of his life. The relatively large number of first-person possessives (*mi nombre, mi parálisis, mi eterno salto, mis poros, mi plegaria, mi derrota, mis semejantes*) and personal pronouns (*de mí; a mí*) stress in the same manner the importance of the projection of the *I*.

From the very first lines, we observe that the modes of this projection vary: preceding the *I* expressing himself (*nací, vivo*) is, beginning with "*mi nombre es,*" a first movement of distancing that soon becomes more marked with "*esta, sangre que me punza*" in which the demonstrative, substituting for the possessive, is the perfect translation of this objectivization. The *I* sees and describes himself as the object of his own observation ("*veo mis poros oscuros*"); he is listening to his body, paying close attention to his own life ("*me punza como filo de maguey*").

This distancing ends up in a veritable play of mirrors ("*Oh faz de mi derrota, faz inaguantable*") in which the *I* is confronted with his past, is aware of his defeat and contemplates it. Thus the reflection of the *self* passes back into time (via the mirroring), a journey which, since it is transcribed by preterits (*exigieron, vedaron, dispensaron*), is presented as if not integrated with the present and thus as if not appropriated by the narrator. The positioning of this duality takes place in three phases: recognized as part of a lived experience through the very strong no-

tional content of "Oh derrota *mía*," this failure is first of all objectivized "*mi* derrota," before being projected in the interpellation "*Oh faz de mi derrota*," which
rejects it into otherness.

We shall keep in mind, then, these fluctuations of the projection of the *Self*,
which at times assumes responsibility for the unity and integrity of its person and
at times repudiates them.

(2) *The first-person plural*

Poses implicitly the problem of the second person, since *nuestro* ("*nuestra*
mano", "*nuestro* baile") is capable of several kinds of extension.

Either: I and he (them)

Or: I and thou (you)

In the absence of any other index, we have every right to wonder whether this
we includes the addressee.

(3) *The third-person plural* (me le vedaron, me dispensaron, me exigieron)

Whereas the presence of the *Self* in the foreground is strongly felt, the in-
definiteness of *vedaron, dispensaron, exigieron* projects the source of authority
and power in the distance, in a certain mode of absence, although the semantic
content of these three verbs expresses all the rigor of a situation of subjection.
Readers may be tempted to see, in the form the allusion to this structure of power
takes, the possible transcription of the structure of the Mexican family, ordered
around the indisputable authority of an absent father; others may think, on the
contrary, of the economic and political weight of a North American power,
which, at the same time it is determinant, remains hidden by the interplay of ideological superstructures. My belief is that this textual structure only repeats the
characteristics of the instance of domination and power in a given society, instances which, as in any society, are recreated from an identical form of
reference.

(4) *The third-person singular*

We note that *él* is perceived both as difference and as likeness ("*flagelado por
su propria [por nuestra] mano. Su danza [nuestro baile]*").

This superimposition of persons (he + I) or (I/thou) leads us to pose the problem of the *I*'s identity.

The *I* is both:

—a man of flesh and blood (*nací y vivo, esta sangre, poros oscuros, mi nombre*)

—the mythical representation of the sun/god: ("*mi parálisis desenfrenada que
todas las auroras tiñe de coágulos*"; "*y mi eterno salto mortal hacia mañana*").

The identification of these two natures is emphasized:

—by the very name of the narrator, Ixca Cienfuegos (literally: 'He who burns with
a hundred fires")

—by the repetition of *afrenta* in which an idea of consubstantiality is being
affirmed (*Afrenta esta sangre, Afrenta mi parálisis*, an idea repeated later in
"*eterno salto mortal*."

We shall add to this series of indexes, all of which refer us to a mythical figuration of the sun, the dual image of the sun's course and the serpent biting its own tail inscribed in *"se caza a sí mismo."*

This very consubstantiality makes the *Self* the site where the contradictory principles of *life* and *death* come together ("eterno *salto mortal*" announced by *"mi parálisis* desenfrenada").

It is quite remarkable that the *yo* assumes (*"mi eterno salto mortal"*) or does not assume this dual nature (*"esta sangre" "mi parálisis"*); these fluctuations repeat, at the mythical level, a systematic duality, which thus far seemed merely a characteristic of discourse.

The third-person plural refers to two different groups:

(a) that of the gods, who have rejected the *Self* in the group of humans ("que me exigieron apaurarla hasta el fin para saber de mí y de mis semejantes");
(b) that of humans, who may be perceived as similar ("mis *semejantes*") but equally as different ("más que a *los otros*"), and whose destiny the narrator seems to share, in any case, despite this difference.

We note that we are still passing through the *Self*, which violently affirms itself here ("saber *de mí* y de mis *semejantes*, dañarme a *mí* más que a los otros") to move toward identity or distinction, making the narrator the site of difference and of sameness where once again contrary principles are being resolved.

This interplay between Identification and Distancing is repeated in the way the two levels of the sacred and the profane are juxtaposed or intersect one another (*"muerto en la guerra florida, en la riña de cantina"*; *"mi plegaria . . . se pierde albur, relajo"*), in a systematics of contradiction (*"lépero cortés, ladino ingenuo"*), in the fluctuations affecting the transcription of a religious and cultural context, seen in both its complexity and its syncretistic tendencies.

The preceding remarks allow us to grasp how the narrator can speak of himself in the third person. Indeed, it is the same character apprehending himself from two different perspectives; this is clear from the relations between the respective images defining him or from the expressions used to describe his attitude. The first refer us, in both cases, to the myth of the sun:

Perspective of yo: "Ixca Cienfuegos," "eterno salto mortal"
Perspective of él: "se caza a sí mismo en une licuación negra de piedras torturadas" (allusion to an intense source of heat)

The second refer to the theme of self-flagellation or sacrifice:

Perspective of él: "flagelado por su propria . . . mano"
Perspective of yo: "dañarme a mí siempre más que a los otros" (the ambiguity of the subject of *dañar* is resolved in the context of these relationships)

This interplay of perspectives is another index of the manner in which the narrator assumes his consubstantiality when he expresses himself in the first person, or declines it when he distances himself with respect to his divine nature. At the level of psychoanalytical discourse these associated phenomena constitute true schizophrenia. Whether it be the situation of communication (play of perspectives), images (interplay of mirroring effects), or discourse (distancing), the law governing the development of the text transcribes a shattering of the self, whose successive figurations create new reflective interplays (see accompanying diagram).

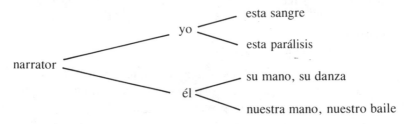

The Internal Organization of the Poetic Text and Psychoanalytic Discourse

The y/o (and/or) Opposition

The dissociative functioning of the *o* ("del premio *o* del castigo," "de un asta de plumas *o* de la defensa de un camión"), which refers us again to the realm of difference and rupture, is opposed by the functioning of the *y*, which creates sequences, recognizes resemblances grouped in sets, and constructs continuity: "y mi eterno salto mortal" (sequence); "piedras torturadas *y* ojos de jade," "oro sangrante *y* tierra seca" (resemblance); "nací *y* vivo" (continuity).

Let us pause to examine the example I have chosen of sequence—"*y mi eterno salto mortal*"—in which coordination is not functioning at the level of the text, but refers to the development of an underlying discourse, for it creates an obvious rupture in the exteriorization of thought, at the same time suggesting a latent problematic coherence in the order of subjectivity. Other indexes of a discourse remaining immersed in the "not said" are connected to this first case; such is the case of "me *lo* vedaron," in which the nature of the interdiction eludes us; we may see in this nonformulation the hiding of a kernel of fixation constructed on a structure of dependency problematized in terms of repression.

Star-shaped Splitting of the Syntagmatic Construction

Whichever of the two perspectives is involved, the relative clauses are not dependent upon a principal clause, but specify the content of a sign describing an attitude or a feeling that is itself connected to a point of origin that, in its turn, eludes us (see the accompanying diagram).

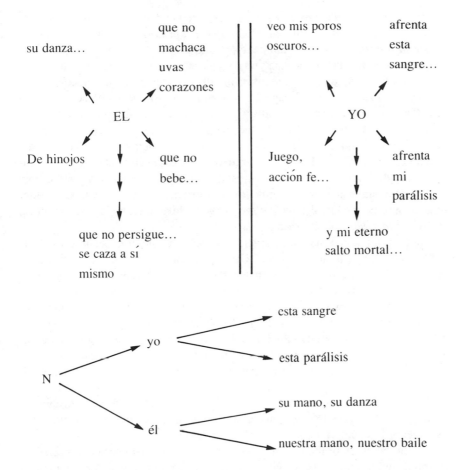

In both cases, the relative clauses refer to a shadowy zone in which the true, deep personalities of the *yo* and the *él* are hidden and protected. Thus, the respective splittings of the *yo* and the *él* repeat in an interplay of mirrors a systematics of diffraction, explicit at the level of the utterance, in the allusion to a body "*fracturado, de trozos centrífugos*" or to a prayer "*desarticulada.*"[2] Here we might state that this corporeal disarticulation (at the level of the utterance) is but the material reflection of a decomposition of the personality, whose symptoms appear through textual structures but which explicit discourse refuses to recognize as such. It is thus essentially with respect to a discourse of the unconscious (at the level of textual structure) that the discourse of the utterance is constantly established. In the same manner, we shall see attempts to recover or reconstruct a coherence in the polarization organized around the axis "*nuestra* mano," "*nuestro* baile," in which, through the plural possessive, *the attraction of unitary forces*

and the quest for a collective authenticity, destined to define itself, in turn, by opposition to the nonself, is affirmed. *Difference is thus born, once again, of resemblance in the framework of a dialectic* operating at every level.

This recourse to the psychoanalytic code is extremely interesting to the extent
that it refers us indirectly to an entire intellectual current that is ideologically
marked and that aims at defining and describing the Mexican character empirically through collective psychoanalysis. The major expressions of this current of
thought are well known: *El perfil del hombre y de la cultura en México*, by Samuel
Ramos (1934), and *El laberinto de la soledad*, by Octavio Paz. Thus, from
Samuel Ramos to Carlos Fuentes, an entire corpus has been established that, running through different historical circumstances (1934–58), is characterized both
by thematic similarities and by functional differences, a corpus whose broader
context may be identified by using the analysis developed by A. Dessau in *La
novela de la revolución mexicana*.[3]

After having noted that nationalistic bourgeois ideology under Porfirio Díaz
is nothing but a "classic liberalism" corresponding to premonopolistic laissez-
faire capitalism, Dessau observes that in the twentieth century this bourgeoisie,
having reached power in 1938, must forge a new ideology capable of responding
to its new situation, which is characterized by a dual confrontation with imperialism and with the working class. In the formation of this new ideology, Dessau
defines two essential points—the reproblematization of the concept of freedom,
which will henceforth be defined as a function of national self-interest, and a
valorization of the notion of Mexican national character, which obscures all
differences in social class.

Despite reservations about certain minor points, I find this thesis entirely convincing, and I propose that we consider the components of this new ideology before seeing how they function in Carlos Fuentes's text.

(1) The ontology of the notion of Mexican national character is supported by
two philosophical ideas of unequal importance. The point of departure for the first
is Samuel Ramos's essay, which, though it attracted little attention at the time of
its publication (1934), was rediscovered in the 1940s and nourished a whole current of thought (Agustín Yañez, "El pelado mexicano," in *Letras de Mexico*,
1940; Octavio Paz, *El laberinto de la soledad*; Emilio Uranga, *Análisis del ser
mexicano*, 1952; Leopoldo Zea, *Conciencia y posibilidad del mexicano*, 1952).
This quest had already been posited by Antonio Caso in 1910:

> Individual and collective life is the quest for absolute happiness, which
> can never be found, and the finding of something better that is con-
> structed each day. Mexico must possess three cardinal virtues in order
> to become a strong people: wealth, justice and enlightenment. . . .
> Turn your attention to the soil of Mexico, the resources of Mexico, our
> customs and traditions, our hopes and our longing, to what we truly
> are.[4]

It was also a part of the objectives of the Ateneo de la Juventud, which, reacting to the materialistic development of capitalism, provoked in large part by the influx of foreign capital, simultaneously glorified spiritual, cultural, and nationalistic values that were, for the most part, taken up and developed in new forms by the *contemporáneos*. Thus dream, imagination, and intuition were valorized as forms of knowledge at the expense of everything having to do with empiricism and experimentalism, and especially important was the *inner universe, the human consciousness, the inner life of the Mexican* that the psychological novel of the 1940s undertook to analyze, as Dessau has shown.

All these investigations, among which there are obvious interrelationships, can thus be grouped around an ontological perspective—the Mexican people—operating at two levels of generalization. However, it is interesting to observe that Samuel Ramos, like the Ateneo de la Juventud or the Gaos school, sought to define the essence of Mexico through the analysis of cultural phenomena presented as authentically Mexican, a methodology that implies the positing, as fundamental hypothesis, of a total identification between the essence of the Mexican national character and the essence of Mexican culture, which at the time could only be the product of an oligarchy and a bourgeoisie. The latter are thus indulging in a narcissistic enterprise, and this Mexican culture is defined as a "Hispanic spirituality transplanted to the New World." This perspective explains certain phenomena that might seem surprising at first glance, in revolutionary or immediately postrevolutionary circumstances: the rediscovery of authors such as Ruiz de Alarcón and Sor Juana Inés de la Cruz; the nostalgia of the colonial period; the glorification of Catholicism and of Hernán Cortés, presented as the father of Mexico—elements found in *El laberinto de la soledad* as well as in the texts of the ideologues of synarchism from approximately the same time (although I would not include Octavio Paz among them).

This current of thought was considerably strengthened at the end of the Spanish civil war by the arrival in Mexico of José Gaos, who taught the historicism of Ortega y Gasset and provided a firmer conceptual foundation for this ontological research.

(2) Insertion of the individual into the framework of a national community: the valorization of the individual is important and represents a constant that, however, does not function as in classic liberalism but, on the contrary, has meaning only in the framework of interrelations between the individual and the community. The individual serves the revolution and, in turn, the revolution permits the individual to flourish. A perfect identification, consequently, is established between the individual level and the collective level ("Individual and collective life is the quest for social happiness"), "the nation is a social being,"[5] and it is no doubt this point of view that accounts for the overlapping of psychoanalytic perspectives (individual/collectivity) in the *Laberinto*. A disciple of Gaos, Leopoldo Zea included this element in his conception of *libertad comprometida*, which Dessau

considers the crux of his philosophic system: "Man is totally obligated to the community. . . . Compromise is not only for the sake of receiving benefits; it is also to receive suffering, if it comes. He who lives in society by this very fact compromises with it."[6]

All of this ontological research, and, more broadly, all of this ideological production, is thus articulated around the identification between the individual and the national community, for this notion of the communal body is essential. It does not exclude the sacrifice of the individual ("Man is totally obligated to the community"), and in that sense, it nourishes a heroic mystique. It underlies the deep structure of a work such as the *Laberinto*, whose authentic value, in Goldmann's sense of the term, it represents under the figure of the *continuous*. No doubt, in other forms that are explicable in terms of the changes that have taken place in the intervening time in the production and circulation of elements participating in the ideology in question, it corresponds as well to the deep structure of Carlos Fuentes's novel. Finally, it is in perfect agreement with the traditional view—which is, moreover, largely justified—but whose relative objectivity is in this manner appropriated by ideological discourse, and which consists in making the Revolution the mortar of national integration.

Let us consider here Carlos Fuentes's direct involvement in this vision, since what interests us is not the discussion of an acknowledged fact, but the analysis of the form the presentation of this fact assumes through the mediation of a veritable mythology.

On the thematic level, a series of indexes in *La región más transparente* repeats the litany of solitude and fragmentation (cuerpo fracturado, trozos centrífugos, las dos orillas, etc.) as well as the quest for unity in the form of allusions to a desire for collectivity (juntos, nuestros), for the concerted effort needed to make the social machinery function (engranaje), for community brotherhood (tocarse los dedos), for a common destiny (el pozo de la gelatina común, la mezcla), or through religious symbolism (hostia). Moreover, the last lines of the text significantly repeat the words said by Ixca Cienfuegos at the very beginning of the novel: "Here we fall, and what are we going to do about it? But cling to me, brother. If only to see if someday our fingers touch." "And the voice of Ixca Cienfuegos which passed, with the tumultuous silence of all memories, through the city dust and wished to touch Gladys García's fingers and say to her, only say to her: Here we bide. What are we going to do about it? Where the air is clear."[7]

This national integration, perceived as the construction of and the quest for ontological wholeness, is presented as a vital necessity allowing us to confront the threatening presence of the *nonself*. González Ramírez stresses this admirably: "The Mexican revolution considered the nation as a social entity requiring integration, with the aim of preventing foreign powers from absorbing it and internal anti-social forces from weakening it. Thus, integration and defense are fundamental factors in Mexican nationalism."[8]

This play between *integración* and *defensa*, wholeness of the *self* and the *non-self*, is but a concrete figuration of the conceptual axis I believe is functioning in the text and that we have defined as a dialectic of sameness and otherness, itself the direct product of a specific ideology that can be summarized as in the accompanying diagram:

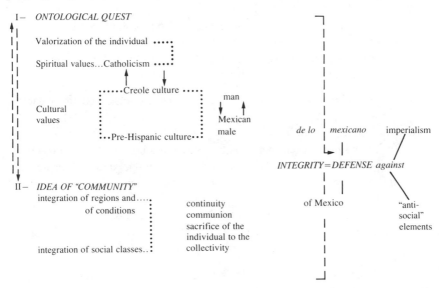

MEXICO: IDEOLOGY OF THE NATIONALISTIC BOURGEOISIE

All these elements make up a galaxy of concepts and notions in play behind the process of economic transformation, and their circulation is closely dependent on changes in the national and international economic situation. They constitute, furthermore, an ideological trace that branches out, grows more complicated, richer, or more schematic in relation to the various contexts and cultural and political structures they penetrate. Their conjuncture alone can describe their original ideological site, but when a period is saturated with them, they are capable of mediating one's whole vision of the facts and, for that very reason, of contaminating different, even contradictory, ideological loci. Thus, they do not serve as indexes of systematic reference in themselves; it is the way they function in thought that alone gives them ideological significance.

It is in this manner, however, that a dominant ideology can exploit for its own profit concepts and attitudes contradictory to it. One is struck by the formal convergence that may exist between the quest for national community proclaimed by a bourgeoisie in power and the goal set by the labor and peasant unions challenging its power—namely, the building of a "classless society," a slogan that sets aside the circumstantial necessity of class struggle in favor of a vision of national community. Similar observations might be made about the struggle between capital and labor, a notion disappearing or becoming secondary in favor of the struggle against American imperialism. This bears witness to a transferral that may be considered evidence of ideological recuperation, and it is in this context that the fundamental question of the interpretation of Marxism in Mexico might well be reexamined.

As we reread this page from *La región más transparente*, we notice the clarity and copiousness with which this ideology has been transcribed in it. At the heart of this transcription is the myth of Quetzacoatl, in its traditional iconographic and conceptual representations:

(a) *Iconographic*: a serpent biting its tail ("se caza a sí mismo en une licuación negra de piedras torturadas").

(b) *Conceptual*: a divinity that
   — forbidding human sacrifice, has become a symbol of love ("no machaca uvas-corazones"; que no bebe licor . . . que no persigue la piel alegre") and sacrifice ("De hinojos, coronado de nopales, flagelado por su propia mano")
   — incarnating the contradictory principles of life and death, represents the site where all contradictions are resolved ("eterno salto mortal . . . lépero cortés, ladino ingenuo").

This myth supports an ideological message that we can now identify. If it is true that the text is marked by indexes referring to the *nahuatl* cultural context (Ixca Cienfuegos, Anáhuac, guerra florida), it includes others that allow it to function in a second cultural context originating in the most authentic Spanish spirituality. Thus the portrayal of the god as a self-flagellant ("De hinojos . . . flagelado por su propria mano") does not correspond to any iconographical tradition of the Aztecs, who seem not to have known flagellation; on the contrary, this portrayal evokes images associated with Christian mythology, in the allusion to a person kneeling, crowned with thorns, and who, when flagellating himself, seems to be flagellated with our hands, for he is expiating not his own sins but ours. Does Jesus not carry our (his) cross in this very way? The symbolism of the passage is thus a clever montage of disparate elements that are at times superimposed, as in the case of "coronado de nopales," for example, and at times particularized, as in the case of the choice of wine ("que no bebe licor . . . su vino") as symbol of the blood of sacrifice, which distances us once again from the pre-Hispanic traditions of a people for whom the spilled blood of victims was held to be a "precious water" nourishing the renewal of life.

This christianization of Quetzacoatl (Jesus/Quetzacoatl) groups two cultural heritages around a symbol highly charged with spiritual values, and which constitutes one of the essential foundations of Catholicism, a symbol tending to assimilate its narratee: "por su propria (por *nuestra*) mano"; "su danza (nuestro baile)." One cannot help thinking of a Christ-like body both one and many (Jesus, each one of the faithful, all of the faithful), that is, the site of individual difference and of similitude (in the All). Here we find again, in a much more elaborate and richly evocative form, that identification of the individual and the collective levels that is the fundamental point of articulation of the ideology produced by the nationalistic bourgeoisie; but certain of its secondary components are noticeably more pronounced, particularly the idea of the necessity of individual sacrifice for the benefit of the community ("El hombre se debe todo a la comunidad" vs. "De hinojos, coronado de nopales, flagelado por su [nuestra] mano"), as well as the valorization of the cultural domain. This text is, in fact, very elaborate and plays on cultural complicity at a high level; on the linguistic level, obvious Mexicanisms (lépero, albur, relajo, camión, rajada) are found alongside words that from a Mexican point of view, can be perceived as true Hispanisms (duende, hinojos) or which, at the very least, lend the discourse a certain literary quality rich in varied connotations (afrenta, faz, duende, de hinojos).

It is the ontological perspective, however, that has undergone the most noticeable changes: this "inner universe" no longer contemplates echoes of sense impressions or dreams, but is the site of hidden phantasms (me lo vedaron, me lo exigieron) and a repressed discourse. Similarly, we are witnessing a reversal of point of view to the extent that this self-questioning and quest for identity have been transformed into a splitting of the self and a realization of the loss of wholeness.

Should we link these two types of gap? How should we interpret the way explicit discourse functions in relation to repressed discourse? What is behind this concealment and how should it be resolved? Emilio Uranga enlightens us on certain points:

> The philosophy of the Mexican was the expression of a vigorous national consciousness. It held a place in the spiritual realm similar to that which Lázaro Cárdenas's "expropriación" had inspired in economic thinking. . . . Mexican philosophy of the last fifty years has culminated in the creation of a humanism that is deemed the most adequate reflection of the achievements of the Mexican Revolution. The consequences of the transition from a feudal regime to one of incipient industrialization and capitalist production have meant for philosophy the definition of a richer model of human existence, with greater opportunities for self-realization than Porfirism allowed. This humanism is threatened today for the same reasons that first promoted it; the bourgeoisie no longer identifies with the humanism proposed by the Mexican Revolution, but rather claims to replace it with a "humanism" imported from the cities it is economically dependent upon. Hence, the oblivion in which so-called Mexican philosophy has fallen today. . . . For this

voracious class, the theme of Mexicanness, as elaborated by the philosophers, has no meaning, does not support any of its interests, says nothing to it, is not its theme. It is for this reason, it seems to me, that this philosophical theme, so flourishing and useful just a few years ago, has disappeared almost completely from public awareness.[9]

This text was written in 1962, four years after the publication of *La región más transparente*, but it makes references to a period that roughly includes the novel's publication date ("just a few years ago"), and seems, at first glance, to contradict everything I have just said, since I am claiming that the "theme of the Mexican" is really at the heart of Fuentes's literary creativity. But when Emilio Uranga writes that "the bourgeoisie no longer identifies with the humanism proposed by the Mexican Revolution but rather claims to replace it with a 'humanism' imported from the cities it is economically dependent upon," is this not tantamount to saying that it no longer identifies with the ideology it has itself produced, that is, that it no longer recognizes itself in its own image, that *it no longer identifies with itself?* There is a striking convergence between this observation and the transcription Fuentes gives of schizophrenia.

Similarly, the views advanced by Uranga ("claims to replace it with a humanism imported from the cities it is economically dependent upon") may be related to the two indexes of Fuentes's text (me le vedaron, me lo exigieron) that refer us to an interdiction, thus to a dependency, both of which remain unexpressed and, for that very reason, are problematized in terms of repression. The relationship established by Uranga between an economic crisis and an economic situation of dependency is perfectly reproduced by the text through the metaphor of a personality crisis, with this exception, however: *this situation of dependency is repressed in the unconscious.*

Returning to our methodological principles we see that this relationship is clearly transcribed by the semiological system we have reconstructed and which appears, once again, as a product of history. But the way this semiological system, which represents the *nonconscious* level, functions with respect to the level of the utterance can be problematic for it expresses what is repressed by explicit discourse and develops an interdiction that is itself marked in the text (me lo vedaron). In that sense, it is in some way retrieved by the utterance, and I am tempted to doubt its autonomy—that is, the relation it maintains with the nonconscious— even if I could accept the dubious notion that authors are in perfect control of their means of expression.

There remains the ideological crisis referred to above. Must it be granted, and if so, how can it be explained? Every ideology is a global response to a specific situation of conflict, yet ideology does not necessarily intervene in the development of these conflicts. We can presume that, the more acute the problems it strives to address become, the more clearly it asserts itself. It was precisely during the presidencies of Miguel Alemán and Ruiz Cortines that this ideology was asserted most clearly—the same time (1946–1958) that Mexico was vulnerable to North American economic and cultural penetration. This is why Uranga's assertions deserve to be nuanced, for the situation to which he refers does not signify the intervention of important ideological change; rather, it seems to refer, on the one hand, to contradictions and conflicts of interest at the very heart of the bourgeoisie and, on the other hand, to the fact that the gap separating this ideology from political reality was growing wider. It is this distortion that is responsible for the fact that the bourgeoisie no longer recognized itself in its own self-image, and above all, it is this distortion that Fuentes's text translates in terms of schizophrenia.

The Continuous and the Discontinuous in Octavio Paz

At the denotative level, the most explicit dialectic in *The Labyrinth of Solitude* is that opposing the closed and the open. Just as the Mexican retreats into himself, he "tries to create closed worlds in his politics and in the arts."[10] Here we shall refer especially to the second essay, "Mexican Masks," in which this idea is developed at length, as in the following significant quotations:

The Mexican *macho*–the male—is a hermetic being, closed up in himself. (p. 31)

The Mexican not only does not open himself up to the outside world, he also refuses to emerge from himself, to "let himself go." (p. 32)

It seems to me that all of these attitudes, however different their sources, testify to the "closed" nature of our reactions to the world around us or to our fellows. (p. 40)

Prudence, restraint, ceremonial reserve, impassiveness, mistrust, irony, apprehension, recourse to Form are the defenses behind which the personality takes shelter:

This predominance of the closed over the open manifests itself not only as impassivity and distrust, irony and suspicion, but also as love for Form. Form surrounds and sets bounds to our privacy, limiting its excesses, curbing its explosions, isolating and preserving it. (pp. 31–32)

Therefore our modesty is a defense, like courtesy's Great Wall of China or like the fences of organ-pipe cactus that separate the huts of our country people. (p. 35)

The body itself is but an organization of boundaries: the body exists, and gives weight and shape to our existence. (p. 35)

Muralla, muro, límites, as well as expressions of confinement and encirclement ("the circle of solitude that surrounds each one of us," [p. 27]), are recurrent images sustaining and repeating at a metaphorical level the allusions to "those plants that survive by storing up liquid within their spiny exteriors" (p. 30), which connote withdrawal into the self ("oblige us to close ourselves in, like those plants" [p. 30]), but are also the symbol of closure ("the fences of organ-pipe cactus that separate the huts of our country people" [p. 35]).

We may add to the image of the mask everything having to do with the associative interplay related to *órganos y cactos* (such as the adjectives *arisco* and *espinosa*), suggesting a protected inside—the other side, as it were, of juices and saps, a changeable and living face. We are thus confronted by two series of images: whereas the first (*muralla, muro, límite*) conveys only confinement, the second evokes a contradictory reality ("storing up liquid within their spiny exteriors"). There is no doubt that the solitude surrounding every individual may be either "closed and mechanical" or "open to the transcendent" (p. 27), authorizing us to see here the affirmation of the existence of a possible communion that nevertheless requires solitude.

This withdrawal into the self originates from self-questioning. The discovery of one's uniqueness involves the sense of otherness. Narcissus does not immediately take responsibility for his own likeness ("he asks himself if the face that appears there, disfigured by the water, is his own" [p. 9]), and at first projects himself in difference, for as reason "tends to split off from itself . . . every time it reflects on itself, it divides in half; every time it contemplates itself, it discovers it is *other.*"[11] The Mexican is twice encircled, alienated both from others and from himself ("The Mexican is always remote, from the world and from other people. And also from himself," [p. 29]). That is why consciousness presents itself metaphorically as a wall ("it is the opening of an impalpable, transparent wall—that of our consciousness—between the world and ourselves" [p. 9]), for discovering oneself as *other*, or discovering *the other*, causes the high walls of solitude to loom around us. Under the effect of an inquiring gaze, this stony universe finally conquers the face ("Eventually these features are seen as a face, and later as a mask, a meaning, a history" [p. 10]). We recognize in *"transparente muralla"* (p. 9) the image of the mirror, which is also associated with the image of stagnant water ("If the solitude of the Mexican is like a stagnant pool, that of the North American is like a mirror" [p. 27]). This imperceptible boundary of consciousness, this mirror's edge, immobilizes in reversibility landscapes that aspire to merge with one another. Here we may think of a poem such as "Himno entre ruinas" (*La estación violenta,* 1948), in which the sea, *araña deslumbrante* (a dazzling spider), a sun under water, is but the reflection of a sky in which "coronado de sí el día extiende sus plumas" ["crowned with itself, day stretches out its plumes"] and in which the principle of reversibility dominates the entire text at the metaphorical level "como el coral sus ramas en el agua extiendo mis sentidos en la hora viva" ["like the branches of coral stretched out into the water I stretch my senses in the living hour"], as well as at the structural level "un puñado de cabras es un rebaño de piedras" ["a few goats are a flock of stones"].[12] No doubt this explains why the moment consecrated by Paz's poetry is that which precedes the rupture of balance, the ultimate point of equilibrium, which is vertigo:

> como surge del mar, entre las olas,
> una que se sostiene
> estatua repentina
>
> ....
>
> vértigo solitario
> tú, delicia, imprevista creatura,
> brotas entre los ávidos minutos,
> alta quietud erguida, suspensa eternidad. (Delicia)

> [As, from the sea, between the waves,
> there rises up
> a sudden statue
>
> ....
>
> Solitary vertigo
> You, delight, unforeseen creature,
> break forth among the avid moments,
> High erect stillness, suspended eternity.][13]

or again fixity (la fijeza):

> "Fixity is always momentary. It is an equilibrium, at once precarious and perfect, that lasts the space of an instant: a flickering of the light, the appearance of a cloud, or a slight change in temperature is enough to break the repose-pact and unleash the series of metamorphoses. Each metamorphosis, in turn, is another moment of fixity succeeded by another change and another unexpected equilibrium. . . . Change is comprised of fixities that are momentary accords."[14]

The reason for this is that stagnant waters are opposed to running water ("We have ceased to be springs of living water" [p. 27]) and that at any moment the water of the mirror may recover its fluidity ("and this astonishment leads to reflection: as he leans over the river of his consciousness" [p. 9]) or again, in "Himno entre ruinas":

> La inteligencia al fin encarna.
> Se reconsilian las dos mitades enemigas

y la conciencia-espejo se licua.
vuelve a ser fuente, manantial de fábulas

[Intelligence finally takes flesh in form
and the two enemy halves are reconciled—
now the conscience-mirror liquifies
and is a spring again, a fountain of legends.[15]

The immanence of communion is opposed to the state of solitude. Thus, in Paz's metaphorical system the fluidity of water and of light connote communion, whereas stone and petrification, minerals, hardness in general, are symbols of solitude. Thus it is this imperceptible mirror's edge that keeps these two metaphorical halves of the system in reversible relation and prevents them from getting lost, from fading and dissolving into one another (cf. in the *Labyrinth* the numerous occurrences of *inmersión, sumergirse, perderse o encontrarse, fundirse, confundirse*). For example, woman as other is obstacle, defense, hostility, and solitude, but "is an incarnation of the life force" and, as such, "an undifferentiated manifestation of life, a channel for the universal appetite" (pp. 36–67). Her contradictory virtualities make her a "piedra del sol" [a sun-stone], a "slim cathedral clothed in light."[16]

This system will be found again in the *Labyrinth*: "[the Americans'] vitality becomes a fixed smile that denies old age and death but that changes life to motionless stone" (p. 24); "the mask that replaces the dramatic mobility of the human face is benevolent and courteous but empty of emotion, and its set smile is almost lugubrious: it shows the extent to which intimacy can be devastated by the arid victory of principles over instincts." (p. 25)

It is in this metaphorical context that we must put back the conception of time, perceived in its dual form as an inexhaustible and continuous source, and, at the same time, a discontinuous atomization, represented by the succession of minutes, hours, and days: "there was a time when time was not succession and transition, but rather the perpetual source of a fixed present. . . . As soon as time was divided up into yesterday, today and tomorrow, into hours, minutes and seconds, man ceased to be one with time, ceased to coincide with the flow of reality" (p. 209).

This analysis, however, is only a superficial view of the problematics of Paz's work. These bulwarks of solitude, apparently built by a "questioning consciousness," also have their source in a series of *breaks* and correspond to the splitting of a *Whole*. We may distinguish between, on the one hand, expressions describing tearing, expulsion, exile, and on the other, those revolving around the idea of *Rupture*.

Tearing

It is a punishment but it is also a promise that our *exile* will end.
(p. 196)

Having been *cut off* from his traditional culture, he asserts himself for a
moment as a solitary and challenging figure. (p. 17)

"The Mexican feels himself to have been *torn* from the womb of this
reality. (p. 20)

We have been *torn* from the *All*. (p. 20)

This desperation, this refusal to be saved by an alien project, is characteristic of the person who *rejects* all consolation and shuts himself up in
his private world. (p. 147)

The feeling of solitude, which is a nostalgic longing for the body from
which we were *cast out*, is a longing for a place. . . . Almost all the
rites connected with the founding of cities or houses allude to a search
for that holy center from which we were *driven out*. (p. 208)

Rupture

We note first of all the semantic ambivalence of *muralla*, which both protects
and imprisons, structures a universe and isolates it, evokes forces of cohesion and
of dispersion, suggests both an aggressive and an evasive exterior, and we shall
consequently oppose an exterior that penetrates, to an interior that exteriorizes
itself.

The first of these wrenchings affects the integrity of the individual, of the personality, or of the world. Here, we think of the *Chingada* myth: "the *Chingada*
is the Mother forcibly *opened*, violated or deceived" (p. 79).

The person who suffers this action [the *chingado*] is passive, inert and
open, in contrast to the active, aggressive and *closed* person who inflicts it. The *chingón* is the *macho*, the male; he *rips open* the *chingada*, the female, who is pure passivity, defenseless against the *exterior*
world. . . . The idea of violence rules darkly over all the meanings of
the word, and the dialectic of the "*closed*" and the "*open*" thus fulfills itself with an almost ferocious precision." (p. 77)

But we also recall that the Mexican is compelled not to open himself up: "*those
who 'open themselves up' are cowards. . . . We believe that opening oneself up
is a weakness or a betrayal.* The Mexican can bend, can bow humbly, can even
stoop, but he cannot *back down*, that is, he cannot allow the outside world to pene-

trate his privacy" (p. 30); "any *opening* in our defenses is a lessening of our manliness" (p. 930).

Within the logic of this imagery, man may open a rift in the universe, violate it, and tear it apart: "man the intruder has *broken or violated* the order of the universe. . . . He has inflicted a wound on the *compact flesh* of the world, and chaos, which is the ancient and, so to speak, *natural* condition of life, can *emerge* [*irrumpir*] again from this *aperture*" (p. 26); "the *macho* commits *chingaderas*, that is, unforeseen acts that produce confusion, horror and destruction. *He opens the world*; in doing so, *he rips and tears it*, and this violence provokes a great, sinister laugh" (p. 81).

Opposed to this rupture of wholeness that originates from aggressiveness toward the outside world are the reverse, always positive, images of exploded inwardness, in the form of: (a) effusiveness, (b) revelation, (c) explosiveness, (d) cracking (*estallido*).

> (a) The Mexican succumbs very easily to sentimental effusions, and therefore he shuns them. We live closed up within ourselves, like those taciturn adolescents . . . who are custodians of a secret that they guard behind scowling expressions, but that only waits for the opportune moment in which to *reveal itself*. (p. 19)
> (b) The Mexican Revolution was an explosive and authentic *revelation* of our real nature. (p. 135)
> (b) In all of these ceremonies . . . the Mexican *opens out*. They all give him a chance to reveal himself *and to converse with God, country, friends or relations*. (p. 49).
> (c) "*¡Viva México, hijos de la chingada!*" This phrase is a true battle cry . . . an *explosion* in the air. (p. 74)
> (c) The Zapatista and Villista movements . . . were popular *explosions*. (p. 145)
> (d) The *pachuco* is impassive and contemptuous, allowing all these contradictory impressions to accumulate around him until . . . he sees them *explode* into a tavern fight, or a *raid* by the police or a riot. (p. 17)
> (d) The Revolution . . . is an *explosion* of reality. (p. 149)

At the level of society, this phenomenon is transcribed by individual rebelliousness: "this sort of conspiracy cannot help but provoke *violent* individual rebellions" (p. 25).

All these images converge around the idea of rupture (of a State, an equilibrium, or an entity) and are associated with allusions to a wound or a tearing of flesh. This associative interplay appears with particular clarity when fiestas are involved: "our fiestas are *explosions*" (p. 53); "if we open out during fiestas, then, or when we are drunk or exchanging confidences, we do it so violently that we wound ourselves. . . .The fiesta, the crime of passion and the gratuitous crime reveal that the equilibrium of which we are so proud is only a mask, always in danger of being ripped off by a sudden *explosion* of our intimacy. . . . Now, every separation causes a wound" (pp. 63–34).

These images are synthesized as well on the metaphorical level in the image of the rocket that on fiesta days lights up the sky before falling back into darkness: "Once again, with a certain pathetic and plastic fatality, we are presented with the image of a skyrocket that climbs into the sky, bursts in a shower of sparks and then falls in darkness. Or with the image of that howl that ends all our songs and possesses the same ambiguous resonance: an angry joy, a destructive affirmation ripping open the breast and consuming itself" (pp. 74–45); and

> El canto mexicano *estalla* en un carajo,
> *estrella de colores* que se apaga.
> *piedra que nos cierra* las puertas del contacto.
>
> [Mexican song exploding in a curse,
> a star of colors that goes dark,
> a stone sealing the gateway of our contact.][17]

Aggression on the outside provokes a rupture of wholeness, but at another level, explosion on the inside is a glimpse of the authentic and an opening out toward communion: that is, a rupture revealing or productive of a certain form or potential for integration is opposed to a rupture in process of disintegration.

Remarkably, however, this notion of rupture goes beyond problems of individual or national personality and applies to a number of visions or entities. I shall add to the notion of fiesta ("Our fiestas . . . are violent breaks with the old or the established" [p. 53]), and of universal order ("Man . . . has broken or violated the order of the universe" [p. 26]), the sensation of life ("We sense the change as separation and loss" [p. 195]), birth ("The cord that united him with life has been broken" [p. 202]), adolescence ("Adolescence is a break with the world of childhood" [p. 203]), death ("Death was not the natural end of life but one phase of an infinite cycle. Life, death and resurrection were stages of a cosmic process which repeated itself continuously" [p.54]), the alternate stages of everyone's life ("In the life of every man there are periods that are both departures and reunions, separations and reconciliations" [p.202]), and the romantic conception of love that "implies a breaking away and a catastrophe" (p. 198). Here one might multiply these examples, as Octavio Paz indeed does ("And the fiesta is only one example, perhaps the most typical, of this violent break. It is not difficult to name others, equally revealing" [p.53]).

It is still more remarkable that history is conceived and analyzed in the following way. At the base of this vision there is, first, the Conquest, seen as a quest for unity, thus of content, in relation to pre-Cortesian cultural and political plural-ism ("Despite the contradictions that make it up, [the Conquest] was a historical act intended to create unity out of the cultural and political plurality of the pre-Cortesian world. . . . If Mexico was born in the sixteenth century, we must agree that it was the child of a double violence, imperial and unifying: that of the Aztecs and that of the Spaniards" [p.100]), a great historical wave that, at the time of Independence, collapsed ("Conquest and Independence seem like moments of flux and reflux in a great historical wave that . . . receded after collapsing into a thousand fragments" [pp. 118–119]). The Indian world whose ties with ancient cultures were broken, but which, through Catholicism, finds new modes of integration with the surrounding universe and with the Sacred: "to belong to the Catholic faith meant that one found a place in the cosmos. The flight of their gods and the death of their leaders had left the natives in a solitude so complete that it is difficult for a modern man to imagine it. Catholicism re-established their ties with the world and the other world" (p. 102); compare again: "in sum, two opposing tendencies struggled within the Independence movement" (p. 120). The colonial world: "the liberals attempted to complete the break with the colonial tradition" (p. 124); "these words reveal how completely the liberals and their heirs had broken with the colonial era" (p. 135). The Reform movement: "this examination ended in a triple negation: of our Spanish inheritance, of our indigenous past, and of Catholicism. . . . Its accomplishments did not consist solely in a break with the colonial world" (p. 126); "the Reform movement founded Mexico and denied the past" (p.126). The Díaz dictatorship: "the Independence movement, the Reform movement and the Díaz dictatorship were distinct and contradictory phases of one continuing effort to break free. The nineteenth century was a complete break with form" (p. 167). Hence this cavalier remark: "Our independent history, from the time we were first aware of ourselves as individuals and of our geographical area as an individual nation, has been a break with tradition, with form, and a search for a new form that would contain all our native particulars and would also be open to the future" (p. 167).

The images synthesizing these historical moments (*superposición* histórica, *disfraz positivista*, *máscara*) show that the latter are closely tied to an outside concerned with a continuity it strives to shatter. Thus Mexican history has been subordinated to universal history, of which it is only a fragment ("But our history is only a fragment of world history" [p. 169]): it is the product of universal projects that have been successively *transplanted* or *imposed* ("As for our ideas, they have never been really ours: they have been either impositions or importations from Europe" [p. 169]). Hence the major idea presiding at this reconstruction by Octavio Paz of his country's history: it is *inauthentic* because it has been *imposed*. Such is the case of the Reform movement: "the Mexican nation was created by a minority that succeeded in imposing its scheme on the rest of the people" (p. 127); and of positivism and the Díaz regime: "the Díaz regime adopted positivist philosophy; it did not father it" (p. 131). It is at this level and in this context that the themes of disguise [*disfraz*], mask [*máscara*], and of clothing [*ropaje*] and nudity [*desnudez*] must be understood when they are applied to the historical realm. In the case of the Independence movement, the question is complex and ambiguous. The development of the situation did not depend on political and economic conditions *inside* the country but, on the contrary, was directly linked to an *external* context:

> A little later, when the insurgent movement had almost been destroyed, the unexpected occurred: the liberals seized power, transformed the absolute monarchy into a constitutional monarchy, and threatened the privileges of the Church and the aristocracy. A sudden change of allegiance took place: the high clergy, the great landowners, the bureaucracy and the *criollo* military leaders, confronted with this new danger, sought an alliance with the remainder of the insurgents and consummated the Independence. . . . The political separation from the metropolis was brought about in order to defeat the classes that had fought for Independence." (p. 124)

I am tempted to liken this external action to an aggression that literally stifled and reified an authentic and vital reality under the weight of juridical and cultural forms productive of isolation in relation to an underlying continuity: "The image that Mexico presents us at the end of the nineteenth century is one of discord. It was a discord more profound than the earlier political quarrels or even the civil war, because it consisted in the imposition of juridical and cultural forms which not only did not express our true nature but actually smothered and immobilized it" (p. 133).

Such is the perspective of a single dialectic of the *continuous* and the *discontinuous*, the open and the closed, Paz's analysis of Mexican ontology in its dual aspect of the individual and the collective: "the whole history of Mexico, from the Conquest to the Revolution, can be regarded as a search for our own selves, which have been deformed or disguised by alien institutions, and for a form that will express them" (p. 166).

Form mutilates to the extent that it represses and isolates; Form is productive of breaks, of discontinuities: "in a certain sense the history of Mexico, like that of every Mexican, is a struggle between the forms and formulas that have been imposed on us and the explosions with which our individuality avenges itself" (p. 33).

Still in the realm of historical vision, we note that the Revolution, in contrast to the other periods in Mexican history analyzed previously, is transcribed in the *Labyrinth* by images that express the explosive invasion of inwardness into history: "the Mexican Revolution was an explosive and authentic revelation of our real nature" (p. 135); "the Revolution . . . was an explosion of reality" (p. 140); "the Revolution was an excess . . . an explosion of joy and hopelessness, a shout of orphanhood . . . an explosion of reality" (pp. 148–149). Closely linked to the images that transcribe phenomena of breaking, in the context of the positive perspective we have already examined, the Revolution is, nevertheless, a return to the notion of permanence, tradition, and continuity: "the radicalism of the Mexican Revolution consisted in its originality, that is, in its return to our roots, the only proper bases for our institutions. . . . The Zapatista movement was a return to our most ancient and permanent tradition" (p. 144); "the Revolution was a sudden immersion of Mexico in her own being . . . a return and a communion" (pp. 148–149); "by means of the Revolution the Mexican people found itself, located itself in its own past and substance" (p. 148); "the Revolution became an attempt to integrate our present and our past" (p. 144).

In the framework of the tension in the text of the *Labyrinth* between the continuous and the discontinuous we shall again oppose, but this time in the context of historical concepts, a major break productive of a dynamics of integration to a whole series of breaks in national wholeness.

History is not only break, it is also continuity: "thanks to the Revolution, the Mexican wants to reconcile himself with his history and his origins" (p. 147); "if we contemplate the Mexican Revolution in terms of the ideas outlined in this essay, we see that it was a movement attempting to reconquer our past, to assimilate it and make it live in the present" (pp. 146–147); "it was a return to the past, a reuniting of the ties broken by the Reform and the Díaz dictatorship, a search for our own selves, and a return to the maternal womb" (p. 148).

When we ask what this historical continuity is for Octavio Paz, we observe that it has three elements or dimensions: the Spanish heritage, the native past, and Catholicism. It is this valorization of Catholicism that makes him conceive of the brief appearance of continuity in colonial society:

> Due to the universal nature of the Catholic religion . . . colonial society managed to become a true order, if only for a brief while. Form and substance were one. There was no wall or abyss between reality and institutions, the people and the law, art and life, the individual and society; on the contrary, everything harmonized and everyone was guided by the same concepts and the same will. No man was alone, however humble his situation, and neither was society: this world and the next, life and death, action and contemplation were experienced as totalities, not as isolated acts or ideas. Every fragment participated in the whole, which was alive in each one of its parts. The pre-Cortesian order was replaced by a universal form that was open to the participation and communion of all the faithful. (pp. 166–167)

Indeed, behind the concept of *Order*, which is one of its primary figurations, this quotation provides a precise description of the *continuous* (absence of breaks: "no wall or abyss"), integration of the parts in a whole. As we noted earlier, for Paz,

Catholicism, at the time of the Conquest, gave back to the Indians their place in the universe ("It is often forgotten that to belong to the Catholic faith meant that one found a place in the cosmos. . . . Catholicism re-established their *ties* with the world and the other world" (p. 102), thus substituting one continuity for another. However, we should not confuse the concept of the continuous with historical continuity, and we shall allow more generally that this systematics of rupture transcribes an authentic value, in Goldmann's sense of the term—that of the *continuous*, a concept whose figurations and meaning we shall now investigate.

The vision underlying the *Labyrinth* is that of universal harmony (*Orden*), in which time and life are merged: "life and time coalesce to form a single whole, an indivisible unity" (p. 209); man and time: "man become[s] one with creation" (p. 211); man and the cosmos: "a creed permitting a genuinely filial relationship between the individual and the cosmos" (p. 128); life and death: "the dead . . . disappeared . . . to return to the undifferentiated country of the shadows, to be melted into the air, the earth, the fire, the animating substance of the universe" (p. 55); space and time: "space and time were bound together and formed an inseparable whole" (p. 55); man and space: "blending with space, becoming space" (p. 44), as well as all the contraries: "we . . . ask it . . . simply for an instant of that full life in which opposites vanish, in which life and death, time and eternity are united" (p. 196).

Man suffers from having been torn from an All, from a center of life, from the womb of a reality (p. 20), from a pure, fixed, continuous present ceaselessly being recreated (pp. 209–212), the negation of those other breaks—succession, the future, and the past.

The discontinuous at other times has the face of difference and of contrariness: "the fiesta is a return to a remote and *undifferentiated* state, prenatal or presocial. . . . The fiesta denies society as an organic system of differentiated forms and principles, but affirms it as a source of creative energy" (p. 52). The poetic sites of the continuous are love, fiesta, myth, poetry (p. 209); its privileged figurations in the *Labyrinth* are the All, Totality, Fusion, Order or Harmony (*orden*), Universality, but also Authenticity, which in turn encompasses *reality, spontaneity, intimacy*. In the text itself a whole system of indexes refers to the continuous: certain adjectives such as *vivo* ("el tiempo vivo," p. 211), *pleno* ("la vida plena," p. 196), *abierta* ("Lo Abierto es el mundo en donde les contrarios se reconcilian y la luz y la sombra se funden" ["The Open is the world in which opposites are reconciled and light and darkness melt together"]), *puro, informe* ("La Fiesta es une súbita immersión en lo informe, en la vita pura" ["The fiesta is the sudden immersion in the shapeless, in life in its pure state"], *infinito, indiferenciado, uno, continuo, perpetuo*; nouns such as *desnudez, realidad, espontaneidad, intimidad, fiesta, redención, inocencia, coherencia, raíces, grito, estallido, alarido, immersión*; as well as, as we have already seen, all the images of fluidity (*fuente, manantial, fluir*).

The avenues of access of the continuous are communion, participation, surrender (*entrega*), immersion, and especially regression, in the form of *retorno, vuelta, regreso*, and of a quest for filiation. For the continuous is not a project but corresponds to a nostalgia and to signs expressive of breaking or tearing away (*des*prendido, *des*garrado, *arr*ancado, *e*xilio); to rupture we may oppose the prefixes of *return* in *re*gresear, *re*descubrirnos, *re*stablecer los lazos, *re*conquistar, *re*-anudacion, which designate as objective the reconstruction of the *un*formed, the *un*differentiated, the *pre*natal, and the *pre*social.

Whatever the scope of his investigation and the outline of his ontological research, Octavio Paz's vision opposes the pressure of the continuous, which occurs on the inside, to the pressure of a superimposed form. Does the fact that the center of this continuity corresponds, among other localizations, to a sort of inner level of the individual, of society, or of history, or, from the structural point of view (which comes down to the same thing), to a past collective experience, mean that it must be reconciled with the author's use of the psychoanalytic code? Of course, since the Superego is related to everything having to do with imposed, transplanted Form, whether it be the individual's mask or, at the level of sociocultural and sociopolitical facts, ideological masks or again, images of petrification that immobilize or "congeal" underlying reality, whereas images of fluidity, spontaneity, and reality are connected to the subconscious level. It is precisely in psychoanalytic terms that the ontological analysis of the Mexican is undertaken: "They are the bad words, the only living language in a world of anemic vocables. They are poetry within the reach of everyone. Each country has its own. In ours . . . we condense all our appetites, all our hatreds and enthusiasm, all the longings that rage unexpressed in the depths of our being" (p. 74). "It is scarcely very strange that a good portion of our political ideas are still nothing but words intended to hide and restrict our true selves" (p. 146), and it is through the same concepts that the movements of history are perceived: "the revolutionary movement was an instinctive explosion, a longing for communion, a revelation of our being; it was a search for, and discovery of, the ties that had been broken by liberalism" (pp. 154–455).

In this context, rupture refers to the trauma in relation to which the collective unconscious is structured. More precisely, this is, with the Conquest, the loss of integrity and rape: "the Conquest had left them orphans, and they escaped this condition by returning to the maternal womb. Colonial religion was a return to prenatal life" (p. 167), and it is to this trauma that, among other things, an expression like *chingar* refers, in which "all of our anxious tensions express themselves" (p. 74).

However, the tension opposing the Superego or *superimposed* Form to subconscious pressures produces neuroses: "Our situation resembles that of the neurotic, for whom moral principles and abstract ideas have no practical function except as a defense for his privacy — that is, as a complex system he employs to deceive both himself and others regarding the true meaning of his inclinations and the true character of his conflicts" (p. 168), and it is no doubt these neuroses that are responsible for the "instinctive explosions," the "revelations of our being," and in general for all inner explosive phenomena. In these circumstances, should we not consider that the relations established between trauma and neurotic symptoms are analogous to those constructed, in the text of the *Labyrinth*, between one series of *rupturas* destructive of integrity, and another series producing or revealing integration? This analogy would oblige us to nuance somewhat our earlier formulation, since the neurotic symptom does not precisely reveal an integration but rather a possibility of integration with the All, through the Freudian "Id," an integration whose full actualization is prevented by the Superego; in this hypothesis, *explosion* becomes a sign that refers to the permanence of the "Id."

To what extent, however, can the "Id," at the level of instinct, intimacy, and spontaneity, merge with the All? The "Id" refers doubly to the continuous, first by means of instinct that establishes a link with life and with others; second, by means of the collective unconscious, "limitless immensity," "unheard of indeterminacy," to use Jungian terms, the realm we have in common with all humanity. This last comparison allows us to differentiate two different extensions of similitude and to distinguish between a collective unconscious produced by specific social and historical structures and a collective unconscious constituted by universal archetypes.

The preceding study seems to me to show how all the great themes of the *Labyrinth* are articulated around this dialectic of the continuous and the discontinuous, whether it be the Freudian perspective in which the unconscious, itself a continuity, is introduced, in the form of a symptom, as a discontinuity in the continuity of daily life, or the central problem of the reflection upon Mexican ontology, or the metaphysical problematic underlying the whole text. Perhaps now we can better understand why the *We* (*Nous*) of Octavio Paz, a point of intersection of the continuous and the discontinuous, is both the site of difference, and through difference, the site of similarity.

Textual Actualizations of an Ideological Community's Latent Utterances in *The Labyrinth of Solitude*

Analogy is the science of correspondences. It is, however, a science which exists only by virtue of differences. Precisely because this *is not* that, it is possible to extend a bridge between this and that. The bridge is the word *like*, or the word *is*: this is like that, this is that. The bridge does not do away with distance: it is an intermediary; neither does it eliminate differences: it establishes a relation between different terms. Analogy is the metaphor in which otherness dreams of itself as unity, and difference projects itself illusively as identity. By means of analogy the confused landscape of plurality becomes ordered and intelligible. Analogy does not eliminate differences: it redeems them, it makes their existence tolerable. . . . *Analogy says that everything is the metaphor of something else.*[18]

This quotation from *Children of the Mire* evokes a semiotic perspective, if we grant the provisional existence, at least, of a new analogy between sign and metaphor, insofar as the latter, in Octavio Paz's definition, refers to something outside itself. A second code, derived from the original code (language), is thus established, and as a result, a semiological community is organized linking the speaker to his addressees.

Whether the analogy's point of support is located in referents or in the initial code, it becomes a sign only to the extent it is accepted as such, after it has been decoded in relation to the new context. Indeed, we must recall that the very purpose of the sign obliges us as senders to situate ourselves in a field of living experience in which we are certain of interacting with our addressees. The sign, one might say, truly acquires its status as sign only when its decoding is accomplished, that is, at the very moment it, in turn, becomes the addressee's sign. Without this intersubjective relationship no sign is possible:

> Signs can only appear on an *intersubjective ground*. What is more, this is a ground that cannot be termed "natural," in the ordinary sense of the word: it is not enough to put two *homo sapiens* together for signs to arise. It is essential that these two individuals be socially organized, that they form a group (a social unit): it is only on this condition that a system of signs can be constituted.[19]

The sign/analogy, moreover, does not depend solely on the point of view of the speaker, but represents as well the reflection and refraction of the addressee's point of view. If it rewrites the world,[20] this new translation of referential reality does not fail to convey, as does the preceding one, specific modes of a social relationship. However brilliant and seductive their expression may be, these correspondences are not only programmed by the respective outlines of the objects or concepts involved, but also by another term that can be defined provisionally as a collective practice produced by the specific forms of social organization underpinning the semiological community. The sign/analogy is not an exception to the essentially ideological status of the sign. Such is our hypothesis.

Octavio Paz's suggestive reflections on analogy represent a kind of refraction of his own writing and make us aware of a major tendency of his textual practice. Earlier, I attempted to reconstruct the network of correspondences structuring *The Labyrinth of Solitude*, suggesting a possible extension of my conclusions to his entire work. I should now like to specify how this system of metaphors reproduces the latent utterances of an ideological community in the form of a series of textualizations whose apparent originality is programmed in the deep structure of an ideological code.

I shall sum up my earlier conclusions by organizing them around three principal analogies suggested by the author: closure (*encerramiento*) → repression (*represión*) → break (*ruptura*), which themselves translate a nostalgia of the *continuous*. The dialectic of the continuous and the discontinuous is the basis of all the themes of the *Labyrinth of Solitude*.

The accompanying table does not include every sign in the text but only the major semantic families and concepts. Its schematic presentation is thus capable of considerable enrichment in the context of a reading that limits itself to the organization of a set of facts. The identification of the relations listed in the table rests, in each case, on specific quotations mentioned in the preceding study of Octavio Paz; when they are my own terms, the signs are placed within brackets.[21]

The two axes of analogy are different in nature. On the vertical axis, correspondences are articulated around a metaphorical system: the antithesis *inside/outside* (deep structure) is actualized in the *husk/sap* (A/E) and *disguise/nudity* (B/E) oppositions, and in a whole series of images: break (C), explosion (D), metaphors of the circle (*muralla, cerca, jacal, castillo fuerte*, A) which comprise a number of isotopies. The analogical vision reactivates this convergence, but in turn operates on all the respective semantic fields involved in order to create a "differential system" it organizes in relation to itself. In fact, it is this analogical vision that selects, in the case of each sign, the difference that renders it doubly meaningful: for example, the seme of artifice in *disfraz* (disguise), of external violence in *abertura* (opening), *herida* (wound), or of internal violence in *explosión*, which open up different levels of meaning (B,C,D). Thus, while repression engenders worlds closed on themselves that cut across the continuous (A/B), these *fragments* recover at another level a status subject to the same external or internal forces of aggression as the first continuity. An explosion of interiority (D) is thus opposed to a rupture of wholeness originating in aggression from the outside world (C).

The horizontal axis (0 → 6) includes groups that do not describe any absolute parallelism. Certainly, the series (4), (5) and (6) can readily be seen as so many different textualizations of the concept of rupture: these juxtapositions bring out the nature of metaphor as a meeting ground that facilitates the transition from individual psychology and individual organisms to national psychology and national organisms. Things become less clear when we approach the initial series (1 to 3). Let us, however, compare series 1 and 2: the first offers us a manifold but oriented translation of the concept. Break or rupture is not perceived either as interruption of succession or as mutilation of a *potential afterward* but as the *tearing away* from a former state (see AB-DE, -EX, -DIS). It is pregnant only with a past (*negar*). This nostalgic dimension filters down to every level of the series, producing secondary interferences around the myth of the innocence (tat-

Table of Analogies

	Denotative Level	Analogical Series 1	Analogical Series 2: Paths to Knowledge	Analogical Series 3: Associated Concepts
A [Rupture of Continuity]	ruptura romper fragmento	arrancamiento desarraigo desprendido separar negar excisión exilio diferenciados AB- EX- DE- DIS-	examinarse contemplarse conciencia reflexión razón filosofia ironia critica (adoptar trasplantar)	cambaio modernidad pluralidad sucesión tiempo lineal
B [Repression]	reprime	superposiciones		sociedad
C [Change of Identity]	impone	chingar, violar desgarrar	se escinde se descubre como	alteridad
D [Revelation of Identity]	revelarse	irrupciones efusiones		
$\frac{\wedge}{\vee}$ vs . . . **E**	$\frac{\wedge}{\vee}$ vs . . .	$\frac{\wedge}{\vee}$ vs	$\frac{\wedge}{\vee}$ vs	$\frac{\wedge}{\vee}$ vs . . .

[Continuity]	continudad
	unidad
	todo
	
	universal
	perpetuo
		regresar, redescubrir,
		  restablecer,
		  reanudar, reintegrar,
		  reconquistar
		prenatal, presocial, ($\rightarrow$
		  inocencia)
		inmersilón,
		  sumergirse,
		  perderse, fundirse,
		  confundirse
		
		PRE-
		RE-
		IN-
			pasmos
			revelación
			entrega
			
			mito
			poesia
			fiesta
			(abierto)
			
			analogia
			
			(engendrar)
				tradición
				dios
				Presente eterno
				
				fusión
				tiempo ciclico
				
				sustancia
				realidad
				pueblo
				vida ($\rightarrow$ vivo)

or Correspondences

Analogical Series 4: Concrete Historical Elements	Analogical Series 5: Psychological/ Psychoanalytic Perspective	Analogical Series 6: Metaphoric Elements	Remarks
el mundo colonial Independencia el siglo XIX Liberalismo Reforma Positivismo Porfirismo	cerrado, hermetico soledad	muralla china, muros, fosa rodear, círculo, límites cerca de órganos y cactos (→ arisco, espinosa) jacales cáscara espinosa castillo fuerte espejo, aguas estancadas transparente muralla [Circle Interior/Exterior Mirror]	catedral vs ↔ vestida de luz piedra vs ↔ de sol estrella vs ↔ colores
principios moral formas juridicas, culturales formulas arte instituciones	[Superego]	disfraz ropaje máscara	
	abrir, abierto rajarse neurótico, conflictos	irrumpir penetrar herida hueco, apertura	abrir: rupture of the closed world, same figuration of the discontinuous
Revolución mexicana Fiesta	rebeliones individuales crimen pasional [Symptom]	cohetes, luces voces, alaridos, gritos estallido explosión	
∧ — vs . . . ∨	∧ — vs ∨	∧ — vs ∨	∧ — vs ∨
historia universal Zapatismo nuestro pasado: herencia española, pasado indigena, catolicismo	communión regreso a la Madre nosotros mismos su propio ser autenticidad intimidad espontaneidad instintos (inconsciente)	jugos, rostro, movilidad dramática desnudez fuente, luz, rio, licuarse, manantial	

tered virginity in *chingar, violar*) of the early ages of humanity (*prenatal/presocial*); the circle here inverts its first connotations (closed world) to recapture a symbolism in which roundness is the traditional representation of perfection. These successive reversals of meaning show how changes in the configuration of a metaphor can be perceived as a mutilation (perfection wounded) or as a liberating outpouring (explosion), making the circle the most adequate sign of solitude according to whether the latter is either "closed and unconscious" or open to transcendence.

Thus continuity is not to be constructed but to be recaptured, as a reading of level E1 will show. From this point of view, the imaginary line joining this series to the evocation of *Zapatism* or to fetal life (*regreso a la Madre, prenatal*) deserves close attention.

The first series gives greater stress to the modalities of rupture (How does it take place? Through tearing, uprooting, schism, separation, etc.) than to what it really represents. This sensitivity to the *How?* in the semiological reading is equally perceptible, at the general level, in the ontological problematics of the *Labyrinth*. The Mexican is defined by the *manner* in which he reveals his personality (outbursts, explosions) or hides it (mask, fortress) rather than by his personality itself. More precisely, it is his nature to express his personality violently or to protect it jealously, which is tantamount to saying that psychological content merges with ways of functioning and is hidden in the blur of tautological notations (revelation of his own nature, of ourselves, authenticity, intimacy, spontaneity), producing an impression of analytical emptiness beneath the wealth of phenomenological observations.

The question *How?* is posed again in series 2, although in a somewhat different form. Whereas the first series led us over the ground of the image (uprooting, tearing away, etc.), this one brings us back to the intellectual level by presenting a series of *factors* of discontinuity. The two series together respond perfectly to the double question inscribed in the *How?* — namely, *in what form? with what effect?* The answer given to the second question (*with what effect?*) is repeated in the series E2, in reverse (What is the source of rupture?/Where can continuity be regained?), in the same way the first had been (through tearing/through return). We can grasp the ideological implications of this more clearly if we group the two subsets and contrast the first group (examination, reflection, reason, philosophy, criticism) with the second (wonder, revelation, surrender, myth, poetry). Two contradictory paths to knowledge are thus confronted, one based on a positivist, empiricist approach sensitive essentially to difference and distance, the other on a sort of osmosis, a participation of the senses with the object, a quest for analogies and resemblances. Here again, the imaginary line joining series A2 to series A4, and especially the mention of positivism, merits reflection.

If we limit ourselves to the *Labyrinth of Solitude*, the stress placed on the double question *How?* in a text inquiring into a national psychology serves as an extremely interesting signal for analysis. In the production of meaning, what role should be attributed to functionalist psychology? to the impact of phenomenology? to existentialist philosophy? All these questions remain open.

In spite of what I have just said, the line of demarcation distinguishing effects, in their modes of functioning, from causes is a fluctuating one: the meaning of the relation is always apt to reverse itself because of the extreme connotative availability of the metaphors underlying this system.[22] Thus, irony, presented as a figuration of the discontinuous ("irony is the wound through which analogy bleeds to death")[23] is itself "the child of linear, sequential, and unrepeatable time,"[24] but it allows us to read the world's discontinuity ("irony shows that if the universe is a script, each translation of this script is different"[25]). What is involved is an associative network in which analogical relations are more or less well marked, complex and of different nature. Moreover, we recall that for Octavio Paz "is" does not transcribe an identity between subject and attribute but is limited to the establishment of a "relation between different terms."[26]

In the somewhat disordered configuration of series 3, the respective outlines of the concepts involved will be defined by the complicated interplay of resemblances and gaps: "modernity sees itself ruled by the principle of change: criticism"; "the modern age is a separation . . . a continual breaking away"; tradition "signifies the continuity of the past in the present . . . the past protects society from change."[27]

By means of internal convergences (Tradition, God, eternal present . . . ← . . .) and by the interplay of serial oppositions (→ change, modernity, linear time), the series cause a semiological reduction of each sign, imprinting it with a specific meaning sometimes giving it the added burden of a value judgment. Thus, within the metaphorical system, the oppositions (jugos ← vs. → cáscara espinosa) or again (rostro ← vs. → máscara) indirectly bring out whatever is negative in change every bit as much as they bring out the fecundity of tradition. Thus metaphor reveals a double system of negative values (change, modernity, succession, society) and positive ones (Tradition, God, eternal present) that have, in that case, a significance that can be termed ideological, at least at a first level. This double system of values underlies both the historical perspective—which glorifies, besides Zapatism, the Spanish heritage, the native past, and Catholicism—and the psychoanalytic perspective, which valorizes instinct (at the expense of reason), spontaneity (at the expense of principles), and the unconscious (at the expense of the conscious), and again is evidence of a nostalgia for the fetal state.

The somewhat systematic and rigid manner in which these two perspectives are treated reveals the genetic role of metaphor (circle, mirror), which does not translate a system of thought but, on the contrary, *is being rewritten in conceptual terms*. We might say that metaphor models and generates a specific vision of history. Preceding thought, the structural metaphor of the circle channels the perception of what historical periods such as Independence, the nineteenth century, the Díaz regime could have been (see A4), immobilizing them in this manner in the schematics of analogy, to the extent that, as presumed actualizations of an instance of breaking away, they are, for that very reason, being projected onto one of the concrete representations of the category of containment (*muralla china, cerca de órganos, castillo fuerte*).

Coming back to the horizontal axis, we note that the whole set of analogies and metaphors is articulated around the image of a roundness traversed in two directions: aggressive exterior/attacked interior (level C); explosive interior/passing dissolution of the confines of the circle (level D). Whereas the exterior is but aridity (*órganos, cactos*), threats (*castillo fuerte, muralla china*), illusions (*disfraz, ropaje*), experienced as aggressive or illusory, the inside appears as a fragile and vulnerable kernel, a center of sweetness (*jugos*) and light (*luz*), a source of living water (*fuente, manantial, licuarse*), the only avenue to cosmic communion, an essentially subjective and new path to perfection solely oriented toward anteriority (see the prefixes pre/re).[28]

This fact shows how the structural metaphor of confinement can be considered as the synthetic realization of a set of ideological utterances.[29] Indeed, we may compare this exaltation of interiority with the manner in which the poetry of the *Contemporáneos*, first, and the "Mexican psychological novel of the 1940s," second, valued intuition as a form of knowledge—as well as the inner universe or the inner life of the Mexican—at the expense of everything empirical (see analogical series 2 in the table of correspondences).

One is struck as well by the way in which the table of correspondences I have established reproduces, in its own way, Dessau's description of the foundations of the ideology of the postrevolutionary, Mexican, nationalistic bourgeoisie—the problematics of the individual's wholeness and quest for the self, the need to defend the self against attack from the outside, the building of a community—around the two essential axes of authenticity and communion.

We thus confirm the conclusions we had reached in the case of Carlos Fuentes's *La región más transparente*: through radically different textual means, the two texts succeed in reproducing the latent utterances of the same ideological community. This would be sufficient to justify, if such justification were necessary, this penetrating remark of Bakhtin's: "Social class and semiological community do not correspond to one another. By the second term, we mean the community using one and the same code of ideological communication. Thus different social classes use one and the same language."[30]

Reproducing an ideology does not mean, for all that, that one supports it. We shall thus be careful not to infer from the preceding analysis any value judgment on Octavio Paz. We shall limit ourselves to the observation that in any act of writing ideological markers filter down to the very heart of the deep structures of texts—a structural metaphor in the case of the *Labyrinth of Solitude*. The more these markers have to do with the realm of the nonconscious, the more easily they elude the control of the supposed producer of the text.

Thus, it seems to me essential to remember that the entire set of images listed in my last column (metaphors) are encountered either directly or in transposed form in Octavio Paz's poetry, where the context does not allow us to see them reproducing collective utterances. Are we in a position to generalize the conclusions that follow from this observation? Can we consider that metaphor is as dependent on the latent discourse of an ideological community as on the "poetic worlds" of individuals, if not more so?

Chapter 10
Social Formations and Figurative Discourse in Mateo Alemán's *Guzman de Alfarache*

The following text develops a *topos,* the praise of the Earth's fecundity. Before we look at the way in which this *topos* is deconstructed by the text, we shall indicate its principal themes and their evolution and impact on Spanish literature of the Golden Age.

In Latin antiquity, the primary major theme of this *topos* is that of early man's life in a natural world that gave its wealth spontaneously. This theme is found in the *De natura rerum*, V, ll. 925–926, in which, instead of a golden age, Lucretius describes the primitive state of humanity, content with Nature's gifts: "*Quod sol atque imbres dederant, quod terra crearat/ Sponte sua satis id placabat pectora domum*" [What sun and rain had given, what earth had produced of her own accord, that was a gift enough to content their minds].[1] Virgil will later glorify this "reign of Saturn" in the *Georgics*, I, 125–128: "*ante Iovem nulli subigebant arva coloni;/ ne signare quidem aut partiri limite campum/ fas erat: in medium quaerebant, ipsaque tellus omnia liberius, nullo poscente, ferebat*" [Before Jove's day no tillers subdued the land. Even to mark the field or divide it with bounds was unlawful. Men made gain for the common store, and Earth yielded all, of herself, more freely, when none begged for her gifts].[2] From that point the primitive state will be positively marked as the representation of both happiness and virtue. Thus, it will appear, among other texts, in the *Elegies* of Tibullus (I, 3, ll. 35–47) and in Ovid's *Metamorphoses* (I, ll. 101–112). It is interesting to note that, echoing line 1006 of the *De natura* ("*Improba navigii ratio tum caeca jacebat*" [The wicked art of navigation then lay hidden and obscure]), the theme in Tibullus and in Ovid is loaded with a condemnation of adventure, whether by land or by sea,

190

or for commercial gain, a condemnation I am tempted to compare with Virgil's praise of community property: "How good the life in Saturn's reign, before/ the world was opened into long roads!/ Pine timbers then had not defied blue waves/or spread billowing canvas to the winds./ No roving sailor seeking profit from strange lands/ had freighted ship with foreign merchandise" (Tibullus).[3] "Not yet had the pine-tree, felled on its native mountains, descended thence into the watery plain to visit other lands; men knew no shores except their own" (Ovid, *Metamorphoses*, I, 95–96).[4]

We shall analyze the following text from *Guzmán de Alfarache*:

> *Conforme a lo cual, siempre se tuvo por dificultoso hallarse un fiel amigo y verdadero. Son contados, por escrito están y lo más en fábulas, los que se dice haberlo sido. Uno solo hallé de nuestra misma naturaleza, el mejor, el más liberal, verdadero y cierto do todos, que nunca falta y permanece, siempre sin cansarse de darnos; y es la tierra.*
>
> *Esta nos da las piedras de precio, el oro, la plata y más metales, de que tanta necesidad y sed tenemos. Produce la yerba, con que no sólo se sustentan los ganados y animales de que nos valemos para cosas de nuestro servicio; mas juntamente aquellas medicinales, que nos conservan la salud y aligeran la enfermedad, preservándonos della. Cría nuestros frutos, dándonos telas con que cubrirnos y adornarnos. Rompe sus venas, brotando de sus pechos dulcísimas y misteriosas aguas que bebemos, arroyos y ríos que fertilizan los campos y facilitan los comercios, comunicándose por ellos las partes más extrañas y remotas. Todo nos lo consiente y sufre, bueno y mal tratamiento. A todo calla; es como la oveja, que nunca le oirán otra cosa que bien: si la llevan a comer, si a beber, si la encierran, si lo quitan el hijo, la lana y la vida, siempre a todo dice bien.*
>
> *Y todo el bien que tenemos en la tierra, la tierra lo da. Ultimamente, ya después de fallecidos y hediondos, cuando no hay mujer, padre, hijo, pariente ni amigo que quiera sufrirnos y todos nos despiden, huyendo de nosostros, entonces nos ampara, recogiéndonos dentro de su proprio vientre, donde nos guarda en fiel depósito, para volvernos a dar en vida nueva y eterna. Y la mayor excelencia, la más digna de gloria y alabanza, es que, haciendo por nosotros tanto, tan a la continua, siendo tan generosa y franca, que ni cesa ni se cansa, nunca repite lo que da ni lo zahiere dando con ello en los ojos, como lo hacen los hombres.*

And therefore (these things considered) it hath ever beene held one of the hardest and difficultest things in the world, to finde out a true and faithfull friend.

Of which sort, many are spoken of in ancient stories, and we finde a great number of them recorded of olde, and painted forth unto us in your feigned fables; but that there either now are, or have beene such heretofore as are there decyphered unto us, I doubt very much, at least I am fully perswaded, they were very rare and few. One only friend have I found to be true, and is of the same nature and condition, as we are. And this friend of ours, is the best, the bountifullest, the truest, and the faithfullest of all other; for this is never wanting to its friend, but continues firme and constant for ever, nor is at any time weary of giving: And this good friend of ours (that I may not hold you any longer in suspence) is the Earth.

This affords us pretious stones, gold, silver, and divers other mettals, whereof we stand in need, and so earnestly thirst after. It bringeth forth grasse, and all sorts of herbes, wherewith are not only fed our flocks of sheepe, our cattell, and other beasts for the use and service of man, but those medicinable simples, which conserve our health, free us from diseases, and if we fall into sicknesse, set us upright againe, preserving this life of ours, in a sound and perfect state of health. It yeeldeth us all sorts of fruits, that are either savourie to the taste, or nourishable to the bodie. It gives us wooll, and flax, and by consequence, all kinde of woven stuffes, wherewith we cloath, and adorne, this naked flesh of ours. It opens its owne veines of its owne accord, whilest from its full brests, sprout forth those sweet and delicate waters, which we drinke; those brookes and rivers, which get the fields with childe, and make them fruitfull, and not only that, but doth facilitate commerce, and make an easie way for trafficke, bringing the strangest and remotest parts of the world to shake hands, and to live in a league of love and friendship together. Nay more, it is so good, and so sweet a friend, that it suffereth, and willingly consenteth to all that we will our selves. Be shee well or ill used by us, all is one to her, so as we be pleased. Shee is like a sheepe, from whom you shall heare no other language, but *Omnia bene*: All is well. Leade her forth to feed, or bring her to the waters to drinke; shut, and penne her up, or let her loose; take her lambkin from her, her milke, her wooll, nay her very life, to all shee alwayes answers *bien*: all is well. And all that *bien*, or good that we have on earth, the Earth gives it us. And for an upshot of all, when we are now dead, and lye stinking above ground, when there is neither wife, father, sonne, kinsman, nor friend, that will abide and endure our companie any longer, but does all of them utterly forsake us, and flie from us; then, even then, doth not shee refuse us, but huggs us, and makes much of us, and opening her owne wombe, takes us in unto her, where we quietly lye, as it were *in deposito*, till shee render afterwards a faithfull account of what shee hath received, and delivers us up to a new and eternall life. And amongst many her other excellencies, one of the worthiest things in her, and deserving most commendation, is; That shee doing so much for us, as shee doth, and that so continually and without ceasing, being so generous, and so

franke-hearted, that shee is never tyred out, never growes weary, yet
doth shee not looke for any requitall, shee neither askes, nor expects
any returne of kindeness, nor doth shee talke and tell of it, nor twit
thee in the teeth with it; which some kinde of friends, more usually,
then commendably, doe. (Part II, Book II, chapter 1)[5]

The second theme develops the idea that the Earth is fecund if it is well cultivated; in return, it provides the peasant with simple and authentic pleasures. It
is encountered especially in Tibullus and Virgil, where it is linked to the notion
of progress in agriculture, a progress ameliorating the quality of life under the
aegis of the gods. It is presented as in contradiction with the first theme on several
points, since Virgil uses it to criticize indirectly all those portrayals of the Golden
Age that glorify man's passivity and inactivity. To the sovereign power of Nature
in Lucretius, Virgil opposes the gods who subjugate Nature and place it in the
service of mankind, which owes its harvests to the beneficent intervention of Jupiter, Ceres, Bacchus, Osiris, Minerva, and others, to whom the first lines of the
Georgics are dedicated. Tibullus writes: "Country I sing & country Gods. Life
as their disciple/ ceased to drive away hunger with the acorn./ They taught men
first to tie rafters together. . . . / They were the first to teach the bull his bond-
age/ & place the wheel beneath the wagon's weight. Then wild fare was forgotten:
fruit-trees then were planted/ & kitchen-gardens drank the channeled stream";
"*Rura cano rurisque deos: his vita magistris*," *Elegiae*, II, ll. 37f.).[6]

The *topos*, at least in the *Georgics*, plays a pragmatic role, since Virgil intends
to celebrate in the exordium: "What makes the crops joyous, beneath what star,
Maecenas, it is well to turn the soil, and wed vines to elms, what tending the kine
need, what care the herd in breeding, what skill the thrifty bees" (I, ll. 1–4). He
certainly does not aim to write a practical manual of agronomy, but to arouse the
interest of the great landowners in farming. Like the first theme, it is joined to
a condemnation of navigation: "*Sollicitant alii remjis freta caeca*" [*Georgics*, II,
l. 503; Others vex with oars seas unknown], to which he adds the rejection of
Court life and luxury: "What though no stately mansion . . . , though their
white wool be not stained with Assyrian dye," in favor of a virtuous and serene
life ("Yet theirs is repose without care, and a life that knows no fraud, but is rich
in treasures manifold" (II, ll. 458–475), in which all hoarding is forbidden ("another hoards up wealth—*Condit opes alius*" [l. 507]). At the same time that he
pays homage in passing to the Earth's spontaneous offerings ("*Quos rami fructus,
quos ipsa volentia rura/ sponte tulere sua, carpsit*" [II, ll. 500–501; He plucks
the fruits which his boughs, which his ready fields, of their own free will, have
borne]), Virgil approves the organization of agriculture ushered in by the reign
of Jupiter, who forged the Roman virtues of energy and know-how in particular.
The social interests vested in the *Georgics* are well known; the work was written
at the request of Maecenas, who "thus gave support to Octavian's plans" to "re-

store in the Roman soul the ancient virtues of the race, especially the taste for agriculture."[7] But in the passage from the first theme to the second, the notion of collective wealth, as well as the portrayal of a social state from which effort and work are banished creates at its heart a space of conflict and unyielding trajectories of meaning, for they organize secondary modeling systems that aim to translate the same thing (happiness and virtue) into contradictory figurative language (effort vs. idleness; private property vs. collectivism). No doubt this explains how Spanish writers between 1590 and 1630 read these works, as Noël Salomon, following Joaquin Costa, reminds us: "In the writers of the period 1590–1630 we constantly find the ancient idea that the introduction of agricultural techniques signaled for humanity the end of the Golden Age."[8]

From Lucretius to Virgil, then, the commonplace of the praise of the Earth changes from an atheistic discourse with philosophical ambitions to an ethicoreligious discourse in the service of a political project whose objective was to persuade the literate sector of the population "possessing vast domains in Italy to return them to their original purpose."[9]

Other themes, secondary to the first two, sometimes accompany these panegyrics: the Earth then becomes the poetic locus of peace (Ovid, *Metamorphoses*, I, 97ff.; Tibullus, *Elegiae*, I, 1; Virgil, *Georgics*, II, ll. 458ff.) and serenity of mind, thus picking up the Horatian reverie (*"Beatus ille quis procul negotiis/ ut prisca gens mortalium"* [*Epodes*, II; Happy the man who, far from business and affairs/ Like mortals of the early times[10]]), in the context of an opposition between town and country. This latter tradition, which only apparently strays from our subject, has been magnificently analyzed by Noël Salomon, who quotes a whole series of "treatises, poems, and dialogues in which, throughout the sixteenth century, the antithesis between village and Court keeps coming back," after having given a convincing interpretation of it. The nobility, he writes, came to

> regret its past, to dream of a mode of existence exactly opposite to the one it was experiencing in reality. The themes of opposition to reality, of flight and escape, of renunciation appropriate to declining classes took hold of the nobility. Thus writers who were noble or who wrote for the nobility began to turn their backs on the Court: this was the theme of the 'menos precio de Corte.' By a second movement complementary to the first, they cast their gaze on the poetically imagined countryside and peasantry as the absolute antithesis of the world of the Court: this was the theme of *alabanza de aldea* (praise of the village).[11]

Besides the thematic differences separating these two motifs, the praise of the countryside or of the Earth, within these two discursive formations, is thus playing different roles. In Salomon's reading of the theme of "scorn for the Court and praise of the countryside," this defense of rural life hides the absenteeism of the nobility attracted by Court life, the exodus impelling the small and medium lan-downers as well as journeymen, to migrate to the cities: "El campo está erial, huidos les labradores de pobreza, cargados de censos y ejecutores" [The land is untilled, the peasants have fled in poverty, burdened with taxes and executions] (Sancho de Moncada, *Restauración política de España y deseos políticos*, 1619). Thus the general state of decay of the Spanish countryside "que las casas se caen y ninguna se vuelve a edificar, los lugares se yerman, los vecinos se huyen y au-sentan y dejan los campos desiertos" [houses are falling down and none are being rebuilt, villages are deserted, the inhabitants are fleeing, leaving the fields deserted"] (*Consejo de Castilla*, 1619, quoted by P. Fernandez Navarrete, *La conservación de monarquías*, Madrid, 1626). This idyllic portrayal of peasant life thus masks on the one hand the relations between classes and, on the other hand, the social interests that explain an economic and social situation *whose representation it is inverting*. By its very functioning, this description is a compo-nent of an ideological formation that is itself the product of a specific social for-mation.[12]

It is difficult to put literary texts in the same category as the economic and polit-ical treatises glorifying the merits of agriculture that flourished from the end of Philip II's reign to the crisis of 1640. Indeed, these treatises denounce a reality that the literary texts disguise (see the texts from Sancho de Moncada and the Council of Castile already quoted) and justify their point of view by an analysis of the national economic situation:

> The evil has come, in Pedro de Valencia's opinion, from the abundance
> of gold, silver, and money, which has always been . . . poison for
> cities and republics. People think money is what provides for their sub-
> sistence, and this is not true. The inheritance of well-tended fields,
> herds, and fisheries, that is what feeds cities and republics. Each man
> ought to work his share of the land. And those who subsist on the in-
> come of the money they invest are idle and useless, only there to eat
> what others have sown and nurtured.[13]

This feeling is shared some forty years later by Saavedra Fajardo:

> The people admired along the banks of the Guadalquivir those precious
> fruits of the Earth drawn from the soil by the toil of the Indians and
> brought to them by our audacity and industry. But the possession and
> the abundance of so much wealth have changed everything. At once
> agriculture gave up the plow and dressed in silk, cared for its hands
> that had been hardened with labor. Merchandise, smitten with nobility,
> exchanged the counter for the saddle and wanted to prance in the street.
> As men always expect from their revenue more than it can provide,
> royal display and ceremonial have grown fat, wages and pay have in-
> creased."[14]

When we compare this monosemic discourse with the figurative system of the literary texts reviewed previously, we can appreciate the acuity of this remark of J. Mukarovsky's: "The relationship between the work of art and the signified object has . . . no existential value, and in that sense the work of art is radically different from purely communicative signs."[15] Similarly, we can perceive the complexity of the discursive formations that are indirectly related to a social formation itself complex in nature, and we shall be careful not to confuse at the ideological level the praise of agriculture with the praise of cattle-raising, each of which transcribes different social interests; likewise, we shall oppose these latter panegyrics to the *arbitrios* who propose the development of industry as the solution to the national crisis.

However, both must be grasped within the context of a polemics opposing "two systems of thought that have coexisted and fought with one another,"[16] concerning the role of gold and precious metals in a State's prosperity. To borrow Vilar's terms, is gold the "only sign of individual prosperity, or of the greatness of a State"? or quite to the contrary, is it "the beginning of the dissolution of true wealth that consists only in the production of the goods necessary for life"?[17] We recognize the terms of a new contradiction opposing the production of agricultural or industrial goods to the accumulation and abundance of money as the best way to create economic prosperity through the growth of business transactions.

The praise of the Earth thus enters into complex networks of meaning, and its ideological significance consequently depends on a number of factors: the typology of themes, of goods selected, of discursive formations, the discursive status (figurative or merely communicative) of the context in which it is inserted.

We shall have to keep all these considerations in mind when we approach this text of *Guzmán de Alfarache*, written at the very moment when the flood of silver coming from the Indies reached its maximum: "When," writes Pierre Vilar,

> under the influence of Mexican silver, and then of silver from Potosí, the volume of imported metal becomes overwhelming—and when, through the effect of successive technical innovations, this silver keeps on getting cheaper, the rise in Spanish prices begins again. Again, apparent growth in wealth masks global problems; no longer do critical analyses like that of Ortiz reappear. But again, the Cortes, frightened by the price increases, frequently raises its voice in protest. And the numerous bankruptcies, the rather premature decline of the fairs of Castile, already provoke 'memorials' on the fragility of the mercantile economy (Toledo, Medina del Campo).[18]

Nor should we forget that this new crisis is accompanied by an awareness of its causes, namely, the malediction of gold: "In fact, Spaniards in the 1600s understood very well . . . that this inflation of money in circulation committing the nation to internal and external expenditures had caused prices to rise, favored nonproductive activities and idleness; that this rise in prices had destroyed the competitiveness of Spanish products in relation to foreign goods."[19]

We may observe that Alemán's text is related especially to the first theme, the one that deals with the spontaneous generosity of the Earth. This is why, in order to follow more closely the mechanisms and the significance of the transformational process the *topos* undergoes in the text, I suggest we do a first reading in juxtaposition with a text by Juan Luis Vives, taken from the *Socorro de los pobres* (I, ch. IX). This overlapping reading will be useful from two points of view, on the one hand, because of the thematic relationship of the two works, which have already been understood simultaneously in the framework of the polemics over charitable works and the reform of begging in sixteenth-century Spain, and, on the other hand, because of the gap separating the conceptual discourse of Vives's text from the figurative language of Alemán.

> Primeramente, la Naturaleza, por la cual quiero que se entienda a Dios, pues la Naturaleza no es otra cosa que la voluntad y mandamientos divinos; cuantas utilidades y con cuanta larguez no nos produce y todas ellas en comun: para comer, hierbas, raices, frutos, mieses, ganados, peces; para vestir, pieles y lanas y demas desto, maderas y metales y las comodidades que se nos derivan de los animales, como perros, caballos, bueyes. Y finalmente todo cuanto derramó de su seno ubérrimo púsolo a la vista en esa gran casa del mundo, no encerrado por vallas ni por puerta alguna, para que de ello participasen indistintamente todos los seres que engendró.[20]

> [First, Nature, by which I mean God, since Nature is nothing else but the Divine will and commandments; how many useful things does it not produce for us, in such abundance, and all of them in common: food—herbs, roots, fruit, grain, livestock, fish; clothing—skins, wools and more; wood and metals and the comforts we derive from animals such as dogs, horses and oxen. And finally all that it brought forth from its fertile womb it displayed in that great house of the world, unenclosed by any fences or gates, so that every being it created could share in it equally.]

We are familiar with the broad context of this passage in Vives, namely, the praise of charity and virtue. I shall limit myself, therefore, to situating the precise immediate context. Chapter IX begins with a denunciation of the concept of property:

> Decía el filósofo Platón que serían felices las repúblicas si desaparecieran del vocabulario del trato humano las dos palabras *tuyo* y *mío*; cuántas tragedias no ocasionan entre nosotros! Con qué énfasis no se hacen sonar expresiones como estas: le di *lo mío*; me quitó *lo mío*, no tocarás *lo mío*; no toqué *lo tuyo*; guardo *lo tuyo*; conténtate con *lo*

tuyo. Como si hubiera algún hombre que poseyera algo que con razón pueda llamar suyo. Aun la virtud misma recibió la de Dios, que nos lo has dado todo, a unos por causa de los otros.

[The philosopher Plato said that republics would be happy if the two words *thine* and *mine* disappeared from the vocabulary of human relations; how many tragedies do they not cause among us? How bombastic do such expressions as these sound: I gave him *mine*; he took *mine* from me; you won't touch *mine*; I didn't touch *yours*; I'm keeping *yours*; be satisfied with *yours*. As if any man could possess anything he could rationally call his own. Even Virtue herself received hers from God, who has given us everything, to some for the sake of others.]

Vives draws from such premises the following conclusions:

Sepa por tanto, cualquiera que posee los dones de la Naturaleza que, comunicándolos con el hermano los posee legítimamente y por voluntad e institución de la Natureleza; pero si no, es ladrón y robador, convicto y robador, convicto y condenado por la ley natural, puesto que retiene y detenta aquellos bienes que la Naturaleza creó no sólo para él.

[Let it be known, therefore, that, by the will and institution of Nature, whoever possesses the gifts of Nature and shares them with his brother, possesses them legitimately; but if he does not do so, he is a thief and a robber, a convicted robber, convicted and condemned by the natural law, since he keeps for himself those goods that Nature did not create only for him.]

Vives's debt to Virgil is obvious even though a situation considered historical and conjunctural (before Jupiter, in the reign of Saturn) is displaced for the sake of affirming a general moral truth. Other minor displacements may be observed: Nature is no longer an autonomous force in the service of the gods, but a representation of divine will. It is differentiated from the Earth, which is identified with the world: "todo cuanto derramó de su seno ubérrimo púsolo a la vista en esa gran casa del mundo." The range of products offered is considerably broadened, owing to the fact that the spontaneous nature of this gift is being erased in order to stress more clearly the total wealth common to humanity; certain goods presuppose a labor either of extraction (*metal, peces*) or of foresight (*mieses*), or, again, of transformation (*lanas*). Finally, in its internal chronology, the *topos* grants special importance to the theme of communal goods by displacing it from the beginning (in the *Georgics*) to the end of the composition. What is striking, however, with respect to the redistribution that takes place in the *Guzmán de Alfarache*, is the economic vision of an autarchic circuit founded on the sole satisfaction of elementary needs.

It is in the hollow of this *topos*, on the contrary, that Alemán's text seems to be operating. The honey and the wild fruit of the Latin descriptions have been left out; all that remains is the much more general form *fruit*. To this, four products are added: metals, grass, cloth, waters. Compared to the preceding text, this one is more selective, thereby giving even greater emphasis to the detailed listing of metals: "precious stones, gold, silver and other metals." Out of eight occurrences of the lexical field of products, four involve metal, and three connote money!

Let us follow the movement of the second paragraph, which opens with the theme of cattle-raising, and after a relatively long and unexpected parenthesis picks up the theme of the textile industry (*dándanos telas*), then loses itself at the end of the paragraph in another allegory of the Earth described in the form of a consenting lamb. Thus, from *yerbas* to *frutas* and *telas* the imagery moves by associative contiguity, constructing a panegyric movement glorifying animal breeding. The last term, *water*, is traditionally linked to life ("for if for a while they lack wheat, they would be able to sustain themselves with other foods as well as with meat . . . but without water no man nor other animal can sustain life. No grass nor plant can produce fruit or seed; all need the aqueous humor and water"[21]). Water's chief merit here is that it permits trade and communication among the most distant peoples of the Earth. This perspective on overseas adventure seen from the viewpoint of its commercial ambitions is doubtless one of the strongest historical underpinnings of the text, and we can see clearly how the internal mechanisms of the deconstruction of a *topos* are direct vectors of the ideological production of meaning. This allows us to stress as well, in passing, how the sign in the cultural object loses the immediacy of its relation to the signified in order to become part of a figurative system; this displacement is all the more perceptible here since water is, at an initial level, metaphorically transformed into milk ("*brotando de sus pechos dulcísimas . . . aguas*"), thereby entering, by means of a point of coincidence which focuses its meaning, into a semiotic text inscribing the preeminence of animal breeding in the deconstruction of a commonplace.

The conjunction of this dual defense of trade and animal breeding gives particular force to the remarkable concision of "dándonos telas." No doubt we can see here a direct trace of the spontaneity of the Earth's gifts; the writing process in this case, however, does not affect the reproduction of *dar* but the nature of this new *gift*, which presupposes a whole process of material transformation as much as it does a human activity. Thus, the text is here unveiling its criteria for hiding: indeed, it erases agriculture and industry in favor solely of activities of direct exchange capable of being translated into monetary gain. Thus *the interdiction of commerce in all the Latin texts is being transgressed and occupies the entire textual space*, and the topos, at the same it remains itself, is being inverted. However, spaces of conflict are perceptible where other voices seem to be invested: such is the case, for example, of the doublet "de que tanta *necesidad y sed* tenemos," in which this obviously mercantilist vision of the economy is being overlain by the *contradictory* moral discourse of the theologians, which itself is wrapped around pretexts (*necesidad*) given to reject them. Such seems again to be the case of this fugitive vision of a bruised, flayed, bloodless Earth sketched out by a final allegory ("*si le quitan el hijo, la leche, la lana y la vida*"), and which transcribes the hidden face of this idyllic vision. I am tempted to see here an articulation of contradictory social interests (*itself hidden in the allegory*) referring to the critical discourse of Sancho de Moncada or of the Castilian Cortes ("El campo está erial, las casas se caen, los lugares se yerman"). Is not the prosperous position of commerce and the great cattlebreeders of the *Mesta* happening at the expense of the agricultural producers and, especially, of this devastated countryside? And, if this is so, is not the discourse I have just described a dominant discourse, one that silences another discourse and prevents it from emerging directly? In that case, allegory would be functioning as the index both of a system of repression and of its transgression, at a dual level—both ideological and psychoanalytic, as we shall see—and it is in this sense that the problem of the unconscious of the text needs, it seems to me, to be formulated.

Let us now investigate the writing itself. Two phenomena of semantic diffraction (or of the deconstruction of set phrases) are evident on a first reading. The first one concerns "*piedras de precio*," a diffraction of the original expression *piedras preciosas*, on which has thus been superimposed the semic plenitude of the concept of monetary exchange of valuable stones, which are worth their weight in something else, at the expense of the metaphorical virtualities of objects that are estimable in relation to other criteria, emotional or aesthetic ones, for example. The second leads to a similar meaning effect, in which the practice of writing deconstructs the traditional expression "*cubrir y abrigar*" and changes it into "*cubrirnos y adornarnos*."[22] From a product of the first necessity, *cloth* becomes adornment, an index of social position, stake and object of covetousness as much as gold or silver; that is, writing poses in a new form the problem of *necesidad* and *sed*. In this manner, the criteria for the selection of the chain of signifiers begin to come into view.

Let us take the case of another deconstruction, even if it may seem more questionable; I mean the theme of the excellence of friendship, for which the most frequently used forms seem to me to be the following: "*buen y verdadero amigo*"; "*el más leal amigo*," "*buena y verdadera amistad*"; which means that even if we grant that it is part of the paradigmatic axis in question, the adjective *fiel* has a relatively low coefficient of possible selection. The fact that it was chosen is not insignificant. What separates *fiel* from *leal* is, if we can rely on Covarrubias, what distinguishes *fe* from *fidelidad*; concerning the former, Covarrubias gives a series of examples ("Yo doy mi fe y palabra"; "Tengo fe con Fulano que vale; fiome dél;" 'Doy fe a lo que Fulano me dixo"; "la fe que da el escribano") that refer, significantly, to his definition of *fiel* ("el que guarda fe y lealtad, *el que trata ver-*

dad y no engaña a otro"). The two semantic fields overlap only partially. (Cf. "*leal*: el que guarda fidelidad y tiene *reconocimiento y amor* al *señor*, al amigo, al que se fia dél. Siempre se dice de inferior a mayor como *vasallo* leal y también de ygual a ygual como amigo leal: oponese a la palabra *traydor*. . . . La mujer guarda lealtad a su marido cuando es casta y honesta y no le intenta hazer *alevosia* o *trayción*.") While *leal*, it seems, refers to a medieval value system, *fiel* seems to me to connote most of all the world of the marketplace, business, and commerce. Two further comparisons will suffice to show this: un criado [a servant] *fiel* is one who does not rob his master; the *fiel executor* is one who "tiene cuydado de mirar las mercaderias que se venden y si se da en ellas el peso justo y *fiel*" (Covarrubias). Writing displays a sequence of signs that originate in the same lexical field: such is the case of "son *contados*," in which *escaso, raros, pocos* have been omitted from the paradigmatic axis in favor of an obviously connoted term; "*estar por escrito*," which, at a certain level, is the antithesis of *fe* ("Tomar por escrito: no fiar en palabras" [Covarrubias]) and, especially, "*guardar en fiel depósito*," which needs no commentary. Let us, nevertheless, recall what Covarrubias says about the verb *depositar*: "cuando los que porfian y apuestan depositan en manos de un tercero alguna cosa para el que salicre con su intencion. O quando la justicia de oficio deposita aquella cosa sobre la qual se litiga o en otra manera."[23] The vehicle of figurative discourse is thus seen as a *representation* in its turn of the world of transaction, seen with its activities, its values, its rules of behavior and juridical organization. *Tracing in this manner the textual markers of a dominant discourse, it reveals the ideological system responsible for the deconstruction of the* topos.

I come finally to the examination of this "galaxy of signifiers" organized in a relational system capable of producing an autonomous meaning. If I apply the analytical principles I have defined elsewhere,[24] I see the following semiotic texts:

1. *Quantification/Qualification*: (24)
← uno, solo, todos^2, contados, partes, todo^3

   tanto, tanta, mas^5, tan^2

→ excelencia, mejor, mayor, malo (digno, alabanza)

2. *Products*: (21)
— Breeding: yerba, ganados, oveja leche, dulcísimas, lana, animales, criar 8
— Mines: piedra, oro, plata, metales 4
— Industry: telas, haciendo, hacer 3
— Agriculture (as such) 0

- Production (polyvalent signs): cosas^2,
  fertilizar, campos, frutos, producir 6
3. *Stability/Instability*: (16)
← Permanence: *cesa, cansa*^{2}, siempre^3, nunca^3, repite (volver a), *falta*, (ampara) a la continua
→ nuevo
4. *Basic needs (use value)*: (15)
- necesidad, sustentarse, valerse, servicio, cubrirse comer
- beber^2, brotar, agua bebemos, arroyos, rios, sed adornar
5. *Situational elements*: (13)
- Time: ultimamente, cuando, después, entonces
- Space: remoto, dentro, donde, hay, hallarse, hallar
- Known/Unknown: naturaleza, misteriosas, extrañas
6. *Generosity*: (12)
- liberal, darnos, da, dándonos, consentir, da, facilitar, dar
- generosa
- franca, dar, dando
7. *Property*: (12)
- tener, nuestra, tenemos, nuestro, neustros, sus, sus, tenemos, bien^3,
  proprio
8. *Life/Death*: (10)
→ salud, eterno (gloria) vida,^{2}

  \
   medicinales, aligeran, enfermedad
  /

← fallecidos, hediondos
9. *Abnegation/Hostility*: (8)
→ consentir, sufra, callar, quiera
← *quiera, sufrirnos*, despide, zahiere
10. *Confidence/Suspicion*: (7)
→ fiel^2, verdadero^2, cierto
← fábulas, por escrito
11. *Ser/Estar*: (7)
- son, haberlo sido, es^3, siendo
- está
12. *Hoarding*: (7)
- conservar, preservándonos, guardar, depósito, encerrar (huyendo),
  recogiéndonos
13. *Adequacy/Inadequacy*: (7)
← conforme, misma, como, juntamente, como
→ *sólo*, otra

14. *Family*: (6)
   − padre, mujer, pariente, amigo[2], hijo
15. *Human Body*: (5)
   − vientre, ojos, hombres, pechos, veras
16. *Speech*: (4)
   − se dice, dice, oir, calla
17. *Exchange*: (4)
   − comercio, comunicándose, (tratamiento), llevar
18. *Robbery*: (3)
   − Quitar, romper, llevar

Subset Groupings

The preceding reading authorizes us to group in a single text, first subsets 10 and 17, and then, with these, groups 3 (basic needs) and 1 (quantification/qualification), around a dialectic opposing *use value* to *exchange value*. These regrouped signs thus number 51 (use value: 22; exchange value: 20; polysemous: 9).

The remarkable preponderance of *Ser* over *Estar* suggests comparison with group 3, increasing it from 16 to 23 or 12.63 percent.

An obvious zone of coincidence is drawn around subsets 6 (generosity), 7 (property), 9 (abnegation), 12 (hoarding), 18 (robbery), for a total of 42 signs.

The minor subsets 5, 8, 13, 14, 15, and 16 do not define any coreferential relations and consequently do not display any pertinent characteristics, at least in this text. Forty-five of a total of 182 signs are involved, or 24.72 percent.

Semiotic Systems

On the thematic axis, which corresponds to the apparent signified in the passage (generosity, abnegation), we note the superposition of a semiotic text that reproduces the values of the mercantile world, as shown in the accompanying diagram.[25]

We can measure the meaning of this chain of signifiers if we compare it with the one that can be observed in the text of Vives, in which four subsets are identifiable:

(a) *Products*: (15)
   hierbas, raices, frutos, mieses, ganados, peces, pieles, lanas, animales, perros, caballos, bueyes, cosa, producir, derivan
(b) *Collective wealth* ← *vs.* → *property*: (9)
   → comun, casa, *encerrado, vallas, puerta*, participasen, indistintamenta
   ← otra, sus
(c) *Quantification* ← *vs.* → *Qualification*: (8)

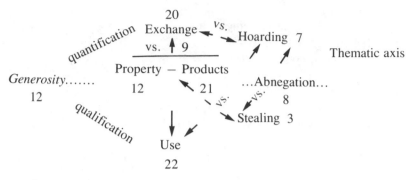

→ alguna, todos, cuantas, todas, todo,
← cuanta, cuanto, gran
(d) *Basic needs*: (4)
   utilidades, comer, vestir, comodidades

No doubt it may seem excessive to make *comodidades* an index of a basic need; however, it is equidistant from basic need and from superfluity or luxury; the same observation holds true for the series *animales*, here perceived as referring to animal husbandry. What emerges from this is the great number of textual markers that negate the concept of property, and consequently the absence of a gap between the two structural chains, that is, between the thematics explicit at the first level ("serían felices las repúblicas si desaparecieran del vocabulario del trato humano las dos palabras *tuyo y mío*") and the linguistic material serving as its vehicle. This difference is doubtless explained by the fact that we have passed from figurative language—*Guzmán de Alfarache*—to conceptual language–Vives. This observation leads us to approach the Alemán passage from another point of view, namely, that of figurative discourse.

This aspect will be clearer if we keep in mind the relative transparency of the text by Vives (*De subventione pauperum*). In connection with the lack of gap between the semiotic text and the explicit thematics, let us take the case in Alemán's text of *sed*, which we have rightly grouped with the indexes of basic needs, and which we have seen functioning in context in a contradictory manner; or again that of *agua*, which sets up a movement (*rios, arroyos, mares*) in which the world of "merchandise" is foregrounded. In both cases, the structural chain of the semiotic text—thirst and what slakes thirst—inverts its first meaning (elementary need and satisfaction of this need) into an image that contradicts this first meaning: desire and the means of satisfying this desire. We see how by that very fact the sign loses its original transparency—the immediacy of its relation to the referent as it has been defined by language—and becomes part of a new code. This new code obviously interferes with the first one, and this interference, in which the chain of signifiers crosses the chain of signifieds and problematizes it, itself carries meaning. Mercantilism is thus seen, for example, not as a choice of economic policy but as a necessity.

Approached from this angle—if, following Yuri Lotman, we consider the whole text as a single sign—it presents us with a first equivalence between the Earth and friendship, seen through two criteria—generosity and stability—that organize the remodeling of the *topos*. When we come to the second of these criteria, we are witnessing a displacement, since the image is being introduced of a victim who does not rebel against the injustices he undergoes, thereby distancing us all the more from the concept of friendship based on a reciprocal relationship; by describing the first term as a victim, the text implicitly defines the second as a tyrant. From that point on, we have left the realm of the signified (friendship), and the supporting image (the Earth), rendered autonomous, develops its own logic. By garbing itself in allegory, it is seen in turn as a signified conveyed by a new figurative sign and as *the object of discourse*. This object remains articulated to the first (friendship) in a single point, namely, the problem of fidelity, but through an implicit network of arguments. The Earth's stability is certainly one of its two essential characteristics, but this stability is not named as such; it is hidden in the allegory and in the "not-said" of the text. It is not immaterial, as we have seen, that the vehicle of this allegory is the image of the lamb, nor is it immaterial, by the same token, that the latter is followed by another metaphorization in the image of the mother, set in place by the preceding movement ("Cria nuestros frutos. Rompe sus venas, brotando de sus pechos" [She raises our fruit. She bursts her veins, gushing forth from her breasts]). It is even more significant that this maternal image is perceived as a subject tempted by a desire for regression to the fetal state ("recogiéndonos dentro de su proprio vientra donde nos guarda en fiel depósito para volvernos a dar en vida" [gathering us within her own womb, where she guards us in safekeeping to return us again to life]), a desire in which a symbolism of quite another sort is invested. Thus, the signified is displaced from one series to the other, for, in that case, it is the characteristic that is common to both friendship and the Earth (stability) that in turn becomes the object of discourse, even if it is seen in the inverted form of a profound feeling of insecurity and of flight.

I readily see in this phenomenon the index of another conflictive space in the very sphere of influence of the deconstructed *topos*. Indeed, the *topos* was originally centered on the glorification of a past portrayed as idyllic or as the crucible of virtue, rejecting the transformations that have altered social organization. Alemán's writing practice creates an inversion of this vision by resolutely opting for modern seafaring and commercial adventure, but in so doing, it clashes once again with trajectories of meaning inscribed in the commonplace, and with their virtual ideological import. Confronted with this uncertain sea, the Earth again becomes a longed-for haven, and this opening onto modernity faces the opacity of earlier discourses. In a general way, everything money contaminates in *Guzmán de Alfarache* is tainted by instability. Such is the case of the false friend won over by favors ("y como anguilla paso a paso en la ocasion se me resbala, dejándome la mano vacía" [and as an eel slowly at that moment slips away from me, leaving me with an empty hand]; "cuando faltaron dineros, faltaron ellos, fallecieron en un día su amistad y mi dinero" [when money is lacking, they are lacking, in one day my money and their friendship died]), as well as material goods ("Presto me hice al trabajo . . . no fiando de bienes caducos que cargan y vacian, como las azacayas tan presto como suben bajan" [Quickly I went to work . . . having little faith in empty goods that come and go, like the waterwheels that, as soon as they rise, fall]).

I am taking this broader context to bring out more clearly the manifold voices in the text that concerns us, in particular, those that are expressed in the judgment made on an Earth "que nunca falta y permanece siempre" [that is never lacking and remains always], in which we can detect in the background of an apparently essentially moral context an economic value judgment that recalls practically word for word a phrase of the *Despertador* of Juan de Arrieta ("que natura ni falta ni jamas ha faltado" [for nature never lacks nor has ever been lacking]),[26] written to glorify agriculture to combat the negative effects of mercantilist thought. Thus, by means of the problematization of instability, the text inscribes in a new form "the ethical theme of the damage done by gold," to use Pierre Vilar's expression.[27] This theme, within the original *topos*, is joined to a contradictory vision of the past, to modalities of deconstruction of the theme in Alemán, in such a way that writing seems to be submitting itself to preconstructed trajectories of meaning, even if those meanings are being reactivated by specific and complex social interests.

Let us now return to the allegory of the mother, which we said was no longer the iconic sign of the Earth, but that of stability. We observe that the word is never uttered again; the mother figure is described both by a series of textual markers (venas, pechos, seno, vientre) and by its significant absence in another series ("no hay mujere, padre, hijo, pariente ni amigo"). The fact that *amigo* is included in this series must not be interpreted as an internal contradiction between *la tierra y el amigo* but as further proof, if it were needed, that the object of the figurative discourse is no longer friendship. No doubt one might question this absence of a psychocritical point of view, but I prefer to pose the problem of the repressed text in other terms. Indeed, I observe that this desire of the subject tempted by regression to the fetal state actualizes at a much deeper level the latencies of an old-fashioned vision contained in the original *topos* that can be seen for that very reason as victims as well of a system of repression, and I am tempted to conclude in favor of an internalized ideological contradiction. The infratext that is the object of repression thus reveals the manner in which the internal contradictions of the *topos* are experienced, as well as the internal contradictions of the mercantilist economy, for the optimistic vision of the first lines has repressed in the "not said" of the text that other reality—the profound feeling of insecurity broadly shared by Spaniards in the 1600s, a feeling that explains why, from a purely economic standpoint, the Earth is the safest of investments.

Even if I have succeeded in relating the Earth to the economic discourse of Juan de Arrieta, its representation as symbol of stability is still problematic. Writing, in fact, is working here on several fundamental *assumptions*–namely, the definition of friendship (generosity, fidelity), on the one hand, and, on the other, the generosity of the Earth. The text's *constructed*, which alone establishes the equivalency of the two terms *Friend* = Earth, is summed up in a single assertion, the stability of the Earth. Thus, figurative discourse models in the hollows of the original *topos*, in that vision attached to the past that is at first glance not reactivated by writing, the coincidence of the ideological subject and the psychic subject.

Chapter 11
Ideology and Textual Genetics

Textual Markers of Ideological Marginalization in Quevedo's *Buscon*

En que cuenta quien es y de donde

*Yo, señor, soy de Segovia. Mi padre se llamó Clemente Pablo, natu-
ral del mismo pueblo; Dios le tenga en el cielo. Fue, tal como todos dicen, de oficio barbero; aunque eran tan altos sus pensamientos, que se
corría de que le llamasen así, diciendo que el era tundidor de mejillas y
sastre de barbas. Dicen que era de muy buena cepa, y, segun él bebía,
es cosa para creer.*

*Estuvo casado con Aldonza de San Pedro, hija de Diego de San
Juan y nieta de Andrés de San Cristóbal. Sospechábase en el pueblo
que no era cristiana vieja, aunque ella, por los nombres y
sobrenombres de sus pasados, quiso esforzar que era decendiente de la
letania. Tuvo muy buen parecer, y fue tan celebrada, que, en el tiempo
que ella vivió, casi todos los copleros de España hacían cosas sobre
ella.*

*Padeció grandes trabajos recién casada, y aun después, porque
malas lenguas daban en decir que mi padre metia el dos de bastos para
sacar el as de oros. Probósele que, a todos los que hacía la barba a
navaja, mientras les daba con el agua, levantándoles la cara para el
lavatorio, un mi hermanico de siete años les sacaba muy a su salvo los
tuétanos de las faldriqueras. Murió el angelico de unos azotes que le
dieron en la cárcel. Sintiólo mucho mi padre, por ser tal que robaba a
todos las voluntades.*

Por estas y otras niñerias, estuvo preso; aunque, según a mi me han dicho después, salió de la carcel con tanta honra, que le acompañaron docientos cardenales sino que a ninguno llamaban "señoría". Las damas diz que salían por verle a las ventanas, que siempre pareció bien mi padre a pie y a caballo. No lo digo por vanagloria, que bien saben todos cuan ajeno soy della.

Mi madre, pues no tuvo calamidades. Un día alabándomela una vieja que me crió, decía que era tal su agrado, que hechizaba a cuantos la trataban. Solo diz que se dijo no sé qué de un cabrón y volar, lo cual la puso cerca de que la diesen plumas con que lo hiciese en público. Hubo fama que reedificaba doncellas, resucitaba cabellos encubriendo canas. Unos la llamaban zurcidora de gustos; otros, algebrista de voluntades desconcertadas, y por mal nombre alcagüeta. Para unos era tercera, primera para otros, y flux para los dineros de todos. Ver, pues, con la cara de risa que ella oía esto de todos, era para dar mil gracias a Dios.

In which is given an account of birth and country

I, Sir, am from Segovia; my father's name was Clement Paul, and he too was a native of the same town—God rest his soul in heaven. He was, they all say, a barber by trade: although his ideas were so exalted that he took it for an affront to be called anything but a shearer of cheeks and tailor of beards. It was said that he came of good stock, and, to judge by his love for the port, this can easily be believed. He was married to Aldonza Saturno de Rebollo, a daughter of Octavio de Rebollo Codillo and a grand-child to Lépido Ziuraconte.

The town suspected that she was not of pure old Christian blood, but she, putting forward the names of her ancestors, proved her descent from the Roman triumvirate. She was comely to look upon, and so renowned that during her life all the rhymsters of Spain made verses on her. Many were her tribulations when first she married, and even after; for slanderous tongues declared that my father was content to wear the horns, so long as they were tipped with gold. It was proved against him that, while busy with the beards of his customers, a little brother of mine, seven years old, was engaged in rifling their pockets. This little angel died of a whipping he received in gaol: my father was greatly concerned at his loss, for the lad was a gifted and willing thief. He himself, indeed, had been arrested for similar trifling affairs: yet, as I was afterwards told, he came out of prison so honourably, that two hundred cardinals accompanied him; although nobody could call them eminent. Ladies, it is said, rushed to their windows to see him pass; for my father had always a good appearance, whether on foot or mounted: I do not say this as an empty boast, for, as the world knows, such would be foreign to my nature.

My mother had no such misfortunes. An old strumpet who reared me said to me one day by way of commending her, that she bewitched all she touched; furthermore, it was whispered that she had an urge from a certain whoremonger to practise her taking arts in public. She had also acquired fame for renewing maidenheads, restoring hairs, and disguising those that were grey. Some called her a contriver of pleasure, and others, a charmer of unsatisfied desires; or, for an ill name, she was dubbed a bawdy procuress and a bottomless pit for all men's money. To see her sweet smile, when she heard such things spoken on all sides, would only ingratiate her the more to you.[1]

Semiotic Texts

In the accompanying list, every sign in the text has been taken into account, with the exception of possessive pronouns and possessive adjectives, personal pronouns, prepositions and prepositional phrases, coordinating conjunctions, and demonstratives. They total 225, but 16 of them are mentioned twice, and two (*tercera*, *oros*) three times; these repeated words are followed by an asterisk (*), thus giving a total of 245 occurrences.

The fields are presented in the order of decreasing importance and, whenever possible, in the form of dialectical oppositions, in which case the first term is the one covering the larger number of signs.

Certain terms do not seem to belong directly to the group proposed for them. They may, however, be related by the effect of what I call *derivative polarizations*, through a sign that dominates in the field in question. This is true for *poner* and *meter*, which are implied by *sacar*. Inside the various fields, these terms are presented in parentheses. Signs that are negatively marked in the text are italicized (e.g., *no . . . cristiana*).

1. *Structuring/Destructuring*: (53)
    1.1. Construction/destruction (8)
        → reedificaba, resucitaba*, hacían, hacía, haciese

        ← > algebrist*, zurcidor*

        ← desconcertadas
    1.2. Orthodoxy/heterodoxy: (15)
        → Dios,[2] cielo, letanía, lavatorio, carenales, San Petro, San Juan, San Cristóbal, resucitaba*, angélico, creer
        ← cabrón, hechizar, *cristiana*
    1.3. Social order/transgression: (30)
        → cepa*, casado, casada, honra*, doncellas, altos, fama*, dinero*, oros*, señor, cardenales, señoría, damas, caballo, oficio, barbero, tundidor, sastre, algebrista*, zurcidora*
        ← alcagüeta, tercera*, (navaja), sospechábase*, probósele*, preso, cárcel,[2] azotes*, salvo

2. *Essence/Designation*: (50)
   2.1. Enunciative function of the verb *ser*: (14)
      soy[2], fue, eran, era[7], es, (fue), ser
   2.2. Vocabulary of designation: (17)
      nombres, sobrenombres, nombre, se llamó, le llamasen, llamaban[2],
      dicen[2], diciendo, decir, dicho, diz[2], decía, se dijo, digo
   2.3. Designated objects: (6)
      Aldonza, Diego, Andrés, Clemente Pablo, cosa, cosas
   2.4. Collective or personal points of view (11)
      sospechábase*, probósele*, saben, celebrada, alabándomela, sé,
      copleros, público, honra*, *vanagloria*, fama*
   2.5. Appearance: (2)
      Parecer, pareció
3. *Quantification/Qualification*: (34)
   → mucho, tanta, todos[7], cuantos, unos[3], otros[3], siete, docientos, dos, mil,
   primera*, tercera*, ninguno
   ← tan[2], grandes, buena, buen, malas, bien[2], cuan, niñerías (agrado)
4. *Giving/Taking*: (17)
   → daban, daba, dieron, diesen, dar, gracia, tenga, tuvo, faldriqueras, oros*,
   dineros*
   ← sacar (→ metia, puso), robaba, volar, levantándoles
5. *Human body and its functions*: (15)
   ——mejillas, barbas, lenguas, barba, cara[2], tuétanos, cabellos, canas, pie,
   ver[2], oía, bebía (agua)
6. *Geographical and family origins*: (14)
   ——padre[3], madre, hija, nieta, pasados, casado*, casada*, hermanica, natural, cepa*, crió, decendiente
7. *Time*: (14)
   vivió, tiempo, recién, después[2], mientras, siempre, día, años, murió, vieja*,
   aún, hubo
8. *Conformity/Nonconformity*: (12)
   → mismo, tal[3], según[2], así, mientras
   ← casi, cerca, ajeno, encubría
9. *Feelings*: (7)
   se corría, pensamientos, sintiólo, voluntades*[2], gustos, quiso*
10. *Card-game vocabulary*: (6)
   bastos, oros*, tercera*, primera*, flux, as
11. *Suffering/Joy*: (6)
   → padecer, trabajos, azotes*, murió*
   ← risa, *calamidades*
12. *Space*: (5)
   Segovia, pueblo[2], ventanas, España

13. *Movement/Absence of movement*: (5)

salió, salían, acompañaron (→ trataban)

14. *Will*: (4)

quiso*, esforzar, voluntades*[2]

Remarks on the formulation and presentation of these semiotic texts

1.1. *algebrista* (in the sense of bone-setter) and *zurcidora* (darner) have to do with a break in wholeness and a desire for restructuring.

1.2. *cristiana*, with a negative sign in the text (*no . . . cristiana*) is italicized and linked to the semiotic text of heterodoxy.

1.3. I shall distinguish the different values (ancestry, marriage, reputation, virginity, nobility, wealth) upon which this social structuring is based, from the terms that refer to a society of Estates: the nobility, the clergy, the *oficios*. To direct references (*Señor, cardenales*) I have added the signs by which they also acquire presence (*damas, caballo* → nobility). *Sospechar* is grouped here since by convergence with *probósele* it belongs to the vocabulary of judicial inquiry.

2.1. I have put in parenthesis the unique use of *ser* as auxiliary.

2.2. *Cosa* is an empty form of designation that can at any time be invested with a variable content according to the context. It belongs appropriately to this group.

2.5. In this network of signs, *parecer* translates the failure of the attempt to designate.

3. *Agrado* could as well be grouped with social values. It is considered here as an index of qualitative valorization.

4. *Oros* is, with *tercera*, the only sign that is grouped in this three different series. *Meter* belongs to this field only to the extent that it is the correlative sign of *sacar*; here we may speak of derivative polarization, as in the case (see "Semiotic Texts," 5. *Human body and its functions*) of *agua* (<*beber*).

8. The formulation of this text might be thought surprising; I am taking account here of concepts of identity (*mismo, tal* ← vs. → *ajeno*), of temporal superimposition (*mientras*), of spatial (non)superimposition (*cerca*), of conformity (*según, así*), that is, of the expression of the presence or the absence of a gap with respect to entities or to norms. In this set, *encubrir* describes an action producing a gap. I might have added the occurrences of *aunque*, in opposition to *según*; as we shall see, it seems that these various occurrences transcribe, at another level, the problematics of structuration and designation.

9. *Calamidades* is in italics for the same reasons as *cristiana* (1.2.).

The Semiotic System

(a) If we are concerned only with the semiotic texts I have presented in the form of dialectical oppositions, an initial observation is necessary: at the level of the utterance, it is the world of social marginality and of religious heterodoxy that is being represented and denounced; on the other hand, the semiotic texts display a very clear imbalance at the expense of the vocabulary of transgression (5/1; 12/3). This remark applies to other realms: the vocabulary of suffering prevails over that of joy (4/2) in a text of burlesque aspect; criteria of value give way to quantification (11/23) under the pen of an author such as Quevedo.

Thus an interesting distortion appears between the sign and the utterance, as well as a kind of systematic consisting in signifying, at every level and in every domain, through the negative.

(b) Certain texts must be combined: social order (text 1), text 4 (giving/taking),and text 6 (geographical and family origin) [total: 84 occ.], and we note the affinity between this new first group and the third semiotic text (quantification/qualification) which problematizes criteria of value. Text 8 can be related either to text 1 or to text 2.

New group 1 [ex. 1 + 4 + 6] and the semiotic texts 2 and 8 total 146 occurrences, or almost 60 percent of all the signs (34.38 percent; 20.40 percent; 4.8 percent). (If we add field 3, we get 75 percent.)

(c) Recalling the relative frequency of the repeated signs:

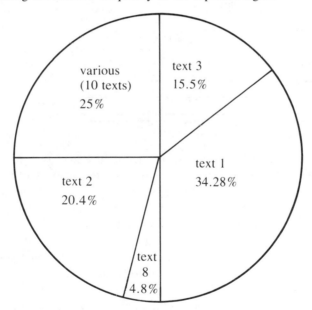

Repeated twice: *casado(a), Dios, parecer, saber, cárcel, ver, pueblo, después, vieja, tener, salir, bueno, tan, bien, según, voluntades.*
Repeated three times: *padre, hacer, tal, unos, otros, nombre.*
Repeated four times: *llamar.*
Repeated five times: *dar.*

Repeated seven times: *todos*.

Repeated ten times: *decir*.

Repeated fourteen times: *ser*.

If we consider that these frequencies begin to be significant at the point of triple repetition, we shall be struck by the observation that in the majority of cases, they are grouped around the axis *essence/designation*, which clearly outweighs the axis *structuring/destructuring* (31/11).

When the affinities among *nombre, llamar,* and *decir* are taken into account, the accompanying diagram displays the importance in the text of the problematic *Ser/Nombre* 14 ⟷ 17.

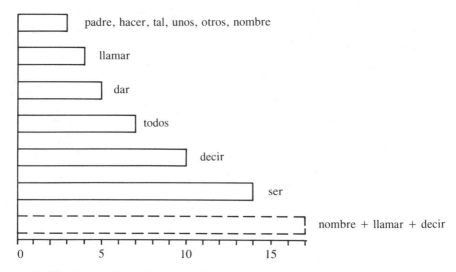

(d) The data gathered here are thus not negligible, since two major polarizations, apparently lacking in any connection, share the majority of the signs and are alternately preponderant, according to the criteria of analysis applied.

Let us return to the manner in which these two polarizations are articulated around text 8. We observe that the instability of the sign or, rather, its problematization in terms of inadequacy applies essentially to marginal individuals (*barbero* → *sastre de barbas*; *alcagüeta* → *zurcidora de gustos*) from and around which the diffraction of the signified (*cepa, celebrada, angélico, robaba, cardenales, hechizaba*) is effected, so that a correspondence between nonconformity in the sociological sense and the inadequacy of the sign seems to be inscribed in the text.

Can we deduce from this that there exists a relation, whose nature remains to be specified, between phenomena of social destructuring and the questioning of the enunciative function of discourse, produced precisely by structures in process of transformation? Even if, in the abstract, this relation seems obvious because every transformation in social structure is, as we have already said, productive

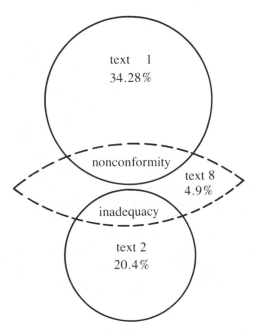

of meaning, it is still necessary to specify its modalities, its functioning, and its meaning in the whole of Quevedo's work.

Lexies *and Set Phrases*

The formulation of these semiotic texts does not, however, entirely resolve the problem posed by convergencies in the meaning of signs, which are independent of the utterance. Let us take, for example, the many uses in the text of *dar* in different acceptations. It is certainly not without significance that on the various paradigmatic axes concerned we find the frequent repetition of the form *dar* + . . . (*Daban en decir, daba con el agua, diese plumas*). In fact, a sort of sign set is thus organized that, beyond the utterance, may, at the time the text is being created, solicit complementarity, whether it be antonymic or not. (We shall find positive or negative sign convergencies of *dar* in field 4: *dar* → *gracias*, but *dar* ← vs. → *robar, levantar, etc.*) *Hence the necessity, justifying my previous step, of taking apart the combined forms: daban en decir, daba con él, diesen plumas.* The fact remains that this operation entails the disappearance of semantic contents (*empeñarse, proyectar, enplumar*) that must be recovered at another level. This is why I propose to complete the lexical map by the regrouping of *lexies* characterized by the fact that the different terms of which they are composed do not add their respective meanings but construct new ones. I shall here differentiate:

a) *soy de* . . .
        (+ *natural de*: a mere reinforcement of meaning)

daban en . . .
daban con . . .

In these cases, the preposition invests the verb with a new meaning.

(b) *cristiana vieja*   (→ purity of blood)
    malas lenguas   (→ scandal)
    dar plumas   (→ repression of sorcery)

This first list does not essentially modify the previous conclusions, except, however, for a slight nuance: *daba con . . .* and, especially, *malas lenguas* and *dar plumas* indicate an idea of repressive violence linked both with field 11 (suffering/joy) and with field 1 (repression of transgression).

Whether transformed or not, stock phrases in the same text may not only form a coherent whole, but also come from an identical source, belong to an identical type of discourse, describe an identical ideological locus. These patterns mark the text in a certain way and suggest intertextual relations.

This is true of the text that concerns us, in which the following expressions, slightly transformed by the narrative context, can be grouped as indicators of a discourse of administrative and legal inquiry:

"*Soy de . . . , Mi padre se llama (ó . . . , natural de . . . , Es (Fue) de oficio . . . , Está (Estuvo) casado con . . . , hija de . . . , nieta de . . .* "

Thus the pattern of lexicalized expressions that emerges, and that are ideologically marked when they are reconstituted as a system, marks in the same way and for that very reason the beginning of the *Buscón*, to the degree that this series transcribes, by means of a transplanted discourse, the powerful presence in the text of structures of social order.

Summary of Lexies and Stock Phrases

A. *Lexies*
1. soy de, daban en, daba con, (natural de . . .)
2. cristiana vieja, malas lenguas, dar plumas

B. *Stock phrases*: (2)
1. Not transformed*:
    a. Dios la tenga en el cielo (1.2), era de muy buena cepa (1.3), es cosa para creer (1.2.), recién casada (1.3.), hacía la barba a navaja (1.3.), muy a su salvo (1.3.), a pie y a caballo (1.3.), dar gracias a Dios (1.2.)
    b. es cosa para . . . era para dar . . . (8)
    c. en el tiempo que elle vivió (7)
    d. padeció grandes trabajos (11)
    e. dos de bastos, as de oros (10)
    f. robaba a todos las voluntades (4 and 9)
    g. no sé qué (2.3.), en público (2.4.), Hubo fama (2.4.), por mal nombre (2.2.)

2.   Transformed: None
3.   With variants: meter . . . para sacar . . .
       ?: Hacer (cosas) sobre elle; Por estas y otras (niñerías)
4.   Organized in a significant pattern
       Soy de . . . , Mi padre se llamó . . . , natural de . . . , de
       oficio . . . , casado con . . . , hija de . . . , nieta de . . .

Sign Combinations, Code, Utterance
Methodological Principles

(1) Just as the text chooses signs at the moment it comes into existence, it chooses combinations of signs from among the various syntactic or other constructions offered by the code.

(2) These combinations are not exclusively at the service of the utterance. They are meaningful in themselves and function at an autonomous level at which they establish their own laws and their own concordances. They will thus be studied according to this dual relation of autonomy and dependency with respect to the utterance.

(3) In the transcription into other forms of the deep structure of the message, the choices made by the text on the textual level refer in turn more or less directly to social structures.

Here I shall study two types of combination: semantic contamination; and syntactic phenomena.

Semantic Contamination

We shall be concerned with relations of identification unrecognized by the code (language) but that the text establishes among different entities, objects, images, and spheres of human activity. This investigation will allow us to set up a list of recurrences that can be perceived as elements constitutive of a particular imaginary world, to which I shall eventually apply a psychoanalytic perspective, and/or as defining the world vision of a transindividual subject. This will lead once again into the realm of sociocriticism. Meanwhile, we shall bear in mind the following principles:

    (a) The pattern of semantic contaminations generally forms a coherent system reproducing itself in the same text according to a law (or laws) that are always identical.

    (b) This system functions in a certain way in the text.

Several categories will be defined here:

1. *Contaminations by derivation* (or false contaminations): such is the case of all the "plays on words" (*era de muy buena cepa, levantándoles la cara para el lavatorio, robaba las voluntades, docientos cardenales*), which rest not on a lack

of pertinence, but on an unresolved polysemy of the sign or, if you will, on the functioning of an unstabilized sign. These are contaminations of the connotative type. This first group is noteworthy in that it converges around the desacralization of social values (ancestry, hierarchy, feelings) and religious values (liturgy, in *lavatorio*). We note that these expressions appear as contaminations only if we leave them in their context or if we relate them to the utterance.

2. I propose that we grant the existence of two subsets of *contamination–reedificaba doncellas, resuscitaba cabellos*, which both appeal to creation or rather to the recreation of human beings and objects — observing the mechanism of inversion designating the reproduction of the object (*cabellos*) by a sign reserved for the description of divine action and presenting the resurrection of human beings (*doncellas*) in the form of a human invention. The examination of the second subset is very interesting, as the accompanying tabulations show:

Main Group of Contaminations

	Identifies
tundidor de mejillas ⎫	artisan's activity / barber's activity
sastre de barbas ⎬	linked to textile
zurcidora de gustos ⎭	industry
tuétanos de las faldriqueras	skeleton / clothing
[algebristas de] voluntades desconcertades	skeleton / feelings

Whole Set of Contaminations

Subject of an implied metaphor	Implied metaphor
Mejillas	*paño*
barbas	*paño*
paño (faldriqueras)	skeleton
gustos	*paño*
voluntades	skeleton
human being (*doncellas*)	object (stone)
object (*cabellos*)	human being

We observe, then, that the pattern of contaminations functions according to a law of systematic inversion.

Note that (1) I am not examining here the phrases *meter el dos de bastos, sacar el as de oros, tercera, primera y flux*, because I do not consider them semantic contaminations (I shall return to them later); and (2) I have formulated a point

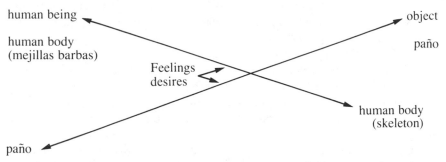

of convergence (*paño*) from *lana, tejidos, vestidos, faldriqueras*, in order to bring out this pattern more clearly.

The sociocritical perspective is also interested in the vehicles of these contaminations.

We shall note the projection in the text of the textile industry, which must be related to the principal locale of the passage, *Segovia*. From this point of view, when we inquire into the meaning of this phenomenon, in the textual context, we observe that this metaphorical transfer may bear witness to the appeal of this activity to the barber's imagination, problematizing his ambition because he *identifies* with a professional group that he places above himself; outlines of social stratification thus begin to appear. On the other hand, however, in the context of an opposite perspective, it is an ironic vision that *identifies* the procuress/sorceress with the same group. We see, therefore, how this sector of activity is taken in two different textual contexts placed in relief by the two parallel phrases: ("él *se llamaba* tundidor . . . sastre ⟷ Unos *la llamaban* zurcidora").

The textile industry, or cottage textile industry, is being presented in this way as an internal center of attraction (a vision of the character) but as well, at the level of narrative objectivity (the vision of the other characters who oppose their own social hierarchy to that projected by the barber), as a point of repulsion.

The protagonist's effort of identification finds an echo in the narrator's concern with the desire for assimilation. Desirous of *identifying himself* with this group, the character is equally *cast down* into this group. Assimilation to this group is, here, a certain form of rejection.

Syntactic Phenomena

Expression of Time/Thematics of Exclusion from the Group

Contrastive use of imperfect and simple past. No doubt the imperfect here transcribes the iterative aspect of the action, but it will be noted that often it is not the only possible form, particularly in the case of "*según él bebía*" and, even more so, in the case of "*hacía la barba a navaja*," in which *hacer*, dependent on a verb expressing a fact, should logically be presented in a form having the value of completion. We can only prove that which has, in fact, taken place, and by opting, with *hacía*, for the aspect of incompletion, the construction comes close to being incoherent, but this preference for incompletion produces meaning effects repeated throughout the passage in different form (*por ser tal que, que era tal su agrado que*): the central characters appear in this manner in their capabilities and not in what they have, in fact, done. Thus, the quest for a globalizing impression is outlined, which, far from being concerned with the balance sheet of an individual life, tends, before anything else, to define a short series of *characteristics*.

In the same way, the text has the choice between the imperfect and the preterit when it is a question of reporting an unrepeated action taking place in the foreground, as in the following examples: "aunque salió, Las damas . . . salían . . . que siempre pareció," 'Un día, alabándomela, una vieja . . . decía," in which the noniterative character of the two episodes leads one to expect a preterit (salieron, dijo). We note that the forms are distributed not according to the aspect to be expressed, but according to the nature of the actants. This choice is even clearer in "fue tan celebrada que, en el tiempo que ella vivió, casi todos . . . *hacían* cosas," in which the meaning of the sentence should have required *hicieron*. But, as in the preceding example, this incoherence is significant: the simple past, the tense of the narrative foreground, is reserved for Pablos's father and mother, while the other characters are relegated to the imperfect, which is the tense of the narrative background.

The present. To the present moment, to which a situational element is added (soy de Segovia), we shall link the immediate past of "*a mi me han dicho después.*"

Thus the past of the *I* is detached from the past of his parents, although it is included in the latter (cf. *alabándomela una vieja*"); between the two is the margin of the indefinite *después*. The *yo* is situated in the present or the immediate past, and situates his parents in the remote past, in this way placing in relief a break that, at first glance, is temporal. We observe, however, that this past is not solely drawn from the narrator's memory, but is reconstructed as well by the collective memory ("*Dicen que era de muy buena cepa . . . , según a mí me han dicho después . . . , Las damas diz que salían . . . , una vieja . . . decía que . . . , Sólo diz que se dijo . . . , Hubo fama*"), and to the extent that the *yo*'s past is drawn sometimes from his own memory and sometimes from the collective memory, we can justly consider that what is really involved is a past that he has or has not taken responsibility for, that is, the transcription of a phenomenon of identification or of nonidentification with oneself. The fluctuations in distancing thus go beyond the mere problem of the transcription of time.

The remote aspect of time, inscribed in the preterit, is protected both by the zone of imprecision of the iterative imperfect that surrounds it and by the mechanism of collective memory that recreates it. The same rejection is meaningful for the relations the narrator maintains with his past and with himself. Just as the preterit allows the individual to abstract himself from the group, the recourse to collective memory allows the narrator to abstract himself from his past.

We shall juxtapose this observation to the opposition constructed in the text between, on the one hand, indefinites and collectives and, on the other, personal pronouns (*todos, se,* third person plural, *unos, otros,* etc. ← vs. → *él, ella, mi, yo, a mí*). Just as Pablos's father and mother are opposed to all the others (*pueblo, copleros, malas lenguas, damas,* etc.), Pablos, in turn, is detached from all others, or from an indefinite collective ("*según a mí me han dicho . . . que bien saben todos*"), or from his parents, according to the following schema:

Todos ⟷ *mi padre*
Todos ⟷ *mi madre*
Todos ⟷ *yo*
mis padres ⟷ *yo*

in which the opposition group ← vs. → individual is being reproduced at different levels.

The grammatical actualizations of aspect transcribe a thematics of the individual's exclusion from the group (individuals exclude themselves or find themselves excluded), because of criteria having to do not with their acts but with their nature. According to the source of the refusal, we shall speak either of nonrecognition (rejection by the group) or of nonidentification (rejection of the group).

A Syntax of Inversion/The Inadequacy of Discourse

To the three uses of *aunque*:

AUNQUE ⟵ *eran tan altos sus pensamientos que . . .*
⟍ *ella . . . quiso esforzar que . . .*
⟍ *según a mí me han dicho después, salió . . .*

we shall add:

SINO QUE a ninguno llamaban señoría . . .

as well as:

SOLO DIZ QUE se dijo no sé qué . . .

observing that we have an inversion of either a point of view (the three uses of *aunque*) or the signified of a word (the two other cases). This double inversion is reduced to a single pattern affecting only the word (*barbero, cristiana vieja, cardenal, hechizaba*); in the first case it is the signifier that changes; in the second case, it is the signified. In other words, what is involved is the inadequacy of the signified and the signifier, that is, the margin separating the object from its projection in discourse. The word hides reality or transforms it (*tundidor de mejillas, sastre de barbas, muy buena cepa, nombres, y sobre nombres de sus passados, docientos cardenales, hechizaba, zurcidora de gustos, algebrista*). But this hiding functions at different levels and according to different modes: the father and mother exhibit their desire to hide a reality behind a word, whereas at other times, it is the narrator who, in the burlesque mode, pretends to mask a reality under a word, before unequivocally destroying this mask. At yet other times, it is others who denounce the character's reality by using the devices this character uses in order to hide himself (*diciendo que él se llamaba . . .* ← vs. → *Unos la llamaban . . .*). The type of discourse serving the character to transform the reality of what he is, is, in turn, used to denounce him, such that this discourse becomes the index of designation and denunciation of the character who is hiding. To hide oneself is to betray oneself. The problem is, who is hiding what?

Inadequacy of Discourse/Break in Social Status

At the center of this means of hiding — discourse — are three groups of expressions that function as "codes of substitution," that is, particular codes that are only decipherable if we know their keys, and behind which the precise meaning of the text is lost:

(1) *tundidor de mejillas, sastre de barbas, zurcidora de gustos*
(2) *Aldonza de San Pedro, hija de Diego de San Juan y nieta de Andrés de San Cristóbal*
(3) *meter el dos de bastos para sacar el as de oros, primera, tercera y flux*

The first two of these codes are attributed to the *barbero/alcahueta* pair, and as a function of what we have just seen (camouflage as an index of detection), they carry in their very encoding the keys of their decoding.

In this matter, we know what is being denounced (ridiculous pretensions, hiding one's origins), but we do not know, at least in the first case, to what that which is being denounced is related (What is this pretentiousness hiding? Why is it ridiculous?) nor do we know who is being denounced (for it is quite obvious that the barber and the procuress are both *substitutes*). In order to clarify this problem, I propose that we use certain distinctions, introduced by the semiologists, that allow us to establish the correspondences shown in the accompanying tabulation. The correspondence existing, in code number 2, between the substance of the signifier and that of the signified justifies, it seems to me, considering code 2 as an

	Code no. 1	*Code no. 2*
Substance of the signifier	Lexical field of cottage textile industry	Lexical field of religion
Form of the signifier	Inadequacy of discourse	Absence of patronymic
Form of the signified	Ridiculous pretension	Hiding one's origins
Substance of the signified	[break in social status]	*No cristiana vieja*

equal mode of transcription of the social reality of code 1. Consequently, I believe I can say that the text denounces attempts to upset a caste society (a break in social status) made by certain elements from the milieu of merchant manufacturers (textile cottage industry).

We may draw another conclusion no less important: the crisis of a discourse perceived as no longer fulfilling its enunciative function is here, once more, connected (in what ways?) to problems of social structuring and destructuring.

The reasons why I posed the principles I have already defined in advance will appear more clearly, no doubt, if we go back to some of the preceding observations. Let us take up again two of the examples that have been studied, showing the double combinations that are possible.

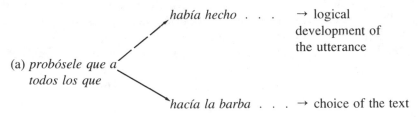

(a) *probósele que a todos los que*

había hecho . . . → logical development of the utterance

hacía la barba . . . → choice of the text

We note that the text's choice mortgages a future not included in *probósele* and that it is thus not programmed in the beginning of the utterance.

(b) *Fue tan celebrada que, en el tiempo que ella vivió* . . .

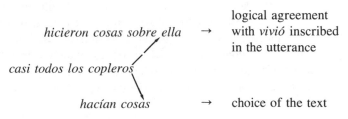

hicieron cosas sobre ella → logical agreement with *vivió* inscribed in the utterance

casi todos los copleros

hacían cosas → choice of the text

Here we see clearly that the syntax does not bend to the utterance and that it obeys its own laws, which, I should like to assert, are imposed upon it by the deep structures of the text. In both these cases, the text's structures inflect the message in a certain direction that repeats what the utterance expresses by what the choice of aspect expresses; the choice of aspect reproduces once again the image of an ordered, caste society in which an individual is defined not through what he does but through what he is (choice of the aspect of incompletion), and which problematizes group/individual relations in terms of social exclusion or of social assimilation (contrastive use of the preterit or the imperfect).

In this connection, we note that, whereas the manner in which the semantic contaminations function with respect to the utterance led us to speak of the juxtaposition of two perspectives, one based on a desire of identification (the barber), the other based on a vision of assimilation (the procuress in the eyes of the public), the grammatical actualizations of aspect, at a less immediate level of the text, take up this problematic but confer upon it a negative sign (refusal of assimilation, refusal of identification).

In the conclusions of this analysis I see the confirmation, at the level of a microtext, of the interpretation I gave of the *Buscón* in *L'Aristocrate et le carnaval des gueux*.[2] Indeed, I observe in these first lines of the narrative the presence of all the structuring elements that have been revealed by rather different methods of approach: namely, a pattern of inversion, oppositions centered on the concepts of assimilation and identification, and a stress on the inadequacy of discourse, comprising several components of the popular carnivalesque festival that problematizes phenomena of social destructuring in Quevedo's text. I can only refer the reader to this interpretation, which, in its main outlines, still seems valid to me, even though I might wish to correct it in the future.

Meanwhile, I should like to stress that we have seen structures of social order fuse with discursive structures through the mediation of a discourse of identification that conservative instances (*Limpieza de la sangre* [the Inquisition's inquiries into "clear-blooded" Christians vs. converts]) or repressive ones (judicial inquiries) cause individuals to impose on themselves (of the type: "I am . . . , I was born in . . . , son/daughter of . . . , grand-son of . . . , married to . . . , occupation . . . ," in which the mention of occupation only confirms social caste). To the question *Who is who?* the text responds by creating systems of hiding and diffraction of meaning ("*Everything is capable of being anything*"), which, by reference and by opposition to the first discourse, are indexes of a challenge (outside the text) to dominant social structures that this first discourse expresses and perpetuates. One might relate this crisis of designation so well transcribed at the beginning of the narrative to phenomena of social mobility (vertical and geographical) that the Spanish picaresque evinces in general, and the *Buscón* in particular.

History and Beyond History: Genetic Markers

Ideología y genética textual[3] had hardly appeared in print when new perspectives opened up that I now realize it would have been desirable to develop. In this study of the *Buscón*, I gave historical meaning to a textual structure previously defined by linguistic and semiotic approaches. At the same time, and this was the central point of my argument, I observed that complex ideological traces, historical vectors, were inscribed in the fictional text through mediating structures. I shall briefly summarize this thesis by reconstructing it from its conclusions. First, the historical facts: in the first place, a classic historical contradiction opposing, in industrial and mercantile Segovia, a bourgeoisie jealously kept from exercising political power to a nobility that feels progressively stripped of economic power; second, attitudes that mediate a particular historical juncture but that do not directly mediate its inscription in the fictional text, and that translate the anti-Jewish bias of the ruling class in Spain at the beginning of the seventeenth century. These sociopolitical and socioeconomic conditions are coded in the text through allusions to two social practices—Carnival festivities and inquisitorial practices. They were comparable, as I had already suggested in *L'Aristocrate*, observing that the former represented a collective phantasm of social destructuring whereas the latter ritualized the reconstruction of the unity of the group's collective consciousness. The *Buscón* links these two practices, showing them to be complementary. It is this complementarity that *Ideología y genética textual* attempted to understand, leading me to see in each of them the reproduction of rites of exorcism, and to define the primordial role played, in each case, by the scapegoat, regardless of whether the sacrifice is accomplished in fact or is merely symbolic. At this point we shall examine all these facts in an attempt to understand their deeper meaning.

Our point of departure is what I have called *the parable of the parodied imitation*, which goes beyond the framework of carnivalesque parody: here what seems to be in question outside the text is, on the one hand, the behavior of the bourgeoisie, an imitative behavior, and, on the other hand—and this is somewhat different—the bourgeois vision of the aristocracy. It is these two elements that we find caricatured in the way in which the narrative voice reconstructs Pablos's observation of Don Diego as surrogate character, as well as in the pattern of textual traces that make up the figure of Don Diego. Thus the bourgeois mentality is inscribed both in the form of a set of observable materials and in that of a parodied point of view supposedly caricaturing the narrative voice. What attracts our attention, in the last analysis, is this deliberately distorted projection of oneself in the consciousness of another, a textual phenomenon that raises new questions. We might be tempted to pose the problem in terms that would lead us to broach the question of Quevedo himself, thus falling into an author-centered criticism. That would take us away from the concerns of sociocriticism. On the contrary, I shall stress the anthropological perspective of the last chapters of *Ideología y genética textual*, giving the preceding remarks a new formulation suggested by René Girard in *Des choses cachées depuis la fondation du monde*.[4] Indeed, we may see in the way bourgeois behavior is being problematized in the *Buscón* the reproduction of an archaic interdiction hanging over every imitative conduct. "A good example of a seemingly absurd interdiction," writes Girard, "is the interdiction in many societies of imitative conduct. One must abstain from copying the gestures, from repeating the words, of another member of the community. The interdiction against using proper names correponds, no doubt, to the same kind of concern; similarly, the fear of mirrors, often associated with the devil in traditional societies."[5]

Rather than speak of "parable of parodied imitation," I shall speak of mimetic escalation and mimetic rivalry to describe the position of a narrative voice that mimetically reproduces the one that caricatures it, thus transforming itself into a simulacrum of itself. One of the advantages of Girard's arguments for my reading of the *Buscón* is that they closely link the mimetic and the violent ("human conflicts are essentially rooted in the mimetic . . . every mimetic reproduction immediately evokes violence. . . . "[6] It is because imitation is a threat to social cohesiveness that every interdict has an antimimetic tenor), and through violence, the mimetic and the sacred. Unaccountably, Girard does not mention Carnival when he speaks of the mimetic crisis, which, according to him, is accompanied by role inversion, reciprocal parody, insulting mockery, and occasionally full-scale battles, a mimetic crisis whose enactment will necessarily consist in violations of interdicts since the latter are antimimetic. In mimetic crisis, "we have to do with a veritable conflictive collapse of cultural organization. At the height of the crisis, men fight over every object that is normally forbidden; this is why there is frequently ritual incest, that is, fornication with women one is forbidden to touch the rest of the time."[7] Does he not invite us implicitly to reconsider our interpretation of the social function of Carnival when he analyzes the extraordinary paradox of the juxtaposition of rituals and interdictions in every religious society? Indeed, "if mimetic crisis is as fearful as our reading of interdicts leads us to think," how can we explain the fact that "rituals persist in reproducing in a perfectly realistic way what societies fear the most, and rightly so, in normal times?"[8] Is it not true that religious institutions, "which appear so timorous the rest of the time, display in their rituals, a literally incredible temerity? Not only do they abandon their customary caution, but they conscientiously mime their own decomposition in hysterical mimetism; everything happens as though they thought that simulated disintegration could keep real distintegration away."[9] But is it not the conclusion of the ritual that gives it its meaning, a conclusion that generally consists in the immolation of an animal or human victim?[10]

If the rites end with sacrifice, it must seem to religious societies as the conclusion of the mimetic crisis enacted by these rites. In many rituals, the entire audience is considered to take part in the immolation, which could easily be mistaken for a lynching scene. Even when the sacrifice is performed by a single sacrificer, he is generally acting on behalf of the entire community. It is the unity of a community that is being affirmed in the sacrificial act, and this unity arises in the paroxysm of division, at the very moment when the community is claiming to be torn apart by mimetic discord, in thrall to the endless circularity of avenging reprisals. The opposition of each against each is suddenly followed by the opposition of all against one. The chaotic multiplicity of private conflicts is followed at one stroke by the simplicity of a single antagonism: on one side the entire community, and on the other the victim. We have no difficulty understanding what the sacrificial resolution consists in; the community recovers its unity at the expense of a victim who is not only incapable of defending himself but totally powerless to wreak vengeance.[11]

I am quoting René Girard at such length because what he says corresponds perfectly to the interpretation I have tried to give of inquisitorial practice and because—here we come to the heart of the problem—the auto da fé, in reproducing the theater of sacrifice, is related to a mimetic crisis. However, if the objective constituting what is at stake in the mimesis of appropriation is obvious in the case of Carnival and in that of the transcription in fictional terms of the struggle for political hegemony, it remains for us to describe the field of mimetic rivalry for the case of the Inquisition. The stakes are certainly social and economic, but the space of confrontation is not limited to that.

In this connection, I refer the reader to the "supplementary explanation" suggested by Henry Méchoulan in *Le Sang de l'autre ou l'honneur de Dieu*,[12] namely, "an attempt to take control of divine choice." To illustrate this notion, Méchoulan quotes a series of examples of the exploitation of Hebrew texts for the benefit of the thesis of a divine alliance with a Spain promoted to the rank of heiress of the chosen people, in, for example, Juan de Salazar's *Política española*. This thesis makes the Jew an obstacle and rival: "Expelled since 1492, the Jews remain present not only as Marranos to be hunted down, but as Jews, heirs of the first divine choice. That election has not been wrested from any gloss but is inscribed undeniably in the sacred texts. Incontestable and uncontested, it makes the Jew a rival who must be eliminated even though he no longer exists as a person on the soil of Spain." This convergence toward one and the same object of desire reproduces *a mimesis of appropriation* that creates conflicts. Read in relation to the fundamental anthropology of René Girard, Henry Méchoulan's observations take on a notable importance when he demonstrates that "the Hebrews are the axis of reference in the contemporary religious history of Spain despite abuse and hatred,"[13] or when he notes that in the dominant ideology of the Golden Age, the Jew remains the undisputed model of relationship with God and a secretly envied rival. One cannot help thinking here of what René Girard says about the logic of the mimetic conflict: "The more the rivalries become intolerable, the more the rivals tend to forget what caused them, the more they become fascinated by each other. The rivalry is purified of all its external objectives, and in sum, it becomes pure rivalry or rivalry for prestige. Each rival becomes the model for the other, the lovable and hateful obstacle that must be both beaten and absorbed." Let us continue the quotation, for it brings us right to the heart of our theme: "Mimesis is more powerful than ever, but it can no longer function at the level of the object since the object does not exist anymore. . . . There is no longer any other area of application possible for mimesis than the antagonists themselves." Thus, the *mimesis of appropriation* threatening to tear the collectivity apart is succeeded by the *mimesis of the antagonist*, which "perforce brings together two or more individuals and causes them to converge upon a single adversary they all wish to destroy."[14]

In light of these fundamental anthropological elements, I propose, then, to recognize, at least provisionally, in the two social practices involved in the *Buscón*, the respective actualizations of the mimetic crisis (Carnival) and the mimesis of the antagonist (auto da fé), which confirms my own interpretation when I suggested that the second be considered as a *redressive* practice of the first. It is true, then, that the unity of the community is reconstructed around a lynching scene, which enlightens us on the necessarily hybrid nature of the scapegoat. Myths have taught us that the scapegoat is generally feeble, or more precisely that he contrasts sharply in one way or another with the general sameness of the community, but, in order to take on himself the collective evil, he must also be, in some way, similar to everyone else. This coexistence in the victim of signs of identity and of otherness means that he is marked by both inclusion and exclusion,[15] and if we consider the problem from this angle, we shall understand better why the Inquisition was not interested in infidels but in heretics. In this sense, the scapegoat bears the distinctive signs of mediation and of the sacred. We know, with Jacques Le Goff, that medieval thought, no doubt reproducing archaic paradigms, defined the monstrous in terms of nonconformity and of what I have called hybridization.[16] Moreover, the monstrous is above all experienced as an index of the sacred, for its hybrid character makes it a bridge to the diabolical or the divine. Here we think as readily of the wild man and the shepherdesses (*serranas*) of the *Book of Good Love*[17] as of the Virgin/Mother and the consubstantiality (another figure of hybridization) of the God/Man.

The preceding remarks will serve as reference points for a new reading of the *Buscón* in which we shall note that in the various "lynching scenes" the distinctive marks of the scapegoat, such as I have just defined them, are curiously reproduced. Thus on the day of the feast of the *Rooster King*, the hero of the day is riding a mount with a long neck like a camel or an ostrich; compare this with the pretext used by the students of Alcalá to attack the new arrival ("Surely this can't be Lazarus raised from the dead—he stinks so!"[18]) and with the nauseating odor given off by certain mythical heros analyzed by Lévi-Strauss. Similarly, Pablos sets off a veritable scalp dance when, to his detriment, he sits in primary school on the side of the "sons of the hidalgos and grandees of the town," despite his humble origins. But this scapegoat, in order to be able to play his sacrificial role, at the very moment of his death must see all the marks of difference he bears done away with; in the contrary case, in fact, if these signs were to prevail temporarily, his sacrifice would be inefficacious. In order to take on the collective evil, it must be seen as belonging to the category of inclusion,[19] hence, no doubt, the necessity, in the ritual of the auto da fé, of obtaining the victim's recantation, which, reconciling the victim with the Church, dissolves all traces of otherness.

These few observations, which may legitimately give the impression of being a mere rewriting in "Girardian" terms of certain analyses in *Ideología y genética textual*, have not been advanced to justify my own conclusions. I am not presuming to pronounce hypotheses, *a fortiori* theses, on fundamental anthropological problems, and I have always limited myself to describing what is functioning in the *Buscón*, and the modalities of this functioning. As we have seen, the fictional text transcribes the existence of a relationship, which I have constantly sought to question, between a mimetic crisis unfolding at several levels and a social practice *inscribed by the same text* in the form of a practice of exorcism that only reproduces the ritual of exorcism operating at the heart of the (carnivalesque) enactment of mimetic crisis. If I have chosen to reformulate the problem in "Girardian terms," this is because René Girard's brillant essay brings me back to methodological concerns.

The reader will have noticed, however, that what the *Buscón* says differs from Girard's thought on a very important point—namely, the legitimacy of the sacrificial reading of the death of Christ, which, for Girard, "must be criticized and exposed as the most colossal and paradoxical misunderstanding in history, at the same time revealing humanity's radical inability to understand its own violence, even when that violence is spelled out to it in the most explicit way. The true function of the Passion is, in fact, to subvert sacrifice, "to prevent it forever from functioning . . . by exposing to view its mechanism of victimization." The fact remains that this reading is a historical fact that permitted "the Christian text to found in its turn what in principle it never should have founded: a culture." We should not be surprised, then, to have spotted it in the complex genetics of the *Buscón*, since "the persecutive character of historical Christianity is linked to the sacrificial definition of the Passion and the Redemption," a judgment that has special importance for the case concerning us. This sacrificial reading is capable of being situated historically, to the extent that the prodigious spread of the Evangelical message throughout the Roman Empire "could only have taken place within the framework of the sacrificial reading, and thanks to it."[20]

In proposing to broaden somewhat the anthropological perspective opened up in *Ideología y genética textual*, I have not strayed from my sociocritical project. This rapid excursus permitted us to glimpse once more the extreme complexity of elements combining to form the genotext and the ways in which precise, locatable, and localized historical facts may reactivate archaic patterns deeply buried in the womb of the cultural context in question and redistributed by the fictional text.

Festival as Space of Social Confrontation

Let us return to Segovia to follow a series of festive ceremonies that took place there at the beginning of the seventeenth century, in particular the procession of the statue of the Virgin of Fuencisla, which occurred September 12 to 22, 1613.[21] These festivals constitute a sort of vast sociodrama in which two gestural discourses signifying contradictory political projects are juxtaposed.

One must first detect in the discourse of the official chronicler of these festivities, Diego de Colmenares, curate of the parish of St. John, the unitary strategy of the local authorities, which tend to give to King Philip III and his court, the official guests of the town, the image of a collectivity unified in its cheerfulness, its loyalty, and its religious fervor. No doubt this discourse itself is organized around a whole system of clichés and ideological practices that combines gestures, rituals, and symbols belonging to radically different texts so as to create a homogeneous production of meaning whose objective is the construction of a vast enactment of allegiance to royal power and of submission to divine authority. This enactment remodeled the human space of the town, placing grandiose altars along the route of the processions, draping the narrow streets of the walled town with hangings of the same colors, each evening illuminating with myriad lights the principal monuments of the city, thus casting in shadow the tangible forms of urban social segregation. Behind these various mediations are facts that I believe we can reconstruct and analyze.

Let us put aside the religious feasts and remain in the realm of civil festivities. For unity's sake, the municipality distributed the tasks and the burden of expense among the different orders and trades: whereas the strictly religious ceremonies are entrusted to the clergy, tradesmen (painters, parchment makers, and weighers) must paint pictures representing the miracles of the Virgin, regild the altarpiece, and provide a velvet canopy. The doctors, surgeons, barbers, and apothecaries will offer the Virgin a golden crown set with precious stones; so much for the preparations. As for the festivities themselves, the bullfights are at the expense of the town and the two courts (*Audiencias*), the fireworks are paid for by the *Audiencias*; the cane games are organized by the knights; and, finally, the three masked cavalcades, the climax of the entertainment, are entrusted, respectively, to the "committee of noble ancestry," the cloth manufacturers, and the menders (*zurcidores*). (We note that two of the three cavalcades are given over to occupations having to do with the textile industry.)

Let us pause for a moment to consider this distribution, which obviously corresponds to a sort of tax assessment. Apart from the case of the tradesmen (painters and parchment makers), from whom only a contribution in kind is required, this tax, which does them honor, hits the highest strata of a society that, despite the strategy of the municipal authority, seems to me to be divided into very distinct categories. If we refer to the classical social structure of the Renaissance city, as it is described, for example, in Jean Bodin's *Republic*,[22] we shall find the same groups at the top of the hierarchy: clergy (religious feasts), consular corps (town), military order (*caballeros*), magistrates (*Audiencias*), doctors. In contrast to this traditional patriarchate, we note nevertheless the extraordinary preponderance of the textile world, whose parade eclipsed all the other ceremonies of the private sector, and its spectacular ascent in the traditional hierarchy. Whereas cloth and fabric makers, and workers in silk, wool, goat hair and camel's hair are relegated to the last part of the symbolic procession imagined by Bodin, they are, at the time of our sociodrama, at the head of the Third Estate, which they are practically alone in representing (with the exception of the medical corps). All the other guilds (teachers, poets, grammarians, merchants, silversmiths, bakers, butchers, fishmongers, etc.), who, however, theoretically precede them in the ideological hierarchy, have disappeared from the scene, at least on the surface. It is true that the privileged position they occupy here explains the ambiguity – or better, the polyvalence – of their occupations, whose activity, as we have seen, extends from production to trade to finance, such that, according to the zone of activity we are willing to grant them, and the group that we single out from this complex body, they can be considered as brazenly out of place in this great celebration of power or, quite the contrary, as quite relatively in their place. This is not at all surprising in a town like Segovia, but we must still understand the way this economic hegemony is translated in political terms, follow the repercussions of this situation in the respective strategies of these opposing forces, and measure the "meaning effects" that these strategies produce upon antagonistic mental structures. We must keep in mind, then, this imposing vertical displacement that decomposes the theoretical social order and plays against a background of social taboos whose acuity we have noted elsewhere.

Thus, the cavalcades of the cloth makers and the noble lineage occupy the streets of the old town on September 20 and 21, projecting their respective phantasms of power, their political projects, values, and alliances in the representational symbolism in which a veiled confrontation will be acted out in the apparent serenity imposed by the royal presence.

The nobles are the first to come on stage: thirty-two participants in all, with four floats commemorating:

(1) the founding of the city in the presence of Hercules;
(2) the courage of the men of Segovia during the conquest of Madrid in 1083;
(3) the courage of the women of Segovia defending the city in the absence of their husbands;
(4) the homage rendered by the town's inhabitants to Isabella the Catholic in 1474.

By honoring the military exploits of a community for which they constitute, in the fullest sense of the word, the head of the lance, the "noble lineages" link their town's destiny to their own collective destiny, significantly connected to their alliance with the monarchy (4). They confuse the town's history and memory, on which they thereby assert proprietary rights, with the history and memory of their class. Whereas in France, it is generally the urban bourgeoisie, in its desire to assert its identity, that seems to have invented for itself a mythical past through the image of a legendary founding of the city, Hercules becomes in the nobles' mythological enactment the guarantor of a semidivine ancestry that draws them closer to the divine right monarch. Ancestry and strength (1), courage and loyalty (2), courage and love (3), loyalty in the framework of the mutual rights and obligations of the bond of feudalism (4), such is the message addressed to the King and the Court. Behind it one cannot help seeing a warning addressed to others.

The next day, the impressive procession of the cloth makers will have as its chief merit that of attaining its goal, that is, to parade under the very eyes of the King, unlike the parade of the nobles, whose cumbersome contraptions could not maneuver the narrow streets and go further than the first part of the predetermined itinerary. We can hardly believe such incompetence, easily lending itself to laughter and derisive comments on aristocratic pretentiousness and the foolishness that ruled over the preparation and execution of their parade. The proud, monumental constructions of the aristocrats will thus remain stalled on the *Plaza Mayor* in testimony to excessiveness. There is no doubt that the cloth merchants had a good laugh over it, all the more since, in contrast to the thirty-two participants of the first cavalcade, they had assembled a crowd of 550 people, nineteen triumphal carts, and thirteen groups of dancers, singers, and musicians.

The presence of dancing in the procession must be stressed, it seems to me, for two reasons: first, because these dances are performed by groups of peasants from the neighboring villages; facing the arrogantly homogenous group of nobles, withdrawn into their shell, the cavalcade of the genealogy of the Virgin seems, then, a composite grouping which assembles around the bigwigs of Segovia distinct social categories. In fact, everything leads us to believe that these country people were hired through the intermediary of several small craftsmen of the town, as was the case during the Corpus Christi festivities from 1608 to 1620.[23] These third-rate impresarios are apparently recruited from the same social level (wool carders, booksellers, cloth shearers, tailors, rope makers, scribes, brassworkers, tavernkeepers, cloth weavers), and textile-related occupations are still predominant. The cloth makers of Segovia thus base the demonstration of their power and wealth on a significant social pyramid in which village and suburban elements overlap closely with each other as well as with the craftsmen's sector of the town. At the same time expressing another conception of the city, they play a role in uniting various social forces against the official authorities. Let us not forget that September 21 is the day of St. Matthew, patron saint of merchants;[24] this explains, among other things, why the iconogaphy of the procession closely follows the text of the Gospel according to Matthew.[25] We see how a social class aspiring to political hegemony diverts for its own benefit the themes of religious celebrations (the Fiesta of the Virgin of Fuencisla) by indirectly paying homage, on this occasion, to the patron saint of its confraternity. The analogical structure of the two iconographies that successively occupy the streets thus repeats the simulacrum of a confrontation in which each of the two classes involved glorifies its own function (military vs. mercantile) within the social body.

Second, the dances are in turn just as significant; they are generally part of the repertory of the religious, civil, and popular fiestas in Spain in the sixteenth century (official visits of important people, royal entries, patron saints' feasts, Corpus Christi, Carnival, etc.) in more or less identical form. Most are peasant dances. To define their function in the case at hand, I propose that we limit ourselves to the reconstruction made possible by the documents published by J. L. Flecniakoska concerning the Corpus Christi fiestas organized at Segovia between 1594 and 1636. The character of several of these dances is easily discernible, such as, for example, that of the bears and shepherds simulating a monkey hunt (April 1608);[26] the eight masked harlequins shaking bells and truncheons (June 1620); the typically carnivalesque characters of fools and transvestites, imitating the wolfmen who ran in the streets of Rome at the Lupercalia, hitting women in the practice of a fertility rite;[27] the "cuckolding of the king of the monkeys" (April 1608), which, like the preceding dance, refers to the erotic gestural code; the dance of the giants (1608–9), belatedly introduced into popular celebrations, according to Van Gennep;[28] the dance of the swords (April 1609), linked to fertility rites, still present at the fiestas at Toledo (February 1555), at Madrid for the Fiesta of St. Isidore (June 18), in the Corpus Christi fiestas in Madrid in the seventeenth century, mentioned by Rabelais, Cervantes, Lope de Vega and Gracián, among others, and characterized by Van Gennep as an apotropaic dance intended to ward off evil spirits that bring sickness and destroy crops;[29] or again the strongly rhythmic dances (*zapateados* and *paloteados*) that are part of what is called paramusic,[30] more or less discordant and cacaphonous, obtained by striking or scraping all manner of instruments at hand—rulers and compasses of stonecutters, sickles, flails (this is the case of the procession of the Genealogy of the Virgin, September 21, 1629),[31] echoing the ceremonial noises of the Tenebrae services, the rattles and noisemakers whose ritual apotropaic meaning is obvious; shepherds' and Moorish dances,[32] which were also part of the Carnival festivities in the Bouches-du-Rhône;[33] people disguised as priests, peasants, valets, pages, halberdiers (Genealogy of the Virgin, September 21, 1613), are found in practically every procession of the same type, "which were organized throughout the Middle Ages and up to the Revolution . . . , during the festival of the patron saint protecting the city, or during important religious ceremonies such as a translation of relics, or during the solemn entry of a king or powerful person, or finally to commemorate the retreat of an epidemic, the winning of a battle, or the deliverance of a town under siege."[34]

Present everywhere were bells, the small round bells on the feet, on the arms, on animals' paws, on tamborines, fools' bells, the many bells of Easter chasing out Lent, the little sonorous drops of cyclical time "redressed."[35] Present too was the mythical hairy "wild man" (Corpus Christi, 1628), striking sticks together while he danced ("the dance of the wild men wearing horsetails and long hair down to their shoulders, and carrying sticks they use to make noise with in rhythm"),[36] whose presence would alone suffice to mark these village festivities with the seal of the King of Carnival. Present were the ambiguous terrors of Carnival in nineteenth-century Languedoc, when during Mardi Gras at Pignan or at Frontignan, for example, boys smeared themselves with jam, or at Castelnaudary, with honey, to "play wild men," fearsome "Pagliacci" of Cournontéral who have survived even today,[37] and the dance of the four wild men in Camacho's Wedding. The wild man is an ancient mythical figure assimilated by Catholic iconography, after many other pagan and primitive elements, and thus by the religious sensibility, as is the case of the joyful and solemn procession that concerns us here. He is a primitive figure we should be careful not to confuse with the Amazons and Africans (Genealogy of the Virgin, September 21, 1513), who come from the illustrated cosmographies of the fifteenth and sixteenth centuries.

Did popular culture in turn misappropriate for the benefit of St. Matthew an homage officially rendered to the Holy Virgin? Is it not, rather, a decidedly hegemonic St. Matthew, under his sway as great financier, who unifies the cultural expression of the various social levels consolidated by the cloth merchants?

Indeed, it is not a matter of indifference that these dances were performed by peasants. No doubt, in sixteenth-century Spain, they had necessarily to be performed by the common people: "Todos los maestros aborrecen a los de las danzas de cascabel y con mucho razón porque es muy distinta a la quenta y de muy inferior lugar y ansi ningún maestro de reputación y con escuela abierta se ha hallado jamás en semejantes chapancadas . . . porque la danza de cascabel es para gente que puede salir a dançar por las calles y a estas danças llama por gracejo Francisco Remo la tarasca del Día de Dios." [Every nobleman abhors the bell dances and rightly so, because they have a very distinctive beat and are of very inferior character, thus no nobleman of good repute and of gentle breeding has ever been found in similar circumstances . . . because the bell dance is for people who can dance in the streets, and Francisco Remo has humorously called these dances the dragon of Corpus Christi].[38]

It is no accident that the participants in these ceremonies come exclusively from a rural milieu. They are performers of their folklore, one profoundly rooted in the cyclical time of seasons and harvests, as the apotropaic and fertility rites underlying the gestures and disguises of most of the figures appearing in the parade attest.

At the heart of the religious procession, the villagers bring back to life the ancient pagan traditions that constitute the transhistorical fund of their culture and beliefs; the fact remains — and this is essential — that they are no longer in control, and that these ancient rites have been cut off from what gave them meaning. It is no longer generational groups, the traditional guardians of sexual equilibrium in the primitive community, that lead the dance. The master of ceremonies has here the face of a rich, bourgeois city-dweller who, in the elaboration of his strategy, makes use of cultural elements foreign to him and appropriates them in the process of his own social ascension in order to confront, as Martine Grinberg suggests, the cultural domination of those classes — clergy and nobility — that are blocking his path to political hegemony.[39]

When we try to perceive this mercantile festivity through the grid of the nobility's abortive cavalcade in a kind of superposition of two texts, we can glimpse an initial conceptual space of confrontation. Military *ancestry* on the one hand; cultural *traditions*, on the other: both of these parades juxtaposed in time speak to us of a quest for origins. The annexation by the former of the foundation myth, a well-worn cliché of the rhetoric of urban description, does not carry much importance.[40] Whether its nature be bourgeois or aristocratic, the municipal power identifies with the town whose interests it embraces and bases its legitimacy on this espousal. The adoption of this myth signifies that one is speaking from a position of power, and from this point of view the example of Segovia is definitive. In other cases cited by Martine Grinberg, for example, a bourgeois elite monopolizes municipal power and functions; henceforth, the discourse of municipal power is its prerogative. However, the alternating semiological reading I am suggesting of the two iconographical patterns clearly draws the major line of force from the first procession, namely, that it is a dramatized historical discourse; the semiological void of the second procession on this point reminds us that the bourgeoisie of Segovia has no memory of social class. On the basis of the facts we have noted concerning the festivities of September 20 and 21, 1613, we should fully accept Martine Grinberg's analysis of the evolution of the function of Carnival when it moves from a rural milieu to an urban one, and the role played in its remodeling by a generally bourgeois magistrature: "Town-dwellers, who have been uprooted from the soil, take with them beliefs and rituals whose function and meaning their new environment will undertake to change and renew. The town must justify its existence on the ideological level; it has but one means of doing that—creating a cultural past—since it lacks a historical one."[41] This is true with the exception that, unlike Metz and Lille, which Grinberg examines, it is impossible to identify town and bourgeoisie in the case of Segovia at the beginning of the seventeenth century. The collective memory of the Segovian bourgeoisie is in part modeled by carnivalesque traditions; thus it is a popular memory appropriated for the benefit of the bourgeoisie. The presence of a dance element in the procession of the Genealogy of the Virgin does not merely represent an alliance of classes. The function it plays transcribes, at another level, the needs of a strategy imposed by circumstances.

I believe it is possible, however, to see this artificial constitution of a collective memory at work elsewhere on the same day. Indeed, let us come back to what might seem, at first glance, the essence of this parade, namely, the floats and *triomphi*. Certainly in the *triomphi*, what is involved is the reconstitution of the Genealogy of the Virgin from Abraham to Christ, following the text of Matthew. But as Flecniakoska observes, "numerous details are drawn directly from various books of the Old Testament, for example, the presentation of Manasseh (II Kings 21, 1–3), the arrangement of Solomon's throne with twelve lions guarding the steps (I Kings 10, 19, 20)."[42] Such a staging to which the choice of subject obviously lends itself (but who is responsible for this choice if not, certainly, the cloth makers' guild itself?), and which has a cavalcade of Old Testament characters parade in the streets of the town, may come as a surprise in the Segovian context insofar as every success in business or wool manufacturing is perceived as an indication that one belongs to the milieu of the *conversos*. What more striking proof of success than this sumptuous parade in which a whole merchant community ostentatiously displays fabrics of great luxury (silks, satins, cloths embroidered in gold and silver, taffetas) set off by precious stones?

If we take into account, as we must, the suspicion hanging over their guild, and it is difficult not to grant that they themselves must have been keenly aware of it, who would doubt that here again we are being confronted with a double message? That the first might be "a veritable hymn to the triumphant monarchy" addressed to King and Court is not impossible.[43] Behind this official and somewhat naive view of things, the meaning of the second is transparent: it responds to the accusations of the Segovian aristocracy by laying claim to an origin and by glorifying cultural roots that they are being reproached for wishing to hide. The problem here is not whether or not the clothiers of Segovia felt themselves to be Jews. Their attitude in this matter must be understood in the context of a polemic:

like the display of their economic power and their aspirations of uniting all the forces of the Third Estate, it takes the form of a provocation and a challenge.

It is in this whole context that we must place the figure of the King dominating the merchants' cavalcade. Surely, "it would be tedious to cite every king figuring in our cavalcade, but, whether Solomon, Roboam, Abias, Joatam or Amon, whether they wear a crown or a turban, they each have a scepter in their hand."[44] Was this multifarious image of royal authority intended to flatter the narcissism of Philip III? Assuming that such would be the decoding officially given to their iconography, while taking shelter behind Holy Scripture and the pretext of religious festivity, did the cloth manufacturers ever dream of opposing to the Spanish monarchy the sacred magnificence of the Priest/King and his primacy over all the Christian dynasties, thereby claiming for themselves a collective history and a collective memory capable of bursting wide open the class memory and class history that had been set against them the day before? These are only hypotheses; we may, however, more safely imagine the impact of this spectacle on the sensibilities of the noble lineages of Segovia. Their streets have been invaded by the federated cohorts of the urban masses, of suburban and rural elements, organized by their adversaries in an impudent display of wealth and strength around a proud symbol of Power, a symbol whose factitious character is denied by the circumstances. We are, in fact, in the presence of two representations of power: if the first is artificial (the scepter of the kings of the Old Testament), the second (the occupation of the street) is laden with actuality and threats; it corresponds to a real, a carnal possessing of the town, and responds to the nobility's metaphorical possession that we saw operating in the cavalcade of September 20 through the reproduction of the myth of the city's founding. Simulacra of possession and power confront one another, then, in games of inversion in which each of the adversaries can read, or thinks he perceives, the hegemonic pretensions of the other.

But, as menacing as it is, this threat of the bourgeoisie ends up in clowning and festivity. These Old Testament kings are only travestied kings, and nothing surrounding them is authentic: these stags, these elephants, these unicorns, these camels, these ostriches, these lions drawing the chariots of triumph or heightening their splendor, are but common draft horses and oxen. The monarchs themselves advance, preceded by their fools, surrounded by a crowd of dancing, grimacing, and gesticulating peasants. We can readily conceive how they might have seemed to malevolent and hostile minds as masquerade and Carnival kings, and how this whole spectacle could have been deconstructed in the eyes of some in a double image in which the burlesque projection of the characters is in turn diffracted to reduce the merchants' parade to the pattern of the processions of victims the Inquisition led through crowded city streets. This is all the more likely since the passage from one image to the other is facilitated by the fact that a whole series of signs belongs to both texts and can thus evoke the space of festival as well as a space of punishment.

By attributing such reactions to the opposition party, we are no longer in the realm of hypothesis, for we have already seen this bourgeois masquerade functioning and producing meaning in our analysis of the *Buscón*, in which it puts in question a vision of the world that corresponds to that of the transindividual subject informing the narrative voice. The respective readings I propose of Quevedo's text and of the iconography of the festivities in Segovia during September 1613 closely overlap. The first serves to decode the background of this sociodrama, whereas the second allows us to understand why and how a socioeconomic and sociopolitical problematic is found at the level of the organization of cultural life, and to *justify the existence of the carnivalesque image as a mediating structure of confrontation*, showing us, in turn, how and why this same mediating structure involves both the textile milieu and problems of religious heterodoxy, as well as a threatened break in social order.

I am not claiming, however, that there was a direct relation between the spectacle presented to the Court in September 1613 and the composition of the *Buscón*, despite the possibility of arguments based on chronology. I am proposing merely that both be considered as isotopic transcriptions of one and the same confrontation of mental structures that have their foundation in the working out of class strategies whose objective is the preservation or conquest of political hegemony. For it would be incorrect to imagine that replacing in its Segovian context the explanation of what is for me the deep structure of the *Buscón* limits the significance of the work. On the contrary, in the perspective I am proposing, new and deeper questions open before us.

The Functioning of Ideological Inscription in *La hora de todos*

The meaning of *La hora de todos* is problematic to the extent that the reader experiences some difficulties in relating the political tableaux to the moral ones and in relating the theoretical moral lesson expressed by Jupiter at the end of the work to all forty episodes. In their introduction, remarkable from every point of view, Jean Bourg, Pierre Dupont, and Pierre Geneste opt for the hypothesis of a providentialist and anti-Machiavelian attitude serving the principal objective of "preserving and preserving oneself" in a world where everything is in process of change: "we can measure," they write, "how small is the distance between the satire of private behavior and political behavior properly speaking. Face to face with crisis, Quevedo, like Jupiter, reacts conservatively."[45]

Josette Riandière La Roche, for her part, ascribes to Jupiter's discourse the functional role of unification: "It unifies by giving a common meaning—the denunciation of the corrupting power of money as the cause of the irremediable nature of human wickedness – to the totality of the work's episodes, bringing to the work an *added* element of cohesiveness."[46]

However, James Iffland[47] challenges this quest for the apparent and illusory unity of literary productions, and basing his argument on both Pierre Macherey's *Pour une théorie de la production littéraire* and Terry Eagleton's *Criticism and Ideology*,[48] he proposes to trace the ideological contradictions operating in the text. This theoretical position leads him to call attention to the subversive content of certain passages that would contradict the author's ideological project; according to this hypothesis, the lopsided character of Jupiter's final speech in relation to the narrative structure of the episodes preceding it expresses Quevedo's conscious or unconscious feeling that what he has represented in his text has gone too far. Iffland explains these contradictory voices by the equivocal modalities of Quevedo's insertion in a class structure; this seems to me entirely convincing. At the same time that it reproduces the ideology of the ruling class, Quevedo's work in fact causes the emergence of the specific discourse of a transindividual subject, who, within this ruling class, is in turn dominated and experiences his position of dependency in bitterness and resentment. Unlike Iffland, however, I do not think that in what would be his criticism of the status quo, Quevedo's point of view can be separated from his own class position and identified with the perspective of the lower classes.

Iffland's analysis is most suggestive in that it stresses the complexity of ideological inscriptions and thereby warns us against any excessively mechanistic and monosemically reductive vision of texts. However, I shall depart from it on a first point – namely, the origin and ideological nature of these contradictions – and rather than construct a coherent argument, I shall limit myself to a series of methodological suggestions or observations:

(1) *La hora de todos*, like any other text, deconstructs a preconstructed matter in which potential trajectories of meaning are already inscribed, as well as latent meanings more or less opaque, more or less resistant to writing. We should be careful not to confuse the ideological traces *invested* in this *preconstrained* linguistic material, which can be complex and contradictory, with the ideological *production* of meaning brought about in the process of their textual transformation. In the case at hand, this "already said" is a transhistorical and transcultural *topos* – the *mundus inversus* – that, as such, may appear to be emptied of all specific historical meaning and conceived only as referring to an archetype in the realm of the imaginary. We shall limit ourselves to this type of observation by noting that it is found in the first half of the seventeenth century in Spanish texts (not only in Quevedo but also in the *Emblemas morales* [1616] of Sebastian de Covarrubias y Horozco[49]), as well as in English texts (Henry Denne, *Grace, Mercy and Peace* [1645][50]), Italian texts (Giacomo Affinati d'Acuto, *The World Topsy-Turvy* [1610][51]), or French texts (Jean Deslyons, *Discours ecclésiastique* . . . [1664], and the French text of the lower cartouche of an engraving by Crispin de Pas

[1635][52]). In this manner, however, the nature of the *topos* appears, not directly articulating social interests but as a secondary modeling system, that is, a cultural code that transforms observable reality, making the transition from denotative to figurative language. Henceforth, through the *topos* of the "mundus inversus," social interests will be given metaphorical form, thus eluding any immediate mono-semic perception. The apparently equivocal meaning of *La hora de todos* must first be related to the ambiguity of the *topos*. No doubt, as Josette Riandière notes, "the discourse that [Quevedo] ascribes to Jupiter rests . . . on a double series of antitheses, one having socioeconomic implications, the other having moral implications," but is not the "mundus inversus" *topos* itself the vector of this double discourse? I shall quote here, following Tristan, a text of Aristophanes in which the denunciation of social injustice and the feeling that it is better not to change the existing order confront each other and are intertwined. Speaking to Chremy-lus and Blepsidemus, who wish to turn the world upside-down so that "the honest and true should enjoy, as their due, a successful and happy career,/ Whilst the lot of the godless and wicked should fall in exactly the opposite sphere," Poverty argues that if what they wish were to happen, they themselves would not profit from it:

> Why if Wealth should allot himself equally out (assume that his sight ye restore),
> Then none would to science his talents devote or practice a craft any more.
> Yet if science and art from the world should depart, pray whom would ye get for the future
> To build you a ship, or your leather to snip, or to make you a wheel or a suture?
> Do ye think that a man will be likely to tan, or a smithy or laundry to keep,
> Or to break up the soil with his ploughshare, and toil the fruits of Demeter to reap,
> If regardless of these he can dwell at his ease, a life without labour enjoying?[53]

We shall be tempted, then, to examine the *topos* itself to recognize in it the coexistence, on the one hand, of a subversive discourse and, on the other, a system that hides this very discourse and that has as its objective the erasure of this display of class relationships by means of an ethicoreligious discourse exploiting universal categories. It is clear, then, that the *topos* draws its primary meaning from the whole "discursive formation"[54] to which it belongs. We may judge this by a rapid comparison of a *cristiano viejo*'s expression of frustration: "I say that everything's going backward and upside down: good men are worth little, and the very good nothing, and those without honor are honored"[55] with the antisubversive discourse of Richard Morrison: "Wouldn't it be mad and unheard of for the foot to say 'I want to wear a hat' just as the head does? Or for the knee to say that he wants eyes or some other fanciful notion, for each shoulder to demand an ear, for the heels to want to be in front, the toes behind?" (*A Remedy for Sedition*, 1536).[56]

If we put Quevedo's text back into the series of *textual* examples of the world upside-down, we can say that, in all known cases, it is a religious discourse that predominates; it revolves about the socioeconomic problematic, which one may think is the original kernel of the *topos*, the better to displace and mask it.[57] It is this strategy that, it seems, has been chosen by writing in *La hora des todos*: when a subversive discourse is reproduced there, it presents itself as a "quoted ideology," to use Claude Duchet's convenient distinction. As for the "quoting ideology," which refers us to the concept of "discursive formation," it likewise revolves around the "quoted ideology" in the attempt to undermine its meaning. Here I shall quote Tableau XL, "The Assembly of Subjects of Princes," in which the narrative voice situates the controversies between partisans of the Republic and partisans of the Monarchy, as well as the demands of women, in a nightmarishly apocalyptic framework:

> There were people of all nations, conditions, and qualities. The number was so great it looked more like an army than an assembly, for which reason they made choice of the open fields to meet in. On the one hand it was surprising to behold the wonderful variety of garbs and countenances; on the other the ears were confounded, and attention itself deceived by the strange diversity of languages. Voices seemed to rend the air and resound in the same manner as when, in the heat of harvest time, the fields ring with the incessant noise of grasshoppers. The most piercing cry was that raised by the women, who tore their throats with an altogether distracted activity. All was full of tumultuous madness and raging discord. The republicans would be governed by princes, and the subjects of princes were for erecting themselves into commonwealths.[58]

The same goes for the *letrado bermejo*, the "ruddy lawyer" condemned by the quoting ideology even before he opens his mouth, "who had set them all a-madding and put into their heads such wild and extravagant demands. Two trumpets gave the signal for silence, when he, standing upon an eminent place in the midst of the multitude, swarmed about, delivered himself in this manner,"[59] a diabolical character who shoulders responsibility for the sedition and discord taking control of this assembly of madmen and demons. There is no doubt, however, that if his speech were artificially taken out of context it would have a certain coherence, with an obviously powerful impact on the reader.

(2) This discourse integrates other voices that, at the same time they are decon-structed in the *topos*, acquire, by virtue of the fact that they are being *represented* in it, a certain degree of autonomy bearing potential *meaning effects* that tran-scribe their resistance to the monosemic project of the quoting ideology. Think of feminist discourse, which, manipulated by the narrative function, is only deri-sion and another actualization of the world upside-down, and in which the reader would be tempted to see an illusory modernity provoked by the way in which a Golden Age figurative discourse is decoded by a twentieth-century discursive for-mation. If this example is obvious, it is probably not unique. One cannot help thinking that these "quoted" voices *represent* that feeling of crisis so masterfully analyzed by J. A. Maravall:

> But it is certain that as soon as the type we have called *modern man* appears—filled with his conquest of nature and his new ideas on society—he begins to develop the capacity to understand that economic life especially, as well as other aspects of collective life are not going well, and what is more important, he begins to think they could be im-proved. Moreover, this awareness of malaise and disquiet becomes stronger at those times in which profound upheavals in the functioning of society begin to make themselves felt, upheavals, the majority of which, are certainly due to the intervention of new forms of behavior in these same individuals, as well as to the pressure that new aspirations, ideals, beliefs, etc., . . . operating in a new complex of economic re-lations, exert on the shape of society. . . . [At such times] relations among different groups, and among individuals, tend, in principle, to become both more complicated and more difficult, changes arise in men's desires, their hopes, their actions, impelled by this same feeling that things have changed . . . And, clearly, that brings with it many conflicts, or better, a very generalized situation that we may call conflictive.[60]

These aspirations find in the imaginary figure of the world upside-down a form that models their signified: "In other cases, the protest against the extremely un-derprivileged social status of the working class cannot be more radical: some claim to invert the terms to the point of designating precisely those who do work for a living as the privileged group."[61]

(3) We must not confuse this first *topos* with that other secondary modeling system consisting of all the Carnivalesque traditions, even if both are articulated around the same polarities (high/low; above/below/; left/right), which are seen in more than one passage and in various guises: allusions to Harlequin figures (Anton Pintado and Anton Colorado), *mayas* (clowns), the *tarasca* (Corpus Christi dragon), etc., which call up in the text popular gestural traditions and which describe a discursive space distinct from, even in contradiction with, the first, since it can be considered as part of bourgeois discourse, at least if my analy-

sis of it in *Ideología y genética textual* is correct. The interdictions weighing heavily against these traditions in both France and Spain during the Counter-Reformation, as Anne Marie Le Coq, Martine Grinberg, and Helen Grant have reminded us,[62] make it abundantly clear that they were perceived as essentially seditious. At any rate, Quevedo seems to have experienced them as such. I think I have shown how, in the *Buscón*, threats of a break in social status and of a subversive movement upward from the bottom are being represented by means of a system of images of this type, which encodes them in this manner before inscribing them in the structure of the text.[63]

We witness a similar phenomenon in the prologue to *La hora de todos* (pp. 295ff.) with the carnivalization of Olympus, projecting the pagan divinities into the "world of the lower body" where they are diffracted: Mars — Don Quixote — guard of the vineyard; Bacchus — lazy simpleton; Neptune — old crone; Venus — animal, and so on. In this type of device two distinct "meaning effects" can be observed: the touch of burlesque can be perceived as the metaphor of a value judgment on the character, which is added to the referent and which is presented as the character's subjective vision, but it can just as well be presented in the form of a direct description of reality; in the first case, writing metamorphoses the character; in the second case, it limits itself to describing appearances. It is this second effect that predominates here, in the obviousness of the disguises: "quijada de vieja por cetro" [an old woman's jawbone for a sceptre], "cara afeitada con hollin y pez" [face powdered with soot and pitch], "cara de azofar y barbas de oropel" [of brazen face and tinsel beard], "a medio afeitar la cara" [her face but half licked], and especially, Neptune/Lady Lent: "Neptuno . . . con su quijada de vieja por cetro . . . y oliendo a viernes y vigilias" [Neptune with his old woman's jawbone for a sceptre . . . and reeking of Fridays and vigils]. The disguises are accompanied by some of the most well-known devices of grotesque realism, such as the "gigantizing" of the descriptions: "Baco . . . y en la boca laga y vendimias de retorno" [Bacchus . . . mouth like a winepress, belching out liquor at second hand]; "vestido de cultos tan obscuro que no le amanecía todo el buchorno del sol" [clothed in such profound darkness that he was scarce discernible, though closely followed by the glaring sun]; or again the choice of specific semantic axes such as drinking and eating: Neptune "hecho una sopa" [dripping Neptune]; Venus "empalagando de faldas a las cinco zonas" [hiding the five zones under her petticoats]; the Moon "con su cara en rabanadas" [with her face cut into quarters]; Mars "sonando a choque de cazos y sártenes" [rattling his armour like the harmony of a tinker's kettle], and so forth.

At the same time, however, writing superimposes on this carnivalization two semiotic texts that curiously change its meaning: the first invokes the world of criminality either directly (mancomunado, doncella de ronda), in the form of images of repression (luz en cuartos), or through *jacarandina* [jargon of world of criminals and prostitution] (*carda, coime*); whereas the second inscribes traces of anti-Semitism (the description of the wandering Jew in "del planeta bermejo y errante') and of Inquisitorial practice (the vision of Venus's wig as a miter of infamy), which, through an echo effect, ideologically semanticize the traditional portrayal of Saturn as "child eater" by incorporating it into the same mental structure (cf. the accusation by *cristianos viejos* against Jews they suspect of practicing ritual sacrifice of children on Good Friday). (The fact that these superimposed texts exist as well in the *Buscón* confirms my reading.)

These semiotic traces cause all the signs in the text to undergo a double displacement that complicates to the same extent the figurative language set up by the secondary modeling system (carnivalization), but at the same time they reveal the text's ideological meaning. In this way, carnivalization appears as the vector of the concept of usurpation and the instance of power as invested by usurpers who represent a danger both for social order and for the unity of religious consciousness. These divinities thus enact, in their figurative interplay, at the very beginning of the work, a scenario that represents straightaway the apocalyptic consequences that an application of the seditious theories of a "ruddy lawyer" might entail. In other words, between the play of the quoting and the quoted ideology that we saw operating in Chapter XL and the representation of the prologue there is only a difference of degree in the modeling. The description of Olympus encodes what Chapter XL decodes, thus justifying the theory of Adorno according to which the literary work says something and hides it at the same time. Both modeling systems—the *"mundus inversus" topos* and carnivalization—play against each other even though the patterns of reversal that structure them are not functioning in the same way, and it is this interplay that is one of the major factors in the ideological production of meaning.

In particular I want to point out that each of these two systems apparently organizes distinct textual spaces: the characters are categorized as upper and lower. The upper are spectators and moving spirits, sheltered, it seems, from the demystifying mechanisms of the "Hour"; however, it is writing that demystifies them by creating an imaginary space in which their authentic nature is revealed. They are frozen in an "untouchable topsy-turviness," probably because their very disguise unmasks them; thus the written word is seen as the double discloser of the "Hour" and as the redressive instance of usurpation, whose function is concretized and metaphorized by the "Hour."

We thereby come to the "decentered" character of Jupiter's theoretical lesson. What is it about precisely? When Jupiter declares: "I have observed that during this *hour* (which gave to every man what he deserved) those who, because they were poor and despicable, were also humble, are become proud and intolerable; and those who being rich and respected, were consequently vicious, perverse, arrogant, and wicked, seeing themselves poor and abject, are become penitent, bashful and pious" (pp. 377–378), he is only answering the complaints of mortals ("They complain that thou givest to villainies those rewards which are due to merit" (p. 297), by denying the category of merit (no mortal deserves the gifts of Fortune). But in fact the carnivalization of the prologue, just as in the forty episodes, is telling us something else, namely, that each individual must stay in the place "in which God wished him to be born and to die"; this is why writing and its double (the hour) do not distribute rewards but are content with unmasking, redressing, and defending Order against chaos. Thus the monosemic project of the quoting ideology is founded on a providentialistic vision,[64] excluding the ethicopolitical notion of merit; at the same time, however, that it is borrowing its garb in the moral spoken by Jupiter, and in this very process of dissimulation, it is revealing itself as ideology.

(4) One last question presents itself, bearing upon the "not said" of the text: does the desire for social transformations overflow the quoted ideology so as to infiltrate and undermine from within the quoting ideology, thus transcribing the aspirations of the dominated groups in the context of the internal contradictions of the ruling class? In order to answer this question, I suggest that we take note of textual phenomena that seem not to have been noticed by critics thus far and that are capable of illuminating fundamental aspects of *La hora de todos*. *La hora de todos* is, to my knowledge, one of the rare texts whose narrative is explicitly dated; it is June 20, the eve of the summer solstice,[65] that is, that time of the year when the flow of time seems on the point of reversing itself, since it is from that day forward that the days begin to grow shorter. This date, then, inscribes a first index of the investment in the text of popular beliefs, in particular those that assume that harmful forces are especially active at the summer solstice. This might explain the fact that the ceremonies organized on this occasion, as on Midsummer's Day, which is close at hand, have a prophylactic purpose. I wonder if it is not appropriate to link this first index to the exclamation of Fortune when she comes on stage to overwhelm everybody with "Fly, wheel: and may the devil drive thee," thereby alluding to a children's game[66] that seems to me to be imitating an apotropaic ceremony, since the participants of the game try to keep away by their kicks the one fate has designated as having to remain on the outside, and who, in such a context, seems to represent evil or the evil destiny that is one of the two faces of Fortune. In the absence of any further documentation on this tradition, I should like to underline this image of the circle that is supposed to protect from evil: I think of the disks and protective wheels of Midsummer's Day, the incandescent circles that are hidden in attics to keep fire away, the crowns of artemisia that in the thirteenth century, Rutebeuf tells us women wore to protect themselves against fire and epilepsy.[67]

A structural study would show us how this image of the circle is organizing the text from the inside, not only in its global configuration (the return to Olympus and to the status quo) of a serpent biting its own tail; in the composition of a number of tableaux: the turning and returning in one direction or another in XI ("The servant deluded by the devil"); the endless "swarm" of "candidates" in XXI ("The lord left them striving to outlive and destroy one another, and went himself away, in a passion to see them protracting their ages beyond doomsday and even coping with eternity" [p. 317]); the successive passing from one character to another that characterizes XVI, "Misers and Cheats" ("The sharper, who heard the other sharper commending the third"); but also in what I shall call the reflexive pattern of the judges' self-condemnation (VII), the tavernkeeper's self-denunciation (XX), the self-execution of the doctor perceived as both his patient's and his own executioner, or in those frenetic sarabands in which the actants, at the end of the episode, exchange objects, attributes, or functions, in those diabolical round-robins of materials, medications, or offal. Similarly, we recognize the specific characteristics of the childish roundelay in the systematics of expulsion and assimilation "van tirando coces al que ha quedado fuera, el cual procura, aunque sea recibiendo algunas coces, coger a otro de los que andan en la rueda y el cogido se queda fuera y siempre van diciendo: Ande la rueda y coz con ella" [translation in note 66], as well as in the interplay of switching, substitution, and interchangeability operating in most of the episodes: "y como se encontraban al salir y al entrar los botes y la basura" [p. 188; and boots and muck were found both coming and going]; "quedando las barbas lampiñas y las uñas barbadas" [p. 194; beards were left hairless and fingernails bearded]; "mandó soltar todos los presos y prender todos los ministros de la cárcel" [p. 202; he freed all the jailed and arrested all the jailors]; "quitando a todos cuanto tienen y enriqueciendolos con quitárselo" [p. 215; taking away from everyone all they have and enriching them by doing it]; "ofrece hacer que lo que falta sobre" [p. 215; he offers to make scarcity abundant]; and so on, and which even model the syntagmatic organization of the sentence: "lo que tiene es sólo lo que no tiene" [what he has is only what he does not have]. It is important to observe that in various forms this structural element inscribes many markers in the text to the extent that they reproduce in it a ritualistic conjuring of an undefined evil whose accomplishment is feared to be imminent at the explicit level ("El mundo está para dar un estallido" [The world is about to explode]). This obsession with evil, capable of transcribing a fundamental anguish face to face with a collective future, leads me to think that even if a desire for change were invested at the level of narrative function—a hypothesis that I do not accept—this desire for change would in the final analysis be exorcised in the deep structures of the text.

Notes

Notes

Unless otherwise indicated, translations of foreign-language quotations are my own – J. S.

Foreword

1. John Fekete, *The Structural Allegory: Reconstructive Encounters with the New French Thought* (Minneapolis: University of Minnesota Press, 1984) Theory and History of Literature, vol. 11.

2. In this connection see Hans Ulrich Gumbrecht, "Déconstruction deconstructed. Transformationen französischer Logozentrismuskritik in der amerikanischen Literaturtheroie," *Philosophische Rundschau* 33 (1986), pp. 1–35.

3. Our reference here is to Derrida's reception in the United States and not to his own, perhaps quite different, political position.

4. The various theory-political connotations of the term "literary sociology" are a good example of the model of culturally specific usage that we outlined above. While in the francophone world Escarpit has defined "literary sociology" as statistics on book distribution, in the German-speaking world – in the tradition of the Frankfurt School – the same term refers to the exact opposition, namely to a critical, analytic, i.e., to a "sociocritical" reading. (A representative example from the German-speaking world is the work of Peter V. Zima, to whom Cros also refers.)

5. Materials and perspectives for a differentiation of the categories "feudal" and "bourgeois" can be found in the volume *La littérature historiographique des origines à 1500* (Grundriss der romanischen Literaturen des Mitelalters, vol. XI/1), Hans Ulrich Gumbrecht, Ursala Link-Heer, and Peter-Michael Spangenberg, eds. (Heidelberg: Carl Winter, 1986–87).

6. Althusser refers not only to public apparatuses like schools as "ideological state apparatuses," but also to private institutions in the realm of civil society, for example, the family. He derives this extreme usage, in our view incorrectly, from Gramsci's category of "hegemony." This produces certain aporia, which can be ignored for our purposes. However, we recommend that any recourse to

Althusser also include a look at Gramsci himself. For a discussion of the whole complex, particularly with reference to Gramsci's central categories of the "historical block" and "hegemony," as well as the relationship between Gramsci and Althusser, see Jürgen Link and Ursula Link-Heer, *Literatursoziologisches Fropädeutikum* (München: Fink, 1980) UTB 799.

7. The term "interdiscourse" can therefore be used to connote two fundamentally different concepts: In Pêcheux, Robin, and Cros it refers to the integration of the "vertical" axis of social stratification, whereas in Foucault it refers to the integration of the "horizontal" axis of functional divisions and the specialization of discourses. For a further examination of Foucault's notion of "interdiscourse" see Jürgen Link, *Elementare Literatur und generative Diskursanalyse* (München: Fink, 1983).

8. In addition to Cros's references, one should mention that Gómez-Moriana is now available in book form: A. Gómez-Moriana, *La subversion du discours rituel*, Collection L'univers des discours (Longueuil, Québec, 1985).

Chapter 1. From Experimental Sociology to Genetic Structuralism

1. Albert Memmi,"Problèmes de la sociologie de la littérature," in *Traité de sociologie*, vol. II, ed. G. Gurvitch, 3rd ed. (Paris: P.U.F., 1968).

2. Gaëton Picon, in "Formes sociales et création artistique" (lecture presented to the Association of Yugoslavian Writers, text reproduced in *Preuves*, Paris, Dec. 1957), quoted by A. Memmi, "Problèmes de la sociologie."

3. See R. Escarpit's remarks at the Colloquium of May 21–23, 1964, organized by Lucien Goldmann, published in *Littérature et société: Problèmes de méthodologie en sociologie de la littérature* (Brussels: Université Libre, 1967).

4. Escarpit, *Littérature et société*, p. 28.

5. "The research presented here is intended to elucidate a problem of literary history by means of a sociological method, which is, in our view, *the specific role of the sociology of literature*" (italics mine), Escarpit, "L'Image historique de la littérature chez les jeunes. Problèmes de tri et de classement," in *Littérature et société*, p. 151.

6. Escarpit, *Littérature et société*, p. 41. See further: "For this reason, commentaries concerning the work of art itself, therefore its structure, remain outside of sociological inquiries on art," in *Fischer-Lexikon*, s.v. "sociologie," ed. R. König, 1967. Quoted by P. V. Zima, *Pour une sociologie du texte littéraire* (Paris: UGE, 1978), p. 103.

7. H. A. Fügen, *Die Hauptrichtungen der Literatursoziologie* (Bouvier, 1964), p. 41. Quoted by Zima, *Pour une sociologie du texte littéraire*, p. 82.

8. K. E. Rosengren, *Sociological Aspects of the Literary System* (Stockholm: Natur och Kultur, 1968). On all these points, as well as on what follows, see Zima, *Pour une sociologie du texte littéraire*, pp. 67–104.

9. Goldmann, *Littérature et société*, p. 42. See "Given the fact that the research objective of sociology is social action, i.e., intersubjective action, it does not consider the literary work as an aesthetic phenomenon, since for sociology the meaning of literature resides exclusively in the particular intersubjective action that literature gives rise to," H. N. Fügen, *Die Hauptrichtungen des Literatursoziologie*, p.14. Quoted by Zima, *Pour une sociologie du texte littéraire*, p. 70.

10. J.-P. Sartre, "Pourquoi écrire?" *Qu'est-ce que la littérature*, in Situations II, vol. I (Paris: Gallimard, 1948), p. 91.

11. B. Berelson and J. P. Salter, "Majority and Minority Americans: An Analysis of Magazine Fiction," in *Public Opinion Quarterly*, 10 (1946), 168–190. Cf. our analysis of *Scarface*.

12. Miltos Albrecht, "Does Literature Reflect Common Values?" *American Sociological Review*, 21 (1956), 722–729.

13. Henri Zalamansky, "L'Etude des contenus, étape fondamentale d'une sociologie de la littéra-

ture contemporaine," in R. Escarpit, *Le Littéraire et le social* (Paris: Flammarion, 1970), pp. 119–129. In the Hispanic field, see, as a good example of this critical approach, the useful study of Liliane Hasson, *L'Image de la révolution cubaine dans la presse française et espagnole: Essai d'analyse de contenu* (Paris: Editions Hispaniques, 1981).

14. Umberto Eco, "James Bond, une combinatoire narrative," *Communications*, 8 (1966), 92.

15. P. Henry and S. Muscovici, "Problèmes de l'analyse de contenu," *Langages*, 11 (Sept. 1968), 38–60.

16. Zalamansky, "L'Etude des contenus," p. 125.

17. Ibid.

18. Yuri Lotman, *La Structure du texte artistique* (Paris: Gallimard, 1970), p. 55.

19. Leo Tolstoy, *Oeuvres complètes*, vol. 62 (Moscow, 1953), pp. 269–270.

20. Leo Tolstoy, *Le Problème du langage versifié* (Leningrad, 1924). Quoted by Lotman, *La Structure du texte artistique*, p. 39.

21. Lotman, *La Structure du texte artistique*, p. 39.

22. Zima, *Pour une sociologie du texte littéraire*, p. 95.

23. Régine Robin, *Histoire et linguistique* (Paris: A. Colin, 1973), p. 93.

24. Gérard Delfau and Anne Roche, *Histoire, littérature* (Paris: Seuil, 1977).

25. Zima, *Pour une sociologie du texte littéraire*, p. 78.

26. Ibid., p. 81.

27. Ibid., p. 101.

28. Lucien Goldmann, "Structuralisme génétique et création litteraire," in *Sciences humaines et philosophie* (Paris: Gonthier, 1966), pp. 151–165 (Goldmann's italics).

29. Ibid. (Goldmann's italics).

30. Ibid.

31. Lucien Goldmann, *Structures mentales et création culturelle* (Paris: Anthropos, 1970), preface, p. xvii.

32. Ibid.

33. Lucien Goldmann, *Le Dieu caché* (Paris: Gallimard, 1959), p. 27.

34. See Lucien Goldmann, *Le Dieu caché*: "L'individu n'a que rarement une conscience vraiment entière de ses aspirations, de ses sentiments, de son comportement" (p. 27) [The individual rarely has a truly complete awareness of his aspirations, his feelings, and his behavior].

35. Ibid., pp. 27–28.

36. Georges Lukács, *Histoire et conscience de classe* (Paris: Minuit, 1960); *L'Ame et les formes* (Paris: Gallimard, 1974). See Zima, *Pour une sociologie du texte littéraire*, pp. 180–182.

37. Ibid., pp. 181–182.

38. Lucien Goldmann, "La Pensée historique et son objet," in *Sciences humaines et philosophie*, p. 29.

39. Goldmann, *Structures mentales*, Preface dated July 1970.

40. Goldmann's responses can be found at the end of *Structures mentales*.

41. Zima, *Pour une sociologie du texte littéraire*, p. 200–201.

42. Lucien Goldmann, *La Communauté humaine et l'univers chez Kant* (Paris: P.U.F., 1948).

43. Zima, *Pour une sociologie du texte littéraire,* pp. 200–201.

44. Goldmann, *La Communauté humaine*, p. 206.

45. "It would be possible to show that for Goldmann even the novels of André Malraux can be 'deduced,' at the level of novelistic structure, from the transition from problematic individualism to the vision of community, in which the form of the novel, inseparable from the destiny of the individual, fades away" (ibid., p. 207).

46. P. V. Zima, *Pour une sociologie du roman* (Paris: Gallimard, 1964), p. 22.

47. Goldmann, *Le Dieu caché*, p. 22.

48. Yuri Tynianov, "De l'évolution littéraire." Quoted by Zima, *Pour une sociologie du texte littéraire*, p. 238.

49. See particularly Pierre Bourdieu, *Un art moyen* (Paris: Minuit, 1965).

50. Lucien Goldmann, *Sciences humaines et philosophie*, p. 110.

51. Lucien Goldmann, *Recherches dialectiques* (Paris: Gallimard, 1959), p. 97.

52. Jacques Leenhardt, "Lecture critique de la théorie goldmannienne du roman," in *Sociocritique*, ed. Claude Duchet (Paris: Nathan, 1979), p. 176.

53. Ibid., p. 174.

54. Ibid.

55. Ibid., p. 176.

56. Jacques Leenhardt, *Lecture politique du roman "La Jalousie" d'Alain Robbe-Grillet* (Paris: Minuit, 1973), p. 36.

Chapter 2. Literature as Secondary Modeling System and Ideological Form

1. Pierre Bourdieu, "Le Marché des biens symboliques," *L'Année Sociologique*, 22 (1971), 49–126.

2. Ibid., p. 51.

3. Ibid., p. 55.

4. Theodor W. Adorno, *Théorie esthétique* (Paris: Klincksieck, 1974), p. 299.

5. Jacques Dubois, *L'Institution de la Littérature: Introduction à une sociologie* (Bruxelles: Labor; Paris: Nathan, 1978). On the same problem, see "*L'Institution littéraire I*," *Littérature*, 42 (Mar. 1981); and "*L'Institution littéraire II*," *Littérature*, 44 (Dec. 1981).

6. Dubois, *L'Institution littéraire*, p. 46.

7. Ibid., p. 50.

8. Ibid., pp. 159, 189.

9. Bourdieu, "Le Marché," p. 56; italics mine.

10. "By becoming the principal object of positions and oppositions between producers, stylistic principles, which always tend to be reduced more to technical principles, are achieved more and more vigorously and completely in works of literature at the same time that they are asserted more and more systematically in the theoretical discourse produced by and for confrontation" (ibid., p. 61).

11. Ibid., p. 62.

12. R. Escarpit, *Le Littéraire et le social* (Paris: Flammarion, 1970), p. 32.

13. Renée Balibar and Denis Laporte, *Le Français national: Constitution de la langue nationale à l'époque de la revolution démocratique bourgeoise* (Paris: Hachette, 1974).

14. E. Balibar and P. Macherey, "Sur la littérature comme forme idéologique – quelques hypothèses marxistes," in *Littérature*, 13 (Feb. 1974), *Histoire et sujet*, 29–48.

15. Ibid., pp. 42–43.

16. Ibid., p. 38. On this problem, see P. Macherey, *Pour une théorie de la production littéraire* (Paris: Maspero, 1966).

17. E. Balibar and P. Macherey, "Sur la littérature," p. 39.

18. Ibid., p. 43.

19. Ibid., pp. 46–47.

20. "After all, 'literature' and 'politics' are recent categories that can be applied to medieval culture, or even classical culture, only by a retrospective hypothesis, and by an interplay of formal analogies or semantic resemblances; but neither literature, nor politics, nor philosophy and the sciences articulated the field of discourse, in the seventeenth or eighteenth century, as they did in the nineteenth century" (Michel Foucault, *The Archaeology of Knowledge*, trans. A. M. Sheridan Smith [New York: Pantheon Books, 1972], p. 22).

21. R. Escarpit, *Le Littéraire et le social*, p. 265.

22. Ibid., p. 268.

23. "Until the end of the eighteenth century, *literature* is, in fact, rarely spoken of when the aesthetic aspect of written works is concerned: Diderot writes a treatise *De la poésie dramatique*, not on the theater; Samuel Johnson narrates the *lives of poets*, not of writers. Poetry, the noble literary form, true to its etymology, is creation *par excellence*." R. Escarpit, "La Définition du terme 'littéraire'," in *Le Littéraire et le social*, pp. 259–272.

24. See R. Robin, *Histoire et linguistique* (Paris: A. Colin, 1973), pp. 107–117.

25. On the historical concept of "historical time," see Althusser: "For each mode of production, there is a peculiar time and history, punctuated in a specific way by the development of the productive forces; the relations of production have their peculiar time and history, punctuated in a specific way; the political superstructure has its own history . . . philosophy has its own time and history . . . aesthetic productions have their own time and history . . . scientific formations have their own time and history, etc. . . . . The fact that each of these times and each of these histories is *relatively autonomous* does not make them so many domains that are *independent* of the whole: the specificity of each of these times and of each of these histories . . . is based on a certain type of *dependence* with respect to the whole" (Louis Althusser and Etienne Balibar, *Reading Capital*, trans. Ben Brewster [London: NLB, 1970], pp. 99–100).

26. See n. 25.

27. Robin, *Histoire et linguistique*, pp. 111–112.

28. Ibid., p. 112.

29. Cascales, *Tablas poéticas*, here reviving the Aristotelian distinction. Cf. Menendez y Pelayo, *Historia de las ideas estéticas en España*, vol. III, 3rd ed. (Madrid: Consejo Superior de Investigaciones Científicas, 1962), p. 237, and E. Cros, *Protée et le gueux: Recherches sur l'origine et la nature du récit picaresque dans* Guzmán de Alfarache *de Mateo Alemán* (Paris: Didier, 1967), Coll. Etudes de Littérature Etrangère et Comparée, p. 96.

30. Robin, *Histoire et linguistique*, p.109.

31. See Edmond Cros, "Sur le fonctionnement des inscriptions idéologiques dans *La hora de todos*," in ed. E. Cros, *Francisco de Quevedo, La hora de todos*, Co-textes, 2 (Montpellier: Centre d'Etudes et de Recherches Sociocritiques, 1981), 99–113.

32. The expression is Josette Riandière La Roche's.

33. Bourdieu, "Le Marché," p. 71.

34. Dubois, "*L'Institution littéraire*," pp. 98–99.

35. Cros, *Protée et le gueux*.

36. Here I am using the terms chosen by A. J. Greimas and J. Courtès, *Sémiotique, dictionnaire raisonné de la théorie du langage* (Paris: Hachette Université, 1979). The reader will notice, however, that my perspective is perceptibly different, insofar as Greimas and Courtès present macrosemiotics as preexisting. See the headings "Discours" and "Sémiotique," pp. 104 and 339.

37. See E. Auerbach, *Vier Untersuchungen zur Geschichte der französischen Bildung* (Bern, 1951).

38. Erich Auerbach, *Literatursprache und Publikum in der lateinischen Spätantike und im Mittelalter* (Bern: Francke Verlag, 1958). Spanish translation: *Lenguaje literario y público en la baja latinidad y en la Edad Media* (Barcelona: Seix Barral, 1969). On the point discussed here, see ch. 4.

39. Auerbach, *Literatursprache und Publikum*, ch. 1, "Sermo humilis." On certain aspects of the specificity of "literary language" in Spain, see E. L. Rivers, "Texto oral y texto escrito en Góngora," in *Estudios filológicos y lingüísticos: Homenaje a Angel Rosenblat en sus 70 años* (Caracas: Instituto Pedagógico, 1974), pp. 459–467.

40. Bourdieu, "Le Marché," p. 82.

41. Ibid., p. 89.

Chapter 3. Discursive Practices and Formations

1. Michel Foucault, *The Archaeology of Knowledge*, trans. A. M. Sheridan Smith (New York: Pantheon Books, 1972), p. 28.

2. Ibid., p. 37.

3. Ibid., p. 42.

4. Ibid., p. 45.

5. Ibid., p. 48.

6. Ibid., pp. 54–55, 63.

7. Ibid., pp. 46, 47.

8. Ibid., p. 44.

9. Régine Robin, *Histoire et linguistique*, (Paris: A. Colin, 1973), pp. 85–89. See also Dominique Lecourt, "Sur l'Archéologie du Savoir, à propos de Michel Foucault," *La Pensée*, 152 (Aug. 1970), 88–99.

10. Foucault, *Archaeology of Knowledge*, p. 45.

11. Robin, *Histoire et linguistique*, p. 110.

12. N. Polantzas, *Pouvoir politique et classes sociales* (Paris: Maspero, 1968), p. 11. Similarly, moreover, the Russia between 1917 and 1927 analyzed by Lenin displays a patriarchal peasant economy, a small commercial sector, and both private and State capitalism.

13. Robin, *Histoire et linguistique*, pp. 98–99.

14. Quoted in Robin, *Histoire et linguistique*, p. 96.

15. Karl Marx, *The Eighteenth Brumaire of Louis Bonaparte* (New York: International Publishers, 1963), p. 124.

16. Michel Pêcheux, *Les Vérités de La Palice* (Paris: Maspero, 1975), p. 130.

17. Claude Haroche, Paul Henry, and Michel Pêcheux, "La Sémantique et la coupure saussurienne; Langue, langage, discours," *Langages*, 24 (Dec. 1971), 102.

18. Pêcheux, *Vérités*, p. 139.

19. Louis Althusser, *Réponse à John Lewis* (Paris: Maspero, 1973), p. 93.

20. Paul Henry, *De l'énoncé au discours: présupposition et processus discursifs* (mimeographed; Centre National de la Recherche Scientifique-Ecole Pratique des Hautes Etudes, 1974), quoted in Pêcheux, *Vérités*, pp. 88, 89. Henry quotes the following example: "It is not the steady growth of the cost of government which calls for an increase in taxes, but the Vietnam war," in which the relative clause functions as a preconstructed.

21. Pêcheux, *Vérités*, p. 152.

22. See, in this connection, Althusser: "God needs to 'make himself' man, the Subject needs to become subject, visible to the eyes, tangible to the hands (cf. St. Thomas) of subjects, as if to show empirically that, if they are subjects subjected to the Subject, this is uniquely so that they may return at Judgment Day, as did Christ, to the bosom of the Lord, that is, to the Subject" ("Idéologie et appareils idéologiques d'Etat," *La Pensée*, 151 [1970], 35).

23. Pêcheux, *Vérités*, p. 153.

24. See Chapter 4.

25. Robin, *Histoire et linguistique*, p. 105.

26. T. Herbert, "Remarque pour une théorie générale des idéologies," *Cahiers pour l'analyse*, 9 (Summer 1968), 74–92.

27. Ibid., 88–89.

28. Robin, *Histoire et linguistique*, p. 105.

29. See Chapter 10.

Chapter 4. Toward a Semiology of Ideology

1. Louis Althusser, "Idéologie et appareil idéologiques d'Etat (notes pour une recherche)," *La Pensée*, 151 (June 1970), 26–28.

2. I quote the text presented by Antonio Gómez-Moriana in the Colloquy "Procédés de véridiction" (Montreal, 1976). See also this passage further along: "The structure of the first picaresque text thus appears to us now as if copied from that of the spiritual confessions, which were apparently commonly read in the Spain of the period, but also from those confidential demonstrations required by the Inquisition which seem curiously familiar to the author of the *Lazarillo* as well as to certain of his readers."

3. Edmond Cros, *Protée et le gueux: Recherches sur l'origine et la nature du récit picaresque dans* Guzmán de Alfarache *de Mateo Alemán* (Paris: Didier, 1967), Coll. Etudes de Littérature Etrangère et Comparée.

4. See Pedro Herrera Pug, *Sociedad y delincuencia en el Siglo de Oro* (Granada: Universidad de Granada, 1971), who quotes lengthy passages from the unpublished manuscript of Pedro de León, and from whom we borrow our quotations.

5. On this point, see the various evidence attested by *Guzmán de Alfarache*: "In Madrid, where I spent my youth, one day I saw two adulteresses taken from prison to be executed. . . . A great crowd—mostly women—ran to see them, overflowing the streets, the square and the windows, all of them pitying their misfortune. And when the husband had cut off his wife's head, the blackamoor shouted "Oh, Lord, and how many there are who might have the same done to them" (*Guzmán de Alfarache*, ed. F. Rico, *La novela picaresca española*, vol. I, [Barcelona: Planeta, 1967], p. 269). "We would go to the comedies at the theater, see executions of those condemned to die, as well as to all gatherings of whatever nature, where we knew there would be many people present," (ibid., p. 635).

6. See Herrera Pug on this point, p. 196.

7. Ibid., pp. 223–224.

8. *Guzmán de Alfarache*, ed. F. Rico, pp. 310, 890, 891, 488, 893. In terms of my preceding argument, I consider these quotations as so many ideosemes referring to ideological practices. (*Translator's note*: English translations are of the author's French translations.)

9. Edmond Cros, *Mateo Alemán: Introducción a su vida y a su obra* (Madrid: Anaya, 1971).

10. See further in the same testimony: "mi maldita vida. . . . Qué locura ha sido la mia? . . . no mireis a mis maldades" (*Guzmán de Alfarache*, ed. F. Rico, p. 231). Henceforth the pagination of the Spanish edition of *Guzmán de Alfarache* is given directly in the text.

Chapter 5. Textual Functions I: Transformational Processes and Codes

1. Mikhail Bakhtin, *Le Marxisme et la philosophie du langage; Essais d'application de la méthode sociologique en linguistique* (Paris: Minuit, 1977), pp. 27, 30.

2. Ibid., pp. 50–51; Bakhtin's italics.

3. Ibid.

4. See Chapter 9.

5. On this point, see Chapter 1.

6. F. de Saussure, *Curso de linguística general* (Barcelona: Planeta, 1985), p. 27. My italics.

7. "Class . . . cannot be conceived as static, passive, in itself, but in its *relation* to other classes" (Jean Guichard, *Le Marxisme: Théorie de la pratique révolutionnaire* [Lyons: Chronique Sociale de France], p. 193).

8. Edmond Cros, "Effets sur la génétique textuelle de la situation marginalisée du sujet," *Imprévue*, 1 (1980), 23–30.

9. L. Cardaillac, *Moriscos y cristianos: un enfrentamiento polémico* (Madrid: Fondo de Cultura

Economica, 1979), ch. 2. The term *aljamiado* refers to a text in Castilian but written in Arabic characters.

10. Nicolav Eimeric and Francisco Peña, *El Manual de los Inquisidores* (Barcelona: Muchnick editores [Colección Archivos de la herejía por R. Muñoz Suay], 1983), p. 148.

11. Bakhtin, *Le Marxisme*, p. 116. On the same problem, see also Bakhtin's *La Poétique de Dostoievski* (Paris: Seuil), ch. 5.

12. See Chapter 6.

13. See Chapter 1.

14. See Chapter 8, pp. 133-136.

15. See Chapter 10, pp. 190-207.

16. Pierre Vilar, *Or et monnaie dans l'histoire* (Paris: Flammarion, 1974), p. 192.

17. See E. Cros, "Pratiques idéologiques et pratiques rituelles. Rendre l'illisible lisible," *Imprévue*, 1 (1980), 129-137.

18. See Julia Kristeva, *Semeiotiké* (Paris: Seuil, 1969), pp. 191, 195, 255.

19. Roland Barthes, *Le Plaisir du texte* (Paris: Seuil, 1973).

20. See Michael Riffaterre, *Semiotics of Poetry* (Bloomington-London: Indiana University Press, 1978) and his highly suggestive study "Sémiotique intertextuelle: l'Interpretant," *Rhétoriques Sémiotiques, Revue d'esthétique*, 1-2 (1979), 128-150.

21. "That for which (a sign) stands is called its *object*; that which it conveys, its meaning; and the idea to which it gives rise, its interpretant," C. S. Peirce, *Principles of Philosophy*, ed. Charles Hartshorne and Paul Weiss, vol. 1 of *Collected Papers* (Cambridge, Mass.: Harvard University Press, 1931), p. 171.

22. J. Molino, F. Soublin, and J. Tamine, "Présentation: problèmes de la métaphore," *La Métaphore, Langages*, 54 (June 1979), p. 14.

Chapter 6. Textual Functions II: Genotext and Phenotexts

1. Julia Kristeva, *Semeiotiké; Recherches pour une sémanalyse* (Paris: Seuil, 1969, coll. Tel Quel). Henceforth I shall put references to this edition directly in the text.

2. S. K. Saumjan-Soboleva, *Le Modèle génératif applicatif et les calculs des transformations dans la langue russe* (Moscow, 1963), and *Fondements de la grammaire générative de la langue russe* (Moscow, 1968).

3. Yuri Lotman, *La Structure du texte artistique* (Paris: Gallimard, 1973), p. 53.

4. P. V. Zima, *Pour une sociologie du texte littéraire* (Paris: UGE, 1978), p. 40.

5. Lotman, *La Structure*, p. 52.

6. Zima, *Pour une sociologie du texte littéraire*, p. 40.

7. Edmond Cros, "La Perception de l'espace dans *Residencia* de P. Neruda, essai sur les mécanismes de production de sens," *Imprévue*, 1-2 (1978), 7-33.

8. See Chapter 9.

9. Zima, *Pour une sociologie du texte littéraire*, p. 40.

10. Quoted by Lotman, *La Structure*, p. 39.

11. Lotman, *La Structure*, p. 54.

12. Sebastian de Covarrubias, *Tesoro de la lengua castellana* (1611; rpt. Madrid: Turner, 1979), entry: *trabajo*.

13. From this point of view, the secularization of ecclesiastical dress, its "banalization," signifies the fact that the Church has lost its function as Ideological State Apparatus.

14. See Chapter 8, p. 150.

Chapter 7. Narrative and Character as Textual Categories

1. Victor Shlovski in *Théorie de la littérature: Textes des formalistes russes*, ed. and trans. T. Todorov (Paris: Seuil, 1965), p. 54.

2. T. Todorov, "Les Catégories du récit littéraire," *Communications*, 8 (1966), 125–151.

3. Roland Barthes, "Introduction à l'analyse structurale des récits," *Communications*, 8 (1966), 1–27.

4. See Gérard Genette, *Figures III* (Paris: Seuil, 1972): "Je propose de nommer *histoire* le signifié ou contenu narratif . . . , *récit* proprement dit le signifiant énoncé, discours ou texte narratif lui-même et *narration* l'acte narratif producteur, et, par extension, l'ensemble de la situation réelle ou fictive dans laquelle il prend place" (p. 72) [I propose to name *story* the signified or narrative content . . . , *narrative* properly speaking the enunciated signifier, discourse, or narrative text itself, and *narration* the productive narrative act and, by extension, the entire real or fictive situation in which it takes place].

5. Jean Ricardou, *Problèmes du nouveau roman* (Paris: Seuil, 1967).

6. Milke Bal, *Narratologie*, (Paris: Klincksieck, 1977), p. 8.

7. Géza Róheim, *The Gates of the Dream* (New York: International Universities Press, 1952); *The Riddle of the Sphinx: or, Human Origins*, authorized translation by R. Money-Kyrle, with preface by Ernest Jones (London: Hogarth Press and the Institute of Psychoanalysis, 1934). On certain of these points, see the remarkable study of Georges Martin, "Continuité des Sphinx—Etude sur *Continuidad de los Parques* de J. Cortazar," *Imprévue*, 1–2 (1978), 35–63.

8. Róheim, *Riddle of the Sphinx*, p. 22.

9. In the following study, I am adopting the code developed by V. Propp in *The Morphology of the Folk Tale*, publication 10 of the Indiana University Research Center in Anthropology, Folklore and Linguistics, Oct. 1958.

10. Claude Brémond, "Le message narratif," *Communications*, 4 (Paris: Seuil, 1964), 4–32.

11. Tzvetan Todorov, *The Poetics of Prose*, trans. Richard Howard (Ithaca, N.Y.: Cornell University Press, 1977), p. 122.

12. On all these problems, see the interesting synthesis of M. Carcaud-Macaire and Y. Mauvais, *La Fiction littéraire: Narratologie*, 2 vols. (mimeographed) (Oran, 1979).

13. Philippe Hamon, "Pour un statut sémiologique du personnage," *Poétique*, 78 (1977), 125.

14. Michel Foucault, *Les Mots et les choses, une archéologie des sciences humaines* (Paris: Gallimard, 1966); translated into English as *The Order of Things: An Archaeology of the Human Sciences* (New York: Pantheon, 1970).

15. *Translator's note: The Rogue: Or, The Life of Guzmán de Alfarache*, trans. James Mabbe (London: Edward Blount, 1623). I have taken the liberty of modernizing spellings, punctuation, and capitalization.

16. Sebastian de Covarrubias, *Tesoro de la lengua castellana* (1611; rpt. Madrid: Turner, 1979), entry: "*prodigio*."

17. Ibid., entry: *cuerno*.

18. Foucault, *The Order of Things*, chapter 2.

19. Claude-Gilbert Dubois, *Mythe et langage au XVIe siècle* (Bordeaux: Ducros, 1970), p. 23.

20. See note 19.

21. Foucault, *The Order of Things*, pp. 47–48.

22. Ibid., p. 56.

23. See Dubois, *Mythe et langage*, pp. 40–41.

24. See E. Cros, *Protée et le gueux: Recherches sur l'origine et la nature du récit picaresque dans Guzmán de Alfarache de Mateo Alemán* (Paris: Didier, 1967), Coll. Etudes de Littérature Etrangère et Comparée.

25. Ibid.

26. On this point, see Foucault, *The Order of Things*, pp. 40–44.

27. Dubois, *Mythe et langage*, p. 32.

28. E. Cros, *L'Aristocrate et le carnaval des gueux* (Montpellier: Centre d'Etudes et de Recherches Sociocritiques, 1975), and *Ideología et genética textual, el caso del Buscón* (Madrid: Planeta, 1980).

Chapter 8. American Films of the Thirties:
The Case of Howard Hawks's *Scarface* (1931)

1. This section presents the results of a research seminar on film criticism that brought together, under the direction of Edmond Cros, the members of the Jean Vigo Club.

2. On these principles of textual analysis, see Chapter 6, pp. 75–92.

3. The notation (Ph.) refers to the numbers of the photograms, which are by Henri Talvat.

4. On the relations between carnivalesque festival practices and the thematics of redemption and exorcism, see E. Cros, *Ideología y genética textual, el caso del Buscón* (Madrid: Planeta, 1980), pp. 17–33 and, in this volume, pp. 225–230.

5. See Jean Delumeau, *La Peur en Occident, XIV-XVIIᵉ siècles* (Paris: Fayard, 1978).

6. The reader may find it profitable to compare these discursive interplays with certain phenomena I have analyzed elsewhere (Edmond Cros, "Effets sur la génétique textuelle de la situation marginalisée du sujet—Eléments pour une synthèse," *Imprévue*, 1 [1980], 23–30).

7. *L'Avant Scène (AS)*, 132 (Jan. 1973), 24. Henceforth, references will be cited directly in the text. The text of *AS* does not use the French subtitles but is based on the translation of the original dialogue.

8. Jerome Lawrence, *Actor: The Life and Times of Paul Muni* (New York: G. P. Putnam's Sons, 1974), p. 161.

9. See John Kopler, *The Life and World of Al Capone* (London: Coronet Books, 1973), p. 65.

10. Geo London, *Deux Mois avec les bandits de Chicago* (Paris, 1930), pp. 101–2.

11. We see only the *other side* or the *aftermath* of the party in Big Jim Colosimo's cabaret, after the *girls* have left.

12. Bernard Berelson and Patricia J. Salter, "Majority and Minority Americans: An Analysis of Magazine Fiction," *Public Opinion Quarterly*, 10 (2) (1946), 168–190.

13. F. Scott Fitzgerald, *The Great Gatsby* (New York: Charles Scribner's Sons, 1925). I thank C. Richard for drawing my attention to this intertext.

14. Fitzgerald, *Great Gatsby*, p. 24. Henceforth, all references will be cited directly in the text.

15. See *Law and Contemporary Problems*, 21 (Duke University, 1956), especially "American Immigration Policy in Historical Perspective." In the following discussion, I am indebted to Norman H. Clark, *Deliver Us from Evil: An Interpretation of American Prohibition* (New York: Norton, 1976), and more especially, to John Higham, *Send These to Me: Jews and Other Immigrants in Urban America* (New York: Atheneum, 1975).

16. Higham, *Send These to Me*, p. 37.

17. Ibid., p. 43.

18. Ibid., p. 26.

19. Ibid., pp. 46–47.

20. Clark, *Deliver Us from Evil*, p. 89.

21. Ibid.

22. Ibid., p. 88.

23. Ibid., p. 188.

24. Ibid., p. 186.

25. Lawrence, *Life and Times of Paul Muni*, p. 156.

26. Clark, *Deliver Us from Evil*, p. 152.

27. Higham, *Send These to Me*. p. 48.

28. René Girard, with Jean Michel Oughourlian and Guy Lefort, *Des choses cachées depuis la fondation du monde* (Paris: Grasset, 1978), p. 32.

29. On the mimetic crisis and the mimesis of the antagonist in the *Buscón*, see Chapter 11, pp. 225–230.

30. See note 28.

Chapter 9. Ideological and Discursive Formations in Contemporary Mexico

1. Carlos Fuentes, *Where The Air Is Clear*, trans. Sam Hileman (New York: Ivan Obolensky, Inc., 1960), p. 3.

2. These phrases are found immediately after the passage being studied here.

3. A. Dessau, *La novela de la revolución mexicana* (Mexico City: Fondo de Cultura Económica, 1972). See pp. 85–103 ("La formación de la ideología de la burguesía nacional"); I borrow the following quotations from him.

4. Victor Alba, *Las ideas sociales contemporáneas en México* (Mexico City: Fondo de Cultura Económica, 1960), pp. 140–043.

5. Gonzalez Ramírez, "Revolución y nacionalismo," *No*, 7 (April 1959), 4.

6. Leopoldo Zea, *La filosofía como compromiso y otros ensayos* (Mexico City: Tezontle, 1952), p. 17.

7. Fuentes, *Where the Air Is Clear* (trans. Sam Hileman), pp. 4, 376. This part would need considerable development.

8. See note 5.

9. Emilio Uranga, "El pensamiento filosófico," in *Mexico, Cincuenta años de Revolución*, vol. 4, *La Cultura*, pp. 553, 524, 554; quoted in Dessau, *La novela de la revolución mexicana*, pp. 98–99.

10. Octavio Paz, *The Labyrinth of Solitude; Life and Thought in Mexico*, trans. Lysander Kemp (New York: Grove Press, 1961), p. 34. Henceforth, page references to this edition will be cited directly in the text.

11. Octavio Paz. *Children of the Mire: Modern Poetry from Romanticism to the Avant-Garde*, trans. Rachel Phillips (Cambridge, Mass.: Harvard University Press, 1974), p. 25.

12. The English translations of the preceding quotations are by Muriel Rukeyser from her bilingual edition of *Selected Poems of Octavio Paz* (Bloomington, Ind.: Indiana University Press, 1963).

13. Octavio Paz, "Delicia," *La estación violenta*, (Mexico City: Fondo de Cultura Económica, 1958).

14. Octavio Paz, *The Monkey Grammarian*, trans. Helen R. Lane (New York: Seaver Books, 1981), pp. 9–10.

15. *Selected Poems of Octavio Paz*, trans. M. Rukeyser, p. 127.

16. Ibid., p. 125.

17. Ibid.

18. Paz, *Children of the Mire*, pp. 72–73.

19. Mikhail Bakhtin, *Le Marxisme et la philosophie du langage. Essai d'application de la méthode sociologique en linguistique* (Paris: Editions de Minuit, 1977), p. 30.

20. "Irony shows that if the universe is a script, each translation of this script is different, and that the concert of correspondences is the gibberish of Babel" (Paz, *Children of the Mire*, p. 74).

21. I place within brackets my own terms (e.g., [Symptom] [Unconscious]) to emphasize the psychoanalytic perspective that, it seems to me, is explicit in the text. Most of the other correspondences come from the *Labyrinth*, some from *Children of the Mire*, and others from the poetical works. This table of correspondences must not be confused with the semiotic texts and systems that I employ in

my studies on the *Buscón* or in Carlos Fuentes's *La región más transparente*. In the case of the present study, my list of correspondences, suggested by the author himself, consists of objective facts and is not the product of a semiological reduction. In most of the analogies with the concept of break suggested by Octavio Paz, the seme of break is not specified. Furthermore, there is no semantic convergence in the various signs involved. The analogical relations are projected by the author, and have no bearing upon the signified of the corresponding words. Cf. "This predominance of the closed over the open manifests itself not only as impassivity and distrust, irony and suspicion, but also as love for Form. Form surrounds and sets bounds to our privacy, limiting its excesses, curbing [*reprime*] its explosions, isolating and preserving it" (pp. 31–32).

22. I might have introduced certain distinctions which would have had the disadvantage of excessively projecting the analyst's own categories into the reconstruction of the system. My aim here is to observe the relations existing between the terms while being careful not to introduce new ones.

23. Paz, *Children of the Mire*, p. 74.

24. Ibid.

25. Ibid.

26. Ibid., p. 73.

27. Ibid., pp. 31, 27, 9. See also for "reason" in series 2: "The dispute between reason and revelation also tore the Arab world apart, but there the victory went to revelation: the death of philosophy and not, as in the West, the death of God. . . . Reason aspires to unity but, unlike divinity, neither comes to rest nor identifies itself with unity . . . Reason becomes identified with change and otherness" pp. 25 and 26).

28. On this horizontal axis the question *How?* is repeated. Whereas at level A the individual's observation of himself and of what surrounds him is what destroys the continuity of the world, at level B this continuity is destroyed as the result of an outside pressure.

29. The structuring role of this metaphor is transcribed in the work's title, in which the image of the labyrinth suggests the idea of confinement without a way out.

30. Bakhtin, *Le Marxisme*, p. 44.

Chapter 10. Social Formations and Figurative Discourse in Mateo Alemán's *Guzmán de Alfarache*

1. [*Translator's note*: The edition used is that of the Loeb Classical Library, 3rd edition (revised), English translation by W. H. D. Rouse (Cambridge, Mass.: Harvard University Press; London: Heinemann, 1937), pp. 406–407.] I should like to take this opportunity to thank G. Devallet for his help in reconstructing this *topos*.

2. Virgil, *Eclogues, Georgics, Aeneid* (Loeb Classical Library), vol. 1, ed. and trans. H. Rushton Fairclough (London: Heinemann; New York: Putnam, 1947), pp. 88–89.

3. *Elegies*, Introduction, text, translation and notes by Guy Lee, 2nd edition (Liverpool: Francis Cairns, 1982), p. 37. The poem continues as follows: "No mighty bull in those days bore the yoke/ or stallion tamely chawed the bit./ Houses had no doors. No stone stood in the fields/ to rule the arable with straight edge./ There was honey from the oak, and heavy-uddered ewes/ offered milk on meeting carefree countryfolk./ Anger and armies and war were not yet known:/ no blacksmith's cruel craft had forged the sword."

4. The text of reference for Ovid is that of the Loeb Classical Library, with English translation by Frank Justus Miller (Cambridge, Mass.: Harvard University Press; London: Heinemann, 1921), vol. 1, pp. 8–9. The passage continues as follows (lines 101–112): "The earth herself, without compulsion, untouched by hoe or plowshare, of herself gave all things needful. And men, content with food which came with no one's seeking, gathered the arbute fruit, strawberries from the mountainsides, cornel-cherries, berries hanging thick upon the prickly bramble, and acorns fallen from the spreading tree of Jove. Then spring was everlasting, and gentle zephyrs with warm breath played with

the flowers that sprang unplanted. Anon the earth, untilled, brought forth her stores of grain, and the fields, though unfallowed, grew white with the heavy, bearded wheat. Streams of milk and streams of sweet nectar flowed, and yellow honey was distilled from the verdant oak."

5. The English text is that of James Mabbe (1623), vol. 3, pp. 182–183 (reprinted by AMS Press [New York, 1967]).

6. Tibullus, *Elegies*, p. 77.

7. See Henri Goelzer's introduction to his edition of the *Georgics* (Paris: Les Belles Lettres, 1926).

8. See Joaquin Costa, *Colectivismo agrario en España* (Buenos Aires: Americalae, 1944), pp. 50–51, and Noël Salomon, *Recherches sur le thème paysan dans la comedia au temps de Lope de Vega* (Bordeaux: Institut d'Etudes Ibériques et Ibéro-Américaines, 1961), p. 205.

9. Goelzer, introduction to the *Georgics*.

10. *The Complete Works of Horace*, translated in the meters of the originals, with notes by Charles E. Passage (New York: Ungar, 1983), p. 99.

11. Salomon, *Recherches sur le thème paysan*, p. 168.

12. I think the complexity of this social formation does not show through in Salomon's conclusion that the treatment of this theme is but the expression of a "Golden Age Physiocratism," and of a single point of view, that of the nobility: "There is no doubt that this 'Golden Age Physiocratism' . . . expresses the self-interest of the great landowners or the large and middle-sized cattlemen who were not traditionally favorable to a manufacturing and monetary economy tied to urban growth. The point of view of a noble class living essentially on its ground rents, incapable of renewing itself and of taking the bold step of commercializing itself, is shared by most of our authors. . . . Yet, at the same time, these nobles, caught up in the thrust toward the cities, are themselves the first to leave the land. . . . The contradiction between theory and practice is here but one of the manifold reflections of the general contradiction tearing Spanish society apart after 1600" (p. 206). My analysis, on the contrary, aims to show how a *topos*, at the same time it is being deconstructed, can transcribe complex and contradictory social interests. In that case, among other oppositions, mercantilism is opposed to "physiocratism"; commerce and cattle-raising are opposed to industry and agriculture; commerce is opposed to nobility, etc. The texts from Sancho de Moncada and Consejo de Castilla are quoted by Salomon.

13. Pedro de Valencia, *Escritos sociales* (Madrid: Vinas Mey, 1945), pp. 36–37. Quoted by Pierre Vilar, "Les Primitifs Espagnols de la pensée économique – 'Quantitativisme' et 'bullionisme,' " in *Melanges offerts à Marcel Bataillon* (Bordeaux: Féret et fils, 1962), pp. 281–282.

14. Saavedra Fajardo, *Idea de un príncipe cristiano*, Empresa LXIX, in *Obras*, I (Madrid: Aguilar, 1947), pp. 527–529, quoted by Pierre Vilar, "Les Primitifs Espagnols," p. 283.

15. J. Mukarovsky, *Kapitel aus der Ästhetik*, p. 139. Quoted by Pierre V. Zima, *Pour une sociologie du texte littéraire* (Paris: UGE, 1978), p. 54.

16. Vilar, *Or et monnaie dans l'histoire, 1450–1920* (Paris: Flammarion, 1974), p. 192.

17. Ibid.

18. Ibid., p. 119–120.

19. Ibid., p. 204.

20. Juan Luis Vives, *De subventione pauperum*, 1525. Spanish text in *Obras completas*, L I, XI, p. 1379a. See Edmond Cros, *Protée et le gueux: Recherches sur l'origine et la nature du récit picaresque dans* Guzmán de Alfarache *de Mateo Alemán* (Paris: Didier, 1967), Coll. Etudes de Littérature Etrangère et Comparée.

21. Pedro Mexia, *Silva de varia lección*, Part II, ch. xxv. ("It does not seem that there is anything among those things that men enjoy and which keep them alive that is as necessary for their life as bread." See also Part II, ch. xxxi.

22. This remark was suggested to me by A. Gomez-Moriana.

23. For all these definitions, see Sebastian de Covarrubias, *Tesoro de la lengua castellana* (Madrid: Turner, 1979), entries: *leal, fiel, fe, depositar.*

24. See pp. 84–92, and about the use of italics and parentheses, see p. 212.

25. The reader will note that the schematization I am proposing here differs somewhat from the one I proposed in *Ideologies and Literature.* The present schema has the merit of showing much more clearly the gap between the two structural chains (signifier/signified).

26. *Despertador* . . . (f. 174 verso). Quoted by Salomon, *Recherches sur le thème paysan,* p. 198.

27. Pierre Vilar, *Or et monnaie,* p. 192.

Chapter 11. Ideology and Textual Genetics

1. Quevedo, "History of the Life of the Great Rascal . . . ," trans. Charles Duff, in Quevedo, *The Choice Humorous and Satirical Works* (London: George Routledge & Sons, Ltd., 1926; reprinted by Hyperion Press. Inc., Westport, Conn., 1978), pp. 3–4.

2. Edmond Cros, *L'Aristocrate et le carnaval des gueux* (Montpellier: Centre d'Etudes et de Recherches Sociocritiques, 1975), and *Idéologia y genética textual, el caso del Buscón* (Madrid: Planeta, 1980).

3. Cros, *Ideología y genética textual* (Madrid: Planeta, 1980).

4. René Girard, *De choses cachées depuis la fondation du monde: Recherches avec Jean Michel Oughourlian et Guy Lefort* (Paris: Grasset, 1978).

5. Ibid., p. 19.

6. Ibid., pp. 20–21.

7. Ibid., p. 29.

8. Ibid., p. 30.

9. Ibid., p. 31.

10. Ibid., p. 32.

11. Ibid., p. 33.

12. Henry Méchoulan, *Le Sang de l'autre ou l'honneur de Dieu: Indiens, juifs et morisques au Siècle d'Or* (Paris: Fayard (coll. La force des Idées), 1979. On the mimetic rivalry between Judaism and Christianity, see again René Girard: "Just as all the oppositions the Judeo-Christian text abounds in, Judaism and historical Christianity are in basic agreement on the essentials; they both give vent to the revelation of human violence, but they resemble one another as much as possible without going so far as understanding that they are doubles of one another and that the only thing that separates them is what also unites them" (*Des choses cachées,* p. 254).

13. Ibid., pp. 148, 149.

14. Girard, *Des choses cachées,* p. 35.

15. See Edmond Cros, "Effets sur la génétique textuelle de la situation marginalisée du sujet. Eléments pour une synthèse," *Imprévue,* 1 (1980), 23–30.

16. "La notion médiévale de normalité s'ordonne autour de l'assimilation de la nature à Dieu et du refus manichéen du mixte (comment peut-on être mi-clerc, mi-laïc comme les béguines et les bégards, mi-animal, mi-homme comme l'homme sauvage)" [The medieval notion of the normal is based on the identification of Nature with God and on the Manichean refusal of mixture (How can one be half-cleric and half-secular like the Beguines and the Begards, half-animal and half-human like the Wild Man?)] (Jacques Le Goff, "Les Marginaux dans l'Occident médiéval" in *Les Marginaux et les exclus de l'histoire,* Cahiers Jussieu, 5 [Paris: Université de Paris VII, 1979]), 20.

17. See Monique de Lope, *Traditions populaires et textualité dans le Libro del Buen Amor,"* (Montpellier: Centre d'Etudes et de Recherches Sociocritiques, 1983).

18. Quevedo, *History of the Life of the Great Rascal . . . ,* p. 25.

19. For René Girard, the scapegoat does indeed belong to the community as real victim, but not

as he is represented in myth (see *Des choses cachées*, p. 120). I should like to express my thanks to my colleague O. Ott for drawing my attention to Girard's study.

20. Girard, *Des choses cachées*, pp. 205, 273, 248, 275.

21. The description of these ceremonies may be found in Diego de Colmenares, *Historia de la insigne ciudad de Segovia y compendio de la historia de Castilla*, vol. 9 (Segovia, 1637).

22. See the Latin edition of Jean Bodin's *Republic* (Paris, 1586), end of the Third Book. This text, which is cited by E. Le Roy Ladurie (*Le Carnaval de Romans*, p. 223), does not appear in the French edition.

23. See J. L. Flecniakoska, "Les Fêtes du Corpus à Ségovie, 1594–1636, Documents inédits," *Bulletin hispanique*, 56 (1954), 14–37, 225–248. These documents are preserved in the Archivo Historico Provincial de Segovia.

24. Originally, Matthew was concerned with taxes, which was to make him an ideal choice as patron saint of commerce. Cf. the confraternity of St. Matthew in Le Roy Ladurie, *Le Carnaval de Romans*, p. 324.

25. Matthew, I, 17. Flecniakoska also points this out; see "Fêtes solennelles du transfert de la statue de la Vierge de la Fuencisla (Ségovie 12–22 Septembre 1613)," in *Fêtes de la Renaissance*, vol.3, ed. J. Jaquot (Paris: Centre National de la Recherche Scientifique, 1975), pp. 485ff.

26. On the dance of the bears, see Arnold Van Gennep, *Manuel du folklore français contemporain* (Paris: Éditions A. et J. Picard, 1947) and C. Gaignebet, "Le Combat de Carnival et de Carême de P. Brueghel (1559)," *Annales*, Economies, Sociétés, Civilisations (March 1972), 313–345.

27. See C. Gaignebet, *Le Carnaval: Essai de mythologie populaire* (Paris: Payot, 1972).

28. For Van Gennep, giants do not appear before the fourteenth century, with the spread of the chansons de geste (*Le Folklore de la Flandre et de Hainaut* [Paris; Maisonneuve, 1935]). According to Jean Robertson, they appear for the first time in the Midsummer Day celebrations in London in 1521–22 ("L'Entrée de Charles Quint à Londres," in *Fêtes de la Renaissance*, vol. 2 [Paris: Centre National de la Recherche Scientifique, 1960], pp. 169–181).

29. The dance of the swords is still called the dance of the *Matassins–Matachines*–in Spanish, or dance of the Clowns. See Thoinot Arbeau, *Orchésographie et traité en forme de dialogue par lequel toutes les personnes peuvent facilement apprendre et pratiquer l'honnête exercice des danses* (Langres, 1589), p. 97. This dance, which is accompanied by special music (see *Fêtes de la Renaissance*, vol. 2), is performed by four fighters dressed in special costumes: short tunics, paper helmets, their arms bare, bells on their legs. There are close resemblances between this dance and the "Moorish" dance. According to Thoinot Arbeau, the latter displays several forms; in fact, it is a solo dance ("a boy in black face with bells for greaves danced the Moorish dance"), or a dance performed on a stage in sumptuous costume, the style especially popular in Italy, or dances performed by several men dressed as fools and forming a circle around a female figure placed in the center whom they are courting, or finally a mock battle between Moors and Christians. The two dances have often been confused; thus Randle Cotgrave, *A Dictionarie of the French and English Tongues* (London, 1611), translates "Dancer les bouffons" as "To daunce a morris." *Moresca* means at other times mimed dance (see Giulio Cesare, *Intravolatura da liuto*). On all of this, see Daniel Heartz's article "Un divertissement à Binche," in *Fêtes de la Renaissance*, vol. 2. On sword dances in Golden Age literature, especially in the theater, see N. Salomon's thesis *Recherches sur le thème paysan dans la "comedia" au temps de Lope de Vega* (Bordeaux: Institut d'Etudes Ibériques et Ibéro-Américaines, 1965), Part III, ch. 3, pp. 512–573.

30. On the notion of paramusic, see Claudie Marcel-Dubois, "Fêtes villageoises et vacarmes cérémoniels," in *Les Fêtes de la Renaissance*, vol. 3, pp. 603–615.

31. Cited by Claudie Marcel-Dubois, "Fêtes villageoises."

32. See note 28.

33. Van Gennep, *Manuel de folklore*.

34. *Fêtes de la Renaissance*, vol. 3, p. 992. The term *supernumeraries*, used by Flecniakoska

in "Fêtes solennelles," does not seem appropriate. We think that what was involved were, in fact, disguises.

35. On the "redressive phase" of the Carnival period, see Victor Turner, *Dramas, Fields and Metaphors* (Ithaca, N. Y.: Cornell University Press, 1975). Anthropologists are in agreement on the differentiation of three phases in the festivities accompanying the end and the new beginning of a cyclical time period: (1) "Preliminary," marking a separation from the period of normal life; (2) "Liminary," the crossing of a threshold, a time "flowing backward," a time of inversion; (3) "Postliminary," a repressive or redressive phase marking reintegration and reincorporation with the time of normal daily life. See Le Roy Ladurie's excellent summary of these complex problems (*Le Carnaval de Romans*, pp. 338–339).

36. "Dança de salvajes de cerdas, o sea vestidos de cerda con cabellera larga que llegue a los ombros y bastones con que an de hacer sus toqueados." The dance of the wild men has often been confused with the Moorish dance (see note 29); thus, to describe the costume of the wild men who fight against knights in the festivities at Binche, an anonymous German text uses the phrase: *Uff morisch gekleidt*. We find the same confusion in the description of the festivities at Tours in 1458: "four young boys and a young girl dressed as savages danced (under very good direction) an excellent *Morisco* in front of the assembled spectators" (cited by D. Heartz "Un divertissement," p. 337). On the presence of the "woodwose" in the festivities in London, see Jean Robertson in *Fêtes de la Renaissance*, vol. 2, pp. 169–181; see also in the same volume, Daniel Devoto, "Folklore et politique au château ténébreux," pp. 311–328. On the general theme of the wild man, see José-Maria Azcárate, "El tema iconográfico del salvaje," *Archivo Español de Arte* (Madrid, 1948), No. 82; and, especially, Richard Bernheimer, *Wild Men in the Middle Ages: A Study in Art, Sentiment and Demonology* (Cambridge, Mass.: Harvard University Press, 1952).

37. See Daniel Fabre, "Occitanie, des rites que l'on croyait perdus," *Autrement* (July, 1976), 55–56.

38. Juan Esquivel Navarro, *Discursos sobre el arte del danzado* (Seville: Juna Gomez de Blas, 1642), ch. 12, p. 44. Quoted by J. L. Flecniakoska in "Fêtes solennelles."

39. Martine Grinberg, "Carnaval et sociétés urbaines XIV-XVIe siècles: le royaume dans la ville," *Ethnologie française*, 99, (1974), 215–545.

40. See Edmond Cros, *Protée et le gueux: Recherches sur les origines et la nature du récit picaresque dans Guzmán de Alfarache de Mateo Alemán* (Paris: Didier, 1967), Coll. Etudes de Littérature Etrangère et Comparée.

41. Grinberg, "Carnaval et sociétés urbaines," p. 239b.

42. Flecniakoska, "Fêtes solennelles," p. 499.

43. Ibid., p. 501.

44. My semiological reading of the fiesta at Segovia should be compared with the judgment made by Fray Luis de Leon: "así que no es maravilla, Sabino, que *los reyes de ahora* nose precien para ser reyes de lo que se precio Jesu Cristo, porque no siguen en el ser reyes un mismo fin. . . . Estos que agora nos mandan reinan para si, y por la misma causa no se disponen ellos para nuestro provecho sino buscan sin descanso en nuestro daño" (*Obras completas castelanas*, prólogo del padre Félix García, 3rd ed., 1959, p. 558). [Thus it is not surprising, Sabino, that kings of nowadays do not value kingship for the same reason as Jesus Christ, because kings do not pursue in life the same purpose. . . . Those who now command us reign for themselves, and for this reason do not provide for our welfare but unceasingly seek our harm.] In this judgment the bitterness of the *converso* seems to be expressed against a cultural background that permits him to set over against this distorted royalty the concept of the God/king of Exodus: "And the Lord said unto Moses, See, I have made thee a god to Pharaoh: and Aaron thy brother shall be thy prophet" (Ex. 7, 1–2). See further: "the kings of the house of David are representatives of the Lord and sit upon the royal throne of Yahweh" (I Chronicles, 177, 14; 28, 5). With this criticism of Fray Luis's as support, it is not inconceivable that every representation of "kings descending from David" is capable of referring, in certain contexts (of which

this one is a striking example), to the negative image of the "kings of nowadays." This remark was prompted by the suggestive article of Alfredo Hermenegildo, "La imagen del Rey y el teatro de la España clásica," *Segismundo*, 12, nos. 1–2 (Consejo Superior de Investigaciones Científicas, 1976), 53–86. The preceding quotations are taken from this article.

45. *La hora de todos y la fortuna con seso*, ed. Bourg, Dupont, and Geneste (Paris: Aubier [coll. bilingue], 1980), p. 50. References in Spanish in the text will be to this edition; English translations are from the 1697 John Stevens translation, *The Hour of All Men and Fortune in Her Wits*, in the previously cited edition of Quevedo's works in English.

46. Josette Riandière La Roche, "La Satire du 'monde à l'envers' et ses implications politiques dans *La hora de todos* de Quevedo," in J. Lafond and A. Redondo, eds., *L'Image du monde renversé et ses représentations littéraires et paralittéraires de la fin du XVIe siècle au milieu du XVIIe* (Paris: J. Vrin, 1979), p. 60.

47. See "Apocalipsis más tarde: Ideología y *La hora de todos* de Quevedo," in *Francisco de Quevedo, La hora de todos*, ed. E. Cros, Co-textes, 2 (Montpellier: Centre d'Etudes et de Recherches Sociocritiques, 1981), 29–97.

48. Terry Eagleton, *Criticism and Ideology; A Study in Marxist Literary Theory* (London: Verso, 1978); Pierre Macherey, *Pour une théorie de la production littéraire* (Paris: François Maspero, 1966).

49.   The world is upside-down, I don't understand it.
         Hell gives the orders and the Lord is his suppliant;
         The rich man weeps, the poor man laughs;
         The mountains are on bottom, the plains in the clouds,
         The hare is chasing the dog
         And the mouse is chasing the cat. But the world asserts
         It is round and that it turns, and so that is why
         We wonder down here who's running after the other.
         (Emblem 79)

This text as well as the following ones have been borrowed from Frédérick Tristan, *Le Monde à l'envers* (Paris: Atelier Hachette Massim, 1980).

50. "It may well be that in everyone's eyes I have been guilty of the crime attributed to the Apostle of having turned the world upside-down and of having placed at the bottom what others judge to be at the top of the edifice, and of having placed on the roof what others have used as a foundation."

51. "He who was destined to live in heaven had hell as his home. He who was to enjoy eternal and celestial joys was condemned to perpetual suffering, and thus glory was changed to punishment, honor to censure, pleasure to torment, joy to sorrow, play into work, wealth into poverty, plenty into want, love into hate, light into darkness."

52.   Voyez ce monde retourné
         Aux biens mondains trop adonné
         Qui pour un Rien se veut périr
         Sans ombre d'aveugle plaisir.
         Et Satan qui toujours veille
         Leur promet des biens à merveille
         Sachant que dessous tel plaisir
         Se cache un mortel repentir.

[Look at this world upside-down, given too much to worldly riches, which would die for a mere bagatelle, without even a glimmer of benighted satisfaction. And Satan, always vigilant, promises them endless wealth, knowing that behind such pleasures lurks mortal repentence.]

See Crispin de Pas's engraving in Tristan, *Le Monde à l'envers*.

53. Aristophanes, *The Plutus*, trans. Benjamin Bickley Rogers (London: George Bell & Sons, 1907), ll. 490–491 (p. 55), ll. 510–517 (p. 57).

54. On the notion of "discursive formation," see Chapter 3.

55. Baltasar Gracián, *Criticon*, III, 3 (*Obras completas*: Aguilar), p. 864b. Quoted by A. Redondo, "Monde à l'envers et conscience de crise chez Gracián," in Lafond and Redondo, eds., *L'Image du monde renversé*, pp. 83–97.

56. Quoted by F. Tristan, *Le Monde à l'envers*, p. 32.

57. In "Effets sur la génétique textuelle de la situation marginalisée du sujet" (*Imprévue*, (1980–1), I attempt to systematize a critical approach to these phemonena of writing.

58. Ibid., pp. 364–365.

59. Ibid., p. 371.

60. J. A. Maravall, *La cultura del barroco: análisis de une estructura histórica* (Barcelona: Ariel, 1975), pp. 55–56.

61. J. A. Maravall, *La oposición política bajo los Austrias* (Barcelona: Ariel, 1972), pp. 220–221.

62. Anne Marie Le Coq, "Le monde à l'envers," *Revue de l'art* 33 (Paris, 1933), 83–102; Martine Grinberg, "Carnaval et société urbaine," in *Fêtes de la Renaissance*, vol. 3 (Paris, 1975), pp. 547–553; Helen F. Grant, "Image et gravures du monde à l'envers," in *L'Image du monde renversé*.

63. See Cros, *L'Aristocrate* and *Ideología y genética textual*.

64. What Bourg, Dupont, and Geneste in their edition of *La hora de todos* have to say on this point seems to me utterly persuasive. (See pp. 17–22.)

65. Popular traditions accord special importance to the vigil on the eve of a holy day, which represents a liminary stage, an initial threshold.

66. "Children's game: which they play by choosing lots to see which one will remain outside the circle formed by the rest, who, joining hands, go round and round, kicking the one who is left outside. The latter, at the risk of getting kicked, tries to grab someone from the wheel to take his place outside, everyone all the while saying: *Ande la rueda y coz con ella*. Let the wheel turn and the kicks with it" (*Diccionario de autoridades*, facsimile edition, vol. I [Madrid: Gredos, 1963], entry: *coz*).

67. On all these points, see Van Gennep, *Manuel du folklore français*, vol. 4, pp. 1096–1097.

Index

Actant: character as, 107; versus narrator, 55, 56

Adorno, T. W., 9, 21, 24

Albrecht, Miltos, 5

Alemán, Mateo, xiii, xvi, 16, 29, 42–43: ideological reading of, 52, 53

Alijamiado: as example of contradictory discourse, 61, 256

Althusser, Louis, x, xii, 26: and idcological interpellation, 39; and materialized ideology, 46–47

Analogy: in Paz, 181–189

Anti–Saloon League, 143

Archaeology of Knowledge, 34

L' Aristocrate: diminutive and conceptist metaphor in, 115

Aristotelian law, 28

Arnauld, Antoine: as analogous to Pascal, 11

Art: defined as social, 21; middlebrow, 32–33

Auerbach, Erich: and the Church, 32; and spiritual unity based on common language, 30–31

Autobiography: as exemplified by confession, 53–57; in Spanish literature, 48–49, 255

Autonomy: and historical time, 253; illusion of, 43; and referentiality, 46; in *Scarface*, 124; writing as, 20–24

L' Avant Scène, 133

Bakhtin, Mikhail, xiii, xiv, xvii: and analysis of the word, 62; and consciousness, 59; and social class and language, 188

Bal, Mike: and narratology, 94

Balibar, Etienne, 24, 25

Balibar, Renée, 24, 25, 28, 29, 30: and the School, 32

Barthes, Roland, 14, 21: and intertextuality, 64; and narratology, 93; and writing/speaking subject, 30

Beckett, Samuel, 22

Benjamin, Walter, 9

Benveniste, Emil: and narratology, 93

Berelson, Bernard: and magazine fiction study, 5, 136

Birth of the Clinic, 34

Bloom, Harold, vii

Bordeaux, 8

Bourdieu, Pierre, vii, 17, 20–23, 24, 28: and mass production, 32–33

Brecht, Bertolt, xi

Bremond, Claude: and elementary sequence, 104

Buscón, xvii, 15, 28: actant versus narrator in, 56; burlesque metaphor in, 88; carnival

269

in, 56, 63–64, 70–71, 152; carnival versus
Inquisition in, 63, 70–71; and character as
textual category, 108, 113–115; conceptist
metaphor in, 72; language/words in,
113–114; semiotic texts/systems in,
210–224; semiotics in, 86, 89, 90; textual
genetics in, 208–246; textual semantics in,
81–82; transformational codes in, 70–71

Calvinism, xiv
Camera: aesthetic sovereignty of, xv
Cardaillac, L., xvii, 61
Carnival, xvii, xviii: in *Buscón*, 56, 63–64,
70–71, 152; and picaresque novel of
Spain, xii; in *Scarface*, 129–130, 151–152
Carpentier, Alejo, 74
Castro, Américo, xviii
Character: defined, 107–108; in magazine
fiction, 136–138; as textual category,
107–115
Chomsky, Noam, xiii, 77
Church: as Ideological State Apparatus,
26–27, 32
Citizen Kane, x, xiv–xv: death image in,
65–70; genotext and phenotext in, 78–79;
philosophic and religious thought in, 58;
signifier/signified in, 46; technical devices
in, 80–81; textual semantics in, 80–81;
transformational codes in, 66–70
Clark, Norman H.: on society and prohibition,
144–145, 149, 150
Class: analysis of, ix, xvii–xviii; defined, 61,
255; and language, 188; and language of
the Universal, 27
Coin: as symbol in *Scarface*, 123
Collective subject, xi, 11, 12, 14, 16, 17, 30,
60. *See also* Transindividual
Confession: as double picaresque discourse,
52, 53–57
Consciousness: collective versus individual,
17; literary text as product of, 59; maximum potential, 11; three levels of, 10, 60
Content analysis, 5–7, 33: of magazine fiction,
136–138. *See also* Textual analysis
Counter–Reformation, 26
Covarrubias, Sebastian de, 15, 86, 109, 110,
201
Cross: as symbol in *Scarface*, 62–63, 91, 121,
128, 129, 133, 134–135

De Man, Paul, vii
Deconstruction, vii, viii
Deleuze, Gilles, viii
Delfau, Gérard, 9
Derrida, Jacques: and reception in United
States, vii–viii
Dessau, A., 162, 163
Discourses, xi–xii, xiii: defined, 30; materi-
alist philosophy of, 59–62. *See also* Dis-
cursives
Discursive formation, 34–44: in contemporary
Mexico, 153–189; defined, 38–39, 40; and
dominant discourse, 43; versus ideological
formation, 41; rules of, 35, 36
Discursive practice, 34–44
Discursive relations, 36
Discursives, xi, xiii, 19: practices and forma-
tions, 34–44; as shaping literature, 32. *See
also* Discourses
Divine Comedy, 31
Le Docteur Pascal, 22
Don Quixote: sign/character in, 111–112, 113
Dubois, Claude–Gibert: on reversibility of
paths of knowledge, 111
Dubois, Jacques, 21–22, 24, 28
Dysfunctional theories, ix

Earth: as symbol in *Guzmán*, 43, 63, 83, 190,
207
Eco, Umberto, 6
Écriture, viii, 24, 77
Elegies: compared to *Guzmán*, 190
Empirical sociology, 8–9
Epístolas familiares, 48
Escarpit, Robert: and literary sociology, ix,
4–5, 8, 24, 249
Execution: as social repression, 50, 255
Exorcism: in *Scarface*, 129–130

Fable: and narratology, 93, 95
Fajardo, Saavedra, 195
Fekete, John, vii
Festival: as social confrontation in *Buscón*,
230–238
Figure III: and narratology, 93–94, 257
Filmic syntax, xiv–xv: in *Citizen Kane*, 81; in
Scarface, 81
Fitzgerald, F. Scott: and *Gatsby/Scarface*
comparisons, 138
Fleming, 6

For Whom the Bell Tolls, 7
Foucault, Michel, viii, xi–xii, 40: and
  episteme, 108; and historical conditions,
  35, 36; importance of, 34; and interdiscourse, 250; and localization as analogy,
  111
Frankfurt School, 249
Fromm, Erich, 9
Fuentes, Carlos, x, 58: sociocritical reading
  of, 153–169
Fügen, H. A., 5

Gallicanism, 26
Gates of the Dream, The: and Oedipal myth,
  100
Gelves, Hernando de: and prison sermons, 51,
  52
Genesis: myth of, in *Citizen Kane*, 66, 68, 70
Genêt, Jean, 13
Genetic structuralism: introduction to, 9–19
Genette, Gérard: and narratology, 93–94
Genotext: in *Citizen Kane*, 78–79; com-
  binatorial structure of, 63; defined, 76–77;
  and interpretant, 65; and narratology, 107;
  in *Scarface*, 91, 125, 129
Genre, 33
Georgics: compared to *Guzmán*, 190
Girard, René, 18: on mimetic rivalry, 150,
  151, 226–229
Golden Age: myth of, in *Guzmán*, 65, 70, 74
Goldmann, Lucien, ix, x–xi, xiii, xvii, 5, 6,
  9, 14, 17–18, 60: and attention to content,
  46; and genetic structuralism, 11–13; and
  transindividual, 9–11; and world vision, 72
Gombrowicz, Witold, 13
Gómez–Moriana, Antonio, xvii, 48–49
Gramsci, Antonio, ix, xv, xviii: and hegem-
  ony, 249–250
Great Gatsby, The: compared with *Scarface*,
  138–140, 142
Guattari, Félix, viii
Guevara, Antonio de, 48
Guillén, Claudio: and spoken epistle reference
  to *Lazarillo*, 48
Gumbrecht, Hans Ulrich, 249
Gutton, J. P., 26
Guzmán de Alfarache, xvi, 15, 16, 28, 31–32,
  42, 49: actant versus narrator in, 56; anal-
  ysis of themes in, 190–203; autobiographi-
  cal narrative in, 52; and character as tex-

tual category, 108–113; and confession,
  53; discursive practice in, 51; Golden Age
  myth in, 65, 70, 74; ideological reading
  of, 52; ideosemes in, 58; and preaching,
  50; semiotic texts/systems in, 90, 91,
  201–207; textual practice in, 57; textual
  semantics in, 63, 64, 82–83; transformational codes in, 70; voice of the Other in,
  55

Hamon, Philippe: on character, 107–108
Hawks, Howard, 119
Hays censors, 63, 130–131, 135: and jour-
  nalistic writing, 91
Hearst, William Randolph, 78
Hecht, Ben, 119, 134
Hegel, Georg Wilhelm Friedrich, xi, 12
Hegelianism, 11
Hegemonics, ix, x, xv, xviii
Hemingway, Ernest, 7
Henry, Paul, 6: and the preconstructed, 39
Herbert, T.: and two forms of ideology, 42
Herrera Pug, Pedro: and prison sermons, 51
Hidden God, The, 13, 18
Higham, John: on minority and majority in
  America between 1920 and 1930, 140–143
Historical time: as defined by Althusser, 26,
  253
History and Class Consciousness, 11, 17
La hora de todos, 27, 45: ideological inscrip-
  tion in, 238–246
Horace, 194
Horkheimer, Max, 9

Ideological form/practice, ix–xiv *passim*, xvi,
  47: in contemporary Mexico, 153–189;
  versus discursive formation, 41; and ideosemes, 50; in *Lazarillo*, 49; literature
  defined as, 24–33, 43; and Pêcheux, 38;
  ritual/textual practice within, 57; as secondary modeling system, 28; and transindividual, 64
Ideological interpellation, 39, 47
Ideological State Apparatus, xii, 24, 26–28,
  41, 88–89: and multiple contradictions of
  social formation, 36; and Pêcheux, 38;
  specificity and fictitiousness linked to, 32
Ideological trace, 28: and character, 108; in
  Scarface, 91, 138

Ideology: toward a semiology of, 45–58; two forms of, 42; versus world vision, 17
Ideosemes, xiii, xvi, xvii: contingent on ideological practice, 50; in *Guzmán*, 58; microsemiotics of, 49
Images, xi, xiv. *See also* Signs; Symbols
Inquisition: in *Buscón*, 63–64, 70–71
Interdiscourse, 41, 64: defined, xii, 39, 250; and intersection with intertext, 64, 75; versus intradiscourse, 39–40
Interpretant: in *Buscón*, 70; defined, 64, 256; and genotext, 65
Intertext: and intersection with interdiscourse, 64, 75; in *Scarface*, 138
ISA. *See* Ideological State Apparatus

Jansenism, 11
Jealousy, 18

Kant, Immanuel, 12
Kantism, 11
Kristeva, Julia, 76
Kuhn, Thomas, vii

Labyrinth of Solitude, The: continuous and discontinuous in, 169–189; signs in, 182–188
Language: in *Buscón*, 114–115; in *Don Quixote*, 113; in *Guzmán*, 113; versus speech, 60–61; of the Universal, 27
Lawrence, Jerome, 133
Lazarillo de Tormes, 28, 48–49: as autobiographical narrative, 114
Le Grivès, Eliane, 133
Leenhardt, Jacques, 18
Léon, Pedro de: and confession, 53, 56; sermon of, 50
Lexicalization, 14–15
Libido: versus transindividual, 10–11
Life and Times of Paul Muni, The, 133
Literary language: defined, 30–31, 32
Literary sociology, ix, xv, 4–5, 24: backwardness of, 3–4; defined by Zima, 7–8; empirical, 8–9; survey of, 3–9; theory–political connotations of, ix, 249
Literature: correlated with society, x, xi: defined, 25–26, 252, 253
Litin. *See Viva el presidente*
London, Geo, 134
Lotman, Yuri, 7, 8: and definition of text, 80; and signs in art, 82–85, 205

Lukács, Georg, ix, x–xi, xiii, 6, 9, 11, 12, 17

Macherey, Pierre, 24, 25: and contradictions in literary text, 36
McLuhan, Marshall, viii
Macrosemiotics, 29–30: in *Stolen Kisses*, 96
Madness and Civilization, 34
Magazine fiction: study of, 5, 136–138
Mallarmé, Stéphane, 22
Malraux, André, 13
Marasso, A., 48
Maravall, J. A., 242
Le Marché des biens symboliques, 24
Marcuse, Herbert, 9
Marginalization, ix
Marxism, 12: and class analysis/problematics, ix, 37; Foucault's attack on, xii; and French peasantry of 1850s, 38; and ideology, x; and literary sociology, ix; and political economy text, vii; and proletariat, 18; and social formation, 36, 41; and the state, 26, 27, 37; and state apparatuses, xii
Mask/Masking, xviii: in *Buscón*, 63–64, 74; in *Scarface*, 126–127
Masonic lodges, 26–27
Mass production: of literature, 21, 32–33
Memmi, Albert, 3, 4, 6, 9
Metamorphoses: compared to *Guzmán*, 190
Metaphor: in Paz, 181–189
Mexico: ideological and discursive formations in contemporary, 153–189
Microsemiotics, 29–30: and consciousness, 60; of ideosemes, 49; intratextual, 72, 74; and materialized ideology, 47
Middlebrow art, 32–33
Molino, Jean, 71
Le Monde, 40
Money: as sign of instability in *Guzmán*, 43
La muerte de Artemio Cruz: analysis of thinking in, 58; textual semantics in, 82–83
Mukarovsky, J., 8, 196
Multiculturism: within discipline of literary theory, vi
Moscovici, S., 6
Myth: as level of semantic transformation, 65

Narrative: defined, 93–94, 257; infra-, 106–107; and narrator, 95; in *Scarface*, 95, 132–133; in *Stolen Kisses*, 95–107; as textual category, 93–107

Narratologie, 94
Neruda, Pablo, 84
Newsreel: in *Citizen Kane*, 66, 68–69, 80
Nicole, Peirre: as analogous to Pascal, 11
Nomen, Lumen, 111
Novel: development of the, 29. *See also* Picaresque novel

Oedipal myth: in *Stolen Kisses*, 100
Order of Things, The, 34
Other: versus Self, 55
Ovid, 190

Paradigm: in literary theory, vii, viii; picaresque novel as, xv–xvi
Parsons, Talcott, ix
Pascal, Blaise, 11, 12, 13
Pauphilet, Albert: and narratology, 106
Paz, Octavio, x, 84, 87: continuous and discontinuous in, 169–189; historical continuity for, 178
Pêcheux, Michel, xi, xii xiii, 39, 40: and discursive formation, 38, 41
Peirce, Charles S., 64, 256
Phenotexts, 91: in *Citizen Kane*, 78–79, defined, 76–77; and narratology, 107; in *Scarface*, 125
Picaresque novel, x, xii, xv–xvi, xvii, xviii: *Buscón* as, 56; as confession, 255; double discourse in, 45–58; *Guzmán* as, 49, 56; textual structures of, 28, 41, 47
Polantzas, N., 37
Polyphony, xiii, xiv–xv, xviii
Polysemics, 64
Pottier, Bernard, 85
Pour une sociologie du texte littéraire, 11
Preaching. *See* Sermon
Preconstructed: in Alemán's work, 42; Henry's work on, 39
Prison: and double picaresque discourse, 51, 52, 56
Prison Notebooks, xv
Problèmes du nouveau roman: and narratology, 94
Prohibition: as setting for *Scarface*, 143–144

La Quête du Saint Graal: Todorov's analysis of, 106
Quevedo, Don Francisco de, xvi, 27, 45: transformational codes in text of, 71

Races of Europe, The, 142
Racine, Jean, 13
Ramos, Samuel, 162
El recurso del metodo, 74
Referentiality, xvi, 7, 14, 30, 32, 46
La región más transparente: internal organization of, 160–169; psychoanalytic discourse of, 160–169; semiological reading of, 154–161; semiotic texts of, 74, 90, 92, 154–157; and social class, 188; sociocritical reading of, 162–169
Residencia, 84
Ricardou, Jean: and narratology, 94
Rico, Francisco, 48
Riddle of the Sphinx, The: Oedipal myth in, 100
Riffaterre, Michael: and intertextuality, 64
Riplay, William Z.: on European races, 142
Robbe–Grillet, Alain, 18
Robin, Régine, xi, xii, 8, 26, 27, 36, 41–42
Roche, Anne, 9
Róheim, Géza: on Oedipal myth, 100
Rosengren, K. E., 5
Royal Prison of Seville, 50

Saint Augustine, 31
Salomon, Noel, 194
Salter, Patricia J.: and magazine fiction study, 5, 136
Sánchez-Albornoz, Claudio, xviii
Sanguineti, Edoardo, 5
Sartre, John–Paul, 5, 21
Saumjan-Soboleva, S. K.: generative theories of, 76
Saussure, F. de: and distinction between language and speech, 60–61
Scarface, x, xv: filmic sign in, 99; genotext in, 125, 129; journalism in, 72; phenotexts in, 125, 129; realism of, 134; semiological reading of, 119–130; semiotic texts in, 90–91, 136; sequences in, 119–124; signs in, 62, 64, 125–136; sociocritical reading of, 79, 130–152; sociocriticism of, 119–130; textual semantics in, 81
Scholarship: levels of, vi
School: as Ideological State Apparatus, 28
Sciences humaines et philosophie, 17
Searle, John, vii, xvi
Secondary modeling system, 65: ideological practice as, 28; language as, 30–31; litera-

ture as, 24–33; textual constraints of, 45
Self: versus Other, 55: in *La región más transparente*, 157–162
Semanalysis, 76
Semantic transformation, 64–65
Semantics. *See* Textual semantics
Seme, xiii
Semiological reading: of *Buscón*, 208–238; of *Guzmán*, 190–207; of Paz, 169–189; of *La región más transparente*, 154–161; of *Scarface*, 119–130
Semiotic texts/systems, 89–92: in *Buscón*, 210–224; in *Guzmán*, 201–207; in *La región más transparente*, 154–157; in *Scarface*, 90–91, 136
Semiotics, xi, xiii, xiv, 8, 17, 29–30: of ideology, 57; and stratifications in textuality, 32
Sequence: in *Stolen Kisses*, 101–106
Sermon: as double picaresque discourse, 50, 51
Sign/analogy: in Paz, 181–182
Sign/character: analysis of, 107–115
Signified/signifier, 84–89: in *Guzmán*, 203
Signs: and character, 107–115: in *Guzmán*, 109–111; in *Scarface*, 124–136; and text, 84–86
Silbermann, A., 5, 8
Social class. *See* Class
Social formation, 36–37: defined by Pêcheux, 38; and transindividual, 64
Social Research Institute of Frankfurt, 9
Sociedades de Amigos del Pais, 27
Society: correlated with literature, x, xi
Sociocritical reading: of Paz, 169–189; of *La región más transparente*, 162–169; of *Scarface*, 130–152. *See also* Sociocriticism
Sociocriticism, xiii–xiv, xv, xvii, xviii, 46: defined, ix–x, xi; versus literary criticism, 33; semiotics of ideology as basic to, 57
Sociology: experimental, 3–9, 33; research objective of, 5, 250. *See also* Content analysis; Empirical sociology; Literary sociology
Socorro de los pobres: compared to *Guzmán*, 197
Soul and Forms, The, 11
Spanish Golden Age: controversies concerning literature of the, 37–38; School and Church in the, 32; texts of the, 27–28, 29

Speech: versus language, 60–61
State: as Ideological State Apparatus, 26
Stereotypes: in *Scarface*, 137–138
Stolen Kisses, x: text versus narrative in, 95–107
Story: defined, 94, 95, 257
Subject: and narratology, 93, 95
Subject–form: individual as, 39, 40–41
Symbols: correlation of, xi, xiv. *See also* Images; Signs
Taine, Hippolyte, 4
Text: defined, 80; and narrative, 93–107; and signs, 84–86; of *Stolen Kisses*, 97–98
Textual analysis, xvi, 17: and production of meaning, 44. *See also* Content analysis
Textual categories: character as, 107–115; narrative as, 93–107
Textual genetics: and ideology in *Buscón*, 208–246; markers in *Buscón*, 225–230
Textual semantics, 80–84
Thematic correlations, xi
Theory of Aesthetics, 21
Theory–political connotation, vii–viii, 249
Theresa of Avila, 48
Tibullus, Albius, 190
Todorov, Tzvetan: and narratology, 93, 106
Tolstoy, Leo, 7, 85
Toward a Sociology of the Novel, 18
Tower of Babel: as myth in *Citizen Kane*, xiv, 66, 68, 79, 80
Transformational codes, 64–74: in *Buscón*, 70–71; in *Citizen Kane*, 66–70; in *Guzmán*, 70; nature and origin of, 71; outlined, 73; in *Scarface*, 143
Transindividual, 9–11, 12, 30, 45, 46
Truffaut, François, x, 95
Tynjanov, Jurij, xvi, 14

Universal, Language of the. *See* Language
Uranga, Emilio, 167–168

Vasconcelos, José, 87
Vilar, Pierre, 196, 206
Virgil, 190
Viva el presidente: intratextual microsemiotics in, 74
Vives, Juan Luis, 197
Volvelle, M., 26

Waiting for Godot, 22

Weber, Max, 9, 11, 28
What Is Literature?, 5, 21
Words: in *Buscón*, 113–114; in *Don Quixote*, 113; in *Guzmán*, 113; meaning of, as defined by Pêcheux, 38; plurality of accent (pluriaccentuation), 62; precise analysis of, 62–64
World vision, 10–11; versus ideology, 17; as keystone of genetic structuralism, 13; as mediating structure, 18–19; of the proletariat, 17–18

Writer: compared to journalist or historian, 7; status of, 21; strategy of, 22
Writing Degree Zero, 21

Your Lordship, 48

Zalamansky, Henri, 5–6, 6–7
Zima, Peter V., 7–8, 9, 11, 12, 13, 24, 249, 250
Zima, Pierre, 82
Zola, Emile, 22

Theory and History of Literature

Volume 28. Edited by Jonathan Arac *Postmodernism and Politics*
Volume 27. Stephen Melville *Philosophy Beside Itself: On Deconstruction and Modernism*
Volume 26. Andrzej Warminski *Readings in Interpretation: Hölderlin, Hegel, Heidegger*
Volume 25. José Antonio Maravall *Culture of the Baroque: Analysis of a Historical Structure*
Volume 24. Hélène Cixous and Catherine Clément *The Newly Born Woman*
Volume 23. Klaus Theweleit *Male Fantasies,2. Male Bodies: Psychoanalyzing the White Terror*
Volume 22. Klaus Theweleit *Male Fantasies, 1. Women, Floods, Bodies, History*
Volume 21. Malek Alloula *The Colonial Harem*
Volume 20. Jean-François Lyotard and Jean-Loup Thébaud *Just Gaming*
Volume 19. Jay Caplan *Framed Narratives: Diderot's Genealogy of the Beholder*
Volume 18. Thomas G. Pavel *The Poetics of Plot: The Case of English Renaissance Drama*
Volume 17. Michel de Certeau *Heterologies*
Volume 16. Jacques Attali *Noise*
Volume 15. Peter Szondi *On Textual Understanding and Other Essays*
Volume 14. Georges Bataille *Visions of Excess: Selected Writings, 1927–1939*
Volume 13. Tzvetan Todorov *Mikhail Bakhtin: The Dialogical Principle*
Volume 12. Ross Chambers *Story and Situation: Narrative Selection and the Power of Fiction*
Volume 11. Edited by John Fekete *The Structural Allegory: Reconstructive Encounters with the New French Thought*
Volume 10. Jean-François Lyotard *The Postmodern Condition: A Report on Knowledge*
Volume 9. Erich Auerbach *Scenes from the Drama of European Literature*
Volume 8. Mikhail Bakhtin *Problems of Dostoevsky's Poetics*
Volume 7. Paul de Man *Blindness and Insight: Essays in the Rhetoric of Contemporary Criticism* 2nd ed., rev.
Volume 6. Edited by Jonathan Arac, Wlad Godzich, and Wallace Martin *The Yale Critics: Deconstruction in America*
Volume 5. Vladimir Propp *Theory and History of Folklore*
Volume 4. Peter Bürger *Theory of the Avant-Garde*
Volume 3. Hans Robert Jauss *Aesthetic Experience and Literary Hermeneutics*
Volume 2. Hans Robert Jauss *Toward an Aesthetic of Reception*
Volume 1. Tzvetan Todorov *Introduction to Poetics*

Edmond Cros is a professor of literary theory and Hispanic studies at the Université Paul Valéry in Montpellier, France, and Andrew W. Mellon Professor of Hispanic Studies at the University of Pittsburgh. He studied at the Universities of Paris and Lyon in the 1950s, concentrating on sociocriticism and the literature of Spain and Latin America, and earned his doctorat d'état in 1967. Cros founded and directs the periodicals *Imprévue, Cotextes*, and *Sociocriticism*. He has published a number of books and articles, primarily in French and Spanish.

Jerome Schwartz is an associate professor of French at the University of Pittsburgh. He received his M.A. and Ph.D. in French literature from Columbia University. Schwartz is author of *Diderot and Montaigne* and contributes to such journals as *Yale French Studies, Esprit Créateur, The Stanford French Review* and *Emblematica*.

Jürgen Link is a professor of German literature at Ruhr-Universität Bochum, West Germany. **Ursula Link-Herr** teaches at Universität Siegen, West Germany. Both are authors of *Literatursoziologisches Propädeutikum* (1980) and editors of *kultuRRevolution*. They served as visiting professors in comparative literature at the University of Minnesota in the fall of 1987.